This edition is created exclusively for Rebo International b.v., The Netherlands by Fire Publishing Ltd, London NW5 2RZ and Book Creation Illustrated Ltd, London W1V 1PH.

Copyright © 1999, 2000 Rebo International b.v., Lisse
2nd edition published 2000

Editorial: Cover (to) Cover
Additional editorial assistance: Fiona Corbridge; Susan Wheatly

Text: Simon Adams
        Viv Croot
        Margaret Crowther
        Will Fowler
        Ann Kramer
        Dan McCausland
        ATH Rowland-Entwistle
        Helen Varley
        Philip Wilkinson

Index: Ingrid Lock

Design and typesetting: Casebourne Rose Design Associates,
Studio assistant: Mat Rose
Additional millennium design: Chuck Goodwin

Project co-ordinator: Tami Rex for Book Creation Illustrated Ltd

Picture research and photography by Anne Hobart Lang and Rolf Lang at AHL Archives, Washington, USA. Additional research by Heritage Picture Collection, London, Mirco De Cet.

The greatest of care has been taken in compiling this book. However, no responsibility can be accepted by the creators and publishers, or by the contributors for the accuracy of the information presented.

ISBN: 978-90-366-1886-1

CONTENTS

INTRODUCTION

THE TWENTIETH CENTURY has been called "the short century".
Perhaps it may seem so but this century has been crowded
with incident, fractured by global warfare and accelerated by
technology and a communications revolution. We have been to the
moon, stared nuclear destruction in the face, cured — and
unleashed — killer diseases, and learned to cope on a planet
whose population has more than doubled since 1900.

Significantly, the end of this astonishing century is also the
end of the second millennium, giving the twentieth century a
particular resonance and interest. Using dramatic pictures and
accessible text, *The Illustrated History of the Twentieth Century*
examines and describes the force of this resonance. The book
begins with three introductory essays outlining the broad themes
that have shaped the century — politics, culture and war. It then
continues to tell the story of the century chronologically, moving
through time decade-by-decade, and, within each decade, year-
by-year. Each year, key events — from significant political
occurrences, through to details of daily life — are presented in
easy to access snippets. Striking black and white photographs,
many of them contemporary, bring events to life in a startling and
dramatic fashion.

At regular intervals feature spreads focus on topics of
particular interest and significance, such as war, revolution,
scientific developments and cultural highpoints. More than 100
major obituaries are also included, and *The Illustrated History of
the Twentieth Century* finishes with wide ranging easy-to-access
reference material on achievements in the fields of sport, cinema,
science and the arts.

POLITICS AND IDEOLOGIES

TO MAKE SOME SENSE of the politics of our own century is to attempt to be objective about our own lives and the events we have lived through, perhaps even witnessed at first hand. Without the measure of distance, the politics of this century appear too personal, crowding together in a seeming confusion of the horrific and banal, the epic and the ordinary. Yet writing at the tail end of a century that is finishing, as it began, with wars in the Balkans, instability in Russia, poverty and exploitation in Africa, and the continuing dominance of the USA, it is possible to make some coherence out of events, to discern some abiding themes which make this century one of the most violent, and most changeable, of this millennium.

ABOVE: The Russian royal family before the Revolution of 1917 brought down the monarchy forever.

AN END TO EMPIRE

To begin the century in 1900 may make chronological sense, but there is nothing to distinguish that year from 1899 or 1901, or indeed 1910. The world order established in the second half of the nineteenth century lived on into the twentieth, an order based on European imperial dominance of trade, technology and colonial possession matched only by the aggressive frontier state of the USA, whose dynamic economy and growing population was fast providing a counterbalance to European hegemony. But while the imperial system of mighty empires was on proud display in Britain, France, Germany, Russia and Austria-Hungary, the edifice was not as strong as it looked. In 1911 the ancient Chinese Empire finally collapsed as a quasi-democratic and republican government took power in Beijing. In 1913 the Ottoman Empire had dwindled to a mere toehold in Europe, having already lost control of North Africa. And in 1914, in Sarajevo in the Balkans, the heir to the Austrian throne was assassinated, bringing the whole imperial system tumbling down. If the nineteenth century ended with the Chinese Revolution, the twentieth began with a gunshot in Sarajevo, the catalyst for the first war in history to be deemed a world war.

A NEW ORDER

The First World War changed the landscape of the world utterly and completely. A total war which mobilized entire populations in Europe and was fought out in colonies on every continent, it ended the certainties of the single world order of the previous century and redrew the map of the world. Gone were the German, Austro-Hungarian, Russian and Ottoman Empires; weakened were the French and British Empires. In their place were three dominant ideologies — the rampant Capitalism and liberal democracy of the United States, the totalitarian, state order of Fascism, and the equally totalitarian although supposed liberating system of Communism. The new order of the world was now disorder.

ABOVE: The image of the swastika dominated the 1930s and 1940s.

For the next 70 years, these rival ideologies strove for world dominance. With Communism confined to one country — Russia — the weakness of Capitalism when faced with the reconstruction of the European economies after the war led to Fascism gaining ground in Italy and then Germany, Spain, and a host of East European countries. Post-war political and economic instability and the collapse of the world economy after the slump of 1929 provided fertile ground for totalitarianism as both a resurgent Germany under the Nazis and an imperial Japan under military control used military might and economic muscle to address the unfinished business of the 1919 Treaty of Versailles which had supposedly ended the First World War. By 1939 the world had returned to war again, a three-sided conflict between rival ideologies that forced Capitalism and Communism together to fight the common foe, Fascism.

ABOVE: Pictures from Hitler's death camps shocked the world.

THE HORROR OF THE HOLOCAUST

To see the Second World War as an equally barbaric continuation of the First makes political sense, with much the same players on the same sides as before. One event, however, stands out as a unique disfigurement to this and indeed any century. Almost 60 years on, the world is still trying to come to terms with the Holocaust, the deliberate attempt by one nation to remove every member of another from the face of the world. The evil banality of the industry of genocide — the camps, the trains, the meticulous record-keeping — revealed the full and horrifying potential of human cruelty, and exposed Western civilization for the sham it really was.

RIVAL WORLD SYSTEMS

The defeat of Fascism by 1945 both simplified and intensified the ideological conflict. The new world order was now based on conflict between the two main victors — Soviet Russia and capitalist USA. This was the Cold War which was to dominate the world for the next 45 years. Despite the obvious flashpoints of Berlin, Poland, Hungary and Czechoslovakia, Europe was in many ways sidelined. Both superpowers, as they became known, poured in money and resources to rebuild their halves of Europe in their own image, while the major European colonial powers — Britain, France, the Netherlands, and later Spain and Portugal — retreated from international pretensions and gave up their colonies, ushering on to the world stage a host of new nations: some old countries such as India regaining their independence, most others new creations with unstable borders and little experience of self-rule. It was here, and in the rest of the so-called Third World, that the superpower conflict was fought out in a series of wars by proxy, with flashpoints in Korea, Vietnam and the rest of Southeast Asia, in Angola, the Horn of Africa, Afghanistan, Cuba and Nicaragua.

ABOVE: Berlin was divided and the wall guarded on both sides.

ABOVE: A US Pershing missile launch.

THE SUPREMACY OF THE SUPERPOWERS

Two responses were evident to superpower dominance. In South America, Africa and Asia, non-alignment became an act of political faith for many newly independent nations, based on the sound principle of a plague on both big houses. In Western Europe, the century-old rivalry between France and Germany was subsumed in an industrial and political partnership to rebuild Europe, which by the end of the century was to include fifteen countries in close political and economic union with a single currency and common institutions and laws. But, inescapably, the superpower rivalry cast a long shadow over the world. It was based on military might, with both sides developing nuclear weapons and space technology to achieve balances of terror in missiles and men. It was also based on ideological conviction, as both sides were convinced of the morality of their position. Oddly, despite protestations to the contrary, both sides soon came to resemble the imperial dinosaurs vanquished in 1914.

In the end it was money, not ideology, which counted. With its ability to generate wealth and develop new technology, the USA outperformed and outspent the USSR, bankrupting the country and causing it to collapse altogether in 1991. By then, however, new forces had emerged which made their conflict irrelevant. Across the world, a growing awareness of human rights and civil liberties led to the emergence of women's liberation and gay rights, of black consciousness movements, and demands for equality of both opportunity and outcome. Oil, and increasingly water, became resources to be fought over. And in the Arab world, the emergence of the state of Israel began a process which led to a fundamentalist renaissance similar to that experienced by Christendom 500 years before. In an increasingly secular age — both superpowers were, after all, based on an ideology of economics, not religion — the arrival of theocracies in Iran, Afghanistan and elsewhere placed in sharp relief the consumerism and commercialism of much of the rest of the world. Where once there were colonial powers, now there is Coca Cola and MTV, Microsoft and McDonalds. Stand in a shopping mall in Seoul or Jakarta and you could be in London or Los Angeles. Such material gains have their price, and just as the Islamic fundamentalists have turned their back on what they see as Western decadence, others have pointed out that such decadence is based on limited world resources and a planet highly susceptible to human maladministration. The world may be glad to turn its back on the horrors of this century, but can hardly face the next with any great comfort.

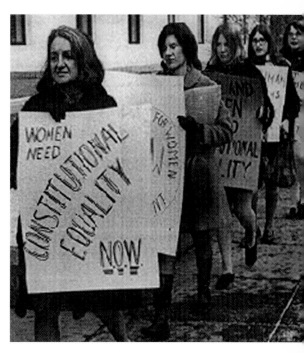

ABOVE: Women marched for equal opportunity.

ABOVE: Ayatollah Khomeini brought fundamentalism to Iran.

THE ARTS AND POPULAR CULTURE

THE RAPID PACE OF CHANGE in the twentieth century affected the arts as much as any other field. Styles and movements followed each other in rapid succession as artists tried to extend their scope, inventing new forms, covering new subjects and using new technology. These trends were accelerated by improvements in communication, giving works of art wide exposure.

Changes in lifestyle, with more leisure for more people, and mass media supplying their needs, had profound effects on the arts. One result was the divergence of "popular" and "high" culture. New forms emerged, whose aims seemed far removed from those of "high" art. Yet, by the end of the century, many artists working in conventional modes have absorbed influences from popular culture and multimedia has brought "high" and "low" culture together again.

LITERATURE AND DRAMA

The century began with some of the most vital, revolutionary literary movements of all time. In poetry, writers such as Frenchman Guillaume Apollinaire and American Ezra Pound invented new forms and transformed readers' ideas about what poetry could be like. Movements such as Dadaism and Surrealism opened up new worlds of experimentation with language and imagery. The scope of the novel was also extended greatly. While many novelists continued writing realist fiction in the tradition of their nineteenth-century forebears, they would eventually include virtually every facet of human life in their work. One writer, James Joyce, extended the scope of the novel further than any other. His masterpiece, *Ulysses*, has influenced countless later works of fiction.

The idea of the "well-made play" reached its fruition in the nineteenth century. Some twentieth-century dramatists, such as George Bernard Shaw, continued to draw on this tradition but others wanted to take drama in new directions. The German Expressionist movement sought a new intensity of language and action; dramatist Bertolt Brecht and composer Kurt Weill brought social comment to musical theatre; the French theatre of the absurd created an elusive symbolism; writers such as Irishman Samuel Beckett pared down

ABOVE: Literary giants of the century — James Joyce, Ezra Pound, Ford Maddox Ford and John Quinn.

dramato into its most basic constituents; French theorist Antonin Artaud inspired the "theatre of cruelty" in which violence, spectacle and religious experience were blended together in a new and potent mix.

MUSIC

Music more than any other art form has shown how popular and "mainstream" culture have diverged during the twentieth century. Composers in the "serious" tradition continued to write for classical ensembles but many others abandoned the concepts of tonality and melody that made earlier classical music accessible to a wide audience.

ABOVE: Igor Stravinsky, one of the century's great musical innovators.

Meanwhile, a flourishing popular culture continued to provide accessible music. Jazz, the music of black America, set the trend. Other cultures soon picked up on its idioms and it began to influence a host of popular styles that sprang up in the second half of the century. Popular music also used the new technologies. It became above all a recorded medium, as successive formats — wax cylinders, 78s, vinyl discs, tapes, CDs — provided better reproduction. "Serious" composers too were fascinated with the new technology. In the 1940s and 1950s, Karlheinz Stockhausen in Germany and Pierre Henri in France pioneered electronic music; later Pierre Boulez founded IRCAM, his Paris centre for research into electronics and acoustics in music.

ABOVE: The first discs.

ARCHITECTURE

The architects of the twentieth century took the materials of the nineteenth, such as steel and reinforced concrete, and put them to wider use. The first result was the rise of the skyscraper. Architects such as Le Corbusier were also at the forefront of social thinking, designing new cities that would provide a better living environment than before. Sadly, few of these cities were built in the way that their architects wished.

And yet the century did produce buildings that have withstood the test of time — the skyscrapers of New York and Chicago, housing projects by JJP Oud, the houses of Frank Lloyd Wright in the USA. Architects in Germany developed a keynote style at the Bauhaus, the

ABOVE: The Seagram Building (1954–8), New York, by Mies van der Rohe and Philip Johnson.

design school started at Weimar in 1919. Driven from Nazi Germany, the Bauhaus designers took their brand of modernism to the USA, where it became known as the International Style.

VISUAL ARTS

With a range of forms from photography to classical portraiture, nineteenth-century artists had achieved some of the most realistic styles in art history. Movements such as Cubism gave a new take on realism, refracting the image and seeming to capture several viewpoints at once. Other artists embraced Surrealism, using realist techniques to portray images from fantasy and dream. Abstraction, the abandonment of the subject altogether, was the route followed in Russia and the Netherlands. Towards the end of the century, in the form of the Abstract Expressionist style, it was favoured by many of the most prominent North American artists.

Another solution was to study the ideas inherent in images. From the "ready-mades" of French artist Marcel Duchamp to more recent conceptual works, many artists have tried to make their audience think, putting this aim before "pure" visual appeal. Artists have also been open to the influence of new media, making use of film and video in recent "installation" art.

ABOVE: Contemporary sculpture

Photography matured, developing its own language, techniques and technology. It became the democratic art form of the century, accessible to all and used for commerce as well as higher art forms.

FILM AND TELEVISION

The art of film grew with the century. Technological advances brought sound, then colour, then a seemingly endless range of special effects. The development of directing and acting techniques suited to film gave the medium its true power but the growth of sizeable film industries in Hollywood, India, and Australia provided finance, and the resources to screen films all over the world. Film became the art form most typical of the century. Television was born in the 1920s, and developed in a similar way to film, becoming the art form that found a place in every home. Television's power lay in its variety and its ability to provide information — documentaries, sports relays, and news broadcasts — that reported the century's events as they happened.

ABOVE: *The Empire Strikes Back*, part of the *Star Wars* trilogy, the pop culture phenomenon of the 1970s.

HOW WAR SHAPED THE CENTURY

I N THE FIRST 50 YEARS of the twentieth century war has directly and indirectly shaped not only the military, but also the diplomatic, social, scientific, technological and economic character of most of the world. Not all the side-effects of war are as grim as the event itself, and the twentieth century has benefited from medical and technological breakthroughs which may not have been made had

ABOVE: A soldier from World War I.

research not been driven by the needs of the military. The damage that war causes to individuals and to a nation's psyche can last long after the last round has been fired and the peace treaties have been signed. The reparations demanded by the Prussians after the Franco Prussian War fuelled the French desire for revenge in World War I. After 1918 the Germans suffered as badly from French demands, and this in turn was a factor in the rise of Hitler and National Socialism and therefore the outbreak of World War II.

THE POSITIVE SIDE OF CONFLICT

However war also gives urgency to research and this included the areas of radar and radio. Penicillin and plastic surgery as well as the more questionable benefit of DDT were all developed or advanced as a result of research in World War II. Nylon — not merely as a substitute for silk in stockings and thus one of the weapons of the American GI's charm offensive in Britain between 1943 and 1945 — replaced silk and cotton webbing material in parachutes.

While war may inspire, finance and accelerate new research, it also creates the climate in which innovation prospers. The tank, developed to break through the barbed wire and trench systems of the Western Front in France and Belgium, would become a key weapon in land war for the rest of the century.

Even explosives — the destructive force of war — have their civil applications. The plastic explosives derived from gelignite, which had been developed by the British in the early 1940s and used for sabotage by resistance groups throughout Europe, is now used in the demolition of redundant industrial plants or high-rise apartments.

ABOVE: War brought women into factories.

■17■

The fire-retardant and bullet proof materials used in tank crew overalls and body armour, find applications in clothing for civilian firemen and even the sails and rigging of modern sailing ships.

World War II accelerated the end of the colonial empires of Britain, France and The Netherlands and created new independent nations in Africa and Asia. As men were called up in huge numbers between 1914–18 to serve in the armed forces, so women went into the factories to take their places. Their work in areas that had previously been the preserve of men did much to accelerate emancipation after World War I. In World War II women again returned to the factories and in the post-war years job opportunities increased for women.

After World War I the first non-stop transatlantic flight was undertaken in an ex-RAF Vickers Vimy bomber. In four short years in World War I, aircraft had changed from fragile powered box kites, to robust machines capable of flying in poor weather. The jet engine that now powers most of the world's passenger aircraft, as well as combat aircraft, was developed in the United Kingdom and Germany during World War II.

ABOVE: World War II troops on Normandy Beach, 1941.

THE ULTIMATE DETERRENT AND UNLIMITED POWER

The research that has had the greatest impact on the world, and received its impetus during World War II, was the development of the atomic bomb. While the Western Allies were developing the atomic bomb, in Germany rocket scientists produced the first ballistic missile, the V2.

The combination of missile and nuclear warhead has made the world since 1945 both a very dangerous and a safer place. As nuclear weapons proliferate beyond Russia, Europe and the USA the threat of global destruction in a "small" nuclear war increases. However in the past this threat kept the peace in Europe between the former Soviet Union and the West until the final collapse of the USSR and the end of the Cold War.

Nuclear power has vociferous critics, but harnessed for peaceful use it has provided electric

ABOVE: Atomic bomb on Nagasaki.

power and propulsion for major ships. The rocket technology that can deliver a nuclear warhead has been used to explore the outer limits of space. While part of the impetus for the drive has come from scientific curiosity the "Space Race" between the USSR and USA financed and drove the programme in its early years.

ABOVE: War in Vietnam.

Navigation and satellite technology, which was first intended for military reconnaissance use, has allowed cartographers to update maps in some of the remotest parts of the world and travellers to visit them using the remarkable accuracy of the Global Positioning System (GPS).

THE BENEFITS OF THE COLD WAR

It must be remembered that one of the remarkable aspects of this century has been the many years of peace — or at least lack of aggression on a global scale — which was the direct result of the East-West split at the end of World War II. With both sides equipped with more than enough fire-power to destroy a thousand Earths, the world

ABOVE: Research into fusion power, a by-product of the arms race.

basked in a kind of stand-off situation and a whole generation in the West has lived to middle age without experiencing the devastation known to their parents. Now that the Eastern bloc has imploded and been reborn as individual states, it seems we are going back to old-fashioned local incidents and skirmishes. What will happen after the millennium has yet to be seen.

War in the twentieth century has been more destructive over shorter periods than any previous conflict. Humanity has harnessed science, technology and perverted medical knowledge in weapon design. War can be, and has been, a degrading, destructive, corrupting and corrosive activity. However it has also been the only option available to governments or liberation movements to defeat tyrants and liberate oppressed or enslaved nations.

A NEW CENTURY

CHANGE is in the air as the new century begins. In Europe, alliances change; in Asia, Japan emerges from isolation and China enters its last imperial phase. Russia experiences its first revolution; industry and technology grow apace in the United States. Women on both sides of the Atlantic opt for militancy in their quest for the vote. Science too is revolutionary: the first manned flight, wireless transmission, new plastics, psychoanalysis, relativity, and the arrival of mass-produced cars — society on the move.

OPPOSITE: World Exhibition opens on April 14 in Paris, France.

1900–1909

KEY EVENTS OF THE DECADE

- BOER WAR
- BOXER REBELLION
- FREUD DEVELOPS PSYCHOANALYSIS
- FIRST SUCCESSFUL MANNED FLIGHT
- RUSSO-JAPANESE WAR
- WOMEN FIGHT FOR THE VOTE
- REVOLUTION IN RUSSIA
- EINSTEIN PUBLISHES THEORY OF RELATIVITY
- HORMONES ARE DISCOVERED
- RADIOACTIVITY IS EXPLAINED

- BLERIOT FLIES THE CHANNEL
- FIRST NOBEL PRIZES AWARDED
- FIRST TRANSATLANTIC RADIO TRANSMISSION
- VACUUM CLEANER INVENTED
- FORD DEVELOPS MODEL-T MOTOR CAR
- PEARY REACHES NORTH POLE
- CUBISM IS BORN
- BALLETS RUSSES FOUNDED
- THE FIRST WESTERN IS SCREENED

WORLD POPULATION: 1,608 MILLION

BOER WAR AND BOXER REBELLION

As a new century opens, conflict remains a common theme. The Boer War continues in South Africa, where the establishment of concentration camps shocks the world, and in China the Boxer uprising gives violent expression to anti-Western sentiment. In the world of science, the findings of Sigmund Freud and Max Planck revolutionize psychology and physics, and in the visual world, Art Nouveau transforms the streets of Paris.

OPPOSITE: Chinese nationalist, member of the Boxer society, "Fists of Righteous Harmony."

1900

Feb	9	Dwight Davis creates Davis Cup tennis tournament
	27	Labour Party founded, U.K.
Mar	19	Arthur Evans begins to unearth Knossos, Crete
Apr	14	World Exhibition opens, Paris, France
May	17	British army relieves Mafeking, South Africa
	20	Second Olympic Games begins, Paris, France
	31	Boxer Rebellion breaks out, China
June	19	Theodore Roosevelt, hero of the Spanish-American War (1898), is nominated for U.S. vice-president
	24	Boxers destroy foreign embassies, China
July	1	Zeppelin makes maiden flight, Germany
	19	Paris Métro opens
	29	Anarchist assassinates King Umberto of Italy
Aug	13	*Deutschland* wins Blue Riband as the fastest transatlantic liner
	14	Allied forces enter Peking, China
	25	Friedrich Nietzsche dies
Sep	19	Alfred Dreyfus pardoned, France
Oct	14	Sigmund Freud publishes *The Interpretation of Dreams*
	26	Britain annexes Transvaal, South Africa
Nov	9	Russia completes annexation of Manchuria
	30	Writer Oscar Wilde dies in exile in France

ABOVE: Count Zeppelin's mighty airship moored in its shed after making its successful flight.

ZEPPELIN TAKES TO THE AIR
Count Ferdinand von Zeppelin of Germany launches his first dirigible (steerable) airship, *LZ 1*, in July. Its flight lasts about 20 minutes.

SALOON BUSTER
In the United States, American temperance agitator Carry Nation campaigns for the closure of saloons. Armed with a hatchet and accompanied by hymn-singing women, she goes on saloon-busting expeditions.

METRO TRANSFORMS PARIS
Art Nouveau architect Hector Guimard transforms the streets of Paris with his entrances to the new Paris Métro. He uses iron and glass in new ways, which are both beautiful in their use of whiplash curves, plant-like forms and distinctive typography, but also highly practical. The roof panels, for instance, are standardized for ease of manufacture.

PETER RABBIT IS BORN
This year sees the writing of *The Tale of Peter Rabbit*, the first of a series of children's stories by English author Beatrix Potter (1866–1943). First published privately, *Peter Rabbit* becomes a firm favorite and will be followed by many similar volumes, which remain popular throughout the century, overcoming fashion. The use of the author's own illustrations and a small format, perfectly suited for children's hands, make this a highly influential book.

TOSCA TAKES THE STAGE
Giacomo Puccini's opera *Tosca* is performed. The full-blooded melodies, violent action, tense emotions, and vivid characters of Puccini's work take traditional Italian opera just about as far as it can go. Puccini is also the chief exponent of the *verismo* or realism style; his plot is so dramatic that audiences can tell what is going on from the music and action, without understanding the language.

MINOAN DISCOVERY
British archaeologist Arthur Evans (1851–1941) uncovers Knossos, capital of the Bronze Age Minoan civilization on the Aegean island of Crete. His remarkable discoveries include the magnificent palace of the legendary King Minos and pottery fragments decorated with Minoan script.

LORD JIM
Author Joseph Conrad's first great novel *Lord Jim* launches the Polish exile on his path. His awareness of the power of evil and how idealism can be corrupted make him a major figure in fiction.

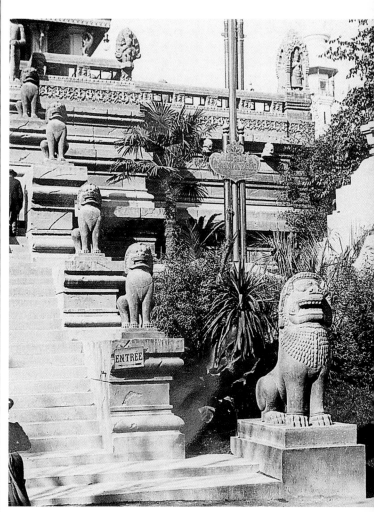

ABOVE: An imposing stairway leads to the Java Pavilion at the World Exhibition, Paris.

PAPER CLIP

The paper clip is patented in Germany by its Norwegian inventor, Johann Vaaler. Before its invention, papers are fastened together with pins.

PLUNGER SUBMERGES

American inventor John Holland has added further refinements to his submersible, the *Plunger*. The first streamlined submersible to be built, it is propelled by electricity when submerged (it was previously steam-driven on the surface). Now Holland has replaced the steam engine with a more efficient gasoline engine.

The invaluable paper clip.

CONCENTRATION CAMPS

British troops conquer the Transvaal and Orange Free State in November and scatter the Boer armies. The British are beginning to intern Boer women and children in concentration camps to prevent them helping Boer soldiers. This move causes an international outrage.

ABOVE: Fashionable shooting outfit for sporting women.

PLAY CAUSES SCANDAL

Austrian writer Arthur Schnitzler publishes his play *Reigen*. It shows the relationships between ten people all connected to each other in a circle of sexual contact, and sums up the corruption and decadence of the last years of the Hapsburg empire. The play causes a scandal and will not be performed until 1920.

CAKEWALK

A strutting dance, the cakewalk, which originated among black American slaves, hits Europe's dance halls.

DARING SWIMSUIT

Annette Kellerman, American aquatic star, introduces the one-piece swimsuit.

SECOND OLYMPICS

The second of the modern Olympic Games is held in Paris, France, from May to October, to coincide with the World Exhibition. However, events are scattered over six months and across northern France, diluting public interest. In contrast to the all-male games of 1896, women compete in a limited number of events.

THE QUANTUM THEORY

German physicist Max Planck (1858–1947) of Berlin University discovers that energy consists of basic units, each of which he calls quanta. This marks the beginning of quantum theory, revolutionizes the study of physics, and wins him a 1918 Nobel Prize.

RADIOACTIVE GAS

German physicist Friedrich Ernst Dorn discovers the dangerous radioactive gas radon, the sixth of the "noble gases." He finds it emanating from a sample of radium.

THE WORLD EXHIBITS IN PARIS

The world's most innovative technology goes on exhibition in Paris, France. The Palace of Electricity, illuminated at night, and escalators from the United States show how the new century will transform daily life. The Rodin Pavilion, France's major exhibit, is a celebration of the great sculptor.

OSCAR WILDE
(1854–1900)

The once-flamboyant Irish writer and brilliant epigramist, Oscar Wilde dies in France aged 44. Author of *The Importance of Being Earnest* and *The Picture of Dorian Gray*, Wilde was imprisoned for homosexual offenses in 1895. He served a two-year prison sentence, which he described in *The Ballad of Reading Gaol*.

YELLOW FEVER

An American army doctor, Walter Reed, discovers that the deadly disease yellow fever is transmitted by mosquitoes. He does this by studying the disease in Cuba with the help of human volunteers. Eliminating the mosquitoes in Panama later enables engineers to construct the Panama Canal.

GAMMA RAYS

French physicist Paul Ulrich Villard discovers that radium puts out a third kind of radiation, in addition to the alpha rays and beta rays already discovered. These new electromagnetic rays are later named gamma rays.

ENTER ELECTRONS

French physicist Henri Becquerel (1852–1908) discovers that the radioactivity from the element radium consists of the subatomic particles, electrons. He also finds that radioactivity can cause one element to change into another.

SISTER CARRIE

The highly realistic novel, *Sister Carrie*, by American master Theodore Dreiser, is effectively suppressed by the publishers because of its alleged immorality — "sin" is not "punished." The book is published, but not publicized.

ABOVE: A Chinese passport signed by statesman Li Hung Chang. A pro-Westerner, Li Hung Chang promoted links with Europe, which were resented by the Boxers.

ABOVE: Severe flooding in Rome creates an unusual image of the Forum.

RADIO, TORPEDOES, AND NOBEL PRIZES

European and Commonwealth countries mourn the death of Queen Victoria. She had reigned for 64 years, giving her name to a particular and remarkable period of history — the Victorian Age. As if to mark the start of a new era, the first-ever transatlantic radio signal is transmitted successfully and a black American is honored at the White House for the first time.

OPPOSITE: British sailors prepare to draw Queen Victoria's coffin through the streets of London.

1901

Jan	1	Commonwealth of Australia comes into being
	10	Oil discovered in Texas, United States
	22	Death of Queen Victoria, U.K.
Feb	26	Boxer leaders publicly executed, China
Mar	1	First monorail opened in Wuppertal, Germany
	17	Students riot in Russia
	13	First Mercedes built by Daimler, Germany
June	24	Unknown artist Pablo Picasso exhibits for the first time
Aug	4	Gold discovered in Rand, South Africa
Sep	6	President McKinley shot; Theodore Roosevelt becomes U.S. President
	7	Peking Treaty ends Boxer Rising, China
	9	Artist Toulouse-Lautrec dies
Oct	16	Black American Booker T. Washington dines at White House
Dec	10	First Nobel Prizes awarded
	12	Marconi sends first transatlantic wireless message

ABOVE: U.S. President McKinley and his cabinet at the White House.

END OF AN ERA

Queen Victoria dies at the age of 82. She has ruled Britain since 1837 and seen it grow into the most powerful economic and military power in the world, with a vast empire on every continent. Through her children and grandchildren, she is related to every monarch in Europe and her funeral is attended by heads of state from around the world.

U.S. PRESIDENT ASSASSINATED

President William McKinley is shot and killed in Buffalo, New York, by Polish anarchist Leon Czolgosz, in a September protest against the American government. Vice-president Theodore Roosevelt is on a climbing holiday when he hears the news and is sworn in as the 26th president at the age of 42.

FIRST TRANSATLANTIC RADIO

Worldwide radio communication becomes possible when the first transatlantic radio signal, the morse letter "S", is transmitted. A team working for the Italian pioneer of radio, Guglielmo Marconi (1874–1937), sends the signal from Poldhu, Cornwall, in the U.K. to St. John's, Newfoundland, on December 12.

MEN IN THE MOON

Creator of science fiction, author H.G. Wells anticipates the future with his new novel *The First Men in the Moon*. The spirit of adventure, the explanation of technology, and the conquest of space are themes which will recur in science fiction of later decades.

EUROPEAN ELEMENT

French chemist Eugène Dumarçay discovers the rare earth element europium, which he names in honor of Europe.

BLACK AMERICAN AT THE WHITE HOUSE

President Theodore Roosevelt (1858–1919) entertains black American Booker T. Washington to dinner at the White House, the first black man to be so honoured. Booker T. Washington is a noted reformer and educator and president of the first university for blacks in the United States in Tuskegee, Alabama. Two weeks later, 34 people are killed in race riots which break out in the American South in protest at the visit.

THREE SISTERS

Konstantin Stanislavsky directs Anton Chekhov's play, *The Three Sisters*, written especially for the Moscow Art Theatre, in a milestone production that brings him fame. His insistence on a permanent, high-quality company of actors, his enthusiasm for a realistic acting style, and his belief in the theatre as a means of educating people, later find expression in the Method style of acting, in which the actor draws on his or her past experiences in creating a role.

MORO WARS BREAK OUT

Violence breaks out in the Philippines when the United States in control of the Philippines since 1898, demands that the Moros, Muslim tribespeople, assimilate with Christian islanders.

ABOVE: Marconi with his radio receiving set.

BELOW: Loading an aerial torpedo — a new and deadly weapon.

ABOVE: Motor racing gains popularity; here a French contestant reaches Berlin.

BLOOD GROUPS

Viennese-born U.S. immunologist Karl Landsteiner discovers that blood can be categorized into three groups, A, B and O, a method of sorting still used today. Landsteiner later discovers a fourth group, AB.

VACUUM CLEANER INVENTED

Herbert Cecil Booth, an English civil engineer, invents the vacuum cleaner. His first machine is mounted on a horse-drawn cart and powered by a gasoline engine. Long tubes are passed into houses to clean them.

MUTATIONS

Dutch botanist Hugo de Vries, who in 1900 rediscovered Gregor Mendel's laws of heredity, discovers that new forms of plants can arise suddenly, and gives this process the name "mutation." He introduces the experimental method of studying plant evolution.

MERCURY LAMP

American electrical engineer Peter Cooper-Hewitt markets the mercury-vapor electric arc lamp. It produces a light that is nearly shadow-free.

BUDDENBROOKS

German author Thomas Mann (1875–1955) publishes his first novel, *Buddenbrooks*. In it Mann portrays the decline of one German family, who lose their money, their creativity, and their very will to live, using this as a symbol for the decline of Germany itself.

WOMEN STUDENTS ENTER ROCHESTER

American feminist Susan B. Anthony persuades Rochester University, New York, to accept women students. She raises nearly $100,000 to pay the tuition costs.

SHAVING TIME

The first safety razor with throwaway blades is made by King Camp Gillette of Boston, Massachusetts. For two years he has to give the razors away until he can find a backer to set him up with a factory. By 1908 he is selling 14 million blades a year.

KORFBALL INVENTED

Dutch schoolmaster Nico Broekhuysen invents the sport of Korfball, similar to basketball. It is played by teams of 12 on a playing area with three zones. In the zone at each end stands a basket 11.5 feet off the ground in which goals are scored.

ANTARCTIC EXPEDITION

Robert Falcon Scott, commander of the British National Antarctic Expedition, sets sail in the *Discovery* from New Zealand. The expedition explores the Ross Sea area, sighting the Transantarctic Mountains, reaching the polar plateau and discovering Taylor Valley.

LEFT: Workmen strengthen wires on the Brooklyn Bridge, the world's largest suspension bridge, crossing the East River, New York City.

CHEAP CYCLES
are
within an Ace of Perfection
when fitted with
DUNLOP TYRES
£3 · 3s.   per Pair.

FIRST NOBEL PRIZES

The first-ever Nobel Prizes for achievements in physics, chemistry, medicine or physiology, literature, and peace are awarded. They were endowed in 1895 by Alfred Nobel, the Swedish chemist and inventor of dynamite. Jacobus Henricus van't Hoff (Holland) is awarded the prize in chemistry for his work on thermodynamics and stereochemistry. Wilhelm Röntgen (Germany) receives the physics prize for his discovery of X-rays. Sully Prudhomme, of France, receives the literature prize, Jean-Henri Dunant (Switzerland), founder of the Red Cross, and Frédéric Passy (France) jointly receive the peace prize.

AUSTRALIAN COMMONWEALTH

The Commonwealth of Australia comes into being in January. The six former Australian colonies are now united within a single federal state, but there are already difficulties over nonwhite immigration and the growing demands of the trade union and labor movement for better working conditions.

ANTI-SEMITISM IN RUSSIA

Anti-Semitism drives many Russian Jews to Palestine to settle in farming colonies set up by Baron Rothschild.

ROCKEFELLER INSTITUTE FOUNDED

American philanthropist and oil magnate, John D. Rockefeller, founds the Rockefeller Institute for Medical Research.

CHRISTMAS TREES ARE LIT UP

Christmas tree lights are among the ideas developed by the Edison General Electric Co. in the United States, founded by the inventor Thomas Edison in 1889.

TEDDY BEAR DEBUT

The Treaty of Vereeniging brings an end to the Boer War, the Japanese and British enter a formal alliance, and France and Italy sign an *entente*. Hormones are discovered and surgery makes a major advance when the technique of suturing is developed. Italian tenor Enrico Caruso becomes the world's first recording star and American president "Teddy" Roosevelt gives his name to what will become one of the world's favorite toys.

1902

Jan	7	Chinese imperial court returns to Peking after suppression of Boxer uprising
	30	Britain and Japan sign peace treaty
Feb	1	Footbinding outlawed, China
Mar	26	Cecil Rhodes, architect of imperialism, dies
May	31	Treaty of Vereeniging ends the Boer War
July	31	96 miners killed in a mining diaster at Port Kembla, Australia
Sep	29	French novelist Emile Zola (b. 1840) dies
Nov	1	Franco-Italian *entente*

ABOVE: Russian novelist and visionary Leo Tolstoy (1828–1910), famed for his novels and rejection of materialism.

ABOVE: The Turin Shroud. Experimenters claim the marks came from vapors emitted by the dead body of Jesus Christ.

ABOVE: Despite appalling conditions in the camps, Boer prisoners maintain their spirits with amateur dramatics.

BOER WAR ENDS

At Vereeniging, South Africa, Britain and the Boer leaders finally sign a peace treaty in May that marks the end of the Boer War, which has lasted for nearly three years. The Boers are forced to accept British colonial rule, with a promise of self-government later, and a substantial grant of £3 million to help rebuild their shattered countries.

VOTES FOR ALL IN AUSTRALIA

Australia grants universal suffrage, allowing women aged 21 and over to vote in federal elections with the same rights as men. This follows New Zealand's example in granting universal suffrage, which is unknown throughout Europe and the United States.

JAPANESE-BRITISH ALLIANCE

Britain and Japan sign a treaty of alliance in January, by which both agree not to make a treaty with a third country without the other's consent. The agreement safeguards Britain's interests in China and Japan's interests in Korea, and is the first alliance Britain has signed for many years.

A TRIP TO THE MOON

Georges Méliès's latest film *A Voyage to the Moon* opens to acclaim. Using innovatory special effects and combining magic and fantasy, it consists of 30 scenes and will bring Méliès, a conjurer by training, international fame.

FIRST TEDDY BEAR

Russian-born Morris Michton, a New York candy store assistant, makes the world's first teddy bear. He was inspired by a Clifford Berryman cartoon in the *Washington Evening Star* which showed President "Teddy" Roosevelt on a hunting trip, refusing to shoot a mother bear.

STITCHES IN TIME

French surgeon Alexis Carrel develops the technique of suturing (sewing) blood vessels (arteries and veins) together end to end, a major development in surgery.

ABOVE: French novelist Emile Zola, author of *Germinal*, and defender
of Dreyfus. He dies this year.

TOP OF THE CHARTS

Italian tenor Enrico Caruso (1873–1921) becomes the first recording star when he makes ten records for the Victor company. They include "Vesti la giubba" from Pagliacci, which will eventually become the first classical record to sell one million copies.

FRANCO-ITALIAN ENTENTE

France and Italy sign an *entente* in which Italy assures France of its neutrality if France is attacked. The French government is increasingly concerned by the growing military and economic might of Germany and is thus ensuring the security of its border with Italy.

RIYADH RECAPTURED

Abdul Aziz ibn Abdul Rahman of the al Saud family recaptures Riyadh from the Turks following a series of campaigns against the Turks and other family groups.

EARLY MORNING TEA

Frank Clarke, a gunsmith from Birmingham, England, makes the first automatic tea-maker. It is powered by clockwork, strikes a match to light a spirit stove, and pours boiling water into a teapot. It then sets off a bedside alarm.

FLATIRON BUILDING

Daniel H. Burnham's twenty-story Flatiron Building in New York City, with its slim lines tapering to almost nothing, shows for the first time how modern concrete-and-steel technology gives the architect scope to create new shapes and forms.

DISASTER IN AFRICA

On the French ruled island of Martinique, West Africa, the volcano Mount Pele erupts. Some 30,000 people are killed.

ABOVE: Franz Josef, Emperor of Austria. His attack on Serbia in 1914 precipitates World War I.

RIGHT: King Edward VII of Britain and Queen Alexandra on board the royal yacht *Victoria and Albert*.

PHOTO-SECESSION GROUP
This group of photographers, based in New York City, is led by Alfred Stieglitz and Edward Steichen. They uphold the right of the photographer to be considered an artist, and publish the influential photographic journal, *Camera Work*, which will run until 1917.

CORONATION DAY
Rulers of Europe gather in London for the coronation of Edward VII on August 9. The coronation has been postponed from June when Edward was forced to undergo an emergency operation for appendicitis. The king, who is 60, has made a good recovery in time for the coronation and the many diplomatic and public events associated with it.

HORMONES DISCOVERED
British physicists Ernest Henry Starling and William Bayliss discover that secretin, produced in the duodenum, acts on another organ of the body, the pancreas. Three years later they name this and other substances "hormones."

FOOT BINDING BANNED
The binding of the feet of Han Chinese women is banned in China by imperial edict after petitions from reform groups. The first reform group was founded in Canton in 1894 and was followed by others in provincial capitals.

IONOSPHERE SUGGESTED
British physicist Oliver Heaviside suggests that a layer of electrical charges in the atmosphere might be reflecting wireless waves back to Earth. Simultaneously, Arthur Edwin Kennelly of the United States puts forward the same idea. It is proved 20 years later, and is now called the ionosphere.

ABOVE: Four years in the making, the now-completed Nile dam.

HEART OF DARKNESS
Joseph Conrad (1857–1924) publishes his novel *Heart of Darkness*. It portrays a journey into the interior of Africa, where Conrad himself had travelled. He brings to life the terrifying consequences of human corruptibility in a colonial setting.

PELLEAS ET MELISANDE
Creator of musical impressionism, Claude Debussy (1862–1918) premières his only completed opera, *Pelléas et Mélisande*. In this work Debussy evokes a nightmarish atmosphere influenced by the ghost stories of American writer Edgar Allan Poe.

MOWING MADE EASY
The first commercially successful motor-mower is made in Britain. It is driven by a gasoline engine.

ELIZABETH CADY STANTON
(1815–1902)

The American feminist, Elizabeth Cady Stanton dies aged 87. In 1848, with the pacifist and antislavery campaigner Lucretia Mott, she launched the American women's rights movement at the Seneca Falls convention. She campaigned for sexual equality throughout her life, and in 1869, with Susan B. Anthony, founded the National Woman Suffrage Association. She acted as president of the Association until 1892. In later life she completed three of the six volumes of *History of Woman Suffrage* (1881–86), with Lucretia Mott and Matilda Joslyn Gage, and her autobiography.

TROUBLE BREWS IN THE BALKANS

Trouble breaks out in the Balkans, where thousands of Bulgarians are massacred. In North America, the U.S./Canadian border is finally settled and in South America, Panama achieves independence. Women in Britain adopt militancy as the best means of achieving the vote, and Marie Curie becomes the first woman to receive a Nobel Prize. Color photography is developed and France's first Tour de France bicycle race takes place.

1903

Feb	24	British forces march against "Mad" Mullah Mohammed bin Abdullah
Apr	16	Jews massacred in Bessarabia
June	15	Cinema audiences flock to *The Great Train Robbery*
July	19	First Tour de France finishes
Aug	2	Uprising begins in Macedonia
Sep	8	Turks massacre Bulgarians
Oct	10	Women's Social and Political Union (WSPU) founded, U.K.
	13	Boston Pilgrims win first baseball World Series
	20	Alaskan boundary decided
Dec	17	Wright brothers make first successful flight

ABOVE: Scott's ship *Discovery* sails south from New Zealand on the Antarctic expedition. On board is a junior officer, Ernest Shackleton.

OPPOSITE: Macedonian revolutionaries dance around a campfire, while their priest looks on.

JEWISH POGROM

Many Jews are killed by local people in the town of Kishinev, Bessarabia, in southwest Russia. The police turn a blind eye to the pogrom, which started on Easter Sunday, as do the government, which has been persecuting Jews since Czar Nicholas came to the throne in 1894.

BOLSHEVIKS BREAK AWAY

At its congress in London in August, the Russian Social Democratic Party splits between the moderate Mensheviks (minority), led by G.V. Plekhanov, and the more radical Bolsheviks (majority), led by V.I. Lenin. The split harms the effectiveness of the opposition to the government of Czar Nicholas II.

DEEDS NOT WORDS

Mrs Emmeline Pankhurst (1857–1928) and other women meet in Manchester, U.K., to form a new women's suffrage society, the Women's Social and Political Union (WSPU). Their aim is the achievement of votes for women "by any means." In contrast to previous women suffragist groups, the WSPU determines a militant approach. Soon, they will be known as suffragettes.

FIRST SUCCESSFUL AEROPLANE FLIGHT

Two brothers, Wilbur and Orville Wright from Ohio, achieve the first successful heavier-than-air-flight in December at Kitty Hawk, North Carolina. Their machine, the *Flyer*, flies a distance of about 120 feet. Orville is at the controls while the plane makes its first flight.

FIRST WESTERN

Edwin S. Porter's film *The Great Train Robbery* is the first U.S. feature film and the first western. It marks the start of a major strand in American popular culture.

RADIUM PRIZE

French scientists Marie and Pierre Curie, with Henri Becquerel, share the Nobel Prize for Physics, for discovering the radioactive elements radium and polonium. Marie Curie (1867–1934) is the first woman to receive a Nobel award.

MEASURING THE HEART

The first electrocardiograph to measure heart beats is made by the Dutch physiologist Willem Einthoven at Leyden University. He uses a simple galvanometer.

BELOW: Scott's Antarctic expedition of 1901–4. The sledge party, photographed by Shackleton, sets out from winter quarters towards the South Pole.

BULGARIANS MASSACRED

In Macedonia, the Turkish army massacres more than 50,000 men, women, and children in its continuing action against separatists in Macedonia. The victims, who are all Bulgarian, are killed by the Turks in their campaign to prevent Bulgaria expanding its territory into Turkish-held Macedonia.

BORDER DECISION

The commission set up to decide the frontier between Alaska and Canada finally agrees on the borderline. The decision of the British representative to favor Alaska infuriates the Canadian government.

FIRST TOUR DE FRANCE

Maurice Garin becomes the winner on July 19 in the first ever Tour de France cycling race, which has lasted for 16 days. The early years of the competition feature marathon stages, often completed in darkness.

SAFETY RAZOR

The safety razor is patented in Boston, Massachusetts, by King Camp Gillette in association with William Nickerson, a mechanic.

PANAMA DECLARES INDEPENDENCE

In November, the province of Panama declares its independence from Colombia in protest at delays by Colombia in agreeing the route for the proposed Panama Canal. In December, a treaty between Panama and the United States sets up the Canal Zone, which is handed over to the United States.

THE WAY OF ALL FLESH

This semiautobiographical novel by Samuel Butler is published after his death. It shows the deadening influence of tradition and family on life, and forms part of the reaction against Victorian views and values that is currently taking place.

THE CALL OF THE WILD

This year sees the publication of *The Call of the Wild* by Jack London. The story of a dog, Buck, who leads a pack of wolves after his master dies, it becomes one of the most popular novels by this socialist writer.

HEADACHE REMEDY

The painkiller, aspirin, is launched by the German drug company AG Bayer.

ABOVE: Under construction — St Louis World's Fair of Industry and Technology. It will open in 1904.

EXPLAINING RADIOACTIVITY

British scientists Ernest Rutherford (1871–1937) and Frederick Soddy, working in Canada, discover that radioactivity is the result of the breakdown of atoms in a radioactive element, producing a new element. They publish this as *The Cause and Nature of Radioactivity*.

VIKING EXCAVATION

The Oseberg longship, found buried inside a peat mound overlooking a Norwegian fjord near Oslo, is excavated. Interred inside it are two women who may have been ninth-century Viking nobles. As well as the women, the longship contains magnificent sledges, carts, furniture, kitchen utensils and textiles.

PAUL GAUGUIN (1848–1903)

Paul Gauguin, the French Post-Impressionist painter, has died. In 1883 Gauguin abandoned his stockbroker career in Paris to become a painter in Brittany. His best-known work was inspired by the art and culture of the South Pacific, where he lived from 1891. His primitive, exotic and dreamlike style (known as Synthesist) is seen in paintings such as *No Te Aha De Riri* (1896), and *Faa Iheihe, Decorated with Ornaments* (1898).

SALIVATING RESPONSE

Russian psychologist Ivan Pavlov (1849–1936) reports that ringing a bell will make a hungry dog salivate, if the bell has always been rung just before the dog's food arrives. Pavlov calls this a "conditioned reflex."

AMSTERDAM STOCK EXCHANGE

HP Berlage's reconstruction of the Amsterdam Stock Exchange, destroyed by fire in 1885, is completed. Based on a grid plan, the building is important for its use of red brick with a glass-and-metal roof.

FIRST CONES

The first ice cream cone made of waffle pastry is patented by Italo Marcioni, an ice cream salesman in New Jersey. The cones will be introduced at the Louisiana Purchase Exposition in St. Louis in 1904.

COLOR PHOTOGRAPHY

Louis and Auguste Lumière of France perfect the first single-plate process for color photography. It will be marketed in 1907 as Autochrome.

PULITZER PRIZE

Joseph Pulitzer, a Hungarian-born American newspaper proprietor, once a journalist on the German-language *Westliche Post*, donates $2 million to found a school of journalism at Columbia University. He endows annual prizes for journalism. The first prizes will be awarded in 1917.

WORLD SERIES

The Boston Pilgrims win the first baseball World Series in the United States. Boston are champions of the American League, formed in 1901, and beat the Pittsburgh Pirates, the champions of the more established National League.

ABOVE: The splendor of the Raj — Indian princes, Bengal lancers and others process into Delhi to proclaim Edward VII Emperor of India.

HOMOSEXUAL SURVEY

Berlin's Scientific-Humanitarian Committee, the world's first organization for homosexual rights, founded in 1898, questions more than 6,000 students and factory workers and concludes that 2.2 per cent of the general population is homosexual.

TIME FLIES

French magazine *Temps* sends a telegram around the world in six hours.

ABOVE: Emigration often provided the only means of escape for persecuted Eastern Europeans.

BELOW: Ellis Island — first port of call for immigrants reaching the United States.

RUSSIA TAKES ON JAPAN

Japan, having emerged from centuries of isolation, and Russia, bent on eastward expansion, clash over conflicting ambitions in Manchuria and Korea, and go to war. By contrast, Britain and France bring to an end centuries of hostility when they sign an *entente cordiale*. In the United States, immigration figures soar as Eastern Europeans flood into the country, fleeing persecution. And the opening of Schlesinger-Meyer in Chicago heralds the arrival of the twentieth-century department store.

1 9 0 4

Feb	8	Russo-Japanese War breaks out
Apr	8	Britain and France sign The Entente Cordiale
	13	Japanese torpedo boats sink the battleship *Petropavlovsk*
	30	World Exhibition opens in St. Louis
May	1	Japanese army defeats Russians at Xinyizhou
	2	Japanese fleet block Port Arthur
	26	Russian forces land in Manchuria
July	1	Olympic Games open in St. Louis
	15	Russian author Anton Chekhov (b.1860) dies
Sep	25	Trans-Siberian Railway is completed
Nov	8	President Theodore Roosevelt re-elected

THE RUSSO-JAPANESE WAR

In 1903 the Japanese had proposed that the Japanese and Russian governments should safeguard each other's special economic interests in Manchuria and Korea. Angered by the Russian lack of commitment, the Japanese ambassador broke off negotiations. In February 1904, 16 Japanese warships under Admiral Togo attack a fleet of six Russian battleships and ten cruisers under Vice Admiral Stark, off Port Arthur. Japanese torpedo boats severely damage two battleships and a cruiser. Others are also damaged and the two countries are at war. In April Japanese torpedo boats sink the Russian battleship *Petropavlovsk*. In May Japanese ships penetrate Port Arthur and block the harbor.

In August the Russian fleet, trapped in Port Arthur and under fire from land batteries, fights to reach the open sea. The Japanese fleet under Togo blocks their exit and forces them back into the harbor.

RIGHT: The Chinese governor of SanSin being carried ashore.

FAR RIGHT: Japanese soldiers execute traitors.

LEFT: Russian troops keep a careful lookout for Japanese from a treetop vantage point.

After a year of fighting, Russia surrenders Port Arthur to the Japanese in January. Japanese losses are 58,000 killed or wounded, and 30,000 sick.

In May the Russian Baltic fleet, including seven battleships and six cruisers, meets a Japanese force of the same size but with greater fire-power and speed, in the battle of Tsu Shima. During the afternoon of May 27, the Japanese sink four Russian battleships and damage one, for no losses. The Russians attempt to escape to Vladivostok but the Japanese destroyers and torpedo boats attack in the night and sink three ships. The battle continues the following day until all but 12 of the Russian fleet are captured, driven aground or sunk.

In September, Russia and Japan finally sign a peace treaty ending the Russo-Japanese War. The treaty marks the first time a European power is defeated in war by an Asian nation.

ABOVE: Siege guns, captured by the Japanese in August 1904, being moved by train before the battle of Liao Yang.

RIGHT: Russian troops inflate a balloon at Mukdon in 1905. The Russians were completely routed.

ANTON CHEKOV
(1860–1904)

This year sees the death of the Russian writer Anton Chekov, whose dramatic voice was so quintessentially Russian and yet universal in its appeal. Also a doctor, he was the author of 13 volumes of short stories, as well as the widely performed plays *The Seagull* (1896), *Uncle Vanya* (1900), *The Three Sisters* (1901), *The Cherry Orchard* (1904), and others. In 1897 he went to live in the Crimea suffering from tuberculosis and died in Yalta.

ENTENTE CORDIALE

Britain and France sign the Anglo-French Entente Cordiale, ending centuries of hostility between the two countries. The Entente settles long-standing colonial disputes between the two countries in North America, Africa, and the Pacific, and continues the British policy of seeking alliances to secure its global interests.

INTERNATIONAL WOMEN'S SUFFRAGE

Veteran American feminist Susan B. Anthony (1820–1906), together with suffrage leader Carrie Catt, founds the International Woman Suffrage Alliance in Berlin.

FIRST LABOUR P.M.

John Watson becomes prime minister of Australia, the first time a Labour politician has led a government anywhere in the world. He holds power only until August, when his government falls and is replaced by a coalition.

IMMIGRATION SOARS

Competitive cuts in steerage rates by rival steamship companies stimulates Eastern European immigration into the States. Slavs, Slovaks, Serbs, Croats, Bosnians, Herzegovinians, and many Jewish immigrants fleeing persecution begin to dominate the immigrant figures.

DIESEL-POWERED SUBMARINE

Maxim Laubeuf of France builds a diesel-powered submarine, the *Aigret*. Its lower flashpoint makes it safer than a gasoline-powered submarine.

GIVE MY REGARDS TO BROADWAY

American musical *Little Johnny Jones* includes this song, which becomes a smash hit and sums up the importance of Broadway and its musicals in the national identity of the United States.

PAIN RELIEF

Organic chemist Albert Einhorn of Germany first produces procaine, also known as Novocaine, which acts as a local anesthetic. It can be used instead of the more dangerous cocaine.

PETER PAN

Scottish dramatist J.M. Barrie's new play *Peter Pan*, with its forever-young hero, Lost Boys, and Never Never Land, becomes an abiding success. Barrie follows it up with a story (1906) and a book (1911).

JEAN-CHRISTOPHE

French author Romain Rolland (1866–1944) publishes the first of his 10-volume novel, *Jean-Christophe*, a long study of a fictional musician. Socialist, idealist, and pacifist, Rolland is important for bringing these values into fiction. He will later win the Nobel Prize in 1915.

CHICAGO DEPARTMENT STORE

One of the finest examples of an early twentieth-century department store is Louis Sullivan's Schlesinger-Meyer. Sullivan's style combines rich ornament on the lower floors with modern steel, glass, and concrete construction. The building also includes public rooms such as an art gallery, restaurant, and lounge.

NONFLAMMABLE CELLULOID

French chemists produce a nonflammable version of celluloid by adding metallic salts during manufacture. This spoils the old joke about the readiness of celluloid to burn: "Please do not smoke as I am wearing a celluloid collar."

ELECTRIC EYE

The first practical photo-electric cell, also called the "electric eye," is invented by Johann Elster of Germany; in the same year, German professor Arthur Korn uses one to transmit a picture over a telegraph wire.

ABOVE: The wrecked pleasure steamer *General Slocum* lies in New York harbor after a fire costing the lives of 1,000 passengers.

ABOVE: Pilgrims flood into Jerusalem to celebrate Christmas.

ABBEY THEATRE FOUNDED

Irish poet W.B. Yeats and Augusta, Lady Gregory (later joined by J.M. Synge as codirector) found the Abbey Theatre in Dublin. The theatre will be identified with a renaissance in Irish culture and many of the important twentieth-century Irish plays will be premièred there.

JUPITER SATELLITE

U.S. astronomer Charles Dillon Perrine discovers Himalia, the sixth satellite of the planet Jupiter.

ST. LOUIS OLYMPICS

The Olympic Games take place in St. Louis at the same time as the World Exhibition. Crowds flock to the Exhibition but, as in 1900, the unfocused games fail to attract large crowds. European involvement is limited because of the cost of travel. Only 680 athletes take part, 500 of whom are American or Canadian.

GIBSON GIRL

Charles Dana Gibson, a New York illustrator with a reputation for capturing aristocratic ideals, creates the Gibson Girl, an elegant beauty. His inspiration is his wife Irene Langhorne, whose fresh-faced image of perfect femininity is printed in society periodicals, such as *Life* and *Harper's*.

THERMIONIC DIODE VALVE

British electrical engineer John Ambrose Fleming patents the thermionic diode (two-electrode) valve (vacuum tube). It allows current to pass in one direction only and will be used for years as a key component in radio and T.V. receivers. After 1947 it will be gradually replaced by transistors.

TEA IN A BAG

Teabags are unwittingly introduced by Thomas Sullivan, a New York wholesaler who sends samples of tea to his customers in small silk bags instead of tins.

RUSSIAN UPRISING AND RELATIVITY

Revolution breaks out in Russia when czarist troops fire on demonstrators outside the Winter Palace in St. Petersburg. A mutiny follows and the czar is forced to introduce reform. After bitter fighting, the Russo-Japanese War comes to an end, with Japan victorious. Norway declares independence from Sweden and Albert Einstein publishes his theory of relativity.

1905

Jan	**2**	Russia surrenders Port Arthur to Japan
	22	Czar's troops massacre peaceful demonstrators in St. Petersburg
Mar	**24**	French writer Jules Verne (b.1828) dies
May	**27–8**	Battle of Tsu Shima. Japanese devastate Russian Baltic fleet
June	**7**	*Die Brücke* exhibition in Dresden
	27	Mutiny on the battleship *Potemkin*
Aug	**19**	Duma (representative assembly) established in Russia
Sep	**5**	Russia and Japan sign peace treaty to end Russo-Japanese War
Oct	**1**	The Fauves exhibit in Paris
	14	English suffragettes Christobel Pankhurst and Annie Kenney imprisoned
	26	Norway separates from Sweden
Nov	**28**	Universal suffrage in Austria

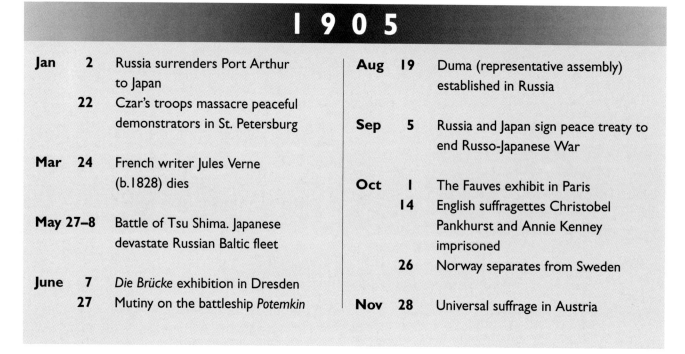

BELOW: Cars for millionaires — a 4-cylinder Fiat on display.

OPPOSITE: Amateur photographers at Burgos, in Spain, wait to photograph an eclipse of the sun.

RUSSIA ARISES

In January, strikers marching through the Russian capital of St. Petersburg, to petition Czar Nicholas II for better conditions, are shot dead by troops defending the Winter Palace. More than 500 are killed and many more wounded. The massacre increases demands for reform in Russia.

In June, Russian sailors on the battleship *Potemkin* mutiny after complaints about conditions on board. Other ships in the port of Odessa join the mutiny, while the city is gripped by a general strike. The mutiny adds to the weakening of the czar's rule, following the St. Petersburg massacre.

In October, Czar Nicholas II agrees a new constitution to turn Russia from an absolute autocracy into a semiconstitutional monarchy. The climbdown is forced on him by a general strike which has paralyzed the country for months, as well as defeat in the war against Japan.

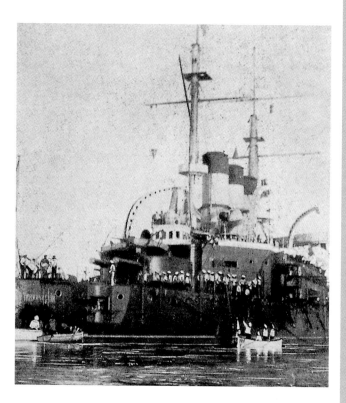

BELOW: *Potemkin* mutiny — a burnt-out railway shed left devastated after mutineers rampage through Odessa.

RIGHT: Battleship *Potemkin*, where the shooting of a sailor sparks off a serious mutiny.

THE KAISER IN AFRICA

The visit of the German Kaiser Wilhelm II (1859–1941) to Morocco leads to tension between Germany and France, who have traditionally claimed "a special standing" in Morocco. The Kaiser claims he is protecting German economic interests.

SALOME AND THE SEVEN VEILS

Based on Oscar Wilde's scandalous 1893 play, Richard Strauss's opera *Salome* opens in Dresden. Its striking harmonies and large orchestra (requiring singers of great power) establish Strauss (1864–1949) as the major German opera composer of the time. The famous Dance of the Seven Veils causes a scandal.

FREE NORWAY

The Norwegian parliament in Oslo declares independence from Sweden in June. The result is approved by the people in a plebiscite in August and Norway becomes an independent nation in October. Prince Charles of Denmark accepts the throne and rules as Haakon VII (1872–1957).

EINSTEIN, RELATIVITY, AND OTHER THEORIES

German-born physicist Albert Einstein (1879–1955) publishes his Special Theory of Relativity, in which he revolutionizes thinking by proposing that time and motion are relative. He also publishes papers on Brownian motion and the photoelectric effect.

SOCIOLOGY RECOGNIZED

The American Sociological Society is formed in Chicago, Illinois, marking sociology's acceptance by the academic world. It follows the founding by the University of Chicago of the world's first sociology department, headed by Albion Small, and the publication of the first sociology journal.

DIE BRUCKE EXPRESS THEMSELVES

A group of German artists in Dresden mount their first exhibition in a lamp factory. They are the first Expressionists — the founding members are Fritz Bleyl, Erich Heckel, Ludwig Kirchner, and Karl Schmidt-Rottluff (who gave the group its name, *Die Brücke*, meaning the bridge). Their bold outlines and strong planes of color enliven European art for several years and have a lasting influence.

SPEED WARNINGS

The Automobile Association is founded in Britain to warn car drivers of police speed traps. The speed limit is 20mph.

RADIOTHORIUM

German radio chemist Otto Hahn (1879–1968) discovers radiothorium, a radioactive isotope produced by the breakdown and decay of the radioactive chemical element thorium.

EARLY STRUGGLE FOR CIVIL RIGHTS

The militant Niagara Movement is founded in the United Staes by 29 black intellectuals from 14 states, led by Atlanta University professor, William Edward Burghardt Du Bois. They demand universal male suffrage and the abolition of discrimination based on race or color.

WILD BEASTS IN PARIS

Work by the artists Matisse, Marquet, Derain, Vlaminck, Rouault, and others is hung in the same room at the Salon d'Automne. The mass effect of bright color and distorted patterns earns them the nickname Les Fauves (the wild beasts).

BELOW: Hussars charge striking workers in Warsaw.

ABOVE: Fishing for sturgeon through ice on the Ural River.

BELOW: Building the Panama Canal.

MAGNETIC NORTH TRACKED DOWN

Norwegian explorer Roald Amundsen (1872–1928) completes the passage from the Pacific to the Atlantic along the Arctic coast. On the way, he finds the current position of magnetic north.

NORDIC GAMES

The Scandinavian nations compete in the first Nordic Games. The event, which features cross-country skiing and ski jumping, is later overshadowed by the Winter Olympics.

FIRST SUFFRAGETTES IN PRISON

In the U.K., Christabel Pankhurst (1880–1958) and Annie Kenney, of the militant women's suffrage movement, choose prison rather than fines. They have been convicted of assaulting policemen after having been forcibly ejected from a political meeting for demanding votes for women.

SILK FOR EVERYONE

Rayon, a new fabric dubbed "artificial silk," is to be produced by the British textile company Courtaulds. They have brought the U.K. manufacturing rights from its British inventor, C.H. Stearn, who patented it in 1898. It is used for underwear and stockings.

WASSERMAN TEST

German bacteriologist August Wasserman (1866–1925) develops a test for the disease syphilis.

PIZZA TO GO

The United States' first pizzeria, Lombardi's on Spring Street in Little Italy, New York City, begins to sell pizza, a Neapolitan dish. It proves a popular fast food with busy New Yorkers.

ANYONE FOR TENNIS?

May Sutton becomes the first American to win a title at the Wimbledon Tennis Tournament; she becomes Ladies' Singles Champion.

TESTING FOR CHILDREN

Alfred Binet (1857–1911), director of the Psychological Laboratory at the Sorbonne in Paris and his colleague, Theodore Simon, produce tests to classify children according to their mental ability. This is in response to the French government's request in 1904 for them to study children with special educational needs.

SPECIAL-NEEDS PIONEERS

The first special-needs schools for educationally disadvantaged children are introduced in the Netherlands and subsidized by the state.

RIGHT: New York's elevated railway.

ABOVE: President Roosevelt watches submarine *Plunger* go through its paces.

EARTHQUAKES AND CORNFLAKES

Cubism is born with the work of Pablo Picasso, who introduces a revolutionary new way of painting the human form. In architecture too, Antonio Gaudí breaks with tradition, introducing startling new designs to the city of Barcelona. The eruption of Mt. Vesuvius in Italy and a major earthquake in San Francisco cause immense suffering and destruction.

OPPOSITE: Wreckage after Russian revolutionaries bomb Premier Stolypin's home.

1906

Feb	**10**	HMS *Dreadnought* launched
Apr	**7**	Mt. Vesuvius erupts, Italy
	8	Treaty of Algeciras ends Moroccan crisis
	18	San Francisco devastated by earthquake
May	**10**	First Duma meets in Russia
	23	Norwegian dramatist Henrik Ibsen dies
June	**26**	World's first Grand Prix, Le Mans, France
July	**12**	Alfred Dreyfus awarded Legion of Honor
Oct	**22**	Paul Cézanne dies
	23	Suffragettes imprisoned after demonstration at Houses of Parliament, U.K.

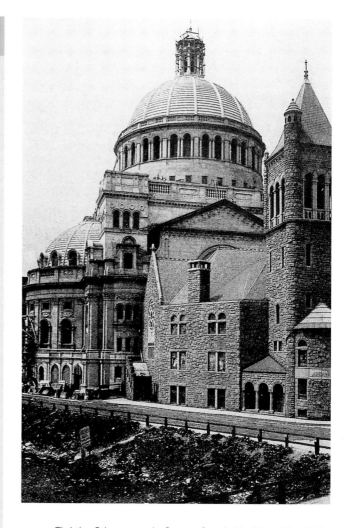

ABOVE: Christian Science temple, Boston, founded by Mary Baker Eddy.

ABOVE: King Alfonso of Spain and his new bride Victoria travel in state through Madrid, minutes before an anarchist hurls a bomb.

MOROCCAN CRISIS
France, Spain, Britain, and Germany meet for a conference in Algeciras, Spain, to decide the future of Morocco. The four powers agree to the continuing independence of Morocco under the Sultan of Morocco, but with Spain and France jointly policing the country. The treaty strengthens the Anglo-French Entente Cordiale and further isolates Germany.

FIRST GRAND PRIX
The world's first Grand Prix motor race takes place in France. The 65-mile event lasts two days and is won by Hungarian driver Ferenc Szisz, who averages a speed of 62mph.

HOT DOG
Hot dogs become fast food after "Tad" Dorgan, a Chicago cartoonist, draws a dachsund inside a Frankfurter bun.

DREYFUS NOT GUILTY
After eleven years, the French government formally annuls the guilty verdict given to Alfred Dreyfus, a Jew and a military officer wrongly accused of treason and spying against France, and awards him the Legion of Honor. The case has split France and revealed considerable anti-Semitism in the country.

MAGNETIC POLE
Norwegian explorer Roald Amundsen (1872–1928) reaches the Pacific Ocean in the *Gjöa*, after a three-year voyage during which he plotted the North Magnetic Pole and discovered the Northwest Passage, the sea route from the Atlantic Ocean through the Arctic archipelago.

BARCELONA TRANSFORMED
Catalan architect, Antonio Gaudí (1852–1926) has designed a house, Casa Battló, for a Barcelona textile manufacturer. Its curving walls, roof like a lizard's back, use of tiles and colored glazing are all distinctive features of Gaudí's style as he emerges from Art Nouveau. After Gaudí, Barcelona never looks the same again.

LEFT: Eighteen bystanders are killed and the state carriage wrecked by the bomb; King Alfonso and Queen Victoria survive.

BELOW: Balloonists prepare to break the long-distance flight record.

VOTES FOR WOMEN

Women in Finland become the first women in Europe to gain the vote. The following year, 19 women have seats in Finland's parliament. By contrast, in the U.K., women's fight for the vote becomes increasingly militant as women throughout the country heckle political meetings in the lead-up to the general election. In June, a deputation representing some half a million women march on the Houses of Parliament to present a petition to the new Liberal government, demanding votes for women. Its rejection is followed by a huge rally in London's Trafalgar Square. In October, women disrupt the state opening of Parliament and ten members of the WSPU are imprisoned rather than pay fines. This year, the militant tactics of WSPU members gain them the nickname "suffragettes," following an insult in the *Daily Mail* newspaper.

IBERIA

Spanish composer Isaac Albéniz begins the suite for piano that will become his most famous work. Inspired by the music and dance rhythms of Andalusia, Iberia shows Spanish composers how they can express national character in music.

SIMPLON TUNNEL

One of Europe's longest rail tunnels, the Simplon Tunnel connecting Brig in Switzerland with Iselle in Italy, is opened. It is about 12 miles long.

CUBISM IS BORN

Pablo Picasso (1881–1973) produces *Les Demoiselles d'Avignon*, the pivotal painting of the early twentieth century. Its angular handling of human forms is so shocking that he is very selective about who sees the picture. From this painting derives Cubism and all the other art movements in which natural subjects are broken up into a new synthesis of form.

ELECTRIC WASHING MACHINE

American Alva J. Fisher patents the first electric washing machine, marking the beginning of a major reduction in household drudgery.

BELOW: City Hall is in ruins after an earthquake and three-day firestorm devastate San Francisco. Above, a policeman stands in the wreckage.

BREAKFAST CEREAL

Will Keith Kellogg and his partner Charles D. Bolin incorporate the Battle Creek Toasted Corn Flake Co. to sell their breakfast cereals. Their new Sanitas cornflakes are lighter and crisper than their first cornflakes, produced in 1898.

NATURAL DISASTERS

Mt. Vesuvius erupts in April destroying the town of Ottaiano and causing damage in nearby Naples. In the United States that same month, a severe earthquake hits San Francisco. The tremors and the following three-day firestorm almost destroy the city.

HMS DREADNOUGHT

Britain launches the battleship HMS *Dreadnought*, the fastest and most heavily armored warship yet built. As an "all big gun" ship, *Dreadnought* also carries the heaviest fire-power with ten 12-inch guns.

PAUL CEZANNE
(1839–1906)

Paul Cézanne, the French painter, has died. His work increasingly concentrated on the underlying forms of nature. It was not widely recognized until the last ten years of his life but will widely influence the development of abstract art. His best-known paintings include *The Card Players* (1890–1892), *Aix: Paysage Rocheux* (1887) and *The Gardener* (1906).

GANDHI, BALLOONS, AND HELICOPTERS

Norwegian women gain the vote, following their Finnish sisters the previous year. Transport makes strides as the world's first "helicopter" makes a successful flight, the liner *Lusitania* crosses the Atlantic at record speed, and French balloonists make the first-ever aerial crossing of the North Sea. Gandhi introduces the idea of nonviolent civil disobedience. Home laundry becomes easier with new washing machines and washing powder.

OPPOSITE: The great nebula of Orion photographed at Yerkes Observatory, near Chicago.

1907

Jan	**14**	Earthquake hits Jamaica
Mar	**22**	Gandhi begins civil disobedience campaign, South Africa
June	**14**	Norwegian women gain the vote
	16	Duma dissolved in Russia
July	**29**	Boy Scouts founded, U.K.
Aug	**4**	French fleet bombard Casablanca after antiforeign riots
Sep	**26**	New Zealand becomes a dominion of Great Britain
Nov	**13**	Cornu makes first helicopter flight, France

ABOVE: Paris rubbish is discharged through huge pipes to be treated and converted into electricity.

CIVIL DISOBEDIENCE

In South Africa, Mohandâs Gandhi (1869–1948) begins a campaign of civil disobedience, or *satyagraha*, against the state government in protest at its new law that requires all Indians to register their presence, submit to being fingerprinted, and carry a certificate of registration with them at all times. Gandhi declares that the new law discriminates against the Indian population in the Transvaal.

DISSOLUTION OF DUMA

In St Petersburg, the Russian Czar Nicholas II (1868–1918) dissolves the Duma, or parliament, when his prime minister, Peter Stolypin, accuses 55 socialist deputies of plotting against the czar. The czar had hoped that the Duma would contain deputies favorable to his conservative policies. Instead it contains liberals and socialists intent on radical reform.

NORWEGIAN WOMEN GAIN THE VOTE

The Norwegian parliament agrees to allow women to vote in elections on the same terms as men. It follows the decision of the Finnish parliament to grant women the vote last year, but since Finland is a province of Russia, Norway is the first independent European country to grant universal suffrage.

MOTHER

Russian novelist Maxim Gorky (1868–1936) publishes *Mother*, an influential novel about revolutionaries.

BELOW: Damming the waters of the Nile threatens the Temple of Isis on the island of Philae.

SUFFRAGETTES BATTLE WITH POLICE

In the U.K., suffragettes demonstrate outside and "rush" the House of Commons. Their actions are met by considerable police brutality. Increasing numbers of women are imprisoned.

TRIPLE ALLIANCE RENEWED

Germany, Austria, and Italy renew the Triple Alliance between their three countries for a further six years, despite Italian reservations. The alliance faces increasingly close links between France and Britain. The following month, Britain signs an understanding with Russia, which draws Russia into their alliance.

NEW ZEALAND

After 48 years as a British colony, New Zealand becomes an independent dominion in the British Empire, joining Australia and Canada.

DYING SWAN

Russian ballerina Anna Pavlova (1885–1931) dances the Dying Swan in *Swan Lake*. Choreographed by Mikhail Fokine, the dance becomes Pavlova's trademark. She will dance it, to Saint-Saëns' music, with the Ballets Russes in Paris, and later with her own company. It becomes an icon of classical ballet.

HENRI MATISSE

The painting *Blue Nude* by French artist Henri Matisse (1869–1954) causes offense to more conservative viewers. The artist painted it after a short visit to North Africa and combined a classical pose with a primitive treatment. It is the primitivism that distinguishes Matisse, and which has caused offence.

ABOVE: World leaders meet for a peace conference at The Hague. They discuss methods of resolving conflict.

RIOTS IN MOROCCO

The French fleet bombards the port of Casablanca and French troops occupy the city after Moroccans riot against foreign workers. More than 1,000 Moors are killed.

BOY SCOUTS FOUNDED

In the U.K., Boer War veteran Sir Robert Baden-Powell sets up a new organization for boys, based on his army experience. The organization is known as the "boy scouts."

PLAYBOY CAUSES RIOTS

Riots follow the première of playwright John Synge's *The Playboy of the Western World*. Performed at the Abbey Theatre, the play's portrayal of Irish life is too realistic for the audience. There are more riots as the play goes on tour, but it will ultimately be recognized as an Irish classic.

THE PRAYER

Constantin Brancusi (1876–1957), the Romanian sculptor, leads the way towards abstract sculpture with his work *The Prayer*. A funeral monument, the statue shows a young girl kneeling in prayer. Its simplified form will soon lead to complete abstraction.

FIRST VERTICAL TAKE-OFF

French bicycle dealer and inventor Pierre Cornu makes the world's first free flight by "helicopter." Cornu's machine has twin motor-driven rotors and a 24-horsepower engine and lifts vertically off the ground.

LUSITANIA: WORLD'S FASTEST LINER

The Cunard liner *Lusitania*, built in 1906, captures the Blue Riband of the Atlantic, a notional trophy for the fastest crossing. She makes the crossing from Liverpool to New York at an average speed of 23.99 knots.

MOTORCYLE RACING

Motorcycle enthusiasts set up a racing festival on the Isle of Man, off the British coast, after racing is banned on mainland roads.

ABOVE: Irish suffragist Miss Maloney rings a handbell, successfully bringing to an end a speech by Liberal candidate Mr. Winston Churchill, noted opponent of votes for women.

"JEWISH MARK TWAIN"

Author Sholem Aleichem has begun to publish his series of stories, *Mottel, or The Cantor's Son*. Written in Yiddish (later translated into English), they give expression to the experiences and humor of ordinary Jewish people in the United States. Publication continues until 1916 and Aleichem becomes known as the "Jewish Mark Twain."

A BETTER VALVE

American inventor Lee de Forest improves the diode valve invented by J.A. Fleming in 1904, by introducing a third electrode. This creates a triode valve. The third electrode, called a grid, has holes in it. By varying the electric charge on the grid, the flow of electrons can be varied.

CAUSE OF SCURVY

The British biochemist Frederick Gowland Hopkins suggests that lack of certain trace substances in the diet can cause diseases such as rickets and scurvy. The substances are later named vitamins.

SUICIDE COUNSELLING

A suicide counselling service is opened in New York City by the Salvation Army.

OVER THE NORTH SEA

The first aerial crossing of the North Sea is made in the balloon *Mammoth* in October by three French aeronauts. The flight is from Crystal Palace, London, to the shores of Lake Vänern, Sweden, a distance of about 725 miles.

ELEMENT DISCOVERED

The French chemist Georges Urbain discovers the heaviest of the rare-earth elements, lutetium. A radioactive isotope of the element becomes useful in determining the age of meteorites.

ITALIAN WINS RACE

Entering the French capital two months ahead of the nearest competitor, Prince Scipione Borghese of Italy wins the Peking-to-Paris Automobile Race by a huge margin. Borghese and his mechanic covered 9,317 miles in 62 days.

NATURAL DISASTERS

In January, a massive earthquake flattens Jamaica. Just one week later, a tidal wave sweeps the Dutch East Indies.

NURSING HONOUR

Florence Nightingale, now aged 87, blind, and an invalid, becomes the first woman to be awarded the British Order of Merit. The honor is conferred by King Edward VII for her services to the nursing profession.

LEFT: Hundreds of acres of tobacco are grown under cheesecloth in Puerto Rico — an American invention for increasing yield.

BELOW: The Cresta Run in Switzerland — the world's most famous toboggan run.

RECORD IMMIGRATION
1907 is a record year for immigration to the States, with more than one million new American nationals admitted.

NEW WASHING POWDER
Persil, a washing powder produced by Henkel & Cie in Düsseldorf, Germany, is marketed in Britain for washing clothes.

AGITATED WASHING MACHINE
Thor, the first electric agitator washing machine, is marketed by the Hurley Machine Company in the States. It was designed by U.S. engineer John Hurley, who has used an electric motor to power a rotating dolly.

NEW ZOO
In Hamburg, Carl Hagenbeck creates a new kind of zoo. Animals live freely in their natural habitats.

DMITRI IVANOVICH MENDELEYEV
(1834–1907)

The Russian scientist Dmitri Mendeleyev dies this year. His work on the grouping of elements according to their atomic weight accurately predicted the properties of several elements that were waiting to be discovered. He also studied the aeronautics and behavior of gases, and, in 1887, took a pioneering ascent in an air balloon.

CARS FOR EVERYBODY

A two-year-old child becomes the last Manchu emperor of China. The first modern version of the Olympic Games is held and the first vacuum cleaner goes on sale in the United States. The largest earthquake ever recorded in Europe devastates the Italian town of Messina, and the dream of motoring for the masses becomes reality when the American car manufacturer, Henry Ford, begins production of the new Model-T motor car.

OPPOSITE: French can-can dancers wow audiences at London nightclubs.

1908

Feb	1	King Carlos and Prince Luiz of Portugal are assassinated
June	21	200,000 attend suffragette rally, U.K., demanding that women be given the right to vote
July	13	Olympic Games begin, U.K.
Aug	12	Henry Ford's first assembly line Model-T appears
	20	Congo, Africa, becomes Belgian colony
Oct	5	Bulgaria declared independent
	6	Austria annexes Bosnia and Herzegovina
Nov	15	Two-year-old Pu-yi becomes Emperor of China
Dec	28	Earthquake devastates Messina, Sicily

ABOVE: Giant bamboo growing in the Botanical Gardens at Peradeniya, Ceylon. In the countryside, these densely packed trees are vulnerable to fire.

ABOVE: Orville Wright prepares for his flight.

BELGIAN CONGO
Leopold II, king of Belgium, hands over his vast private estate in central Africa to the control of the Belgian government. Belgium thus acquires its first colony, which is more than 90 times its own size.

EARTHQUAKE DEVASTATION
A massive earthquake, the biggest ever recorded in Europe, destroys the town of Messina in Sicily, southern Italy. Thousands of people are killed and made homeless.

THE BALKANS
In the Balkans King Ferdinand I (1861–1948) declares Bulgaria independent from Turkey and takes the title of czar. At the same time, Austria annexes the Turkish province of Bosnia-Herzegovina, and Crete proclaims its union with Greece. The Ottoman Empire continues to disintegrate.

MAKING AMMONIA
German chemist Fritz Haber (1868–1934) invents the Haber process for making ammonia artificially by combining nitrogen and hydrogen.

ABOVE: Orville Wright swoops over Fort Myer, Virginia. An accident during this military air trial kills Wright's companion, TE Selfridge.

CHILD EMPEROR
After the deaths of the Emperor Kuang Hsu and the Dowager Empress Cixi, the two-year-old Pu-yi becomes emperor of China with the name Emperor Hsuan T'ung. Real power lies with the various warlords who control the Chinese throne.

MASS-PRODUCED MODEL-T
American car manufacturer Henry Ford (1863–1947) begins the mass production of his Model-T Ford car, using an innovative assembly line method. He sells the new model for $850, but by 1925 has cut the price to $260. When production stops in 1927 he has made 15 million Model-Ts.

THE WAR IN THE AIR
In this prophetic novel, H.G. Wells describes the military use of aircraft, a form of warfare which will soon become all too well-known. This prediction later helps to give Wells the status of modern prophet.

POWER AT LAST

After earlier failures, American inventor Thomas Alva Edison (1847–1931) perfects his alkaline storage battery. It stores more than twice as much power as a lead-acid battery.

DETECTING RADIATION

While working in Manchester, England, German physicist Hans Geiger (1882–1945) invents the Geiger counter, a device which detects radiation. It works by detecting and counting alpha particles emitted by a radioactive substance.

"THE EIGHT"

A group of American painters who have had work rejected from the National Academy of Design form "the Eight," part of what will later become known as the Ashcan School. They are ridiculed as "apostles of ugliness" and exhibit together only once.

MAGNETIC SUNSPOTS

American astronomer George Ellery Hale (1868–1938) discovers that sunspots have strong magnetic fields — the first magnetic fields detected outside the Earth. He also installs a 59-inch reflecting telescope at Mount Wilson Observatory in California.

SPACE–TIME LINK-UP

Professor Hermann Minkowski, a Lithuanian mathematician, puts forward the view that space and time are interlinked as the "space-time continuum."

CELLOPHANE

Swiss chemist Dr Jacques Edwin Brandenburger patents a thin, transparent, flexible film made from wood cellulose. He calls it Cellophane.

EXPEDITION TO ANTARCTIC

Ernest Shackleton and Edward Wilson, with the National Antarctic Expedition, travel to latitude 88° 22' S, closer to the South Pole than any previous expeditions.

LIQUID HELIUM

Dutch physicist Heike Kamerlingh Onnes (1853–1926) discovers how to make the gas helium into a liquid. This strange liquid expands instead of contracting as it cools, and conducts heat well.

INTERNATIONAL PSYCHOLOGY CONGRESS

The first International Congress of Psychology is held in Salzburg in April. It is attended by the leading figures in this controversial new branch of medicine, including Sigmund Freud and his colleagues Alfred Adler and Karl Jung.

A NEW CHAMPION

Texan Jack Johnson becomes the first black heavyweight boxing champion of the world.

FIRST PSYCHOLOGY TEXTBOOK

The first social psychology textbook is published by William McDougall, a British psychologist who argues for a biological rather than a philosophical approach to psychology. He believes people inherit instincts and characteristics that direct them to unconscious goals.

MARATHON RUNNER DISQUALIFIED

London, England, steps in to host the Fourth Olympic Games after Rome, Italy, withdraws. Large crowds watch as the games are held as a self-contained event. The marathon ends in drama when Italian runner Dorando Pietri is helped across the finish line in first place. He is stripped of his gold medal as the help is against the rules, but wins public sympathy.

DISPOSABLE CUPS

Disposable paper cups are introduced into the States by the International Paper Company, a conglomerate of American and Canadian paper companies.

CHAMPAGNE DISASTER

Champagne, in France, the last European wine region to be devastated by the vine-destroying phylloxera aphid, has its worst harvest failure this century. The year's total production equals little more than that normally produced by one vineyard.

VACUUM CLEANER

The first commercial vacuum cleaner is produced in the States by William Hoover, a leather manufacturer.

ABOVE: Residues of pitchblende are stirred in these tanks to produce radioactive radium, first discovered by Pierre and Marie Curie.

BLERIOT AND BALLETS RUSSES

Louis Blériot makes headlines when he successfully flies across the English Channel — the first man to do so. The Ballets Russes is formed, bringing dramatic innovation to the world of ballet, and the AEG Turbine Factory in Berlin proves that modern architecture can blend perfectly with the demands of industry. The world's first synthetic plastic is invented and the first newsreels appear in cinemas. Neon lights shine in the night. In Holland, the first organized 11-city ice skating tour takes place. In Britain, imprisoned suffragettes go on a hunger strike.

1 9 0 9

Jan	1	Old-age pensions introduced, U.K.
Mar	31	Pathé News shown in Paris
Apr	6	Robert Peary reaches the North Pole
	23	Armenians massacred in Turkey
	27	Young Turks depose Sultan Abdul Hamid
May	18	Ballets Russes performs in Paris
Jul	16	Twelve-year-old Soltan Ahmed Mirza becomes the Shah of Persia
	25	Blériot flies the Channel
Oct	26	Japan's first prime minister, Prince Ito Hirobumi, is assassinated
Dec	16	President Jose Zelaya resigns in Nicaragua

ABOVE: Royal England meets Imperial Russia — the Prince of Wales and the Czar with their sons.

ABOVE: Polar camp — from here, on April 6, American commander Robert Peary reaches the North Pole, the first man to do so.

ARMENIAN MASSACRES

Thousands of Armenians are killed by Turks in the province of Cilicia in April. Sultan Abdul-Hamid (1842–1918) orders the killings after Armenian revolutionaries, demonstrating against oppressive Turkish rule, provoke the inhabitants and officials in Armenia. The United States and various European countries intervene to halt the killings. Following these events, Abdul Hamid is deposed by a unanimous vote in the two houses of parliament he was forced to set up last year. Opposition to the sultan is led by the Young Turks, who are pressing for reform in the vast and ramshackle Ottoman Empire. The sultan is replaced by his brother, Mahmud Reshad.

BLERIOT FLIES THE CHANNEL

The first man to fly across the English Channel is Louis Blériot (1872–1936) of France, flying a monoplane he has designed and built himself. His historic flight, from Calais to Dover, takes just 37 minutes.

MOROCCO

French and Spanish forces fight Rif tribesmen in Morocco as the Moroccan War continues.

NICARAGUAN CIVIL WAR

War begins in Nicaragua with a conservative revolt against liberal dictator President Jose Santos Zelaya. Dr. Jose Madriz is elected to succeed him.

BALLETS RUSSES FOUNDED

Russian impresario Sergei Diaghilev (1872–1929) founds the company that will have the greatest influence over ballet in the twentieth century. Many of his dancers, choreographers and artists are Russian exiles, including Nijinsky, Pavlova, Karsavina, Fokine, and Stravinsky, but he also draws on the best of French talent. The company is notable for its new fusion of passion, fantasy, color, and sound with classical ballet.

HUNGER STRIKES

In the U.K., imprisoned suffragettes begin to go on a hunger strike. The British government orders them to be forcibly fed and there is a public outcry.

GLASGOW SCHOOL OF ART

Charles Rennie Macintosh brings Art Nouveau and Viennese Secession styles to Scotland in his own unique idiom. This building is one of the finest examples. It is famous because of its innovative use of space, unusual ornament, and inspired use of vertical elements. The library is finished in 1909 and is the best of all.

INDUSTRY MEETS ARCHITECTURE

Designed by pioneering German architect Peter Behrens (1868–1940), the AEG Turbine Factory in Berlin shows for the first time that the modern architectural idiom is well-suited to industrial buildings — and that such buildings can in themselves be fine examples of architecture. Huge windows provide lots of light, and metal uprights and roofing members give a broad roof span. No ornament is used but the structure itself has an austere elegance.

BAKELITE, FIRST SYNTHETIC PLASTIC

A Belgian-born American industrial chemist, Leo Hendrik Baekeland, markets the world's first heatproof synthetic plastic. It is called phenolic resin but is better known under its trade name, Bakelite. It proves to be an excellent electrical insulator.

FIRST CINEMA NEWSREEL

French film pioneer Charles Pathé (1863–1957) begins making and showing the first cinema newsreel in Paris. He takes the idea to the United States in 1910.

DARING TO BE GAY

His novel, *Strait is the Gate*, launches Parisian writer André Gide (1869–1951) on a courageous career as a novelist. He defends his own right to be gay, but in this book pays tribute to his wife who appears as the character Madeleine.

LIGHTING UP WITH NEON

French scientist Georges Claude invents the neon tube, in which a glass tube containing a small quantity of neon gas glows red when a current is passed through it. Different colors are produced by adding other gases.

AUTOMATIC TOAST

The first electric toaster is sold in America by the General Electric Company. It toasts the bread on only one side at a time, and doesn't eject the toast.

PENSIONS FOR THE ELDERLY

In Britain, old-age pensions are introduced for people aged 70 and over. France introduced old-age insurance in 1850, followed by Germany, Denmark, and New Zealand. Britain's is the first twentieth-century scheme, and the most comprehensive so far.

ABOVE: Louis Blériot stands in his monoplane before take-off. Later that day he becomes the first man to fly the Channel, flying from France to England in just 37 minutes.

ABOVE: Following his inauguration, President Taft and his wife drive to the White House. He succeeds former president Roosevelt.

78

RADIO SEA RESCUE
The first use of radio to save life at sea is made when the ship *Republic* collides with another vessel in the Atlantic and calls for help; rescuers arrive in time to save nearly all the passengers.

SIX PIECES FOR LARGE ORCHESTRA
This pivotal work of the Second Viennese School, composed by Anton Webern, is notable for his use of wind and percussion instruments to produce a unique orchestral color and sense of space.

ORGANIZED ELFSTEDENTOCHT
This year sees the start of an organized 11-city ice skating tour — Elfstedentocht. Skaters visit 11 cities in the Frisia area of the Netherlands in a loop beginning and ending in Leeuwarden. The first event is more of a tour than a race and the skaters start by heading north rather than south. Twenty-two skaters start and Minne Hoekstra is the first of the nine who finish 13 hours and 50 minutes later.

LILIOM: PLAY, MUSICAL AND FILM
Hungarian writer Ferenc Molnár publishes *Liliom*, his most famous play. Subsequently it is turned first into a musical (1945) and then the film *Carousel* (1956).

PEARY REACHES POLE
Robert E Peary, a U.S. naval commander, is the first person to reach the North Pole (on his second attempt), having been accompanied during the final stages by his colleague, Matthew Henson, and four Inuit.

A NEW WORD
The National Conservation Commission, appointed by President Roosevelt, publishes the first inventory of the United States' natural resources. Advised by his chief forester, Gifford Pinchot, who has coined the term "conservation," Roosevelt has already introduced several legislative measures designed to preserve the natural environment.

GERONIMO
(1829–1909)

The Apache leader Geronimo, who led the Apache Indians in their struggle against Mexican, and later North American, usurpers, has died. After finally surrendering in 1886 he became a Christian and farmed in Oklahoma. His Native American name was Goyathlay which translates as "One who yawns."

THE WORLD AT WAR

This is the decade that literally shakes the world. The war that breaks out in 1914 is the first, but sadly not last, incidence of global conflict that this century will endure. It will change lives and social customs forever and redraw the maps of the world. More than nine million people die and over twelve million are wounded. The Treaty of Versailles, which concludes the war, contains the seeds for conflict 20 years later. On a happier note, exploration has a good decade, with the rediscovery of Macchu Picchu and the pinning down of the South Pole.

OPPOSITE: The Palace of Peace in The Hague, Netherlands, brainchild of Andrew Carnegie.

1910–1919

KEY EVENTS OF THE DECADE

- UNION OF SOUTH AFRICA FORMED
- REVOLUTION IN CHINA
- BALKAN WARS
- MEXICAN REVOLUTION
- THE ARMORY SHOW, NEW YORK
- WORLD WAR I
- EASTER RISING IN DUBLIN
- EINSTEIN PUBLISHES HIS THEORY OF GENERAL RELATIVITY
- DADAISM INVENTED

- FIRST BIRTH CONTROL CLINIC IN UNITED STATES
- REVOLUTION IN RUSSIA
- ATOM SPLIT
- WOMEN GET THE VOTE IN UNITED KINGDOM
- LEAGUE OF NATIONS FOUNDED
- MUSSOLINI STARTS FASCIST PARTY IN ITALY
- ALCOCK AND BROWN FLY THE ATLANTIC
- AMRITSAR MASSACRE

WORLD POPULATION: 1,712 MILLION

THE THRILL OF SPEED AND SOUND

The Union of South Africa is formed and Japan annexes Korea. Black Americans unite to campaign for an end to racial segregation, and slavery is abolished in China. International police work moves into a new dimension when radio is used for the first time to capture a criminal. The Dutch government introduces state pensions and a new, passionate dance, the tango, sweeps Europe. In Italy, a group of artists produce the Futurist Manifesto, an attempt to sweep away the past and welcome speed and power.

OPPOSITE: Fire at the Great Brussels Exhibition in Belgium leaves ruin and destruction in its wake.

1910

Feb	10	First woman pilot flies solo	**Aug**	20	Florence Nightingale, founder of modern nursing, dies aged 91
Apr	21	U.S. novelist Mark Twain dies aged 74		24	Korea annexed
May	6	Death of King Edward VII of Britain; George V succeeds	**Sep**	7	Marie Curie and André Debierne isolate pure radium
	31	Union of South Africa formed			
	31	Girl Scouts movement established	**Oct**	5	Portugal becomes a republic
				30	Red Cross founder Jean-Henri Dunant dies aged 82
June	19	Father's Day introduced in the United States by Mrs John B. Dodd			
			Nov	11	Russian writer Leo Tolstoy dies aged 82
	25	First performance of Igor Stravinsky's ballet The Firebird			
			Dec	10	Dutch physicist Johannes Diderik van der Waals is awarded the Nobel Prize in physics
July	1	Union of South Africa is proclaimed a dominion of Great Britain			
	31	Dr Crippen, murderer, arrested after a radio tip-off			

ABOVE: Infrared photography, developed in the United States, shows scenes taken in the full sun as moonlit snowscapes. The technique will later be adapted for night espionage.

RACE RELATIONS

In New York, African-American liberals form the National Association for the Advancement of Colored People (NAACP), with the goal of ending racial segregation and discrimination. The organization publishes a newspaper, *The Crisis*, edited by American writer and professor W.E.B. Du Bois (1868–1963), which reports on race relations around the world.

SOUTH AFRICA UNION FOUNDED

The Union of South Africa is created out of the former British colonies of Cape Colony and Natal, and the former Boer states of Transvaal and the Orange Free State. The new country joins other former British colonies as independent dominions in the Empire.

U.S. SUFFRAGE

In Washington State, women gain the right to vote.

COUNT LEO NIKOLAYEVICH TOLSTOY (1828–1910)

The great Russian writer Leo Tolstoy has died of pneumonia in a railway siding at Astapovo station, while in flight from his wife. After service in the Crimean War and a socialite life in St. Petersburg and abroad, he married in 1862 and settled in his Volga estate. While he and his wife produced 13 children, he wrote *War and Peace* (1863–69), *Anna Karenina* (1874–76) and *The Death of Ivan Ilyitch* (1886). From 1879 he espoused an extreme ascetic form of Christianity, condemned his own works as worthless, was excommunicated for his unorthodox views, and irreconcilably alienated his wife.

KOREA ANNEXED

The Japanese government formally annexes the peninsula of Korea. Japan occupied Korea during the Russo-Japanese war of 1904–1905 and has exercised increasing control ever since.

REVOLUTION IN PORTUGAL

King Manuel of Portugal is deposed in a revolution and flees on his yacht to Gibraltar. The revolution comes after a decade of revolt against the monarchy. Portugal becomes a republic and adopts a liberal constitution the following year.

FIRST WOMAN PILOT

In February, Baronne Raymonde de Laroche, a French aviator, becomes the first woman to fly solo. She is the first woman ever to be granted a pilot's license. The Baronne, born Elise Deroche, worked as a model and actress. She claims her title is Russian.

SLAVERY ABOLISHED IN CHINA

The Chinese imperial government has abolished slavery. Until now, the Manchu ruling elite enslaved prisoners of war, and their servants kept slaves. Family members, usually women, were often made to be slaves.

BLACK MIGRATION

The founding of the NAACP marks the beginning of a great migration that brings some two million black people into the northern United States.

GASES INTO LIQUIDS

Dutch physicist Professor Johannes Diderik van der Waals (1837–1923) is awarded the Nobel Prize in physics for his work on the relationship between gases and liquids, which helps later scientists turn so-called "permanent" gases into liquids.

ABOVE: The Eiffel Tower stands witness to devastating floods in Paris when the Seine bursts its banks and almost drowns the city.

FIREBIRD

The Firebird by Russian composer Igor Stravinsky (1882–1971) is performed in Paris. Danced by the Ballets Russes, it is based on traditional Russian tales but displays strong rhythms, unusual harmonies and joy through the tone colors of individual instruments. This will mark the composer's later works.

CATCHING CRIPPEN

The first use of radio for catching criminals occurs in July when the captain of a New York-bound Atlantic liner radios Scotland Yard, in London, to say he thinks he has suspected murderer Dr. Hawley Harvey Crippen on board. Crippen, an American born in Michigan, is later tried, found guilty of poisoning his wife, and executed.

MODERN HOUSING

The modern house makes its appearance with the Steiner House in Vienna. Designed by Austrian architect Adolf Loos (1870–1933), who is influenced by American industrial buildings, the house has no ornament, the pale exterior is symmetrically arranged, and there is a flat roof. Everything is highly functional.

MARY (MORSE) BAKER EDDY (1821–1910)

The founder of Christian Science, Mary Baker Eddy dies. Her work *Science and Health with Key to the Scriptures* (1875) expressed her belief that disease is illusory. With her third husband, Asa G. Eddy, she founded the Church of Christ, Scientist in Boston in 1879.

FUTURIST MANIFESTO

Italian artists Umberto Boccioni and Giacomo Balla produce the Technical Manifesto of the Futurist Painters. The artists aim to celebrate speed and movement, especially of machines such as cars and airplanes. The painters develop a particular style to do this, taking up the fragmented idiom of Cubism to suggest movement through space.

ELECTRIC FOOD MIXER

The first electrically-driven food mixer for domestic use is made by the Hamilton Beach Manufacturing Company of America.

ABOVE: Princess Hélène of Portugal goes hippo hunting in Portuguese West Africa.

ISOLATING RADIUM
French scientists Marie Curie and André Debierne isolate the first sample of pure radium from the uranium ore pitchblende. They do so using an electrolytic process.

LET'S TANGO
A new dance, the tango, which originated in Argentina, has become a major dance craze in Europe and the United States, inspiring an ankle-length tango dress and tango shoe.

HALLEY'S COMET
In May the Earth passes through the tail of Halley's Comet, which returns every 76 years. Unwarranted fear of "poisonous gases" from the tail leads to brisk sale of a so-called antidote, "Comet Pills."

LEFT: Black Hussars, the paramilitary mounted police, use maces and revolvers on strikers in Philadelphia. The strike had started with tramway workers and escalated into a general strike.

MARK TWAIN
(1835–1910)

Born Samuel Langhorne Clemens, Mark Twain, the American author of *The Adventures of Tom Sawyer* (1876) and *The Adventures of Huckleberry Finn* (1884), has died. Journalist, humorist, and lecturer, he incorporated his experiences as a Mississippi boatman, Nevada gold-digger, and foreign traveler into his writing.

ABOVE: A skeleton of steel tubing supports the tandem biplane, designed by naval lieutenant J.W. Seddon to carry six passengers.

PENSIONS
The Dutch government introduces pensions for people aged over 70, although they will not be implemented until the 1930s.

FIRST ABSTRACT WATERCOLOR
This untitled new work by the Russian painter Wassily Kandinsky (1866–1944) signals the birth of abstract art as it is to become known in later decades.

ROBIE HOUSE
American architect Frank Lloyd Wright (1867–1959) designs a series of houses in which long, low, horizontal lines appear to ground the buildings, making them seem at one with the earth — an aspect of what Wright calls "organic architecture." Inside, the houses are notable for a flowing use of space. The Robie House in Chicago is one of the finest.

STANLEY CUP
The Stanley Cup, named after governor general of Canada, Lord Stanley of Preston, is presented to the winner of the professional ice hockey play-offs. Until this year, it had been fought for by Canada's best amateur teams. Now it is the goal for the Canadian and American teams in the National Hockey League.

DEATH OF BRITISH MONARCH
Edward VII dies and is succeeded by his son, who becomes George V. Edward was a much-respected king whose love of foreign travel and public ceremony increased the popularity of the British monarchy.

POLAR TRIUMPH AND INCA CITY

Norwegian explorer Amundsen reaches the South Pole, one of the last of the great unexplored regions of the world. And in the Peruvian jungle, an American explorer uncovers the remains of a great Inca city. On the political stage, revolutions break out in Mexico and China, Germany announces her intention of achieving a "place in the sun," and Italian troops invade Tripoli. The first aircraft carrier is born and the first torpedo is tested.

OPPOSITE: Captain Robert F. Scott, leader of the ill-fated expedition across the Antarctic.

1911

Jan	18	Eugene Ely lands airplane on battleship
	26	First performance of Richard Strauss's opera *Der Rosenkavalier*
Feb	3	Ulrich Salchow becomes world figure-skating champion for the tenth time
May	18	Austrian composer Gustav Mahler dies aged 50
	25	Mexican dictator Porfirio Díaz resigns
	30	First Indy 500 motor race takes place in the United States
Apr	23	French and Algerian troops enter Morocco
June	9	U.S. temperance campaigner Carry Nation dies aged 65

July	2	Germans send gunboat to Moroccan port of Agadir; leads to international incident
Aug	22	The painting *Mona Lisa* is stolen from the Louvre in Paris. It will be recovered in 1913
Sep	30	Italy attacks Ottoman Empire's port of Tripoli in Libya
Oct	9	Revolution begins in China
Nov	4	"Agadir Crisis" ends, Morocco
	14	First airplane take-off from a ship
Dec	14	Roald Amundsen's Norwegian expedition reaches the South Pole
	31	Marie Curie wins a second Nobel Prize

MEXICAN PRESIDENT RESIGNS

Porfirio Díaz (1830–1915) resigns as president of Mexico after ruling the country as dictator for almost 35 years. Although popular abroad, Díaz is hated at home for his corruption and brutality. Discontent with his rule erupted when he imprisoned his opponent on the eve of the presidential election last year. With the fall of Díaz, Mexico descends into seven years of revolution and civil war.

GERMAN PLACE IN THE SUN

German Kaiser Wilhelm II (1859–1941) states that Germany intends to achieve "a place in the sun," secured for it by its increasingly powerful navy. Germany's intention to obtain an empire alarms both Britain and France, especially after the dispatch of a German gunboat, *Panther*, to Agadir in July threatened French control over Morocco.

ITALIANS ATTACK TRIPOLI

Italian warships attack the Libyan port of Tripoli in September, after Italy declares war on the Ottoman Empire. Libya is the only part of North Africa still under Ottoman rule; by November, the Italian conquest of the country is complete.

BELOW: The unearthed palace at Knossos, Crete, the center of the ancient Minoan civilization and legendary home of the Minotaur. It is being excavated by a team led by British archaeologist Arthur Evans. These pits are storage galleries, still containing pots and jars.

REVOLUTION IN CHINA

Revolution breaks out in China against the government of the Manchu Emperor Hsuan T'ung, who abdicates the following January. China becomes a republic and elects Sun Yat-Sen (1866–1925), leader of the nationalist Kuomintang Party, as the first president.

THE BLUE RIDER

Wassily Kandinsky and Franz Marc found *Der Blaue Reiter* (the blue rider), named after one of Kandinsky's paintings. This diverse group of artists, which includes Paul Klee, value the Expressionist use of brilliant colors. There is no stylistic common denominator but the group provides a forum for the European avant-garde.

FIRST AIRCRAFT CARRIER

The first aircraft carrier comes into being when American civilian pilot Eugene B. Ely, in a Curtiss biplane, lands on a specially-built platform on the quarterdeck of the battleship USS *Pennsylvania*, using wires attached to sandbags on the platform as arresting gear. After lunch, he takes off again. Ely had already made the first-ever take-off from a ship the previous year.

THE DEVIL'S DICTIONARY

An amusing and sometimes vitriolic collection of definitions and epigrams is published by American journalist Ambrose Bierce. It will prove an enduring classic of American humor.

FIRST SEAPLANE
French aviation designer Henri Fabre makes the first take-off from water near Marseille in a plane fitted with floats.

THE EGOIST
A new literary magazine *The Egoist*, under the editorship of American poet Ezra Pound (1885–1972), provides a home for some of the most notable writing — prose and poetry — of the early twentieth century. The magazine has its origins in *The Freewoman*, an outspoken feminist journal.

SUPERCONDUCTIVITY
Dutch physicist Heike Kamerlingh Onnes (1853–1926) discovers superconductivity, the property of materials that can conduct electricity, in frozen mercury. Later, the principle is used in magnets used in particle accelerators.

MAIL TAKES TO THE AIR
Airmail is first carried from London to Berkshire in England by Gustav Hamel in a Blériot aeroplane.

DER ROSENKAVALIER
Probably his greatest and most successful opera, *Rosenkavalier* is a triumph for German composer Richard Strauss (1864–1949) and his librettist, the poet Hugo von Hofmannsthal. Called "a comedy in music," the opera is set in eighteenth-century Vienna and is full of tuneful waltzes and colorful characters.

TREEMONISHA
American ragtime composer Scott Joplin (1868–1917) puts his musical ideas into operatic form in *Treemonisha*, about a mythical black leader. Only performed once during his lifetime, Joplin considers it his most important work.

TORPEDO TEST
Italian Capitano Guidoni makes the first-ever torpedo drop when he releases a 353-pound Whitehead torpedo from a Farman biplane as a test exercise.

FIRST GASTROSCOPE
London doctor William Hill invents the gastroscope, a tube which a patient swallows, enabling a doctor to examine the interior of the stomach.

GYROCOMPASS
U.S. engineer and inventor Elmer Ambrose Sperry invents the gyrocompass, a device that is more accurate than an ordinary magnetic compass. It points to true north, as opposed to magnetic north, and is not affected by the movements of the ship in which it is installed.

ELECTRIC HEATER ON SALE
The first commercially produced electric heater is marketed in Britain by the General Electric Co. (GEC).

GUSTAV MAHLER
(1860–1911)

Bohemian composer and conductor Gustav Mahler dies while conductor of the New York Philharmonic Society. His nine symphonies, the orchestral song cycles *Kindertotenlieder* (1902), and *Das Lied von der Erde* (1908), lead the way from nineteenth-century romanticism to twentieth-century atonality.

NICARAGUA
Unrest continues in Nicaragua. With assistance from the United States, the conservative Adolfo Díaz replaces liberal president Jose Santos Zelaya.

MOTOR SPEEDWAY
The first Indy 500 motor race takes place at the Indianapolis Motor Speedway in the United States. It holds 77,000 spectators for the inaugural event. Ray Harroun wins, the only one of the 40 competitors not to carry a mechanic in his car.

MASS MARCH
Between 40,000 and 60,000 women march through London in a mass demonstration demanding votes for women.

AMUNDSEN REACHES SOUTH POLE
Norwegian explorer Roald Amundsen (1872–1928) reaches the South Pole, having crossed more than 2,000miles of snow and ice. Relying on huskies and with a well-organized and efficient team, he arrives at the Pole just over a month ahead of British explorer Sir Robert Scott, who, together with four other members of the team, dies on the return journey.

INCA CITY DISCOVERED
Macchu Picchu, a long-deserted Inca city, is discovered beneath jungle growth at an altitude of 52,000 feet in the Peruvian Andes by American explorer Hiram Bingham, an archaeologist heading an expedition from Yale University.

CARNEGIE CORPORATION FOUNDED
The Carnegie Corporation is founded to administer the fortune of Andrew Carnegie, the Scottish-born founder of Carnegie Steel. Since selling the company in 1901, Carnegie has founded many philanthropic, educational and research institutions in Scotland and the States.

BAN ON SEAL FISHING
The North Pacific Fur Seal Convention ends with agreement by the United States, Britain, Japan, and Russia to stop fishing for seals out at sea as a conservation measure, since the fur seal population has declined to about 200,000 animals.

THE TITANIC GOES DOWN

War breaks out again in the troubled region of the Balkans. Civil war threatens Ireland and a liberal revolt in Nicaragua is suppressed. The "unsinkable" SS *Titanic* hits an iceberg and sinks with the loss of more than 1,500 lives. Neon lights are used for advertising displays and Cellophane is produced commercially. German scientist, Alfred Wegener, suggests that continents were once one landmass that has drifted apart.

1912

Mar	1	The first parachute jump from a moving airplane
Jul	6	The Fifth Olympic Games open in Stockholm
	15	Yoshihito becomes emperor of Japan
Aug	13	French composer Jules Massenet dies aged 70
	11	Sultan abdicates, Morocco
Sep	1	French troops quell uprising in Morocco
Oct	8	First Balkan War breaks out
	25	Battle of Kirk-Kilissa, Balkan peninsula
Nov	5	Woodrow Wilson is elected president of the United States
	5	Battle of Monastir, Balkans
Dec	18	"Piltdown Man" discovered in England

ABOVE: Survivors from the sinking *Titanic* in lifeboats on their way to the *Carpathia*.

ABOVE: Survivors coming ashore in the United States.

BALKAN WAR

War breaks out in the Balkans as Bulgaria, Serbia, Greece, and Montenegro unite in an effort to take possession of the remaining Turkish territory in the Balkan peninsula, and invade the Ottoman province of Macedonia. Turkey has already lost Libya, Rhodes, and the Dodecanese Islands to Italy in a separate dispute. In October, at the battle of Kirk-Kilissa, the Bulgarians throw back the Turks, inflicting heavy losses. In November, Serbs fighting at Monastir, assisted by Greek forces, drive back the Turks, causing 20,000 casualties.

TITANIC DISASTER

The mighty liner SS *Titanic* strikes an iceberg during her maiden voyage and sinks. Out of 2,224 passengers, more than 1,500 lose their lives, many freezing to death in the icy water of the Atlantic. The liner, which was the most luxurious in the world, had been declared unsinkable because of watertight compartments. In the event, these failed to prevent the disaster and lack of sufficient lifeboats exacerbated the tragedy.

MEASURING X-RAYS

Max von Laue, a German physicist, passes X-rays through a crystal and finds that this enables him to measure the wavelengths of the rays.

CIVIL WAR THREATENED IN IRELAND

In Britain, the House of Commons passes the Home Rule Bill, which promises home rule for Ireland. Unionists in the north of Ireland refuse to recognize the new parliament if it is set up and threaten civil war.

NEW U.S. PRESIDENT

Woodrow Wilson (1856–1924), governor of New Jersey, wins the presidential election for the Democratic Party and is elected 28th president. He is the first Democrat to be elected since Grover Cleveland in 1892.

MOROCCAN CRISIS ENDS

In Morocco, the sultan signs the Treaty of Fez, making Morocco a joint protectorate with France and Spain. This averts the threat of a European war over Morocco, following the arrival of the German gunboat *Panther* to the region.

UNITED STATES SUPPRESSES REVOLT IN NICARAGUA

In Nicaragua, liberals rise up against conservatism and U.S. influence, under the slogan "Down with Yankee imperialism." President Díaz is forced to ask for U.S. help, which comes in the form of 2,500 U.S. marines. The rebellion is quelled within two months.

AUTOBIOGRAPHY OF AN EX-COLORED MAN

The first black barrister in Florida and consul to Venezuela and Nicaragua, James Weldon Johnson (1871–1938) publishes *Autobiography of an Ex-Colored Man*. Johnson does more than anyone in the early twentieth century to make Americans aware of the richness of black American culture.

WALKING

Ukrainian-born American sculptor Alexander Archipenko bores holes into otherwise solid figures, to convey the notion of inner space. His sculpture, *Walking*, marks the first time that holes have been made in solid sculpture in this way.

QUO VADIS

The big, silent, Italian film *Quo Vadis*, by director Enrico Guazzoni, is the longest film yet produced. It is the first of several film versions of the novel by Henryk Sienkiewicz and is an influential cinematic epic.

PILTDOWN MAN

A fossilized skull and jawbone are found in Sussex, England. The remains, nicknamed "Piltdown Man," are hailed as the missing link in human ancestry. Many years later Piltdown Man is proved to be a hoax.

PARACHUTE ESCAPE

Albert Berry, an American stuntman, makes the first parachute jump from a moving biplane over St. Louis in March. He falls some 397 feet before his parachute opens and his exploit proves that it is possible to save life in this way.

KEYSTONE KOPS

The Kops make their riotous appearance in the first of scores of films made by Mack Sennett (1880–1960), an uneducated Irish-Canadian who began as the apprentice of D.W. Griffith. His films with the Kops are made in his own studio, however, which will be highly successful until the arrival of sound.

NAMING VITAMINS

Polish-born American biochemist Casimir Funk (1884–1967) coins the name "vitamines" (later shortened to vitamins) for the substances discovered by Frederick Hopkins in 1907.

ADVERTISING LIGHTS

The first neon advertising sign — for the aperitif Cinzano — lights up in Paris. A red neon tube light was first demonstrated in Paris by French physicist Georges Claude in 1910.

ABOVE: The revived Olympic Games attract a great deal of publicity. This detail from a multilingual poster is the first attempt at international marketing.

LEFT: Five sisters working as "pit-brow" lasses in a coal mine in the north of England.

RIGHT: Still no vote, but women work the same shifts as men digging and sorting coal in mines all over Europe.

NUDE DESCENDING A STAIRCASE

This landmark painting by French artist Marcel Duchamp (1887–1968) uses the futurist technique of breaking up the image to suggest movement. It causes a scandal, but becomes one of the most influential works of modern art.

POST OFFICE SAVINGS BANK

Otto Wagner's Savings Bank in Vienna becomes famous for exposing its structure to view — even the rivets are left visible. The whole form of the building follows the structure, with much use of metal and glass. Glass bricks in the floor allow light to enter the basement.

MONTESSORI SCHOOLS

Italian educationalist Maria Montessori (1870–1952) founds schools in Europe and New York City following the success she achieved in the school for neglected children, which she opened in Rome in 1907. The Montessori method involves stimulating children's natural desire to learn by using toys and puzzles.

ELECTRIC COOKER

The electric stove invented by British engineer Charles Belling is the most successful of a number of attempts to apply electricity to the kitchen. However, as yet electric stoves do not have temperature control.

ABOVE: The national Republican convention in Chicago. The election of William Howard Taft as presidential nominee forces Theodore Roosevelt to quit the party in order to oppose him.

ABOVE: Russian peasants in the Novgorod area. This decade will see a revolution in their lives.

CONTINENTS DRIFT

German scientist Alfred Wegener (1880–1930) suggests that Africa and South America were once one mass, and have broken apart by a process that he calls continental drift. Because he is a meteorologist, not a geologist, geologists mock his theory.

PIERROT LUNAIRE

This work, by Austro-Hungarian composer Arnold Schoenberg (1874–1951), shocks its first audiences but will become a classic of modern music. It is a "melodrama" in which a female performer (dressed as a male pierrot figure with a whitened, masklike face) half-sings, half-speaks the words of the text. The half-singing, half-speaking technique is known in German as *Sprechstimme*. Although the form was not invented by Schoenberg, *Pierrot* shows its potential for the first time.

GITANJALI

Indian poet Rabindranath Tagore (1861–1941) translates his collection of poems, *Gitanjali*, into English, bringing this mystical Indian poet fame in the West. Irish poet W.B. Yeats writes the introduction, helping to publicize Indian poetry in the Western world for the first time.

OLYMPIC GAMES

Athletes from five continents compete at the Fifth Olympic Games, held in Stockholm, Sweden. More women participate and the photofinish and electric timing are introduced. American athlete Jim Thorpe wins two gold medals, but is stripped of them for previously having been paid to play baseball.

WOMEN'S SUFFRAGE

Arizona, Kansas, and Oregon grant women the right to vote. In Britain, suffragettes raid the House of Commons and break shop windows in a coordinated campaign of protest. More than 200 women are arrested.

JUNG AND FREUD DISAGREE

Karl Gustav Jung (1875–1961), the pioneering Swiss psychologist who became president of the International Psychoanalytic Society in 1911, publishes *Psychology of the Unconscious*. This sets out his disagreements with his colleague Sigmund Freud on the sexual origins of unconscious motivations.

COMMERCIAL CELLOPHANE

Cellophane, invented by Jacques Brandenberger, a Swiss chemist, is produced commercially in Paris for use as a wrapping material.

JOHAN AUGUST STRINDBERG (1849–1912)

August Strindberg, the controversial Swedish writer, has died. His work has been a major influence on twentieth-century writing for the theater. His novel *The Red Room* (1879) introduced naturalism to Sweden, and his plays and chamber plays such as *The Father* (1887), *Miss Julie* (1888), and *The Ghost Sonata* (1907) combine naturalism and psychological analysis.

WAR CLOUDS MASS IN THE BALKANS

Trouble continues in the Balkans as the world drifts towards war. Revolution intensifies in Mexico, where the first air-to-air combat takes place. Stravinsky's *Rite of Spring* causes a riot, and in New York the Armory Show gives Americans their first chance to view examples of European modern art. Also in New York, the new Woolworth Building is the world's tallest. Vitamins A and B are isolated and state-funded insurance is introduced into Britain.

1913

Feb	2	Grand Central Station, the world's largest train station, opens in New York
	23	Deposed president shot in Mexico
Mar	18	King George I of the Greeks is assassinated in Salonika
May	10	Bombs dropped on Mexican gunboats
	29	Igor Stravinsky's ballet *The Rite of Spring* performed in Paris to riots
	30	Treaty ends the First Balkan War
June	8	British suffragette Emily Davison killed by horse
July	31	Second Balkan War breaks out as Bulgaria attacks Serbia
Aug	10	Treaty of Bucharest ends the Second Balkan War
Sep	29	Rudolf Diesel, inventor of the diesel engine, dies aged 55
Oct	10	Last rock barrier on the Panama Canal is blasted away
Dec	10	Dutch scientist Heike Kamerlingh Onnes is awarded the Nobel Prize in physics

OPPOSITE: British suffragette Emily Davison lies fatally injured after falling under the king's horse, Anmer, during the annual Derby race.

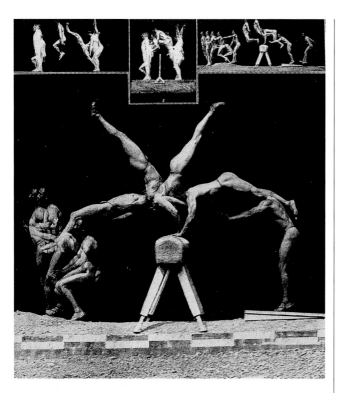

ABOVE: One of Eadweard Muybridge's remarkable photographs capturing the body in movement. Muybridge's work has great influence on artists of the day.

BALKAN WARS

In March, Adrianople surrenders to the Bulgarians, who have been beseiging the city, and in May a peace treaty is signed with the Turks. However, war breaks out again and the Turks reoccupy Adrianople. After bitter fighting, in August peace is finally restored to the Balkans after a year of war. The treaty limits the Ottoman Empire in Europe to Constantinople and its surrounds, creates the new state of Albania, doubles the size of Serbia and Montenegro, and confirms Greece as the most important power in the Aegean Sea. Both Bulgaria and Turkey bitterly resent the new settlement.

MEXICAN REVOLUTION

Right-wing general Victoriano Huerta seizes power from elected president Madero, who is murdered. Huerta's dictatorial regime leads to revolts led by General Alvaro Obregon, and revolutionaries Francisco "Pancho" Villa and Emiliano Zapata. In May, pilot Didier Masson, a supporter of the rebels, drops the first-ever bombs on to an enemy warship when he attacks Mexican gunships in Guayamas Bay. In November, the first air-to-air combat takes place when an aircraft piloted by Phillip Rader, in support of President Huerta, exchanges pistol shots with a rebel plane flown by Dean Ivan Lamb.

A BOY'S WILL

American poet Robert Frost (1874–1963) publishes his first volume of poetry and an authentically American voice is heard in modern poetry for the first time.

PANAMA CANAL OPENS

The canal connecting the Pacific and Atlantic oceans is finally opened. The canal flows through a U.S.-controlled zone and shortens the journey between the east and west coasts of America by many days.

GREEK KING ASSASSINATED

King George I of Greece is assassinated by a madman, Alexander Schinas, in Salonika, newly won from the Ottoman Turks. George had been king since 1863; he is succeeded by his son, Constantine I.

WOMEN'S SUFFRAGE

In the United States, Alice Paul and Lucy Burns lead a parade of 5,000 through Washington, D.C. demanding women's suffrage on the day before President Wilson's inauguration. In the U.K., British suffragette Emily Davison dies after falling under the hooves of the king's horse in the Derby.

LES GRANDES MEAULNES

In his one completed novel, *Les Grandes Meaulnes*, French writer Alain-Fournier (1886–1914), who will die in the first weeks of World War I, evokes a dream world and a world of childhood, both of which are finally lost. It is one of the few successful novels to come from the symbolist movement in art and literature.

THE FOURTH OF JULY

In this new work, American composer Charles Ives (1874–1954) creates a unique sound world, full of snatches of American tunes. Its technique and harmonies anticipate many later developments. Ives is an insurance executive who composes in his free time.

SPRING RITE CAUSES RIOTS

The *Rite of Spring*, a new work by Russian composer Igor Stravinsky (1882–1971) is premièred in Paris. Staged by the Ballets Russes, it portrays a fertility rite that ends in a ritual sacrifice, and it causes a riot in the theater. With its strong rhythms and vibrant orchestral colors, the work will later become one of the most popular in twentieth-century music.

SWANN'S WAY

The first part of French writer Marcel Proust's great novel, *A la Recherche du Temps Perdu* (1913–1927) is published. Its evocation of memory and character over a large canvas make it one of the most important of literary works. Proust's literary goal is to release creative energies derived from past experience, from the hidden store of the unconscious.

ISOTOPES

British chemist Frederick Soddy (1877–1956) invents the term "isotope" to describe atoms of the same element that have different masses, for example, carbon-12, the most common form of that element, and carbon-14, which is radioactive.

ARMORY SHOW

Some 1,600 works are exhibited at the Armory Show in New York City, including around 400 modern European works. This gives Americans the chance to see many European modern works for the first time, and gives modern artists much publicity. Some of the paintings, such as Matisse's *Blue Nude* (which was burned in effigy) and Duchamp's *Nude Descending a Staircase*, cause controversy.

WORLD'S TALLEST BUILDING

The Woolworth Building in New York City, architect Cass Gilbert's Gothic-style skyscraper is 790 feet high, the tallest building in the world. It is so high that it influences the decision to introduce zoning, whereby tall buildings have to be set back to provide light and improve wind flow.

SOCIOLOGY PROFESSOR

Pioneering French sociologist Emile Durkheim (1858–1917) becomes the first professor of sociology at the Sorbonne, Paris. In *The Rules of Sociological Method* (1895) he advocated using the scientific method to study society. He believes that studying anthropology will throw light on the way society is organized.

PRIZE FOR ONNES

The Dutch scientist Heike Kamelingh Onnes is awarded the Nobel Prize in physics for liquefying helium.

BELOW: Members of the Scott expedition to the Antarctic, including Captain Scott (center) and Captain Oates (second from the right). Five of the group died, including Scott himself.

STAINLESS STEEL

Metallurgists Henry Brearley (U.K.) and FM Becket (U.S.A.) produce stainless steel, an alloy of iron and chromium which resists rust.

GAS-FILLED BULBS

American chemist Irving Langmuir discovers that electric light bulbs last longer if they are filled with an inert gas such as nitrogen or argon.

NATIONAL INSURANCE

In Britain, payments are to be made to British workers under a new National Health Insurance Act. Under this, state and employers will give limited financial support during ill-health and unemployment. The state insurance scheme is based on pioneering schemes set up by Scandinavian governments in the late nineteenth century and the Dutch government in 1901.

OZONE LAYER FOUND

French physicist Charles Fabry discovers that there are quantities of ozone in the upper atmosphere, between 6 and 26 miles above the Earth.

SCHWEITZER'S HOSPITAL

Albert Schweitzer's new hospital is opened in Lambarene, French Equatorial Africa. It will treat thousands of people suffering from tropical diseases.

VITAMINS A AND B

American biochemist Elmer Verner McCollum discovers fat-soluble vitamins A and B.

DEN NORWEGERN

BEHAVIORISM

In *Behaviorism*, John Broadus Watson (1878–1958), an American psychology professor, argues that psychology is the study of observable behavior, which is a response to physiological stimulus. His approach to psychology is well received by psychologists who question the value of studying the unconscious.

ARTIFICIAL KIDNEY

Medical theories come close to reality when American pharmacologist John James Abel and his colleages make the first artificial kidney. However, it is not completely practicable.

DOMESTIC FRIDGE ON SALE

The first domestic electric refrigerator goes on sale in Chicago. Called the Domelre, its compressor (which compresses air to reduce the temperature) is driven by an electric motor instead of the steam engine used on earlier refrigerators.

HARRIET TUBMAN
(1821–1913)

American former slave, Harriet Tubman, has died at her home in Auburn, New York. A courageous woman, known as the "Moses of her people," she smuggled more than 300 slaves to freedom via the so-called Underground Railroad after her own escape from slavery.

LEFT: An impressive present from the German Kaiser to the people of Norway, the colossal statue of Frijthof.

BELOW: Diamond hunters race to peg their claim at Killarney, dubbed the new "Eldorado" of South Africa.

THE END OF THE GOLDEN SUMMER

Archduke Ferdinand is assassinated in Sarajevo. The rival European powers mobilize and by August, France, Britain, and Russia are at war with Germany and Austria-Hungary — the world's first global conflict is under way. Elsewhere, the Panama Canal opens and Mother's Day is invented.

OPPOSITE: Soldiers struggle to maneuver in the muddy trenches characteristic of World War I.

1914

June	28	Serbian student Gavrilo Princip assassinates Archduke Franz Ferdinand of Austria at Sarajevo
July	28	Austria-Hungary declares war on Serbia
	29	Russia mobilizes its army
	30	In Britain the Irish Home Rule Bill is shelved
Aug	1	Germany declares war on Russia because of Russian mobilization
	3	Germany declares war on Russia's ally, France
	4	Germany invades Belgium in order to reach France; Britain declares war on Germany
	5	First traffic lights are introduced in the United States
	6	Austria-Hungary declares war on Russia
	14	Official opening of the Panama Canal
	23	Battle of Mons: British army sent to help Belgium begins to retreat

	26–30	Battle of Tannenberg: massive German victory against Russians
Sep	5	Germans capture Reims, France
	6–8	Battle of the Marne: German advance halted
	19	South African troops invade German West Africa (Namibia)
	23	Germans sink British cruisers off the Netherlands
Oct	13	The Ottoman Empire (Turkey) joins the war on Germany's side
	23–24	Battle of Mons
	30–Nov 24	Battle of Ypres
Nov	11	Trench warfare fully established on the Western Front in France
Dec	11	Battle of the Falklands: four German cruisers sunk
	25	Christmas Day truce on the Western Front: German and Allied troops play football

WORLD WAR I BREAKS OUT

In Sarajevo, Bosnia, Archduke Franz Ferdinand, heir to the Austrian throne, is assassinated by a Serb, Gavrilo Princip, in June. The Austrian government suspects Serbia of complicity in the killing and threatens reprisals. As a result of the assassination in Sarajevo, the rival European powers mobilize their armies. Austria declares war on Serbia, which is supported by Russia, and invades. Germany declares its support for Austria and declares war on Russia. France supports Russia and prepares for war. In August, Germany invades Belgium on its way to invade France. As a result, Britain declares war on Germany to protect Belgian neutrality. Italy, the Netherlands, Spain, Portugal, and the Scandinavian countries stay out of the war, which engulfs the whole of the rest of Europe. In September, the war spreads to the Pacific and Africa as British and Empire troops invade and seize the German colonies of Togo, Cameroon, German East Africa, German Southwest Africa, New Guinea, and the Caroline Islands. Fighting is now taking place around the world.

BELOW: Aircraft soon join the conflict on both sides.

ABOVE: HMS *Iron Duke* battles through the North Sea.

ABOVE: American artillery plays a crucial role in the final year of the war. This is a 16-inch pack gun that can be mounted on a railroad carriage for ease of maneuvering and firing.

ABOVE: Dropping bombs from an airplane.

ABOVE: German submarine crew in the North Sea.

LEFT: German high command plan tactics and strategy in the field.

RIGHT: Going over the top. As soldiers emerged from the trenches, they were only too often mown down.

OPPOSITE BELOW: Austrian troops shoot blindfolded prisoners.

FIRST SCREEN GODDESS

American actress Mary Pickford (1893–1979) stars in Edward S. Porter's film, *Tess of the Storm Country*. This is her first famous movie, and one of the hits that launches her as the "first screen goddess."

FIRST TARZAN

Written by Edgar Rice Burroughs, *Tarzan of the Apes* is published. It is the first of a series of books featuring Tarzan, a British aristocrat who is abandoned in the jungle and brought up by apes.

PANAMA CANAL OPENS

The Panama Canal is officially opened to traffic in August, having taken ten years to build at a cost of $380 million; it shortens a voyage from New York to San Francisco by about 7,750 miles.

A PORTRAIT OF THE ARTIST AS A YOUNG MAN

The seminal autobiographical novel, *A Portrait of the Artist as a Young Man*, by Irish writer James Joyce (1882–1941) begins serial publication in *The Egoist*. It is the archetypal *Bildungsroman*, and inspires other writers. *Dubliners*, Joyce's volume of short stories, also appears this year.

FIRST TRAFFIC LIGHTS

As motor vehicles increase in number, the first two-color electric traffic lights, red and green, are installed in Cleveland, Ohio, at the junction of Euclid Avenue and 105th Street.

SUFFRAGETTES SIGN FOR WAR

After fighting the British government for many years, suffragettes Emmeline and Christabel Pankhurst urge women to join the war effort. Many respond to the call; some join an international women's peace movement.

HORMONE ISOLATED

American biochemist Edward Calvin Kendall (1886–1972) isolates the hormone thyroxin, in crystalline form. This hormone is essential for physical growth and mental development.

A BLUE NOTE

Black composer W.C. Handy (1873–1958) becomes known as "the father of the blues" with numbers such as *St Louis Blues*. He integrates ragtime and jazz styles, and produces a characteristic effect with a "blue note" — a slightly flattened seventh note of the scale, which comes from traditional black music.

MOTHER'S DAY

Mother's Day is introduced in the United States. This follows lobbying by Anna Jarvis of West Virginia, who marks May 10, the day her mother died, with prayers. Congress signs a resolution that the second Sunday in May is to be a national holiday.

EARTH'S CORE

By studying earthquake waves, American geologist Beno Gutenberg decides that the Earth has a central core, a theory now generally accepted.

EARLY BRASSIERE

The first brassière is marketed, based on a design by Mary Phelps Jacob, a New York socialite; her first model is made from two handkerchiefs and some elastic.

FOOTBALL IN THE TRENCHES

During a Christmas Day truce, German and British soldiers fighting in France play football together in the no-man's land between their trenches. The following day, they return to killing one other.

GAS, GALLIPOLI, AND ZEPPELIN RAIDS

Far from ending by Christmas, the Great War intensifies. Improved technology makes the machine gun a terrible weapon of war and both sides make use of poison gas, with awful results. Zeppelins bomb British cities. Italy enters the war. The *Lusitania* is sunk by a German submarine. And while men make war, some women travel to The Hague to discuss possible ways of achieving peace. Radio waves are sent across the Atlantic and in the United States the white racist organization the Ku Klux Klan is revived.

OPPOSITE: Turkish troops at Gallipoli, the campaign that lasted for almost a year.

1915

Jan	9	German zeppelins bomb English towns	Aug	30	Germans capture the Russian fortress of Brest-Litovsk
Feb	2	Germany begins U-boat blockade of the British Isles	Sep	5	Czar takes command of the Russian army
	19	British ships shell Turkish forts guarding the Dardanelles Strait	Oct	12	British nurse Edith Cavell is shot in German-occupied Belgium
Apr	22–	First use of poison gas by Germans at Ypres			
May	25		Nov	5	An airplane is catapulted from a U.S. warship, the first such launch
	25	British, Australian and New Zealand troops land at Gallipoli, in the Dardanelles	Dec	10	The 100th car rolls off the Ford assembly line
May	7	German U-boat sinks the British liner *Lusitania*		20	The Gallipoli campaign is abandoned
	23	Italy declares war on Austria-Hungary			
June	1	Zeppelins bomb London			

ITALY ENTERS THE WAR

After renouncing the Triple Alliance with Germany and Austria, Italy enters the war and seizes Italian-speaking territory from Austria. Despite its early successes, the Italian army fights a series of inconclusive battles on the River Isonzo against the Austrians.

HOLLAND REMAINS NEUTRAL

Holland remains neutral during the course of World War I.

SINKING OF THE LUSITANIA

The liner *Lusitania* sinks off the coast of Ireland after it is torpedoed without warning by a German submarine. More than 1,100 of the 1,978 on board are drowned, including 128 American citizens. The sinking increases anti-German sentiment in the United States, which is trying to remain neutral in the war.

NURSE SHOT

In Belgium, the British nurse Edith Cavell (b. 1865) is shot by a German firing squad for sheltering Belgians fearful of conscription and helping young British and French soldiers escape to safety across the Dutch border. Her death causes an international outrage against the German action.

SYNCHRONIZED MACHINE GUN

Germany introduces a device that synchronizes a machine gun so that its bullets can be fired through an aircraft's rotating propeller without hitting the blades; it is fitted to a Fokker E-1 fighter plane.

POISON GAS

German armies use chlorine gas for the first time against the British at Ypres. Its effects are devastating and over the next four years, both sides develop phosgene and mustard gas, causing terrible injuries and deaths. English physicist Hertha Ayrton (1854–1923) works on a fan for dispersing gas; it is later known as the Ayrton fan.

WOMEN AT THE HAGUE

In April, 2,000 women, delegates from many countries, meet at The Hague in Holland to discuss ways of ending the war. They set up the Women's International League for Peace and Freedom (WILPF) and agree to lobby governments for peace. By November women have formed peace groups in 11 European countries including Austria, Belgium, Britain, Germany, Italy, France, and Hungary.

ABOVE: The ominous Ku Klux Klan regroup in Atlanta, Georgia.

LEFT: The passenger ship *Lusitania*, soon to be a victim of war.

KKK REVIVED
The Ku Klux Klan white supremacist movement, which arose after the Civil War in the American South, is revived in Atlanta, by ex-preacher William J. Simmons.

THE GOOD SOLDIER
The publication of *The Good Soldier* by English novelist Ford Madox Ford (1873–1939) brings him fame. The novel is valued for its subtle treatment of life's illusions and realities. Ford is also known for his championing of experiment in fiction and his support for important writers, such as D.H. Lawrence, at early stages in their careers.

HIGHER EDUCATION FOR CHINESE WOMEN
Ginling College, the first institution of higher education for women, opens in Nanking, China.

THE BIRTH OF A NATION
The most famous of American film director D.W. Griffith's great silent epics, *The Birth of a Nation*, is screened this year. It covers the Civil War and is remarkable for its use of such cinematic techniques as close-ups, fade-outs, and flashbacks. But Griffith (1875–1948) is criticized for the film's racial bias and glorification of the Ku Klux Klan.

HERLAND
Having written a famous short story *The Yellow Wallpaper* (1892), about a young Victorian woman's mental breakdown, American feminist Charlotte Perkins Gilman (1860–1935) publishes *Herland*, a feminist utopia.

CALLING LONG DISTANCE
In January the first North American transcontinental telephone service between New York City and San Francisco is opened by the inventor of the telephone, the Scottish Alexander Graham Bell (1847–1922), and his former assistant Thomas Watson.

BELOW: Cruiser *Eleucher*.   ABOVE: German ship sinking.

ABOVE: Despite logistics and planning, the Gallipoli campaign is unsuccessful.

CATAPULTED INTO THE AIR

In November, a flying boat is catapulted from the deck of the US battleship *Carolina* in Pensacola Bay, Florida — the first aircraft launched at sea in this way.

BLACK SQUARE

Going further than the Cubists, Russian painter Kasimir Malevich (1878–1935) reaches abstraction by reducing his paintings to pure arrangements of flat geometrical shapes. He calls this style suprematism.

TRANSATLANTIC SPEECH

Radio transmits speech across the Atlantic Ocean for the first time; it is sent from a U.S. naval base in Virginia and received in Paris by a station on the Eiffel Tower.

HEATPROOF GLASS

By adding boric oxide to the mix, the Corning Glass Works in New York makes the heat-resistant glass known as Pyrex™. Ideal for ovenware, the new substance is developed by technologists Eugene Sullivan and William Taylor.

PAUL EHRLICH
(1854–1915)

Chemist, bacteriologist, haematologist, German-born Paul Ehrlich has died. He pioneered the use of chemotherapy, formulated a successful treatment for syphilis, and in 1908 shared the Nobel Prize for medicine with Ilya Mechnikov for their work in immunology.

NO QUIET ON THE WESTERN FRONT

War continues to engulf the globe. As always, war stimulates technology and a new weapon appears: the tank, first used on the Somme. Plastic surgery, too, develops as a result of terrible injuries and the term "shell shock" comes into use. The Easter Rising in Ireland is put down brutally. Rasputin the monk is murdered in Russia. The art movement dadaism appears as a protest against the carnage of war.

OPPOSITE: Tanks first come into use in World War I. They are a British invention and first see service at Cambrai in France.

1916

Jan	**6**	British House of Commons votes to introduce military conscription
	16	Battle of Gallipoli ends after nine months, with Allied withdrawal
Feb	**21**	Battle of Verdun begins with German attack, ends Dec 18
Apr	**25**	The Easter Rising in Ireland begins; it is crushed within a week
May	**21**	Battle of Jutland begins; it continues until June 1
June	**6**	Field Marshal Lord Kitchener, British War Minister, is drowned at sea
	21	Arab leader Hussein, Sheik of Mecca, opens a rebellion against the Turks who control Arabia
July	**1**	First Battle of the Somme begins on the Western Front; it lasts until November 18. Losses on both sides amount to more than 1,260,000 killed or wounded
Sep	**15**	British first use tanks during the Battle of the Somme
Nov	**21**	Emperor Franz Joseph of Austria-Hungary dies aged 86
Dec	**7**	David Lloyd George becomes prime minister, U.K.
	30	Grigori Rasputin, self-styled "holy man" and adviser to the Czarina of Russia, is murdered by a group of noblemen

ABOVE: Armored cruisers, or Dreadnoughts, steaming in formation.

MEXICAN REVOLUTION

In Mexico, soldiers of the rebel leader Pancho Villa cross into the United States and kill 18 Americans working for a mining company. In response, U.S. troops under General Pershing march into Mexico and attack Villa, killing 30 of his men and routing his army.

EASTER RISING

Rebel Irish republicans seize strategic buildings in central Dublin on Easter Sunday and declare an Irish Republic. The British bombard the city to end the rebellion, which spreads to other cities in Ireland, and execute the leaders. As a result, support for Irish independence increases throughout Ireland.

RASPUTIN

In Petrograd, a group of Russian nobles murder Rasputin, the Siberian monk and mystic who has held considerable power over the czar's wife and is blamed for exercising a malign control over affairs of state.

EASTER 1916

The Irish poet W.B. Yeats (1865–1939), who is already well known, writes the poem "Easter 1916" on the Dublin Easter Rising. The poem is famous for its celebration of Irish nationalist heroes and for its line "A terrible beauty is born." Later, in 1922, after the Anglo-Irish War, Yeats will become a senator in the Irish Free State.

ARAB REVOLT

Arabs rise in revolt against their Ottoman rulers in Hejaz, Saudi Arabia. The revolt is led by Emir Feisal and his son Hussein and is supported from December by Colonel T.E. Lawrence, a British soldier known as "Lawrence of Arabia."

BRITISH CONSCRIPTION

In the United Kingdom, the House of Commons agrees to introduce conscription to increase the size of the army. The government has been relying on single men to volunteer, but losses on the Western Front mean that volunteers can no longer be relied upon to ensure the army remains at full strength.

AUSTRO-HUNGARIAN EMPEROR DIES

Franz Josef, emperor of Austria-Hungary, dies at the age of 86 after ruling his country since 1848. He is succeeded by his grandnephew, Charles I.

BIRTH OF THE TANK

First trials of a military tank take place in Britain. It is first used in battle on the Somme. The name "tank" is used to confuse German spies. This new weapon of war is an armored vehicle, which can cross the most difficult terrain and withstand powerful artillery.

PLASTIC SURGERY AND SHELL SHOCK

British surgeon Harold Gillies sets up a plastic surgery unit to deal with 2,000 cases of facial damage after the Battle of the Somme. This year too the term "shell shock" comes into use to describe the psychological disorder caused by battle fatigue and experiences in the trenches. It is often mistakenly regarded as a form of cowardice.

SCHEEPVARTHUIS

A striking new building, Scheepvarthuis, has appeared in Amsterdam, Holland. This office building, used by six shipping companies, is built using a concrete shell covered with bricks and reliefs depicting different aspects of sea trade. The nautical theme is continued in the interior and the stained glass. The building is notable for marrying a modern material (concrete) with a striking use of ornament.

DADAISM

In Zurich a group of young artists found the Dada movement, an anti-art movement that has its roots in their protest against the carnage of World War I. They start the Cabaret Voltaire, where they put on bizarre lectures and weird entertainments. They revel in nonsense and the irrational, and many of their number (who include Marcel Duchamp, Jean Arp, and the Romanian poet Tristan Tzara) will later become prominent surrealists.

UNDER FIRE

French writer Henri Barbusse (1873–1935) publishes *Under Fire*. An antiwar novel, it is based on Barbusse's own experiences at the front. It portrays, unusually for these patriotic times, the squalid side of war and the lives of ordinary men in the trenches.

RELATIVITY

German theoretical physicist Albert Einstein publishes his General Theory of Relativity, which argues that the gravity of a mass (such as a heavenly body) distorts space.

DETERGENTS

German scientist Fritz Gunther develops the first synthetic detergents to replace soap; they prove too harsh for domestic use.

THE PLANETS

British composer Gustav Holst (1874–1934) writes this suite for large orchestra, inspired by his own studies of astrology. Despairing of the chances of such a large-scale work getting performed, he puts the score away. When friends discover the work and have it performed for Holst, the composer's handling of rhythm and orchestral color will win over both audience and musicians alike.

FIRST GUIDE DOGS

In Austria and Germany the first guide dogs for the blind are trained to help soldiers blinded in battle.

BOEING TAKES OFF

U.S. industrialist William E. Boeing (1881–1954) founds the Pacific Aero Products Company, later the Boeing Company, one of the largest aircraft manufacturers.

NO OLYMPICS

The First World War forces the cancellation of the Olympic Games.

BIRTH CONTROL CLINIC

America's first birth-control clinic opens in New York City, run by Margaret Sanger (1883–1966), a public health nurse. Like the pioneering clinic opened in 1878 in Amsterdam, the Brooklyn clinic is technically illegal. Mrs. Sanger was jailed in 1914 for distributing birth-control literature.

FIRST CONGRESSWOMAN

Jeannette Rankin (1880–1975), a worker for women's rights, becomes the first woman to be elected to the U.S. Congress. Her stance on the war in Europe is pacifist, and she will fight for independent citizenship for married women.

NATIONAL PARKS

The National Parks Service is set up by the U.S. government. President Cleveland pioneered the creation of parks and preserves during the nineteenth century. Since 1872 the United States has protected more than 20 areas of natural and scientific interest.

HORATIO HERBERT KITCHENER (1850–1916)

Lord Kitchener, the Irish-born British field marshal, has been lost at sea after his ship HMS *Hampshire* was mined off Orkney in June. He was veteran of the Sudan campaign (1883–1885), and commanded British forces in South Africa during the second Boer War (1900–1902) and in India (1902–1909). Appointed British secretary for war in 1914, he was responsible for a highly successful recruitment campaign.

WORLD WAR I

Sometimes called the Great War or "the war to end all wars", World War I is fought in Europe, Africa, and the Middle and Far East. On one side are the Central European powers (Germany, Austria-Hungary and allies); on the other are the Triple Entente (Britain and Empire, France, Russia and allies) together with the United States of America, which enters the war in 1917. An estimated 10 million people die and twice that number are wounded.

❖KEY DATES❖
WESTERN FRONT 1914–18 FRANCE AND BELGIUM

- **NAMUR August 20–25, 1914.** German heavy artillery including 540 heavy guns batter Belgian fort into surrender, inflicting over 30,000 casualties.
- **MONS August 23–24, 1914.** The British 2nd Corps conducts a fighting withdrawal in the face of heavy German attacks. For losses of 1,600, British marksmen inflict 3,000 casualties on the Germans.
- **FIRST BATTLE OF THE MARNE September 6–8, 1914.** The battle that saves Paris. The Germans commit 44 infantry and seven cavalry divisions, the Allies 56 infantry and nine cavalry divisions. German casualties are 200,000, French 250,000 and British 1,071.
- **YPRES October 14–November 11, 1914.** The German offensive. It costs Germany 130,000 casualties, the French 50,000, the British 2,368 officers and 55,768 men, and the Belgians 32,000.
- **YPRES April 22–May 25, 1915.** Germans use poison gas against the British. Its use and subsequent fighting cause 60,000 Allied casualties and 35,000 German.
- **VERDUN February 21–December 18, 1916.** A grim battle of attrition. The Germans fire 40 million shells. Initially one million Germans attack 500,000 French; at the close, the Germans have lost 434,000 and the French 543,000.
- **FIRST BATTLE OF THE SOMME July 1–Nov 18, 1916.** British lose 57,470 men on the first day. By November 18, the Allies have advanced 7 miles over a 20-mile front. The British lose 418,000, the French 195,000 and the Germans 650,000 (killed or wounded).
- **CAMBRAI November 20–December 4, 1917.** The first great tank battle in which 324 tanks are committed and made a 6-mile gap in the German lines. The Germans counterattack and when the fighting is over the British have lost 43,000 including 6,000 prisoners, the Germans 41,000 including 11,000 prisoners.
- **YPRES July 21–November 6, 1917.** A British offensive designed in part to take the pressure off the French. German counterattacks and use of bunkers cause heavy casualties of 400,000 while the Germans suffer 65,000, including 9,000 prisoners.

- **VILLERS-BRETONNEUX April 24, 1918.** The first tank versus tank action; three British Mark IV tanks fight a drawn engagement with three German heavy A7Vs.
- **SECOND BATTLE OF THE SOMME March 21–April 4, 1918.** A massive assault by 71 German divisions with 6,000 guns, the Germans advance 40 miles but are halted by exhaustion and lack of supplies. The Allies lose 160,000 battle casualties and 70,000 prisoners, the Germans 150,000 killed or wounded.
- **SECOND BATTLE OF THE MARNE July 15–August 6, 1918.** A major German attack by 52 divisions which is stopped by 36 Allied divisions, French, American, British, and Italian. The Germans lose 100,000 the Allies 60,000, including 20,000 dead.

❖KEY DATES❖
EASTERN FRONT 1914–17 RUSSIA, POLAND, AUSTRIA, HUNGARY, ROMANIA

- **TANNENBERG August 26–30, 1914.** A massive German victory against the Russians. Russian losses 30,000 killed or wounded and 92,000 prisoners. The Germans lose 13,000 killed or wounded.
- **GORLICE-TARNOW April 28–August 5, 1915.** Germany and Austria advance through Poland and the Ukraine. Pounded by heavy artillery the Russians lose one million killed and wounded and one million prisoners as well as huge areas of valuable agricultural land.
- **LAKE NAROTCH March 18, 1916.** After initial successes the Russian infantry are counterattacked and lose more than 80,000 men.

❖KEY DATES❖
NAVAL WAR

- **CORONEL November 1, 1914.** Five German cruisers, the *Gneisenau*, *Scharnhorst*, *Nürnberg*, *Dresden*, and *Leipzig*, meet and destroy HMS *Good Hope* and HMS *Monmouth*, the smaller faster HMS *Glasgow* is able to escape.
- **FALKANDS December 8, 1914.** HMS *Invincible*, *Inflexible*, *Kent*, *Cornwall*, *Glasgow*, *Bristol*, *Otranto*, and *Macedonia* meet and destroy the German squadron that was victorious at the Coronel. Only *Dresden* escapes.
- **DARDANELLES February 19–March 18, 1915.** Abortive Franco-British attempt to force the narrows of the Dardanelles. A combination of mines and coastal batteries sinks three heavy ships and damages three.
- **JUTLAND May 21–June 1, 1916.** Germans lose four cruisers and five destroyers. They claim victory because British navy lose three battle cruisers, three light cruisers, and eight destroyers. British claim victory because German fleet does not venture to sea again and the Allied naval blockade of Germany remains intact.

❖KEY DATES❖
AIR WAR IN THE WEST 1914–1918

- **August 14, 1914.** First bombing attack of World War I, undertaken by an aircraft of French Aviation Militaire against zeppelin sheds, at Metz-Frescaty.
- **August 30, 1914.** First bombing attack on a capital city, Paris. German Taube drops five bombs and a message; one person killed, two wounded.
- **October 5, 1914.** First aircraft is shot down in air-to-air combat.
- **April 15–26, 1916.** First aerial resupply mission, Kut-el-Amara, Mesopotamia. Food, mail, currency, gold, silver, and wireless parts are delivered by the RFC and RNAS.
- **April 5–6, 1917.** First British night bombing begins, hitting aircraft hangars at Douai airfield.
- **June 13, 1917.** German Gotha bombers make first and most costly mass bombing raid on London. Fourteen Gotha bombers drop 72 bombs killing 162 and injuring 432 people.

❖KEY DATES❖
MEDITERRANEAN AND MIDDLE EAST 1914–18 EGYPT, PALESTINE AND MESOPOTAMIA

- **GALLIPOLI April 25, 1915–January 16, 1916.** Amphibious landing on the Turkish coast which through British mismanagement fails to block the narrows of the Dardanelles. After heavy fighting the Allies are obliged to withdraw. Allied casualties: 252,000; Turkish casualties 251,000, including 66,000 deaths.
- **KUT-EL-AMARA December 8, 1915–April 29, 1916.** Initial British successes are followed by a decision to fortify and hold Kut, leading to a siege and British defeat. Ten thousand starving and sick survivors surrender to the Turks.
- **ISONZO RIVER (Italian Front) June 23, 1915–October 1917.** Eleven battles in all. Italian troops launch attacks against Austrian positions on the Isonzo River. Four battles fought in 1915 cost the Italians 66,000 killed, 185,000 wounded, and 22,000 taken prisoner, for no real gains.
- **GAZA March 26–7, April 17–19, 1917.**
- **CAPORETTO October 24–November 12, 1917.** Seven German and eight Austrian divisions attack General Capello's mutinous 2nd Italian army. The Italians are driven back to the Brenta valley. At Caporetto, and subsequently, Italians lose 40,000 killed and wounded.
- **JERUSALEM December 11, 1917.** General Allenby enters Jerusalem following the defeat of the Turks at Nebi Samwil ridge. He guarantees religious toleration to all.
- **WADI FARA 1918.** First major fighter ground attack victory.
- **VITTORIO VENETO October 24–November 4, 1918.** Italians with 57 divisions and 7,700 guns attack the Austrians with 52 divisions and 6,000 guns. Italians, with British and French assistance, force crossings over the Piave and capture Vittorio Veneto. Victory leads to the collapse of the Austro-Hungarian empire. Austrians lose 5,000 guns and 300,000 prisoners; Italian casualties: 36,000.

WAR AND REVOLUTION

The United States enters the war on the Allied side. A revolution occurs in Russia that ends with the Bolsheviks victorious and the setting up of the world's first Communist state. Its effects will be felt for most of the century. In science too, a development occurs that will dominate the century: Rutherford splits the atom, paving the way for the nuclear age.

OPPOSITE TOP: Poison gas in the trenches. First used by the Germans, gas had devastating effects.

OPPOSITE BELOW: Australian troops being treated at a dressing station near Ypres.

1917

Jan	10	William F. Cody, better known as Buffalo Bill, dies
Feb	3	The United States severs diplomatic relations with Germany
Mar	8	Count Ferdinand von Zeppelin, airship designer, dies aged 78 Revolution breaks out in Russia
	14	Provisional government set up in Russia
	15	Russia's ruler Czar Nicholas II abdicates
	16-17	German U-boats sink three U.S. ships
Apr	6	United States declares war on Germany
	16	With German help, Bolshevik revolutionary Vladimir Lenin returns to Russia after ten years in exile
June	24	First American soldiers land in France
July	16	Alexander Kerensky becomes prime minister of Russia
	31	On the Western Front, Battle of Passchendaele begins in a sea of mud; it lasts until November 10
Sep	17	Germany captures Riga
Nov	2	Balfour Declaration: British Foreign Secretary Arthur Balfour promises the Jews a homeland in Palestine
	7	"October Revolution" in Russia; Lenin and Bolsheviks seize power
	17	French sculptor Auguste Rodin dies aged 77
	20	Ukraine declares itself a republic
Dec	6	Finland declares independence from Russia
	15	Russia signs an armistice with Germany

UKRAINE AND FINLAND INDEPENDENT

As a result of the Russian Revolution, Ukraine declares itself a republic and breaks away from Russia. Finland follows the next month, and is recognized by the new Russian government as an independent state.

UNITED STATES ENTERS THE WAR

In April, the United States enters the war on the Allied side against Germany. President Wilson declares that "the world must be made safe for democracy." U.S. resources, including shipbuilding and steel production, are put to work for the war effort as thousands of troops prepare to sail for Europe.

WOMEN'S WAR WORK

British and French women sign up for war work in munitions factories, agriculture, transport, and the auxiliary military units from 1915, and American women after April 1917. In the United States and Britain especially, their contribution softens attitudes to women's emancipation.

JEWISH HOMELAND

Arthur Balfour, British Foreign Secretary, issues a declaration promising the Jews a homeland of their own in Palestine. The British government hopes that the declaration will lead to Jewish support for the war effort.

DE STIJL

Dutch painter, poet, and architect Theo van Doesburg (1883–1931) founds the magazine *De Stijl* (the style). The De Stijl artists (including Mondrian and Gerrit Rietveld) embrace a theory of art that can also be applied to painting, architecture, and the decorative arts. They use primary colors and right angles, and reject art that takes its inspiration from nature.

RADIOACTIVE ELEMENT FOUND

Two teams of scientists independently discover the element protactinium, a radioactive metal; they are Otto Hahn (1879–1968) and Lise Meitner (1878–1968) of Germany, and Frederick Soddy and John Cranston of Britain.

MATA HARI SHOT

Mata Hari is executed in France as a spy. She was Netherlands-born Margaretha Geertruida Zelle, who, after divorcing her Scottish husband became a dancer in Paris. In 1907 she joined the German secret service and betrayed military secrets confided by unsuspecting Allied officers.

DETERGENT

The first artificial detergent, called Nekal, is produced commercially in Germany during World War I for washing clothes, to conserve soap for other purposes. Synthetic chemical detergents wash clothes cleaner than soap.

HILAIRE GERMAIN EDGAR DEGAS (1834–1917)

Edgar Degas, the French impressionist painter and sculptor, dies at the age of 83. His paintings and pastel work portray the movement and line of horses and their riders, circus artists, and ballet dancers. Among his best-known and best-loved works are *Absinthe* (1876–1877), *Dancer Lacing her Shoe* (1878), and *Miss Lola at the Cirque Fernando* (1879).

HUGE TELESCOPE

American astronomer George E Hale (1868–1938) instals a 3-yard refracting telescope at Mount Wilson Observatory in California, of which he is director. Hale's telescope is the world's largest to date.

SPLITTING THE ATOM

British scientist Ernest Rutherford (1871–1937) bombards nitrogen atoms and breaks up the nucleus, thus becoming the first person to split the atom. He does not publish his results until 1919 but his achievement will have enormous and long-lasting implications.

SONAR BEGINS

French physicist Paul Langevin (1872–1946) invents a method of detecting sound under water; it is later developed as sonar (an acronym of Sound Navigation And Ranging) and used for locating submarines.

FIRST AIRMAIL STAMP

Italy issues the first airmail stamp in May by overprinting a 25 centime express letter stamp with ESPERIMENTO POSTA AEREA MAGGIO 1917 TORINO-ROMA-ROMA-TORINO.

BOBBED HAIR

A short haircut known as the bob, pioneered by Irene Castle, is adopted for safety by women workers in munitions factories and becomes the latest fashion in hairstyles.

DIXIELAND JAZZ

The Original Dixieland Jazz Band makes its first recording: *The Darktown Strutters' Ball.*

NAIL VARNISH

Transparent liquid nail varnish is first manufactured by Cutex.

RUSSIAN REVOLUTION

Czar Nicholas II (1868–1918) abdicates in March as revolution breaks out across Russia. Discontent with the unpopular war against Germany and Austria, high loss of life on the Eastern Front, and food shortages at home combine to weaken the czar's authority. A provisional government is set up after the czar's brother refuses to accept the throne. In July, the Bolshevik party, led by Vladimir Ilych Lenin (1870–1924), fails to take power in Russia after an abortive coup. Lenin flees in disgrace and Alexander Kerensky (1881–1970), a socialist member of the Duma and Minister of War in the provisional government, becomes prime minister. He promises to continue the war against Germany. In November (October in the Russian calendar) the Bolsheviks overthrow the provisional government of Alexander Kerensky and seize power in a bloodless coup. The Bolsheviks promise "Peace, land, bread, and all power to the Soviets." The new government, led by Lenin, opens peace negotiations with the Germans.

ABOVE: The luxurious lifestyle of the czars clashed with the deep poverty experienced by most Russians.

ABOVE: During the Revolution of 1917 important buildings were protected from damage and looting.

ABOVE: Crowds outside the Winter Palace, St. Petersburg, scene of the revolution.

RIGHT: The ex-czar Nicholas II, in exile under guard, the last of the Russian royals this century.

PEACE COMES AND EUROPE IS REDRAWN

Germany surrenders and World War I ends. Postwar peace settlements involve the breakup of the old Austro-Hungarian empire and redraw the map of Europe. In Russia, the Romanovs are shot and civil war breaks out as the Bolsheviks fight to protect the revolution. Women in Britain gain the vote. Airmail services begin in the United States.

1918

Jan	9	U.S. President Woodrow Wilson lists 14 points for U.S. war aims
Mar	3	Russia signs Treaty of Brest-Litovsk with Germany
	21	Germans begin series of three offensives on Western Front
Apr	22	German flying ace, the "Red Baron," is shot during the Second Battle of the Somme
July	16	In Russia, Bolsheviks execute Czar Nicholas and his family
Sep	26	Final Allied offensive begins on the Western Front
Nov	3	Austria signs an armistice with the Allies
	9	After riots in Germany, Kaiser Wilhelm II abdicates and Germany becomes a republic
	11	World War I ends Austria's emperor Karl abdicates
	13	Austria and Hungary are declared republics

ABOVE: British nurses celebrate the end of the carnage.

OPPOSITE: The guns fall silent at last on the 11th hour of the 11th month, 1918.

WILSON'S 14 PEACE POINTS

In a speech to Congress, in January, U.S. President Wilson sets out 14 points for a peace settlement. Among them are the breakup of Austria-Hungary, the independence of Poland, and the establishment of an international organization to guarantee the independence and integrity of all nations.

RUSSIA OUT OF THE WAR

Germany and Russia sign a peace treaty at Brest-Litovsk in Poland, which takes Russia out of the war. Russia is forced to cede Poland and the Baltic states to Germany and large areas of the Caucasus to the Ottoman Empire, as well as recognize the independence of Ukraine. The treaty allows Germany to transfer its large armies to the Western Front.

CZAR SHOT

As Russia collapses into civil war, the former Russian czar, Nicholas II, and his family are shot by the Bolsheviks to prevent them falling into counter-revolutionary hands. The Bolsheviks organize a Red Army under Leon Trotsky (1879–1940), commissar for war, to fight for the revolution.

WAR ENDS

As Germany collapses, Kaiser Wilhelm II flees into exile in the Netherlands. On November 11, Germany and the Allies finally sign a peace treaty. The Ottoman Empire and Austria also sue for peace. After more than four years of bitter fighting, World War I comes to an end. As an approximate estimate, more than ten million people have been killed.

NEW NATIONS

Following peace settlements, four new nations emerge out of the old multinational Austro-Hungarian empire. Austria and Hungary become independent republics, as does Czechoslovakia. The South Slavs form a new kingdom, later called Yugoslavia, which is ruled by King Peter of Serbia, who led his country to victory in the war.

WINNING THE VOTE

After a 67-year struggle, women in Britain finally gain the vote. New legislation gives the vote to women over the age of 30 and men over 21.

WILFRED OWEN
(1893–1918)

The young English poet Wilfred Owen is killed in action just one week before the end of World War I. His friend, the poet Siegfried Sassoon, will collect his unpublished work, for publication in 1920. Owen's famous poems "Dulce et Decorum Est" and "Anthem for Doomed Youth" are heartfelt appeals against war and its brutality.

ACHILLE-CLAUDE DEBUSSY
(1862–1918)

Claude Debussy has died after a long battle with cancer. The Parisian composer was responsible for the creation of musical Impressionism and has had a strong influence on contemporary composers. His works include the orchestral tone poem *Le Mer* (1905), chamber music, piano pieces, and many lovely song settings.

THE TWELVE

Set in St. Petersburg during the Bolshevik revolution, "The Twelve," a poem by Russian poet Alexander Blok, describes a group of 12 Red Guards. A tribute to the revolution that uses techniques as diverse as folk songs and revolutionary slogans, the work portrays the revolutionaries as if they were the Apostles of Christ.

CALLIGRAMMES

The second of French writer Guillaume Apollinaire's two volumes of verse, *Calligrammes*, is published (the first was *Les Alcools*, 1913). It develops the technique of making the physical shape of the poems match their content. Thus rain is depicted in type that pours vertically down the page, and typography mirrors the shapes of field guns and cathedrals.

THREE-COLOR LIGHTS

Three-color traffic lights, with a yellow phase between green and red, are introduced in England and in New York City.

SUPERHET RADIO

The superheterodyne (or "superhet") radio receiver is invented by U.S. army major and electrical engineer Edwin Armstrong (1890–1954). It makes radios easier to tune. Subsequently, all radios will work on this principle.

AUSTRALIAN RADIO LINK

Using Morse code, the first-ever radio link is made between Britain and Australia.

FOOD MIXER

The universal food mixer and beater is invented by the Universal Company of America. It consists of a bowl and two beaters powered by electricity.

SUPREMATIST COMPOSITION

With his painting *White on White*, Russian artist Malevich takes his suprematist style to its logical conclusion, painting white shapes on a white background. The work becomes the symbol of extreme modernism in painting.

RIGHT: Women take up heavy work in wartime.

ABOVE: American soldier getting ready for action. Over 116,000 U.S. troops die.

RIGHT: The Red Baron, Manfred von Richthofen, the German air ace killed in action this year.

AFTERMATH OF WAR

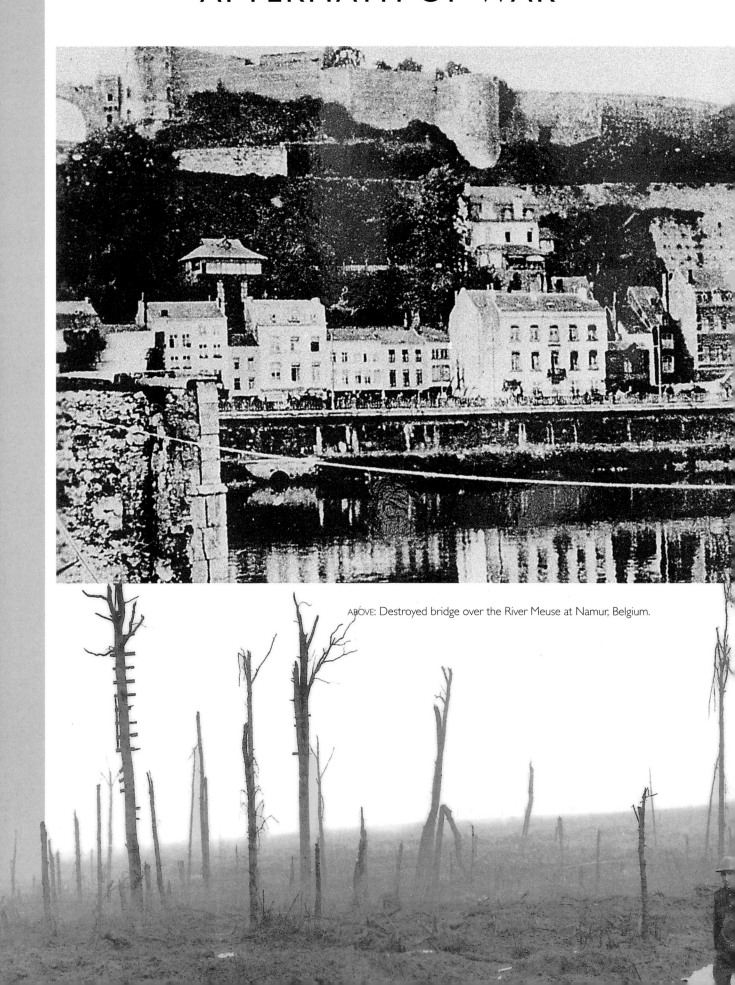

ABOVE: Destroyed bridge over the River Meuse at Namur, Belgium.

ABOVE: Ruined fortifications near Liège, Belgium.

ABOVE: Paris, devastated by heavy artillery.

ABOVE: German POWs in a French camp.

BELOW: Passchendaele — a barren sea of mud.

PEACE OF PARIS AND THE WEIMAR REPUBLIC

The League of Nations is set up by a world temporarily sickened by the carnage of war. The Treaty of Versailles imposes reparations on Germany. In Germany, a new constitution establishes the Weimar Republic. In Italy, Mussolini founds the Fascist party. British troops fire on Sikhs in the town of Amritsar and war breaks out between British India and Afghanistan. Aviators Alcock and Brown make the first transatlantic flight.

OPPOSITE: French tennis star Suzanne Lenglen wins the Ladies' Singles at Wimbledon.

1919

Jan	5	Spartacist uprising begins in Berlin; it is quickly suppressed
	6	Former U.S. President Theodore Roosevelt dies aged 60
	18	Peace conference begins at Versailles, near Paris
	21	Sinn Fein MPs set up an unofficial "parliament" in Dublin
Feb	6	Bolsheviks capture Kiev, Ukraine
	14	The League of Nations is founded
	14	Bolsheviks invade Estonia
	20	Emir of Afghanistan murdered
Mar	23	Italian journalist Benito Mussolini founds the Fascist party
Apr	13	British troops massacre 379 unarmed rioters at Amritsar, India
May	3	War begins between British India and Afghanistan
June	15	Aviators Alcock and Brown complete the first nonstop flight across the Atlantic Ocean
	28	Peace of Paris between Germany and the Allies is signed at Versailles
July	5	French tennis star Suzanne Lenglen wins the Ladies' Singles at Wimbledon
	13	British airship R-34 completes the first two-way Atlantic flight
	31	The Weimar Republic is founded in Germany
Aug	8	Afghanistan achieves independence
Oct	7	Dutch airline KLM is founded
Nov	3	French artist Pierre Auguste Renoir dies aged 78
	15	Red Army captures Omsk

THE TWENTIES START ROARING

The 1920s kick off with prohibition in the United States. Banning the manufacture and sale of alcohol leads to an unprecedented crime wave. The Treaty of Trianon redraws the map of Europe and the former Ottoman Empire is split into protectorates policed by France and Britain. The Netherlands begins a literal expansion plan, reclaiming land from the Zuider Zee. Marcus Garvey raises black consciousness in the United States, establishing the Universal Negro Improvement Association. In Czechoslovakia, the robot is born.

OPPOSITE: Civic guards take a break during street demonstrations in Berlin.

1920

Jan	16	Prohibition (of alcohol) goes into force in the United States	July	9	Greek forces, with U.K. approval, capture Bursa in Asian Turkey
Feb	20	U.S. polar explorer Robert Peary dies aged 63	Aug	10	Treaty of Sèvres robs Turkey of 80 percent of the Ottoman Empire
				14	Olympic Games open in Belgium Little Entente between Czechoslovakia and Yugoslavia
Apr	7	French troops occupy Germany's Ruhr			
	25	League of Nations awards Middle East mandates to U.K. and France	Nov	16	Civil war in Russia ends after three years QANTAS airline set up in Australia
May	16	Pope Benedict declares Joan of Arc a saint		21	In Ireland the IRA kills 14 British soldiers, the first "Bloody Sunday"
June	4	Treaty of Trianon redraws the map of Eastern Europe	Dec	10	Woodrow Wilson (1856–1924) is awarded the Nobel Prize for peace

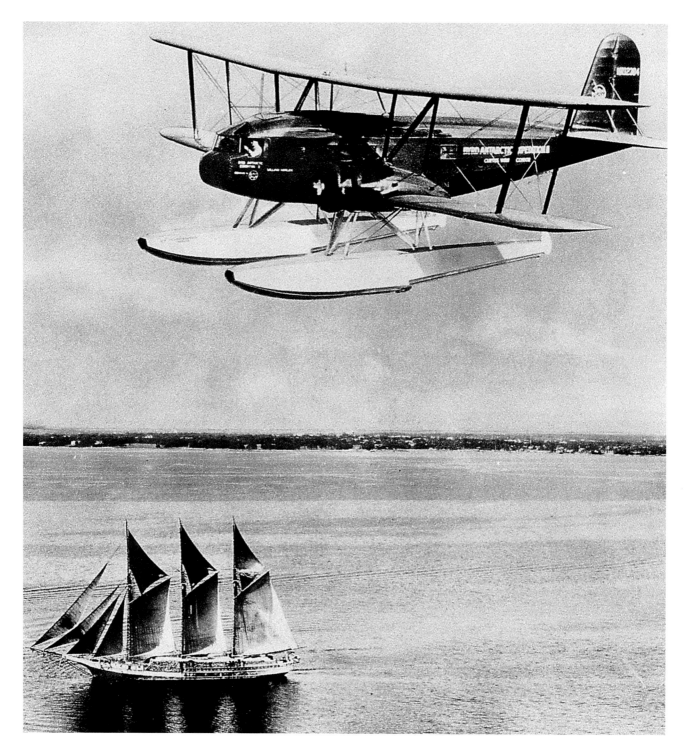

MANDATES FOR FRANCE AND GREAT BRITAIN
In April, at San Remo, Italy, the League of Nations gives France a mandate over Syria and Lebanon, and Britain a mandate over Iraq and Palestine, all former Ottoman territories. Britain is thus free to abide by the Balfour Declaration of 1917 and allow Jews to settle in Palestine.

PEACE WITH TURKEY
In August, at Sèvres, France, a peace treaty is signed with the former Ottoman Empire, which cuts it back to one-fifth of its former size. The treaty is opposed by Turkey, which resents giving land to the Greeks.

ABOVE: Airmail service is introduced, using seaplanes which can land anywhere there is water.

END OF RUSSIAN CIVIL WAR
In November, the Red Army, under Trotsky, wins its final battle against counterrevolutionary forces in the Crimea, bringing an end to the three-year-old Russian civil war.

SOUND ON FILM
American scientist Lee de Forest invents a system of recording synchronized sound on a separate track on cinema film, to be "read" by a photoelectric cell.

THE TREATY OF TRIANON

In June, the Treaty of Trianon (Paris) is signed with Hungary, redrawing the map of Eastern Europe. Former Hungarian lands are divided between Czechoslovakia, Poland, Austria, Yugoslavia, and Italy, leaving Hungary a third of its former size. The treaty follows on from Versailles, St Germain, and Neuilly, which together have settled the frontiers of Germany and Austria-Hungary.

THE LITTLE ENTENTE

In August, Yugoslavia and Czechoslovakia sign a treaty of friendship known as the Little Entente. Romania will join in April 1921. The countries are united in their desire to keep the current borders in Eastern Europe and not to allow any revival of the Hapsburg empire in either Austria or Hungary.

THE AGE OF INNOCENCE

The greatest book of the American writer Edith Wharton (1861–1937) is a study of American high society at the turn of the century, showing how human values such as love can be destroyed by the obligation to stick to outdated moral codes. In it Wharton condemns people "who dreaded scandal more than disease, who placed decency above courage."

BELOW: Prohibition starts and teams are sent to dismantle bars and drinking clubs all over America.

THE INKBLOT TEST

Swiss psychiatrist, Hermann Rorschach (1884–1922), develops a test by which the personality, intelligence, and emotional stability of patients can be assessed by analyzing their interpretations of random patterns made by inkblots.

BONJOUR CHERI

In the first of her mature novels, the French writer Colette (Sidonie Gabrielle Colette, 1873–1954) describes a liaison between a young man and an older woman. *Chéri* will be followed by many other books, remarkable for their vivid evocations of sights, sounds, and smells, and for their frank depictions of the lives of women in the France of her time.

QANTAS TAKES TO THE AIR

Queensland and Northern Territory Aerial Service (QANTAS) is set up as Australia's commercial airline on November 16.

BLACK POWER

Marcus Garvey, Jamaican editor of *The Negro World* published in New York City, leads the first meeting of the Universal Negro Improvement Association (UNIA) in August. On the agenda for discussion by 3,000 delegates from across the United States is a bill of rights for Negroes.

BABE RUTH SOLD

In January, the Boston Red Sox sell Babe Ruth to the New York Yankees for $125,000 in the most infamous transaction in American sports history. After the sale the Red Sox will never win baseball's World Series — attributed to the "Curse of the Bambino" — while the Yankees will become the most successful team ever.

HUGH SELWYN MAUBERLEY

Mauberley, a collection of linked poems by the American poet Ezra Pound (1885–1972), describes the literary life of London just after World War I. For its classical, ironical style, its compression of language, and its use of allusion, it quickly becomes one of the most influential works of the modern movement in literature.

THE SEVENTH OLYMPIC GAMES

In August, the Seventh Olympiad is staged in Antwerp, Belgium. It is the sixth actually held, as there were no Games in 1916. The Olympic flag of five linked rings, symbolizing the continents, is used for the first time. American diver Aileen Riggin became the youngest winner at 14.

LAND FROM THE SEA

The Wieringen Polder, the greatest-ever land reclamation scheme, begins in the Netherlands. Embankments built from over one million cubic feet of earth taken from the Zuider Zee will join north Holland to the Island of Wieringen, and that to Friesland.

THE TATLIN MONUMENT

Soviet artist Vladimir Tatlin (1885–1953) designs this great project, a construction which evokes technology and social progress in an upward-spiralling form containing cylinders and a glass pyramid. Although the monument is never built, and is known only in the form of a model, it is a lasting symbol of the kind of art embraced by the Soviet Union in its early years.

ABOVE: British troops are sent in to impose order on the streets of Londonderry where Sinn Féin and the Unionists are fighting.

RUR: THE BIRTH OF THE ROBOT

Karel Capek's play (the initials stand for Rossum's Universal Robots) introduces the word "robot" into the vocabulary. The robots are part of an anti-utopia, in which people try to use machines to improve their lot, but the machines are so effective that they take over and dominate their creators.

RADIO CONTACT

The first U.S. commercial broadcasting station, Pittsburgh KDKA, begins regular weekly broadcasts in November by announcing the Harding-Cox presidential election results. The new station, run by the Westinghouse Co., is also opening in France, Germany, and Argentina.

ENTER THE TOMMY-GUN

U.S. gunsmith John T. Thompson patents a sub-machine gun, which later becomes known as the tommy-gun.

OLIVE SCHREINER
(1855–1920)

The writer, pacifist, and feminist Olive Schreiner whose husband was persuaded to take her name when they married (in 1894) has died. Born of a German father and English mother in South Africa, where she spent most of her life, she published her first book *The Story of an African Farm* (1883) under the name Ralph Iron. Works under her own name include *Trooper Peter Halket* (1897) and *Woman and Labor* (1911).

NO MORE DRINKING

On January 16 it becomes illegal to manufacture, sell and transport intoxicating liquor in the United States when the Volstead Act, the 18th Amendment to the U.S. Constitution ratified on January 29, 1919, comes into effect.

LEGAL ABORTION

Abortion becomes legal for the first time in a modern European state, in legislation introduced in Russia. Since 1918 the new Bolshevik government has made marriage a civil ceremony, facilitated divorce, and introduced free maternity care. The new Czechoslovakia also legalizes abortion this year.

A NEW SAINT

Pope Benedict XV declares Joan of Arc a saint.

ROBERT EDWIN PEARY
(1856–1920)

The American naval commander and explorer Robert Edwin Peary, believed to be the first man to reach the North Pole in 1909, and veteran of eight Arctic expeditions, has died. The region of Greenland, Peary Land, is named in his honor.

BELOW: A nail bomb explodes outside the U.S. Assay Office in Wall Street, under the gaze of George Washington. Over 300 people are injured and 35 killed, but no perpetrator is ever found.

THE RISE OF FASCISM AND COMMUNISM

There is mutiny and economic collapse in Russia. In China, the young Mao Zedong helps to establish Communism. The Irish Free State is ratified, dividing the island. Greece and Turkey are at war. Marie Stopes introduces birth control to the United Kingdom. In the United States, heavyweight Jack Dempsey knocks out Georges Carpentier. Band-aid is invented. The lie detector is introduced and the first woman priest ordained. In Italy, Mussolini becomes Il Duce and Enrico Caruso sings his last.

OPPOSITE: Crowds outside the Kremlin display religious icons as well as red flags.

1921

Jan	**6**	Release of *The Kid*, Charlie Chaplin's first feature film
	21	Tanks patrol Dublin in search for IRA snipers
Mar	**12**	Lenin relaxes strict controls on Russia's economy
	17	Russia's Red Army crushes anti-Bolshevik rebellion at Kronstadt naval base
Apr	**12**	President Warren Harding says United States will not join the League
June	**22**	In Ireland King George V opens the first Ulster parliament
	30	First meeting of China's Communist Party is held
July	**2**	First $1 million "gate" at a boxing match
July	**10**	Outer Mongolia gains independence from China
Aug	**3**	Italian tenor Enrico Caruso dies at 48
	5	Mustafa Kemal becomes virtual ruler of Turkey
Nov	**5**	Crown Prince Hirohito of Japan becomes regent for his father
	7	Benito Mussolini becomes head of Italy's National Fascist Party with the title of Il Duce, "the Leader"
Dec	**7**	Peace in Ireland: 26 southern counties become independent, six northern counties stay in the U.K.
	10	Albert Einstein wins Nobel Prize for physics
	16	French composer Camille Saint-Saëns dies at 86

MUTINY AND ECONOMIC COLLAPSE IN RUSSIA

In March, Russian sailors mutiny at the Kronstadt naval base (Petrograd, once St. Petersburg) in protest at the new Communist government's policies. The sailors are demanding free elections and other reforms. The mutiny shakes the government, as the sailors were previously in the forefront of the revolution.

At the same time, in Moscow, Lenin announces to the Communist party Congress that he is relaxing controls over the economy, ending state planning, and encouraging private enterprise. The move is forced on Lenin because of the collapse in the economy as a result of the civil war.

CHINA TURNS RED

In July, the Chinese Communist Party holds its first meeting, electing Chen Duxiu, a Beijing university professor, as its first president. Among its founder members is Mao Zedong.

EINSTEIN TOWER, POTSDAM

Designed by German Erich Mendelsohn (1887–1953), this building houses an observatory and laboratory. It is designed in a wholly "plastic" form, consisting almost completely of curves, which owes nothing to previous styles. The original intention was for the building to be constructed from poured concrete, but it is actually built of brick covered with cement.

A FREE STATE FOR IRELAND

In December, Irish Republican negotiators finally agree a settlement with the British government, setting up an independent Free State in the south of Ireland. The British government decided in 1920 to divide Ireland, offering home rule to both the Catholic and Republican south and to the Protestant and Unionist north, but the south refused to accept limited home rule. The settlement comes after three years of vicious civil war in the south.

PROKOFIEV'S FIRST HIT

Russian composer Sergei Prokofiev (1891–1955) sees the première of his Piano Concerto No. 3, one of the most important (and most popular) of the works from his early Russian period. It helps establish him as a composer with his own distinctive style.

A MILLION-DOLLAR GATE

In July, Jack "The Idol" Dempsey knocks out Frenchman Georges "The Orchid Kid" Carpentier in front of 80,000 fans. The heavyweight championship bout is the first million-dollar gate in boxing and boosts boxing's popularity enormously.

FAST FIRST AID

Band-aid, the first stick-on bandage, is introduced in the United States by Johnson & Johnson.

LEFT: Mountaineer Captain Finch nears the summit of Mont Blanc, the giant of the French Alps.

ABOVE: President of the Irish Republic Eamonn de Valera, invited by Lloyd George to try to answer the Irish Question.

WAR IN THE AEGEAN

In January, war breaks out between Greece and Turkey with the Greeks invading western Anatolia, on the shores of the Aegean Sea. Fighting between the two countries continues in the region, which is home to many thousands of ethnic Greeks into 1922.

FIRST LIE DETECTOR

U.S. medical student John Larson invents the world's first lie detector, which shows by means of heart rate, breathing rate and blood pressure if a subject is under stress.

A HOUSEBOAT IN AMSTERDAM

Dutch architect Michel de Klerk, a member of the Amsterdam School, designs Het Scheep housing complex, notable for its decorative use of brickwork, tiling, and a variety of window shapes and glazing arrangements. Its nickname, meaning "the ship," derives from its wedge shape.

BIRTH CONTROL IN THE UK

In March, Marie Stopes (1880–1958), opens the U.K.'s first birth control clinic in London amid great opposition from the establishment. In 1918 she published *Married Love*, the first sex education manual, and *Wise Parenthood*, which advocated birth control and sex education for women.

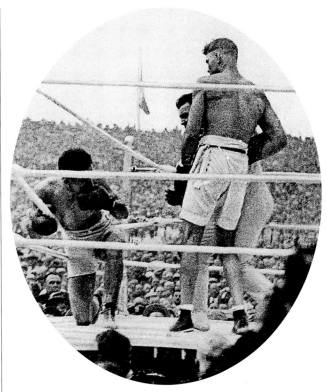

ABOVE: Georges Carpentier wilts under the onslaught of champion Jack Dempsey.

BELOW: Suzanne Lenglen and partner play to victory in the Wimbledon mixed doubles.

UNITED STATES COAST TO COAST
In February Lieutenant William D. Coney of the U.S. Air Service makes the first coast-to-coast flight across North America, from California to Florida.

FIRST EXPRESSWAY
The world's first express highway, the Avus Autobahn, is opened in Berlin, foreshadowing the Autobahn network to be built in the 1930s.

ENRICO CARUSO
(1873–1921)

The world-renowned Italian tenor Enrico Caruso has died in Naples. He leaves a wealth of gramophone recordings to ensure that his voice will be appreciated by future generations. His first performance was in Naples in 1895, and international fame came in 1902 when he sang in *La Bohème* with Dame Nelly Melba at Monte Carlo. He made over 600 appearances at the Met in New York City, where he held his final performance on Christmas Eve 1920, and he sang some 40 roles.

ABOVE: Queen Wilhemina of the Netherlands, Prince Hendrik, and Princess Juliana make an informal canal tour of their country.

FIRST WOMAN PRIEST
Rev. Antoinette Brown Blackwell becomes the first woman to be ordained in the Anglican Church in the United States.

LYSOZYME DISCOVERED
Scottish bacteriologist Alexander Fleming (1881–1955) discovers the existence of lysozyme, an enzyme present in saliva, tears, and nasal mucus, which helps to kill bacteria naturally, and so prevent infection.

SEXUAL REFORM
The World League for Sexual Reform is set up in Berlin by Magnus Hirschfeld, a homosexual doctor and founder, in 1919, of the Institute for Sex Research in Berlin.

GAMES FOR WOMEN
In Monte Carlo, the first Women's World Games are held in protest at women not being allowed to take part in Olympic track and field events.

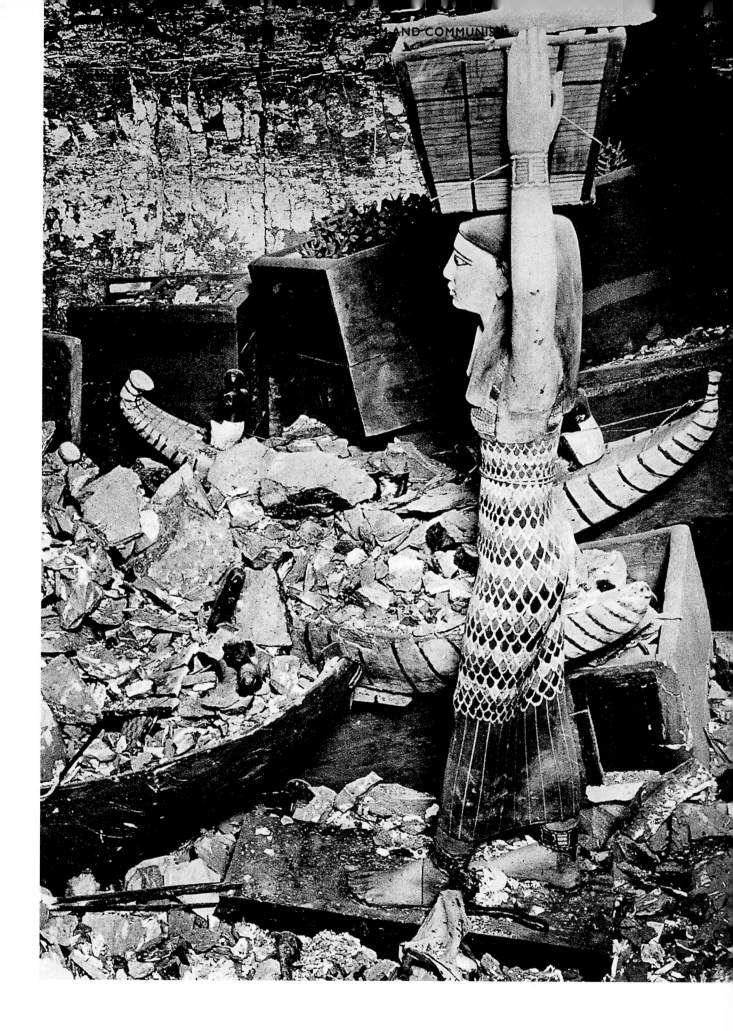

SECRETS FROM AN EGYPTIAN TOMB

A year of alliance and excavation: Russia and its satellites become the mighty U.S.S.R., and Germany makes an alliance with the Soviets. Mussolini seizes power in Italy. The ancient city of Ur is unearthed in Iraq, and in Egypt the tomb of the young Tutankhamun yields its secrets. Retail therapy is introduced with the first shopping mall in the United States. Insulin is discovered and in Ireland Michael Collins is shot dead. French novelist Marcel Proust eats his last madeleine and Alexander Bell, inventor of the telephone, finally hangs up.

OPPOSITE: Mask of Tutankhamun, whose tomb is discovered this year.

1922

Jan	5	British explorer Ernest Shackleton dies at 49
Feb	5	The first issue of *Reader's Digest* is published in the United States
Apr	16	German and Soviet Russia sign a secret treaty
	21	Alessandro Moreschi, the last known castrato, dies
May	3	Four Canadian scientists announce the discovery of insulin
Aug	2	Telephone inventor Alexander Graham Bell dies at 75
	14	British newspaper owner Viscount Northcliffe dies aged 57
	22	In Ireland, Sinn Féin leader Michael Collins is shot dead, aged 32
Sep	4	U.S. aviator James H. Doolittle flies from Florida to California in one day
Oct	11	Treaty of Mudania ends the war between Greece and Turkey Benito Mussolini and the Fascists take power in Italy
Nov	15	British Broadcasting Company broadcasts its first wireless news bulletin
	26	The tomb of the Egyptian pharaoh Tutankhamun is found in Egypt
Dec	30	Soviet Russia changes its name to the Union of Soviet Socialist Republics (U.S.S.R.)

ABOVE: A huge explosion rocks the Four Courts in Dublin, the result of a mine. Thirty Free State troopers are killed in the explosion and fighting continues for four hours afterwards.

GERMAN AND SOVIET ALLIANCE

In April, Germany and Soviet Russia sign a secret peace treaty at Rapallo, Italy, under which they reestablish full diplomatic and trading relations, agree to waive reparations payments, and commit to full cooperation between their armed forces. The treaty shocks Europe, as it allows Germany a way of rebuilding her army in defiance of the Versailles Treaty.

IL DUCE SEIZES POWER

In Rome, 24,000 members of the Italian Fascist Party march from Naples to Rome to seize power. Their leader, Benito Mussolini, waits in Milan, ready to flee to Switzerland if the coup fails. However, there is no opposition in Rome and King Victor Emmanuel asks Mussolini to form a government.

RUSSIA BECOMES U.S.S.R.

Russia formally changes its name and becomes the Union of the Soviet Socialist Republics, a confederation with Belarus, Ukraine, and the Transcaucasian Federation.

THE WASTE LAND

The major work of the American poet T.S. Eliot (1888–1965) uses imagery from myth and past literature to evoke the desolation of modern humanity and the breakdown of modern values and belief systems. Its mixture of styles, ranging from everyday Cockney speech to literary allusion and quotation, baffles but impresses its first readers.

COLLINS SHOT

The Irish prime minister, Michael Collins, is assassinated in County Cork by opponents of the treaty signed with Britain last December. Although the Irish parliament accepted the treaty in January, opponents have taken up arms against their former friends and civil war is now raging throughout the Free State.

TALES OF ULYSSES

Irish writer James Joyce's groundbreaking novel is published. It incorporates major innovations in the use of interior monologue, cinematic scene-setting, and use of language. It will be valued for these modernist features and also for its realistic portrayal of its main characters, for its humor, and for its vivid depiction of Dublin. Because of alleged obscenity, the book is printed in Dijon and published in Paris.

AIRCRAFT CARRIER

The USS *Langley* becomes the first U.S. aircraft carrier; she is converted from a coal ship, the *Jupiter*.

DISCOVERY OF INSULIN

In February a group of Canadian scientists, Frederick Banting, Charles Best, James Collip, and Professor John Macleod, jointly announce the discovery of insulin, and its use in treating diabetes.

ABOVE: The New Lincoln Memorial is a huge but benign statue of Abraham Lincoln by American sculptor Daniel Chester French.

THE EARLIEST CITY

Ur, an ancient city on the River Euphrates in Iraq, is excavated by a British Museum and University of Pennsylvania expedition headed by Charles Leonard Woolley (1880–1960), the English archaeologist who has just excavated the ancient Egyptian site of Tel-el-Amarna. The discovery of a Sumerian temple proves that Ur flourished in Mesopotamia as early as 2600 BC.

IMPERIAL HOTEL, TOKYO

Asked to design a building that will withstand earthquakes, architect Frank Lloyd Wright (1869–1959) develops a system of concrete posts which support the structure while allowing it to "give" during an earthquake. About two years after completion, the building is shaken by a severe quake and remains standing — providing a refuge for those left homeless.

SAVING THE KOALA

The koala bear, a native marsupial found only in Australia, is now protected by rigidly strict legislation, because fur trappers have killed some eight million animals over the last four years alone.

IMMORTALIZING THE LIVING DEAD

Nosferatu, the first major vampire movie, is also the first major film directed by F.W. Murnau. It includes effects such as negative imagery (black appearing as white and vice versa) to intensify the atmosphere of strangeness and horror. Many imitators will follow in its wake.

PEACE BETWEEN TURKEY AND GREECE

The war between Greece and Turkey ends when they sign the Treaty of Mudania. Greece withdraws from Anatolia and the area around Constantinople. As a result, the British wartime leader, David Lloyd George, loses power as prime minister and is replaced by the Conservative leader, Andrew Bonar-Law.

SOUND-ON-FILM MOVIE

The first commercial sound-on-film motion picture is *Der Brandstifter* (*The Arsonist*) made in Germany. But it does not immediately lead to the end of silent films.

TUTANKHAMUN COMES TO LIGHT

The tomb containing the sarcophagus of the ancient Egyptian boy king, Tutankhamun, who reigned during the Eighteenth Dynasty (fourteenth century BC), is discovered in November by two British archaeologists, Howard Carter and his sponsor, the Earl of Carnarvon.

MARCEL PROUST
(1871–1922)

One of the most influential writers of modern times, the French novelist Marcel Proust has died. Born in Paris, where he spent his life, he was a semi-invalid, and spent his last 17 years writing reclusively in his apartment. His 13-volume work *A la Recherche du Temps Perdu* (translated into English as *Remembrance of Times Past*) has won great acclaim. The second volume won the Prix Goncourt in 1919 and an international reputation followed. At the time of his death three final volumes are awaiting publication.

ALEXANDER GRAHAM BELL
(1847–1922)

Alexander Graham Bell, the inventor of the telephone and founder of the Bell Telephone Company (1877) has died. This American, of Scottish birth and education, established a training school in Boston for teachers of deaf people and later became professor of Vocal Physiology. The telephone sprang from experiments with acoustical devices to aid deaf and dumb people. His other interest was aeronautics.

MR. LINCOLN COMES TO WASHINGTON
The Lincoln Memorial, Washington, D.C., becomes a place of national pilgrimage with the completion of Daniel Chester French's memorial statue.

DAY TRIP
Lieutenant James H. Doolittle makes the first one-day flight across the United States from Florida to California; time 22 hours 35 minutes, including a refuelling stop.

ABOVE: The largest telescope in the world at Mount Wilson in California. It incorporates an instrument for measuring the diameter of stars and is to be significant in the discovery of galaxies.

RETAIL THERAPY
The world's first shopping mall, the Country Club Plaza, opens in the United States in July.

DANISH SUCCESS
Danish scientist Niels Bohr wins Nobel Prize for physics.

FIRST GLIMPSES OF NAZISM AND HITLER

Nazism rears its head as the first rally is held in Munich. At the same time, French troops occupy the Ruhr, impatient at the slow delivery of war reparations. The German mark collapses. Turkey becomes a republic, signaling the death of the once mighty Ottoman Empire. Far from the troubled Earth, galaxies and nebulae are discovered. A Spanish engineer flies the first rotor-driven flight machine and French actress Sarah Bernhardt takes her final curtain.

1923

Jan	25	French troops march into Germany's Ruhr to collect war reparations
	27	The first National Socialist (Nazi) rally is held in Munich, Germany
Feb	10	German X-ray discoverer Wilhelm Roentgen dies aged 77
Mar	9	Russian leader V.I. Lenin suffers a stroke and there is speculation about who will be chosen to be his successor as leader of the Soviet Union
	29	Legendary French actress Sarah Bernhardt dies at 78
Apr	28	Wembley Stadium, London, hosts its first football cup final
Aug	2	U.S. president Warren Harding dies aged 69; he is succeeded by Vice President Calvin Coolidge
Aug	12	Italian Enrico Triboschi swims the English Channel in a record 16 hours 33 minutes
Sep	16	An earthquake destroys Tokyo and Yokohama in Japan. At least 300,000 people die and two million are left homeless
Oct	29	Mustafa Kemal proclaims a republic in Turkey, with himself as president
Nov	12	Adolf Hitler tries to seize power in Bavaria, Germany, and is arrested
	15	German mark collapses to 20,142 billion to the pound sterling; a loaf of bread costs 201 billion marks
Dec	7	British general election results in a "hung" Parliament
	28	French engineer Gustav Eiffel dies at 91

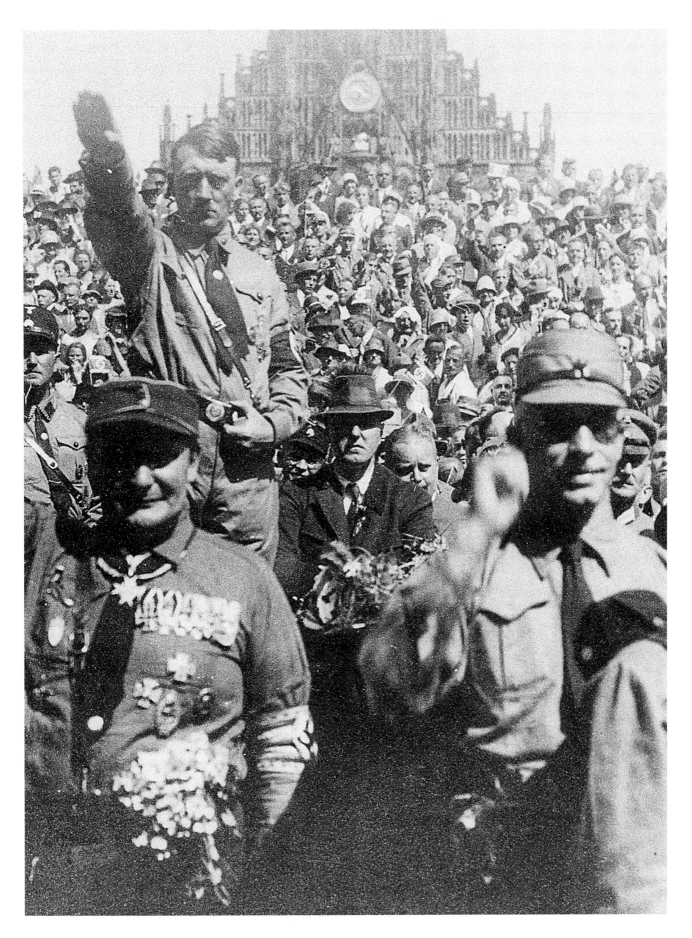

ABOVE: Adolf Hitler is jailed then released and begins his rise to power in Germany.

THOMAS WOODROW WILSON
(1856–1924)

Woodrow Wilson, the 28th American president (1913–1921), and winner of the Nobel Prize for peace in 1919, has died. President Wilson reluctantly led the United States into World War I in 1917 and helped to bring the war to an end. A Democrat, he was instrumental in forming the League of Nations, which the Senate prevented the United States itself from joining.

DEATH OF LENIN
Vladimir Ilyich Lenin, the founder of the Soviet Union, dies in Moscow aged 54. He had suffered the first of three strokes in May 1922 and control of the government had been passed to other people, notably Joseph Stalin, general secretary of the Communist Party.

FIRST BRITISH LABOUR GOVERNMENT
A Labour government takes power in Britain for the first time ever. Led by Ramsay MacDonald, the Labour government is supported in power by the Liberals, but soon collapses and loses in the general election called in October.

NAZIS BECOME ESTABLISHMENT
In May, the Nazis enter the Reichstag, the German Parliament, for the first time, taking 32 seats in the general election. The Social Democrats remain the largest party, but both the Nationalists and Communists gain ground.

SURREALISTS SHOW THEMSELVES
French writer André Breton (1896–1966) publishes his Manifesto to mark the official beginning of the surrealist movement, which aims to break down the distinctions between dream and reality, madness and rationality, in art of all forms.

A PASSAGE TO INDIA
English writer E.M. Forster (1879–1970) publishes what is probably his greatest book, the last of his novels to be published in his lifetime. A picture of life in India under British rule, the book lays bare the prejudices that both Britons and Indians have about each other and the clashes that result.

LIVING IN STIJL
With its white walls, clean lines, and primary-color details, the Schröder-Schräder house, Utrecht, designed by Gerrit Rietveld, is a classic example of De Stijl design. The right angle is everywhere in this building. Even the windows can only be opened so that they are at 90 degrees to the façade.

GOODBYE TO WASHDAY BLUES
The spin drier, consisting of a spinning drum built into a washing machine, which extracts water by centrifugal force, is produced by the Savage Arms Corporation in the United States and used to dry wet clothes.

GERMANY SETTLES HER DEBTS
Germany and the Allies accept the Dawes Report to settle the issue of reparations by establishing a plan for annual payments. As a result, the German Reichsbank introduces a new mark to stabilize the economy, which is supported by a foreign loan.

QUICK-FROZEN FOOD
Birds Eye Seafoods launches the first commercially produced fast-frozen food. U.S. fur trader Clarence Birdseye (1886–1956) experimented with preserving perishable foods by freezing, after visiting Labrador in 1917 and eating palatable fish that had been preserved in ice. Now he sets up a company to produce quick-frozen food for the retail market.

CONTROVERSY ON STAGE
Paul Robeson and Mary Blair play an interracial couple in *All God's Chillun Got Wings* by American dramatist Eugene O'Neill (1888–1953). It is a controversial play attacking racism.

MY LIFE IN ART
Konstantin Stanislavsky (1865–1938), the great Russian director, looks back over his life and his experience in the theater. In the book he outlines various theories that have influenced the way many modern theater directors have approached their work. The Method becomes increasingly popular in the 1920s as the result of Stanislavsky's books.

PARTICLES = WAVES
French physicist Louis de Broglie discovers that electrons and other particles can behave as waves, as well as particles, thus becoming the founder of the science of wave mechanics.

JOSEPH CONRAD (JOZEF TEODOR KONRAD NALECZ KORZENIOWSKI)
(1857–1924)

The Polish-born, naturalized British writer Joseph Conrad has died. At the age of 21 he joined a British merchant ship, and six years later gained his master's certificate. He spent many years at sea but settled in Kent after his marriage in 1896. There he became a writer, using his experiences as inspiration. Among his best-known works are *Lord Jim* (1900), *Nostromo* (1904), *Heart of Darkness* (1902), and *Victory* (1919). He was working on a novel, *Suspense*, when he died.

RHAPSODY IN BLUE

American composer George Gershwin (1898–1937) writes this popular piece — originally for Paul Whiteman's jazz band. It will later become better known in the form of an arrangement for classical symphony orchestra. The work is the first distinctively American piece of concert music, although if Charles Ives had been better known the story would have been different.

THE SOUTHERN APE

Australian anthropologist Raymond Dart (1893–1988) discovers a skull in a South African quarry. It is a primitive hominid which Dart names Australopithecus (southern ape).

ELECTRIC REFRIGERATOR

Swedish engineers Balzer von Platen and Carl Munters patent the first refrigerator using an electric motor to drive the compressor; they call it the Electrolux.

WINTER OLYMPICS

In January, the International Winter Sports Week in Chamonix, France, is retrospectively declared the First Winter Olympics. The Scandinavians dominate the event, which is organized by the French Olympic Committee. The success of the event leads the International Olympic Committee to stage Winter Games in tandem with Summer Olympics.

ROUND-THE-WORLD FLIGHT

Two U.S. Douglas DCW biplanes, *Chicago* (piloted by Lieutenant Lowell H. Smith) and *New Orleans* (piloted by Lieutenant Erik Nelson), make the first round-the-world flight between April and September in 175 days; two others fail to make the full journey.

FRANZ KAFKA
(1883–1924)

The Czech writer of German-Jewish parentage Franz Kafka has died of tuberculosis in Berlin after many years of ill health. His novels, written in the German language, express the angst of the sensitive individual in a seemingly irrational society, and the adjective "Kafkaesque" will soon be familiar to those who have not even read his books. The books include the short story "Metamorphosis" (1916) and the unfinished novels *The Trial*, *The Castle*, and *Amerika*, all to be published after his death.

ENTER KLEENEX

U.S. firm Kimberley Clark introduces the first tissues, called Celluwipes — and now known as Kleenex™.

THE EIGHTH OLYMPIAD

Finnish athlete Paavo Nurmi wins five golds as the Olympics returns to Paris for the Eighth Olympic Games. The Olympic Village, where athletes live, makes a return, and events are broadcast on radio for the first time. Eric Liddell and Harold Abrahams, later to be immortalized in the film *Chariots of Fire*, win sprint medals for Britain.

FREE EDUCATION

An educational experiment is launched with the founding of Summerhill, a self-governing coeducational boarding school, by a British schoolmaster, Alexander Sutherland Neil. Pupils are allowed to develop in their own way without the constraints of discipline, direction, moral or religious instruction.

SWEDISH HEAT

The Aga, a cooker that uses solid fuel cleanly and has an efficient temperature control, is invented by Gustav Galen, a blind Swedish scientist.

HIGHWAY NETWORK

Italian companies begin building a 310-mile network of *autostrada*, toll highways; the first opens in September.

LEFT: Artists and writers in exile — James Joyce, Ezra Pound, Ford Maddox Ford, and John Quinn gather in Ezra Pound's Paris studio.

STALIN GETS A TIGHTER GRIP

Three men who will dominate the world are active this year. In the U.S.S.R., Stalin seizes power. In Germany, Hitler publishes *Mein Kampf*. And in China, Chiang Kai-shek succeeds as leader of the People's Party. In the United States, the Scopes trial focuses on fundamentalism and evolution, and the Ku Klux Klan march is unopposed by the establishment. Charlie Chaplin films *The Gold Rush* and Sergei Eisenstein films *Battleship Potemkin*. The first frisbee is thrown.

OPPOSITE: The Murrumbidgee River hits the Burrin Jack Dam during Australia's May floods.

1925

Jan	16	In Russia, Stalin sacks Leon Trotsky as commissar for war	**July**	21	Biology teacher John Scopes is fined $100 in Tennessee for teaching evolution
Mar	12	Dr Sun Yat-sen, leader of the Kuomintang, China's People's Party, dies aged 69; he is succeeded by General Chiang Kai-shek	**Aug**	16	Première of Charlie Chaplin's film *The Gold Rush*
	23	State of Tennessee bans the teaching of evolution theory	**Oct**	16	Belgium, Britain, France, Germany, and Italy sign the Locarno Pact, promising to keep peace with one another
Apr	25	Field Marshal Paul von Hindenburg is elected president of Germany	**Nov**	14	First Surrealist art exhibition in Paris includes work from Picasso and Klee
May	1	Cyprus becomes a British colony			
July	18	Adolf Hitler's book *Mein Kampf (My Struggle)* is published	**Dec**	10	George Bernard Shaw is awarded the Nobel Prize for literature

THE LOCARNO PEACE

A major peace conference between Germany and the Allies agrees a security pact for western and central Europe, guaranteeing frontiers and settling outstanding disputes. The treaty appears to guarantee peace between Germany and her former enemies.

NICARAGUAN CIVIL WAR

1925 sees the start of the civil war in Nicaragua. It will last until 1933. President Calles is opposed by three separate guerilla groups led by Generals Moncada, Díaz, and Sandino. Díaz and Moncada eventually become allies, but Sandino remains independent. The United States backs the president and sends in the marines. General Sandino escapes to Guatemala, but returns when the marines leave. The war is eventually won by the presidential forces, but the rebel Sandinistas (named for General Sandino) keep up guerilla warfare.

TROTSKY DISMISSED

Leon Trotsky is dismissed as commissar for war by Joseph Stalin and placed under house arrest. Many of his supporters are imprisoned or exiled to Siberia. The moves consolidate Stalin's grip on power in the Soviet Union after the death of Lenin.

THE GREAT GATSBY

F. Scott Fitzgerald (1896–1940) was already famous as a writer and representative of the "jazz age" when he published this, his greatest novel. It portrays the doomed passion of rich Jay Gatsby for Daisy Buchanan, and evokes the sophistication and squalor of New York. The book is remarkable for describing the glamour and the dream of Gatsby, showing the hollowness of this vision as it turns to dust, and yet convincing us that the dream does have some value after all.

GERMANY ELECTS A PRESIDENT

In April, Field Marshal Paul von Hindenburg becomes the first directly elected German president. Hindenburg is supported by right wing and nationalist parties, many of which want to see the German monarchy restored.

COSMIC RAYS

U.S. physicist Robert Millikan (1868–1953) coins the term "cosmic rays" for radiation from outer space.

RUDOLF STEINER
(1861–1925)

The founder of the Anthroposophical Society (in 1912), the Croatian-born Austrian, Rudolf Steiner has died. Influenced by theosophy, he believed that our spiritual development has been blocked by modern materialism. Many Steiner schools for children have developed since his founding of the first one in 1919.

ERIK ALFRED LESLIE SATIE
(1866–1925)

The French composer Erik Satie (whose mother was Scottish) has died in Paris. After training at the Paris Conservatoire he at first earned his living as a pianist in a Montmartre cabaret. His compositions for the piano, such as *Gymnopédies* (1888), and *Three Pear-shaped Pieces* (1903), were eccentric and avant-garde. He composed the music for the Diaghilev ballet *Parade* in 1917, and was part of the circle of surrealists and dadaists.

DRINKING IN STIJL

Designed by JJP Oud, the Café De Unie in Rotterdam is a De Stijl building that makes a bold statement. In a city street flanked by two old, traditional-style buildings, its brightly colored façade and bold sans-serif signage shine out as symbolic of the modern era.

THE FIRST FRISBEE

The frisbee is improvised by Yale University students using tin plates meant to hold pies baked by the Frisbie Baking Company of Bridgeport, Connecticut. An aerodynamically designed version is later marketed as a game.

THE TRIAL

Franz Kafka's novel is published a year after his death. It is the story of Josef K., caught in a labyrinth of law and officialdom, and powerless to escape or control his fate. More than any other of Kafka's books, it has given us the term "Kafkaesque" for this situation.

THE BATTLESHIP POTEMKIN

The brutalities of the czarist regime are dramatized in Sergei Eisenstein's landmark film about a mutiny during the 1905 revolution. Eisenstein's most famous work shows the effectiveness of his technique of montage, a method of editing that boldly exploits visual metaphor.

BETTER VACUUM PACKS

Thermos vacuum flasks covered in plastic go on sale. They are lighter, longer-lasting, and cheaper than their predecessors, patented in 1902 by a German, Reinhold Burger. These were large, cumbersome, fragile, and rather expensive because they were covered in nickel.

THE RISE OF THE KLAN

The Ku Klux Klan suffers a setback when its Kentucky leader, D.C. Stephenson, is imprisoned for assault, rape, and kidnapping. The Klan's political power and membership have grown in recent years — over 40,000 members attend its first national congress on August 8, complete with a parade through Washington.

A NEW BAUHAUS, DESSAU

Walter Gropius (1883–1969) designs this landmark building for a landmark institution, which moves to Dessau after political pressure forces it to leave Weimar. The elegant but austere building, like the institution it houses, seems to unite art and industry. Inside, some of Europe's greatest artists and designers (such as Kandinsky, Moholy-Nagy, and Gropius himself) teach the arts of design and architecture, and spread the ideals of modernism.

THE NEW DUTCH SCHOOL

The Vondelschool is built in Hilversum. Impressive for its sober, elegant use of brickwork and its strong horizontal lines, this is one of many such buildings by Dudok in the new town to the southeast of Amsterdam.

PIAGET'S THEORY

A pioneering study of children's mental development is published by Jean Piaget (a Swiss psychologist who studied under Jung and worked with Alfred Binet on children's intelligence tests). He theorizes that the development of mental processes is determined genetically and always occurs in four stages.

MEXICAN INSURRECTIONS 1926–29

In this year, anticlerical provisions in the Mexican 1917 Constitution are implemented. Clerical land is seized, church property is nationalized, and bishops are exiled. A guerrilla group calling themselves the Cristoferos, fight on the side of the clergy. There are no major outbreaks but many skirmishes. In 1929, agreement will be reached between the two parties.

CLAUDE MONET
(1840–1926)

The French impressionist painter Claude Monet, whose painting *Impression, Soleil Levant*, exhibited in 1874, initiated the term impressionism, has died. His technique was to build up a painting from patches of pure color, and his paintings often consist of a series examining the same subject again and again in different lights, as in his *Argenteuil* series (1872–75), *Views of London* (1902), *Rouen Cathedral* (1892–95), and the countless *Water-lilies* (1899–1926).

The Italian-born actor and heartthrob has died unexpectedly of peritonitis in New York. He emigrated to the States in 1913, and worked first as a stage dancer, then as a Hollywood extra. With his flashing eyes, handsome and athletic bearing, and dramatic talent, he soon became the leading man in a series of silent films of the 1920s. His funeral caused hysterical public displays of grief.

FIRST T.V. DEMONSTRATED

In January Scottish inventor John Logie Baird (1888–1946) demonstrates the first true television transmission to 50 scientists at the Royal Institution in London, using a mechanical scanner.

NORGE OVER THE NORTH POLE

Italian aviator Umberto Nobile flies across the North Pole in his airship *Norge*, accompanied by explorers Roald Amundsen (Norway) and Lincoln Ellsworth (U.S.).

WATERPROOF WATCH

The first waterproof watch is made by the Rolex Company of Switzerland, and marketed as the Oyster.

METROPOLIS

This important film by Austrian director Fritz Lang (1890–1976) uses the genre of science fiction to create a vision of a nightmare urban landscape, which influences many other moviemakers. Set in a mechanized, slave-served society in the year 2000, the film uses expressionistic sets and techniques to depict the horrors of the city — and of the class warfare that breaks out.

ROCKET LAUNCH

In March U.S. physicist Robert Goddard (1882–1945) launches the first liquid-fuel propelled rocket near Auburn, Massachusetts; it flies 184 feet.

NATIONAL PARKS INVENTED IN THE STATES

The U.S. Forest Service identifies 55 million acres of American wilderness area in the initiative to preserve regions of natural beauty and geological and ecological importance.

THIAMINE ISOLATED

Thiamine (vitamin B1) is the first vitamin to be isolated in its pure form. This is achieved by American scientist Robert Runnels Williams (1886–1965).

LEFT: The Gothic-style Woolworth Building, at 792 feet high, one of the distinctive New York skyscrapers. It will soon be dwarfed by even more upwardly reaching buildings.

ABOVE: The Italian airship *Norge*, which successfully flew over the North Pole this year, carrying an international crew.

ZIP UP
Zip fasteners, invented in Chicago in 1891 by Whitcomb L. Judson, redesigned in 1913 by Gideon Sundback, and used by the U.S. military from 1914, are being used to fasten jeans.

CHANNEL CROSSING
American Gertrude Ederle is the first woman to swim the English Channel from France to England. She takes 14 hours 31 minutes, knocking two hours off the record.

POWER TO THE WOMEN OF INDIA
Indian women are permitted to stand for public office.

MAYAN CIVILIZATION REDISCOVERED
Archaeologists guided by descriptions in books by the nineteenth-century American travel writer, John L. Stephens, rediscover five ancient Mayan cities in the Yucatan, Mexico, and prepare to excavate the largest sites, the cities of Chichen Itzá, Uxmal, and Coba.

BIGGER AND BETTER
Safeway Stores becomes America's largest chain store when Marion B. Skaggs unites the Safeway chain of grocery stores he founded in Maryland in 1923, with a Californian company, to create a chain of 466 stores.

FLYING OVER THE NORTH POLE
On May 9 U.S. aviators Richard Byrd and Floyd Bennett are the first to fly over the North Pole. They make the round trip in 15 hours from Spitsbergen, Norway, in a Fokker trimotor aircraft piloted by Bennett, with Byrd as navigator.

A NEW EMPEROR
Hirohito is crowned Emperor of Japan. He became regent for his ailing father, Yoshihito, in 1921 and succeeded him to the throne on his death in December.

HARRY HOUDINI (ERICH WEISS)
(1874–1926)

The American escape artist and president of the American Society of Magicians, Harry Houdini, has died. Famous for his ability to withstand any blow, sadly he developed peritonitis after being punched by a member of his audience when unprepared. Houdini, who was born Erich Weiss in Budapest, Hungary, could extricate himself from any form of restraint and frequently escaped from imprisonment in underwater boxes or when suspended in midair. He was a vigorous campaigner against charlatanry.

THE MOVIES SWITCH TO SOUND

Civil war rages in China but it is also a year of American triumphs: aviator Charles Lindbergh flies the Atlantic solo and sound is introduced to the movies. In the Soviet Union, Stalin rises to supreme power by exiling, imprisoning, or executing his opponents. Swiss architect Le Corbusier establishes the canons of modern architecture.

ABOVE: A "flapper" with bobbed hair, short skirt, and a new attitude.

OPPOSITE: General Chiang Kai-shek, bracketed by his guards, visits the Ming Tombs at Nanking.

1927

Feb	9	Revolution in Portugal is crushed after heavy fighting
Mar	21	In China, the Nationalists capture Shanghai
May	20–21	US aviator Charles Lindbergh makes the first solo airplane flight across the Atlantic
July	15	In Austria, troops crush a riot in Vienna
Sep	14	Dancer Isadora Duncan dies in an accident aged 49
	30	Baseball player Babe Ruth hits 60 home runs in one season
Oct	6	Première of *The Jazz Singer*, first film to contain live dialogue
Nov	3	Lt. General A. Montgomery-Massingberd forecasts war with Germany within 20 years
Dec	19	In China, Nationalists execute 600 alleged Communists

ABOVE: American aviator Charles A. Lindbergh lands safely at Le Bourget near Paris after his pioneering nonstop flight from New York City.

ABOVE: The single-engine *Spirit of St. Louis*, Lindbergh's record-breaking plane. It was funded by the citizens of St. Louis.

STORMY WEATHER
Freezing blizzards in Britain end a year of disastrous weather, devastation, and casualties. Floods hit Britain in February, devastate America's Mississippi Valley in May, Galicia in Poland in September, and in November, the northern States and even Algeria.

CIVIL WAR IN CHINA
Kuomintang Nationalist forces capture the port of Shanghai from northern warlords and continue their campaigns to unite the country under the leadership of Chiang Kai-shek. The Kuomintang soon remove Communists from the party, leading to increasing tension between the two sides and eventual civil war.

TROUBLE IN VIENNA
Riots and a general strike break out in the Austrian capital after three anti-Socialists were acquitted of the murder of two Communists. Troops loyal to the government crush the strike, but the Austrian government is now seriously weakened.

STALIN TRIUMPHS
Stalin finally wins total control of the Communist Party when he expels Trotsky and Zinoviev from the party. The following year, Trotsky is sent into internal exile near the Chinese frontier, while other opponents are imprisoned.

CLOSER SHAVES
The first commercially successful electric shaver, with a cutting surface that moves backward and forward, is patented by Colonel Jacob Schick in the United States.

ABOVE: Manchurian warlord Chang Tso Lin being received at the American HQ in Tientsin, China. America supports Manchuria in the Chinese civil war.

CBS ABD BBC
CBS (Columbia Broadcasting System) is formed in the United States when William S. Paley buys a small radio network. In January, the BBC (British Broadcasting Corporation), founded in 1922 from a consortium of radio manufacturers and now incorporated under royal charter, makes its first broadcasts.

LE CORBUSIER SETS THE STYLE
Villa Les Terrasses, Garches, near Paris, is one of a group of Le Corbusier's great houses, and shows all the features associated with this important modernist architect at this point in his career: white walls, long bands of windows, roof terrace; no load-bearing walls and thus large open interior spaces.

DEATH COMES FOR THE ARCHBISHOP
American writer Willa Cather (1876–1947) writes most movingly about pioneers and missionaries — the difficulties they have in adjusting to their new surroundings, their relationships with the local people, and so on. This novel is remarkable for her understanding of the outlook of both missionary Roman Catholics and of native Americans.

PEKING MAN
Canadian anthropologist Davidson Black discovers fossilized prehistoric human remains near Beijing (Peking), which he names "Peking Man"; they prove to be an example of *Homo erectus*.

YOU AIN'T HEARD NOTHING YET

The sound era in the movies is inaugurated with *The Jazz Singer*, the first major sound picture, starring the Jewish minstrel singer Al Jolson.

FLESH AND THE DEVIL

Greta Garbo's first Hollywood film is also said to be the best of her silent dramas. She is already creating the air of mystery that surrounds her in her later sound films.

ISADORA DUNCAN (ANGELA DUNCAN) (1878–1927)

The American-born dancer and choreographer Isadora Duncan (born Angela) has died in a tragic motoring accident. The pioneer of contemporary dance, which incorporates the fluid movements of birds and animals, as well as walking, running and skipping, and classical poses, she founded schools of dance in Berlin, Salzburg, and Vienna. Internationally known, and with an ardent following, she has led an unconventional life. In 1922 she married the young Russian poet Sergei Yesenin, who died by committing suicide in 1925. Shortly before her untimely death she published her autobiography, *My Life*.

ABOVE: The Utitsky Palace in Leningrad inscribed with the Soviet hammer and sickle.

RIGHT: New York from the air: 300 square miles of Big Apple taken at one bite.

COUNTING THE WORLD

First international World Population Conference is organized by U.S. feminist Margaret Sanger.

RECORD RUTH

Babe Ruth hits a record 60 home runs in a single season for the New York Yankees. Ruth's achievement and more home runs around the game, due to a livelier ball, rekindle America's enthusiasm for baseball.

UNDERWATER COLOR

In January *National Geographic Magazine* publishes the first natural color photographs taken beneath the surface of the sea, following months of experiments by ichthyologist W.H. Longley and photographer Charles Martin.

ATLANTIC SOLO FLIGHT

On May 20–21, U.S. aviator Charles A. Lindbergh (1902–74) makes the first solo nonstop flight across the Atlantic in his plane *Spirit of St. Louis*, covering 3,590 miles in 33.5 hours.

THE DEVELOPMENT OF THE CAR

LEFT: President William Taft riding in the White Model touring car that formed part of the presidential motor fleet. The steam-powered, seven-seater car was built around 1910 and cost $4,000 to buy.

ABOVE: Henry Ford driving his "999" racing car at the Grosse Pointe horse-racing track in 1903. Racing with him is Harry Harkness in a Simplex.

Since Henry Ford rolled his Model Ts off the production line in 1908, the car has become part of American life. Early models are driven by steam power, gasoline, and even electricity, although gasoline will eventually be the fuel of choice. Women take up driving enthusiastically and a roadster suits the fast-living flapper style very well.

RIGHT: The Model T is the first car to go into mass production, pouring off the line in this Highland Park factory.
ABOVE: Mr. Ford publicizes the arrival of the 15 millionth model.

ABOVE: The first electric car, built between 1917 and 1919 — the Detroit Electric coupé — recharging its batteries. On a full charge it could travel over 210 miles on a test run, but 80 miles was an average distance.

LEFT: Amanda Preuss at the wheel of the 1915 Oldsmobile Model 44 eight-cylinder roadster which she has driven from San Francisco to New York City in 11 days 5 hours and 45 minutes.

BELOW: The stylish La Salle roadster, which was being produced in 1927.

FIVE-YEAR PLANS AND VOTES FOR WOMEN

All British women get the vote in the same year that suffragette Emmeline Pankhurst dies. Emperor Hirohito comes to power in Japan, and Japan and China go to war. Germany, Britain, France, and 24 other countries sign the Kellogg-Briand Pact to outlaw war. Small pleasures include chewing gum and Scotch™ tape. Mickey Mouse makes his first appearance. In Australia, the Flying Doctor service takes off.

OPPOSITE: Health and strength: a German swimming pool with wave effects and sunshine.

1928

Jan	14	British novelist Thomas Hardy dies, aged 87
	16	In Russia, Stalin sends all his political rivals into exile
Feb	11	The Second Winter Olympics open at St. Moritz, Switzerland
Mar	29	In Britain, all women aged 21 or over are given the vote
May	11	In China, Japanese forces beat off a Chinese army that is trying to recapture Jinan, capital of Shandong province
	15	Australia's Flying Doctor service starts
June	14	British suffragette leader Emmeline Pankhurst dies, aged 69
	20	Roald Amundsen dies in a plane crash while going to rescue Umberto Nobile, who had crash-landed in the Arctic

July	12	Nobile and his crew are rescued by an icebreaker
	30	George Eastman demonstrates color motion pictures in the United States
Aug	12	The Eighth Olympic Games open in Amsterdam
	27	Twenty-three countries, including Germany, sign the Kellogg-Briand Pact for the Renunciation of War
Sep	19	First screening of the animated cartoon film *Steamboat Willie*, featuring Mickey Mouse
Oct	1	In Russia, Stalin begins a Five-Year Plan to boost industry
Nov	6	Republican Herbert Hoover is elected President of the United States some say because his opponent, Alfred E. Smith, was a Roman Catholic

NEW BROOM FOR PORTUGAL

António de Oliveira Salazar (1889–1970) becomes minister of finance, with wide-ranging powers. He soon transforms the Portuguese economy, taking dictatorial powers for himself when he becomes prime minister in July 1932.

CHINA TAKES ON JAPAN

Nationalist forces clash with the Japanese army as they advance towards the old imperial capital of Beijing. Although the Nationalists capture the city in June, uniting China under one leader for the first time since the revolution of 1911, tension grows between China and Japan for control of northern China. The Kuomintang leader, Chiang Kai-shek, is elected president of China in October.

PEACE IN OUR TIME

Twenty-three nations, including the United States, France, Germany, and Britain sign a pact in Paris outlawing war. The pact is the work of the U.S. secretary of state Frank Kellogg and the French foreign minister, Aristide Briand.

THE FIRST FIVE-YEAR PLAN

The first Five-Year Plan begins, designed to transform Russia into a major industrial power. In the countryside, smallholdings are being merged into vast state-owned collective farms, freeing up farmers to work in the new factories and towns.

THE NINTH OLYMPIAD

Established stars Paavo Nurmi and Johnny Weissmuller shine again but there are significant changes at the Ninth Olympiad in Amsterdam, Holland. The rise of a rival organization forces the International Olympic Committee to allow women to compete in track-and-field events. The ritual of lighting the Olympic flame is begun in the new Olympic stadium.

ABOVE: Japanese imperial banners are seen in China, but the struggle between the two countries goes on.

CIVIL WAR IN AFGHANISTAN

Amanullah Khan is still trying to introduce reform but is meeting opposition. He puts his brother on the throne, becomes a rebel himself, and leads a band of guerrillas to depose his brother. Khan's cousin, Nadir Khan, joins in the fight and kills Amanullah. The British support Nadir Khan's claims to the throne. He brings in modern practices, placates the rebels, and calms things down. By 1929, it is all over.

STEAMBOAT WILLIE

Walt Disney introduces Mickey Mouse in this animated film. It is also the first animated film with sound. The mouse is instantly popular, sequels appear, and eventually the character becomes the ubiquitous symbol of Disney and one of the best-known logos of the century.

EMMELINE PANKHURST (NEE GOULDEN) (1858–1928)

The English campaigner for women's rights, Emmeline Pankhurst, has died. Married to a barrister, and advocate of women's suffrage and women's property rights, she was a vociferous campaigner for the cause. She founded the Women's Franchise League in 1889 and both she and her daughter Christabel suffered frequent imprisonment and ill-treatment in the cause. The Representation of the People Act,1928, passed shortly before her death, was the end of her 40-year campaign and a just and fitting tribute to her.

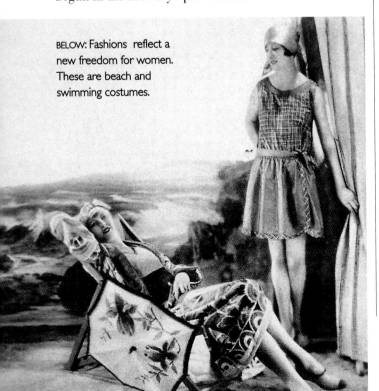

BELOW: Fashions reflect a new freedom for women. These are beach and swimming costumes.

ABOVE: Swimming is a major event in the Ninth Olympics in Holland.

ROALD ENGELBRECHT GRAVNING AMUNDSEN (1872–1928)

Roald Amundsen, the Norwegian explorer, is missing, feared dead, having disappeared while searching by plane for his fellow-explorer Umberto Nobile in the region of the North Pole. During his expeditions in the Arctic he located the Magnetic North Pole, and he was the first man to reach the South Pole in December 1911. In 1927 his book *My Life as an Explorer* was published.

THE WELL OF LONELINESS

With its treatment of lesbian relationships, Marguerite Radclyffe Hall's novel creates controversy and is banned in some countries, including Hall's native Britain, where its description of the relationship between a young girl and an older woman causes scandal. An American court, however, decides that the book should not be banned.

THE THREEPENNY OPERA

Bertolt Brecht and Kurt Weill create a form of musical that admits biting social comment. Weill's music combines memorable tunes and bitter harmonies, while Brecht's words embrace vivid characterization and social satire.

SOLO TO AUSTRALIA

In February the first solo flight from England to Australia is made by Squadron-Leader Bert Hinkler of the RAF, touching down sixteen times on the 10,981-mile journey.

WOMAN PASSENGER

In April American pilot Amelia Earhart becomes the first woman to fly across the Atlantic — as a passenger; the journey is from Newfoundland to Wales.

SCOTCH™ TAPE

The first cellulose adhesive tape is invented by Richard Drew of the 3-M Corporation in America; it is marketed under the brand name of Scotch™ tape.

FLYING DOCTOR SERVICE

On May 15 the first flight of Australia's Flying Doctor Service, founded by Presbyterian minister John Flynn, takes place from Cloncurry, Queensland; the service provides medical help for people living in the remote outback.

PENICILLIN DISCOVERED

Scottish bacteriologist Alexander Fleming (1881–1955) accidentally discovers a mold that produces a substance that kills bacteria; he calls the substance penicillin, but does not study it further.

THE SECOND WINTER OLYMPIAD

The Second Winter Olympics in St Moritz, Switzerland, sees the return of German athletes banned after the war. Warm weather forces the cancellation of some events and while Norway again leads the medal table, the United States disrupts Nordic dominance by finishing second. Norway's Sonja Henie, though just 15, captures figure skating gold and spectators' hearts.

WALK AND CHEW GUM

Fleer's Dubble Bubble gum is marketed in the States.

LEAVING AFGHANISTAN

The RAF undertake first large-scale civilian evacuation by air: 568 people and 24,194 pounds of baggage flown from Kabul December 23, 1928 to February 25, 1929. They are flown in eight Vickers Victoria transports of the RAF's No 70 Squadron, and a Handley Page Hinadi.

UN CHIEN ANDALOU

The quintessence of surrealism is reached in this short film by Luis Buñuel and Salvador Dali. At a time when filmmakers are trying to be as realistic as possible, this piece, with its often grotesque imagery, comes as a shock to artists and audiences alike.

BIG BAND VENUE

In New York City, The Cotton Club is established. It quickly becomes a favorite venue for the new style of big band jazz, attracting artists such as Duke Ellington and many enthusiastic jazz fans.

FINANCIAL RUIN AS WALL STREET CRASHES

In the United States, Wall Street crashes and the world trembles. The Pope teams up with Mussolini and the Graf Zeppelin airship floats around the world in three weeks. Tintin and Snowy have their first adventure. The universe is proved to be expanding. Foam rubber enters the home. Doomed British dirigible, the R101, has its test run.

1929

Jan	13	Former U.S. marshal Wyatt Earp dies in his sleep, aged 80
	30	Stalin orders Leon Trotsky to leave the U.S.S.R.
Feb	1	Popeye the Sailor Man makes his debut
	11	In Italy, Mussolini and the Pope sign a treaty guaranteeing Vatican sovereignty
	13	Trotsky seeks refuge in Turkey
Aug	29	The Graf Zeppelin completes the first airship round-the-world flight
Sep	5	French Prime Minister Aristide Briand proposes a United States of Europe
Oct	24	Black Thursday: Wall Street stock market crashes, and 13 million shares are hurriedly sold
	29	Even heavier selling on Wall Street: 16,400,000 shares are sold
Nov	28-29	U.S. aviator Richard Byrd makes the first airplane flight over the South Pole

POPE ALLIES WITH IL DUCE
Mussolini signs the Lateran Pact with the Pope, which guarantees the sovereignty of Vatican City. The pact ends 59 years of tension between the Pope and the Italian state, since the Papal States were annexed by Italy in 1870. In July, Pope Pius X becomes the first pope to leave the Vatican since 1870.

WALL STREET CRASHES
The New York Stock Exchange on Wall Street crashes, with many shares losing up to half their value. The crash brings to an end a decade of rising share prices and prosperity in the United States, and sends the economy into depression.

FLYING OVER THE SOUTH POLE
Richard Byrd, U.S. naval commander, makes the first flight over the South Pole as navigator of an aircraft piloted by Bert Balchen, in a 19-hour round trip from Little America, the expedition's base on the Ross ice shelf.

HOMOSEXUALITY DECRIMINALIZED
Homosexuality is decriminalized in the Weimar Republic. After lobbying by the Coalition for Reform of the Sexual Crimes Code, the German Reichstag committee approves a penal reform bill removing Clause 175 from the Penal Code, which made homosexuality illegal.

ROUND THE WORLD AIRSHIP
In August the German airship Graf Zeppelin makes the first round-the-world flight by an airship, starting and finishing at Lakehurst, New Jersey; the journey takes 21 days, 7 hours, and 34 minutes.

OPPOSITE: Crowds wait in London's Trafalgar Square for the general election results. Vote numbers and the final result will be affected by newly enfranchised women.

GERMAN PAVILION, BARCELONA EXPOSITION
Ludwig Mies van der Rohe (1886–1969) is the German architect of this, one of the simplest of all modernist buildings. The large expanses of glass, simple form, and high-quality materials are all typical of the work of this architect in Europe and, later, in the United States.

VICEROY'S HOUSE, NEW DELHI
In total contrast to the modernist buildings being designed by people like Mies van der Rohe and Le Corbusier, Edwin Lutyens' Viceroy's House is a mixture of traditional styles and elements — domes, minarets, and details influenced by the Renaissance.

OPPOSITE: A spectacular eruption from the crater of Mt. Vesuvius: its most powerful outpouring since 1906.

ABOVE: The Middle East is in turmoil. Arabs demonstrate against the Jewish population of Jerusalem.

THE SOUND AND THE FURY
American writer William Faulkner's novel depicts the decline of the American South through the eyes of a number of different characters, the "idiot" Benjy Compson, the mean Jason, and the sensitive Quentin. This is probably the most ambitious use of different narrative perspectives in fiction to date.

HUBBLE'S LAW
U.S. astronomer Edwin Hubble confirms that the more distant a galaxy is from our own, the faster it is moving away; this discovery, known as Hubble's Law, proves that the universe is expanding.

GEORGES EUGENE BENJAMIN CLEMENCEAU (1841–1929)

The great French statesman, orator and journalist Clemenceau has died at the age of 88. First elected to the National Assembly in 1871, he took a principled stand on many issues, including, most famously, the Dreyfus case (as a Dreyfus supporter). He was prime minister of France during the years 1906–09 and 1917–20, and presided over the 1919 Paris Peace Conference, which negotiated the Treaty of Versailles at the end of World War I.

SERGEI PAVLOVITCH DIAGHILEV (1872–1929)

The legendary Russian dancer and impresario Sergei (Serge) Diaghilev, director of the Ballets Russes de Diaghilev, has died. Diaghilev first brought Russian dance to Paris in 1908 and established the Ballets Russes there in 1909. Under his spell the company has attracted the greatest dancers, choreographers, artists, and composers of the century, including the dancer/choreographers Nijinsky and Massine, the artists Matisse and Picasso, and the progressive composers Ravel, Prokofiev, Poulenc, Satie, and Stravinsky.

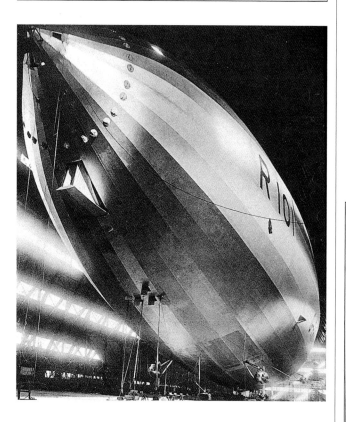

ABOVE: The airship R101 on its test bed.

TROTSKY EXILED

Trotsky goes into exile in Constantinople after being expelled from the U.S.S.R. at the end of January. Many of his supporters are exiled or imprisoned.

ALL QUIET ON THE WESTERN FRONT

German writer Erich Maria Remarque's novel of World War I, seen from the point of view of an ordinary soldier, is an enormous success, and it is said to speak for an entire generation. It shows war in its horrific and nonheroic aspects.

BIRTH OF TINTIN

The first appearance of Tintin, Snowy, Captain Haddock, Professor Calculus, and the Thompson Twins as Hergé produces his first adventures. Although Belgian, he becomes an icon of French culture. Hergé will later be suspected of sympathizing with the Nazis.

FIRST IRON LUNG

American engineer Philip Drinker develops the first iron lung, a machine that helps people paralyzed by poliomyelitis to breathe; it saves many lives.

FOAM RUBBER

Scientists at the Dunlop Rubber Company develop foam rubber, made by whipping air into latex, the white juice of the rubber tree.

ELECTROENCEPHALOGRAPH

German psychiatrist Hans Berger develops the electroencephalograph, a device that measures electrical voltages produced in the brain; a print-out of these voltages is called an electroencephalogram (ECG).

HAIR AND BEAUTY

Colorinse, the first commercial hair colorant for home use, is launched by Nestlé in the United States.

ALETTA JACOBS (1849–1929)

The Dutch doctor's daughter Aletta Jacobs who, as a result of petitioning the prime minister, became the first woman to study medicine in the Netherlands, has died. After qualifying she set up in practice with her father, offering free treatment for the poor. A committed feminist, she set up the first birth control clinic in Amsterdam in 1882 and was a vocal spokeswoman for women's health education, women's suffrage, and reform of legislation affecting women.

THE GREAT DEPRESSION

A frightening decade of extreme ideologies, economic disaster, and war. Communism, Fascism, and Nazism confront each other, each led by fanatical leaders. Adolf Hitler's image, stage-managed rallies, and swastika sign dominate these ten years. Gandhi takes the opposite path, advocating nonviolent resistance. Financial depression leads to global poverty. In the United States, Roosevelt introduces the New Deal while in China Mao Zedong leads the Long March. Nothing can stop the inevitability of World War II, which brings the decade to an end.

OPPOSITE: Adolf Hitler and his followers at one of the many Nazi rallies of the decade.

1930–1939

KEY EVENTS OF THE DECADE

- CIVIL WAR IN CHINA
- THE RISE OF STALIN
- GANDHI AND CIVIL DISOBEDIENCE
- AIRSHIP DISASTERS
- NAZISM IN ASCENDANCY
- THE CULT OF HITLER
- PLASTIC AND NYLON
- JET AIRCRAFT
- SPANISH CIVIL WAR
- RADIO FROM SPACE

- FINANCIAL DEPRESSION
- THE NEW DEAL
- THE LONG MARCH
- THE OKLAHOMA DUSTBOWL
- WAR BETWEEN ITALY AND ETHIOPIA
- KEYNESIAN ECONOMIC THEORY
- WORLD WAR II BEGINS
- REPEAL OF PROHIBITION

WORLD POPULATION: 2,295 MILLION

PLASTICS, PLUTO, AND THE RISE OF NAZISM

The new decade brings civil war in China and revolt in India as Gandhi shows civil disobedience to the British. The new material, plastic, is taken up with enthusiasm by designers working in the new art deco style. Haile Selassie is crowned emperor of Ethiopia, and in Germany, the jackboot stamps into the Reichstag as Hitler's Nazi Party proves a vote-winner. In France, André Maginot takes the threat of German expansionism to heart and begins constructing the defensive Maginot Line. Triumph is in the air: Amy Johnson is the first woman to fly from Europe to Australia and the prototype jet engine is patented. A new planet swims into view: it is named Pluto, after the god of the underworld.

1930

Feb	18	American astronomer Clyde Tombaugh discovers the planet Pluto
Apr	6	Gandhi and his followers end their march to the sea in protest against the salt laws imposed by the British in India
	24	Amy Johnson lands in Australia after flying from Britain
July	1	In the United States, the first Greyhound bus pulls out of the garage
Nov	2	Haile Selassie crowned emperor of Ethiopia

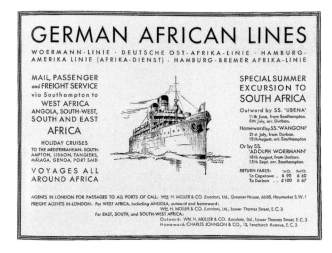

ABOVE: Europe and the great African continent are linked by fast, regular mail steamers offering every modern comfort and convenience for their passengers.

OPPOSITE: The British airship, the *R101*, crashes into a French hillside on its maiden voyage.

CIVIL WAR IN CHINA

This year sees the start of the war fought between the Kuomintang (KMT) (Nationalist) armies of Chiang Kai-shek and the Communists, which is to last until 1934. The KMT drive the Communists out of their bases in the southern mountains of China and force them on to the Long March to new bases. Mao Zedong is among the marchers.

COLLECTIVIZE OR DIE

Following the success of the Five-Year Plan in collectivizing all smallholdings, Stalin extends the program to larger farms, ordering the kulaks, or rich peasants, to hand over their land. Millions of kulaks are subsequently killed as collectivization is ruthlessly enforced.

THE SALT MARCH

In India, Gandhi begins a campaign of civil disobedience against British rule by protesting against the government monopoly of salt production. He leads a march to the sea, to make a symbolic amount of salt from sea water. His arrest and imprisonment in April causes widespread rioting and strikes across India.

FIRST CYCLOTRON

An American team led by Ernest O. Lawrence build the world's first experimental cyclotron, a device that accelerates atomic particles in a circle.

ABOVE: Children in a Russian collective are cared for in a kindergarten so that their mothers can work on the land. This was part of Stalin's first Five-Year Plan for the collectivization and industrialization of agriculture.

FIRST WORLD CUP

Only 13 nations, of which just four are from Europe, compete in the first football World Cup in Uruguay on July 30. The United States is one of four seeded nations. The hosts win, beating neighboring Argentina 4–2, starting a trend of victories by host nations. The competition is the brainchild of Frenchman Guerin and Dutchman Hirschman.

FLYING SOUTH

English pilot Amy Johnson (1903–41) arrives in Australia in her Gipsy Moth on May 24, the first woman to make a long-distance solo flight from London. She sets a world record of six days from London to India and reaches Darwin in 19 days.

HAILE SELASSIE

In April, Ras Tafari, regent of Ethiopia, becomes emperor on the death of the empress. He takes the name Haile Selassie, and will be crowned in November. Rastafarians in Jamaica, British West Indies, hail him as a living god, the fulfilment of a prophecy by American black nationalist leader Marcus Garvey.

PLUTO DISCOVERED

American astronomer Clyde W Tombaugh, working at the Lowell Observatory in the United States, discovers Pluto, then considered the outermost planet.
Its existence has been predicted by Percival Lowell; it proves to have an irregular orbit around the Sun.

WHITE VOTES IN SOUTH AFRICA

In May white South African women win the vote, but black men and women remain disenfranchised.

EXTREMISM COMES TO POWER

The Nazis make huge advances in the general election in September, gaining 107 seats, second only to the Socialists. The growing economic crisis in Germany after the Wall Street Crash causes many to support the party in the hope that it can provide strong government for Germany.

FIRST LARGE COMPUTER

A team led by American scientist Vannevar Bush develops the world's first big analogue computer, an electromechanical machine.

FANTASTIC PLASTIC

Solid, clear plastics made from acrylic acid (discovered by scientists in Britain, Canada, and Germany in the 1920s). They will go on the market as Perspex in Britain, and as Lucite and Plexiglas in North America.

ABOVE: Mahatma Gandhi, marked by an arrow in the picture, watching as his followers scoop up sand and salt water at Dandi, defying the government.

ABOVE: Amy Johnson, in her Gipsy Moth *Jason*, becomes the first woman to fly solo from England to Australia. A year later, she will make a recordbreaking solo flight to Cape Town.

ABOVE: Adolf Hitler inspires the party faithful at a vast open-air rally held to celebrate the recent election success of the National Socialists (Nazis).

ABOVE: Plastic frames for glasses encasing lace and other fabrics become a fashionable designer accessory as makers experiment with this new acrylic material.

ART DECO REACHES NEW HEIGHTS

The Chrysler Building in New York, designed by William van Alen, is completed. Phantasmagoric art deco detailing (the steel-faced, seven-story spire, the curving lines of the top storys, the interior decoration, the doorways) make this perhaps the most beautiful of all skyscrapers. Until the Empire State Building is completed, it will remain the highest building in the world at 1,056 feet.

THE BEST THING SINCE ...

Sliced bread is introduced in the United States under the Wonder Bread label by Continental Baking — in the year that the first successful automatic electric toaster is produced by the McGraw-Electric Co. of Elgin, Illinois.

BRIDGES IN SWITZERLAND

Swiss engineer Robert Maillart creates a series of elegant bridges in reinforced concrete, of which the Salginatobel Bridge, with its fine lines and dramatic gorge setting, is the most striking. Functional simplicity produces beauty in Maillart's work.

AMERICAN GOTHIC

This memorable painting of a Midwestern farmer and his wife seems to sum up rural America and becomes a lasting symbol of the rural way of life. Painted in Iowa by Grant Wood (1892–1942), it becomes the most famous painting of the American regionalist group of artists (which also includes Thomas Hart Benton and John Steuart Curry).

THE FIRST JET ENGINE

British aero-engineer Frank Whittle (1907–96) patents a jet engine for aircraft use.

DISASTER IN THE AIR

The British airship R101 crashes into a French hillside on its maiden voyage, killing 47 people. The disaster signals the end of the British airship industry.

FRIDTJOF NANSEN
(1861–1930)

The Norwegian explorer, zoologist, and oceanographer has died. His first Arctic adventure was in 1882 on board a sealer, and from 1893 to 1895 he tested his theory that he could reach the North Pole by drifting with an ice floe. He went further north by this method (86°14'N) than anyone had so far reached. After independence (1905) Nansen was Norwegian ambassador in London (1906–08). He was League of Nations commissioner for refugees from 1920 to 1922, devising the Nansen passport for stateless persons, and won the Nobel Peace Prize in 1922 for his Russian relief work.

TREE SICKNESS
Dutch elm disease, first seen in Holland in 1919, spreads to the United States and is attacking American trees.

MIND MATTERS
Karl Menninger, who in 1920 founded with his father the pioneering Menninger psychiatric clinic in Kansas, publishes *The Human Mind*. Although written for medical students, it is widely read because it explains how psychiatry can help mentally disturbed people.

HAYS RULES
Motion Picture Production Code established in response to calls for censorship of motion pictures. It is spearheaded by Will H. Hays, president of the Motion Pictures Producers and Distributors (known as the Hays Office). The code consists of a detailed list of what is and is not acceptable on screen.

FRENCH DEFENCE
French workmen begin building the Maginot Line, named after French war minister André Maginot; it is a series of forts built to protect France against possible German invasion.

COUP IN PERU
After an army coup in August, Colonel Luis Sánchez Cerro becomes president of Peru, overthrowing the elected government. A month later, an army revolt in Argentina overthrows the reformist president, Hipólito Irigoyen, and installs a military government under General José Uriburu

TICKET TO RIDE
The Greyhound Bus Company opens up bus routes all over the United States.

RIGHT: The two spans of the Sydney Harbor Bridge inch towards each other to form the world's largest arch bridge. It will enable pedestrians and road and rail passengers to cross 170 feet above even the largest of the harbor's ocean liners.

WAR IN THE EAST, BUILDING IN THE WEST

Japan flexes its imperial muscle and poaches Manchuria from China, initiating the Sino-Japanese War, which will last until 1945. In Spain, a republic is declared, but this will not prevent eventual civil war. In America, despite the Depression, building is on the up and up and towers begin to scrape the sky. In France, Swiss architect Charles Jeanneret, better known as Le Corbusier, establishes the canon of modern architectural orthodoxy. Conquering the skies is still very much on the agenda: Swiss scientist Auguste Piccard reaches the stratosphere in a balloon. The disputed father of the light bulb, Thomas Alva Edison, dies.

1931

Feb	**5**	British racer Malcolm Campbell sets a new world land speed record at Daytona: 245 miles per hour
Mar	**3**	"The Star-Spangled Banner" becomes the official national anthem of the United States
Apr	**14**	Spain becomes a republic
May	**1**	Empire State Building opens in New York City
	28	Swiss scientist Auguste Piccard balloons to the stratosphere
Oct	**17**	Al Capone imprisoned for tax crime

ABOVE: Robert Frost (1874–1963) wins the Pulitzer Prize for the second time this year. He is one of America's most popular poets.

BIRTH OF THE SPANISH REPUBLIC

King Alfonso abdicates in April and goes into exile in London as Spain is declared a republic. The collapse of the monarchy follows gains made by the Republican party in the local elections. The new government is headed by Alcalá Zamora. In the general election in June, the Socialists make huge gains.

AUSTRIA TRIGGERS EUROPEAN RUIN

In May, the collapse of Credit-Anstalt, a minor Austrian bank, leads to a major financial crisis throughout Central and Eastern Europe. The crisis spreads to Germany in July and to Britain in August, causing the minority Labour government to fall and a National government, under the leadership of the Labour prime minister, Ramsay MacDonald, to take office. Britain comes off the gold standard and devalues the pound in September, causing financial turmoil around the world. Unemployment soars across Europe.

A COMMONWEALTH CHARTER

The British Parliament passes the Statute of Westminster, which defines the independence of the five dominions within the British Empire. The statute becomes the basic charter of the modern British Commonwealth as British colonies gain their independence.

NIGHT FLIGHT

French writer and aviator Antoine de Saint-Exupéry (1900–44), author of the well-known children's book, *The Little Prince* (1943), publishes *Night Flight*, probably his best book, about a new South American airline and its chief pilot. The book, which draws on his experiences as a pilot, contributes to the 1930s literary love affair with everything to do with the air and aviation.

EMPIRE STATE BUILDING

The latest of New York's skyscrapers is now the world's tallest building. It is famous for its great height of 1,250 feet, later increased by antennae to 1,472 feet, for the speed of construction, for its shimmering walls, (many clad in metal alloy) and its fine foyer. It opens during the Depression, much of the office space remains unlet, but the owners reap revenue from sightseers.

MAIGRET STONEWALLED

Belgian writer Georges Simenon (1903–89) creates Inspector Jules Maigret in this novel (originally titled *M. Gallet décédé*), and elevates the *roman policier* to a psychological novel of some subtlety. Maigret is notable for being perhaps the first of the "caring" policemen in fiction, a man who solves crimes by understanding the criminals. The books are also famous for their depictions of the atmosphere and even the smells (Simenon had an extraordinary nose) of Paris.

ABOVE: New York City's George Washington Bridge, opened on October 24, spans a recordbreaking 3,609 feet.

ANNA PAVLOVA
(1885–1931)

The Russian ballerina has died. She left Russia in 1909 to work with Diaghilev's Paris-based Ballets Russes, and later set up her own company, becoming internationally known for performing highlights from the classic ballets — perhaps the most celebrated being the dying swan. Pavlova cake is named in her honor.

VILLA SAVOIE

This house at Poissy, France, is one of the most famous by Swiss architect Le Corbusier, and is the physical manifestation of his famous *Five Points of Architecture*. It popularizes the use of concrete pillars (or *pilotis* as Le Corbusier calls them) to raise the living floor above the ground. Other typical features include ribbon-windows, white walls, a flat roof, and large terraces.

THE WAVES

English novelist Virginia Woolf (1882–1941) publishes her most experimental work. In it she describes the lives of a group of friends, from childhood to middle age, through their own words and thoughts. Between the characters' thoughts come poetic mood-setting passages describing a seascape with the rising and setting sun, the shore, and the breaking waves.

FRANKENSTEIN'S MONSTER COMES TO LIFE

English-born actor Boris Karloff (1887–1969) stars as the monster in *Frankenstein*, directed by James Whale, a film loosely based on Mary Shelley's novel of 1818. This is the most popular of many films based on the story.

IONIZATION

French modernist composer Edgard Varèse (1885–1965) writes the first piece of Western music solely for percussion. The piece relies on the contrast between the deep, rich sound of the tam-tam and the drier sound of the military drum.

POPULATION CONTROL

Contraception is forbidden to Roman Catholics by Pope Pius XII in his encyclical Casti Connubi, but approved for Anglicans by the Archbishop of Canterbury. As the world population approaches two billion, abortion is outlawed in Italy by Mussolini.

UP UP AND AWAY

Auguste Piccard (1884–1962), a Swiss physicist, and Charles Kipfew, his assistant, become the first people to reach the stratosphere. They ascend to 55,000 feet in an enclosed, pressurized aluminium sphere carried by a balloon.

KNOW YOUR MARKET

The Starch Ratings are introduced by Daniel Starch, director of the American Association of Advertising Agencies, to measure advertising readership and radio audiences.

FLASH BANG

Electronic flashguns for photographers are invented. This does away with expendable flashbulbs.

LEFT: Smog-bound Pittsburgh (top) gags for controls on air pollution, and sighs with relief at the result (bottom).

THOMAS ALVA EDISON
(1847–1931)

The Ohio-born inventor has died. He took out over 1,000 patents during his prolifically industrious life, his inventions ranging from a vote-recording machine and the stock exchange ticker tape, to the phonograph, the incandescent electric light bulb, the humble megaphone, the first electricity power plant and the "talking" movies.

BRIGHT LIGHTS, BIG CITY?

The first study of air pollution is carried out by the U.S. Public Health Service. It estimates that one-fifth of the natural light of New York City is cut out by smoke pollution.

FASTER SHAVES

The electric razor, patented in 1923 by Colonel Jacob Schick, is produced and marketed by his own company, Schick Dry Shaver Inc.

RADIO FROM SPACE

U.S. radio engineer Karl G. Jansky discovers radio waves emanating from outside the solar system; this marks the beginning of radio astronomy.

SAFETY KETTLE

British manufacturer Walter Bulpitt invents an electric kettle that automatically ejects a resettable safety plug if the kettle overheats.

ENTER TELEX AND TWX

The American Telephone and Telegraph Company introduces two-way teleprinter services, called TWX in America and telex in Britain, which can be used by subscribers in their own offices.

THE MORNING AFTER

Alka Seltzer, a new painkiller produced as a tablet that effervesces when dissolved in water, is introduced by Miles Laboratories of Indiana. It contains an antacid indigestion agent and is a popular treatment for hangovers.

SUSPENSION RECORD

The George Washington Bridge over the Hudson River, connecting New York City with New Jersey, is opened; its suspension span is 3,609 feet — a record for the time.

ELECTRON MICROSCOPE

German scientists Ernst Ruska and Max Knoll construct the first electron microscope, which gives a much greater enlargement than ordinary microscopes.

ABOVE: Thomas A. Edison dies. Physicist and world-famous inventor, he is shown outside the office of a mining plant seeking his famous "one percent inspiration."

DAME NELLY MELBA (HELEN PORTER ARMSTRONG, née MITCHELL)
(1861–1931)

The renowned Australian soprano has died in Sydney. Born Helen Mitchell near Melbourne, she took her stage name from the city. Having been trained in Paris she performed in the world's great opera houses, and such was her reputation that she could command the casting. Among the many roles she made her own were Mimi in *La Bohème*, Gilda in *Rigoletto*, and Desdemona in *Othello*, and like Caruso, with whom she sang, she was among the first opera singers to make recordings. Peach Melba and Melba toast are named in her honor. She was famous for her many "last" performances.

SINO-JAPANESE WAR

Japanese troops attack a Chinese garrison at Mukden, in the northern province of Manchuria, in September and speedily occupy the entire province. The following February, they set up the puppet state of Manchukuo, with the former Chinese Emperor Pu Yi as emperor.

In January of 1932, Japanese troops enter the city of Shanghai, starting an invasion of China. Although the Chinese drive them out of the city in March, the Japanese continue acts of aggression against Chinese territory for the next five years.

LEFT: Invading Japanese forces encounter stiff resistance and, backed by armored vehicles, fire from the safety of a reinforced emplacement.

BELOW: Defending Chinese soldiers return rifle fire from behind a hastily constructed barricade on Paoshan Street.

ABOVE: Japanese soldiers place logs across a river for their tanks to cross.

RIGHT: An armed convoy of Japanese sailors races through the city.

BELOW: General Tsai, commander of the 19th Route Army, observes the damaging effect of one of his howitzers.

THE WEST SINKS INTO DEPRESSION

Depression tightens its grip on the Western world in the continuous fallout from the Wall Street Crash of 1929. In the United States, Franklin D. Roosevelt comes to power on his promise of a New Deal to fight poverty; in Germany, Adolf Hitler's policies are equally attractive to a nation still recovering from World War I. The world of physics concentrates on detail: The development of particle accelerators allows scientists to observe what are at the time considered to be the smallest building blocks of the universe. Amelia Earhart becomes the first woman to fly the Atlantic.

1932

Jan	**31**	Japan captures Shanghai
Mar	**2**	The infant son of aviator Charles Lindbergh is kidnapped. Sadly he will be found dead two months later
May	**10**	President Paul Doumer of France assassinated
	21	Amelia Earhart flies from Canada to the United Kingdom
July	**5**	Antonio Salazar becomes dictator of Portugal
Aug	**6**	First Venice Film Festival
Nov	**8**	Democrat Franklin D. Roosevelt elected president of the United States

ABOVE: Mies van der Rohe is director of the Bauhaus (1930–33). The Seagram Building (completed in 1958) epitomizes Bauhaus principles.

LAND FROM THE SEA

The drainage scheme of the Zuider Zee in the Netherlands is completed, vastly increasing the amount of available arable farmland and reducing the risk of flooding from the North Sea.

GRAN CHACO WAR

War breaks out between Bolivia and Paraguay over their disputed border, the Chaco Boreal or Gran Chaco, which is a potential shipping route to the sea for oil. Paraguay declares war, but Bolivia is better trained and equipped, and has successes. Paraguay then fully mobilizes and counterattacks. The war drags on until June 1935. Both sides became war-weary and, at a peace treaty in 1938, Paraguay receives the Chaco region and Bolivia gains access to the Atlantic via two rivers.

DE VALERA LEADS IRELAND

Éamon de Valera wins the Irish general election and becomes prime minister the following month. He begins to loosen Irish ties with Britain, adopting a new constitution in 1937, which renames the Irish Free State as Eire.

THE INTERNATIONAL STYLE

This work on architecture, by Philip Johnson and Henry-Russell Hitchcock, publicizes the modernist style and influences a whole generation of architects. The book, together with the arrival of exiled scholars and architects from Nazi Germany, will influence the development of architecture, first in North America, then all over the world. The book describes a style in which form follows function.

FDR FOR PRESIDENT

Franklin D. Roosevelt wins the presidential election by a landslide for the Democrats, defeating the sitting Republican president, Herbert Hoover. Roosevelt, who is in a wheelchair as a result of polio, wins all but six of the 48 states of the Union.

ANDRE LOUIS RENE MAGINOT
(1877–1932)

The French politician André Maginot has died this year. During the 1920s, in preparation for a possible further war with Germany, he organized fortifications around the Franco-German border, known as the Maginot Line. When war came, the Germans invaded through Belgium, rendering these defenses useless. Maginot's name is doomed to go down in history attached to a useless mega-project.

NEUTRON DISCOVERED . . .

English physicist James Chadwick discovers the neutron, a particle with no electrical charge found in the nuclei of all atoms except hydrogen.

. . . AND POSITRON DISCOVERED

U.S. physicist Carl D. Anderson discovers the positron (positive electron), the first subatomic particle of antimatter to be found.

HINDENBURG BEATS HITLER

President Hindenburg wins reelection in the German presidential election in a close-run contest with Adolf Hitler. In the general election in July, the Nazis become the biggest party, although they do not have a majority and so cannot form a government.

PARTICLE ACCELERATOR

Physicists John Cockroft of England and Ernest Walton of Ireland build the first linear atomic particle accelerator; with it they bombard lithium with protons and transform it into helium — the first artificial atomic transformation.

BELOW: Jobless Californians contemplate a bleak future as they wait in line for unemployment compensation.

ABOVE: Amelia Earhart, set to become the first woman to fly solo across the Atlantic — from Harbour Grace, Newfoundland, to Londonderry, Northern Ireland.

BROTHER CAN YOU SPARE A DIME?

This plangent tune, written by E.Y. Harburg and Jay Gorney, is the archetypal song of the Depression. It will later become popular sung by Bing Crosby and Rudy Vallee.

WOMAN'S ATLANTIC SOLO

American aviator Amelia Earhart (1898–1937) becomes the first woman to fly the Atlantic solo, from Harbour Grace, Newfoundland, to Northern Ireland.

DOUBLE DUTCH

Flemish, a language almost identical to Dutch, becomes the official language of Belgium's Flemish provinces, which border on Holland. French becomes the official language of the Walloon provinces.

BRAVE NEW WORLD

Aldous Huxley's seminal dystopian novel is published. It depicts a society in which humans are "programmed" from birth to accept their social destiny, and are graded in a pseudoscientific caste system (from intellectual to "semi-moron"). The novel describes what happens when a savage from a reservation confronts the World Controller, and plays out the debate between social stability and individual freedom.

AMERICAN OLYMPICS

In February, worldwide economic depression and warm weather leave competitors and snow thin on the ground at the Third Olympic Winter Games in Lake Placid, New York. Again, the North Americans (who make up half of the competitors) and the Scandinavians dominate. Nineteen-year-old Sonja Henie of Norway repeats her success in the women's figure skating.

In July, Los Angeles hosts a Tenth Olympic Games depleted by economic turmoil. Only 1,400 athletes, half the 1928 tally, travel to California. The International Olympic Committee block Olympic hero Paavo Nurmi from adding to his 9 golds and three silvers, for breaking rules on his amateur status. With two golds and a silver, American Mildred "Babe" Didrikson is the star of the games.

LEFT AND BELOW: Los Angeles is home to the Tenth Olympic Games and, despite the world's money worries, thousands attend to cheer the athletes to ever greater feats.

THE NEW DEAL VERSUS NATIONAL SOCIALISM

In Germany the Reichstag burns, Adolf Hitler takes power, and his secret police, the Gestapo, begin the process of what will become known as ethnic cleansing. In the United States, Roosevelt deals with financial collapse by putting his New Deal into practice. Everyone can celebrate as prohibition ends in this year. The League of Nations, formed after World War I to prevent any future global warfare, disintegrates. Cuba becomes a dictatorship. American aviator Wiley Post flies round the world in just over a week, and in the cinema, *King Kong* storms the box office.

1933

Jan	30	Hitler apppointed chancellor of Germany
Feb	27	Reichstag burns down
Mar	5	Roosevelt closes banks for cooling off period; follows with other measures
May	27	Japan leaves the League of Nations
June	23	Hitler dissolves all opposition parties
Oct	14	Germany leaves the League of Nations
Dec	5	Prohibition repealed in the United States

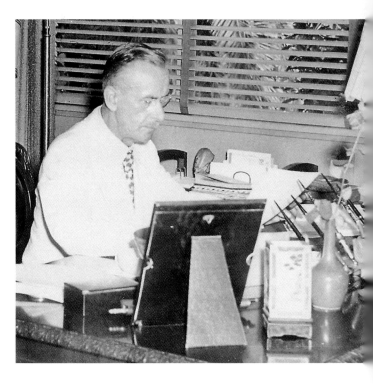

ABOVE: Thomas Mann speaks out against the increasing dangers of political extremism and, after 1933, moves from Germany to Switzerland. He settles in the United States in 1936.

NEW DEAL, NEW ENERGY
Franklin D. Roosevelt takes power in the United States and begins to tackle the economic crisis. New Deal legislation is soon introduced to control industry and production, money is pumped into public works, farmers and banks are bailed out with public money, and a vast scheme is introduced to revive the Tennessee Valley. Three million acres will be restored to cultivation, erosion halted, and 42 dams and eight hydroelectric projects built. The energy of the new government does much to lift depression in the United States.

LEAVING THE LEAGUE
Japan withdraws from the League of Nations in May; Germany follows in October.

ABOVE: Prohibition sees millions of gallons of illegal alcohol go down the drain and an increase in crime. The Eighteenth Amendment that brought it about is repealed in December 1933.

ART DIASPORA
Nazi Germany drives out "degenerate" artists. They include composers Kurt Weill (1900–50) and Arnold Schoenberg (1874–1951), and writers Thomas Mann (1875–1955) and Bertolt Brecht (1898–1956).

BACK TO MOTHER
The dominion of Newfoundland, which received its independence from Britain in 1917, reverts to colonial status after complete financial collapse.

ABOVE: The New Deal offers encouragement to American farmers, and the summer's harvest is savored by this young crop-picker.

ABOVE: The Marx Brothers' antiwar satire *Duck Soup* stars the hapless team delivering their distinctive brand of irreverence.

DUCK SOUP

The Marx Brothers star in this antiwar satire. Their rapid-fire irreverent humor has a lasting influence on cinema comedy.

ABOVE: The New Deal offers encouragement to American farmers, and the summer's harvest is savored by this young crop-picker.

THE REICHSTAG BURNS

In February, fire guts the Reichstag, the parliament building in Berlin. A young Dutchman is arrested but the new Nazi government blames the Communist party, using the excuse to suspend civil liberties such as freedom of speech and of the press and to crack down on political opponents.

CUBAN DICTATOR

In Cuba, the army, led by Fulgencio Batista and supported by the United States, overthrows President Machado and takes power in a coup in August. Batista becomes increasingly dictatorial, and although he will go into voluntary exile in the Dominican Republic in 1944, he will return to power by another coup in 1952, hanging onto power until 1959.

PAINLESS CHILDBIRTH

Grantley Dick-Read publishes *Natural Childbirth* in the United States, a manual of exercises and procedures for childbirth without drugs.

POLYTHENE BY CHANCE

British chemists accidentally discover the plastic polythene (polyethylene) while doing experiments on high pressures. Its discovery is based on research by a Dutch chemist, AMJS Michels of Amsterdam. It is the first true plastic made by the polymerization of ethylene.

LEFT: "Tea, anyone?" The all-electric Teasmade is launched in Britain by Goblin.

TUBERCULOSIS SANATORIUM

Finnish architect Alvar Aalto (1889–1976) is the leading modern architect in Scandinavia. His Sanatorium Paimio, Finland, shows how the modernist style adapts well to buildings with a humanitarian purpose. The clean lines and sound planning of the building are praised by Le Corbusier, Mies van der Rohe, and Walter Gropius.

MAN AT THE CROSSROADS

Eminent Mexican muralist Diego Rivera (1886–1957) completes this work for the Rockefeller Center's RCA Building. Because of its content (it includes a portrait of Lenin), the mural is destroyed.

42ND STREET

Busby Berkeley (1895–1976) is the choreographer of the elaborate set pieces in this musical, which immediately becomes a classic. It is the second of such films, and a number of other films follow in which Berkeley is given full rein to include similar set pieces, in which special effects produce kaleidoscopelike patterns of precision dancers.

MORNING TEA

The Teasmade, the first all-electric automatic teamaker, invented in the U.K. by Brenner Thornton in 1932 and stylishly designed, is marketed by the British company, Goblin.

NOT CRICKET

During the "Bodyline" cricket tour of Australia, the tactics of the English team cause anger and draw diplomatic protests. A number of Australians are hit as England bowls at the bodies of the batsmen in the hope of catches as they fend the ball off or hook it in the air. The most demonic of the demon bowlers is Harold Larwood.

SOLO WORLD FLIGHT

Pioneer American aviator Wiley Post makes the first solo flight around the world, using a single-engined Lockheed airplane; the flight takes him seven days 18 hours 49 minutes.

THE BIG BANG

Belgian astronomer and priest Georges Lemaître (1894–1956) publishes *Discussion on the Evolution of the Universe*, which first states the theory of the Big Bang. It is based on his 1927 theory of the cosmic egg, the beginning of all things.

GESTAPO CRACKDOWN

In Germany the Gestapo begin closing gay institutions, bars, clubs, journals, and libraries, burning magazines and books, and hunting down and imprisoning homosexuals. They dissolve the Bund Deutsches Frauenverein and other women's organizations, remove women from the government and professions, and award "Aryan" women cash for producing children.

CONSERVATION WORK

The Civilian Conservation Corps is founded in the United States to create work, enlisting three million young men for environmental conservation work. They plant more than two billion trees, build small dams, aid wildlife restoration, and tackle soil erosion.

TECHNICAL PROGRESS

The Chicago Exposition portrays technical progress since the city's foundation in 1833. Rocket cars carry millions of visitors along the elevated Skyride. General Motors shows off its fast vehicle assembly line, and soya products are displayed in the Ford Motor Company's Industrialized American Barn.

MONKEY BUSINESS

King Kong, a film directed by Merian Cooper and Ernest Schoedsack, breaks all box office records. It stars Fay Wray, Robert Armstrong, the Empire State Building, and special effects by Willis H O' Brien.

RIGHT: Pretty in polythene, despite the weather.

THE LONG KNIVES AND THE LONG MARCH

Hitler consolidates his position by despatching the enemy within during the Night of the Long Knives. In China, the Long March begins as Chinese Communists, including Mao Zedong, begin their epic walk to escape from Chiang Kai-shek's Nationalist troops. In the Soviet Union, Stalin's purges continue unchecked. In the United States, the first stirrings of black Islam are heard. Tornadoes tear across the Dust Bowl of the Midwest, devastating already-depleted prairies. In Italy, Fascist dictator Mussolini hitches his star to the Italian football team's triumph in the second World Cup.

1934

May	23	Bonnie Parker and Clyde Barrow die in a hail of bullets
June	10	Italy wins football's second World Cup
	30	The Night of the Long Knives among Germany's Nazis
July	2	Lázaro Cárdenas, revolutionary leader, becomes president of Mexico
	25	Chancellor Dollfuss assassinated in Austria
Sep	26	Liner *Queen Mary* launched
Oct	21	The Long March begins in China

STORMTROOPERS STORMED

German chancellor Hitler crushes the S.A. (Sturmabteilung), known and feared as the Brown Shirts, and kills their leaders in the Night of the Long Knives. The excuse for the killing is that the S.A. were plotting a coup, but as a result, Hitler now has complete control over his party. Other opponents of the regime are also killed.

PURGE AND PURGE AGAIN

Stalin begins a massive purge of his opponents following the assassination of the Communist Party leader in Leningrad, Sergei Kirov. It is possible that Stalin ordered Kirov's murder himself, but over the next four years more than seven million people are arrested and three million people killed through execution or forced labor. Those killed include more than half the generals in the Red Army, as well as many leading Communist party members.

HEIL HITLER

Germany: President Hindenburg dies and Hitler takes absolute power, abolishing the presidency and making himself Führer and Reich chancellor. More than 90 percent of voters approve of the action in a referendum held later in the month.

DOLLFUSS ASSASSINATED

Members of the Austrian Nazi Party attempt a coup by killing the chancellor, Engelbert Dollfuss. The unsuccessful coup follows the attempt by the Socialists to seize power in February, and further weakens Austrian independence. The Nazis keep up the pressure to unite Austria with Germany.

THE LONG MARCH

Chinese Communists begin the Long March to escape attacks from the Nationalist government. An estimated 100,000 people leave Jiangxi in southern China and march 6,000 miles to safety in Yanan in the northern province of Shaanxi. They will arrive in October 1935.

CONNUBIAL RADIOACTIVITY

French husband and wife physicists Jean-Frédéric and Irène Joliot-Curie discover how to make radioactive elements artificially; they share a Nobel Prize in 1935.

DIONNE QUINTS

Oliva Dionne gives birth to five girls in Callanda, Ontario. Canada's Dionne quints are the first recorded case of quintuplets to be born in one delivery and survive. They are taken away from their parents and raised in a nursery as a kind of public spectacle.

STREAMLINED CARS

Four manufacturers introduce streamlined cars at the International Car Exhibition in Berlin: the models are the Chrysler-Airflow, the Steyr 32 PS, the Tatra 77, and the 1-litre DKW.

ABOVE: Alcatraz prison, on an island in California's San Francisco Bay, opened in 1836 as a military penitentiary and is a state prison from 1934 to 1963.

CAT'S-EYE ROAD STUDS

English road engineer Percy Shaw patents cat's-eye road studs, invented for marking out roads to make them easier to see while driving in fog or at night. They will be in use in 1935.

FORZA ITALIA

Italy triumphs on home soil in the second football World Cup. Thirty-two countries take part but holders Uruguay do not participate. The Italians beat Czechoslovakia 2–1 in the final. This is a great propaganda coup for Mussolini and the Fascists and the Italian team gave the Fascist salute before kick-off.

BLACK ISLAM

Black Muslims at the Temple of Islam, a black sect organized in Detroit by Walli Farrad (W.D. Fard), are led by former Baptist teacher Elijah Poole (Elijah Muhammad), Farad's assistant until his disappearance in 1934, who styles himself the "Messenger of Allah" and advocates black separatism.

DUST DISASTER

Dust storms blow 300 million tons of topsoil from the U.S. Midwest into the Atlantic; some 300 million acres are damaged, the result of the plowing of virgin lands when wheat prices were high during World War I.

DIVING FOR GRAVITY

Dutch Professor Felix Andries Vening Meinesz, who has been using submarines to investigate gravity, makes his longest, deepest, and most widely reported dive so far in the submarine K18.

CULTURAL STUDIES

Ruth Benedict, a social anthropologist at Columbia University, publishes *Patterns of Culture*, a groundbreaking work that disseminates the concept of culture and, by describing Native American and contemporary European cultures, helps combat current racist attitudes.

DAWN OF THE PLASTIC AGE

Perspex, a colorful, transparent acrylic plastic, is produced commercially in the U.K. by ICI. The process, discovered in 1930 by ICI chemist Roland Hill, was improved in 1932–33 by John W.C. Crawford. It incorporates research carried out earlier in the century by German chemists.

COLLECT $200

Monopoly, the game that makes a capitalist of everyone, is launched in the United States. It will be translated to suit the property map of many other countries.

BELOW: Representatives of the German army honor their dead from World War I as they rearm for the next conflict.

SOMETHING FOR THE WEEKEND

In Britain, Durex manufacture condoms for male contraception. Trojan is a popular U.S. brand.

CHEESE PLEASE

The cheeseburger is the inspiration of a restaurateur in Louisville, Kentucky, who places a slice of cheese on top of grilled meat inside a hamburger bun and lets it soften, before serving it in his restaurant.

THE BACHELORS

French novelist Henri de Montherlant publishes *The Bachelors*, a study of two aging aristocrats. It combines humor with tenderness and comments on a society in which such people no longer fit. Probably his best work, the book is moving because it finds emotional accommodation for the senile and foolish.

WE ROB BANKS

Bonnie Parker and Clyde Barrow, lovers and thieves, die in a hail of machine-gun bullets in Louisiana. Their two-year crime spree has made them famous and they have become a regular feature in the local media. They will be immortalized by Faye Dunaway and Warren Beatty in Arthur Penn's film *Bonnie and Clyde* (1967).

DUCKS ON FILM

Irascible fowl Donald Duck joins the animated Disney menagerie.

ABOVE: Marie and Pierre Curie work together on the characteristics of magnetism and on radioactivity, a word Marie herself coined in 1898.

DEATH AND THE ARTIST

German graphic artist Käthe Kollwitz begins her series of lithographs (her last such series) that anticipates images from concentration camps. She combines her compassion with self-portraiture.

PENGUIN CLASSIC

Penguins at London Zoo move into a concrete rookery designed by internationally acclaimed Russian architect Berthold Lubetkin and his London-based group Tecton. One of Britain's best modern buildings, it uses dramatic curving concrete ramps to stunning effect — not only are they beautiful to look at, but they provide an ideal environment for the pool's inhabitants.

MARIE CURIE
(née MARIA SKLODOWSKA)
(1867–1934)

The Warsaw-born French physicist has died of leukemia, having spent some 40 years working with radioactivity. In Warsaw she worked as a governess to save the money that would enable her to study physics in Paris. She and her husband Pierre Curie were awarded the Nobel Prize for Physics for work on the study of magnetism and radioactivity, with Antoine Becquerel, in 1903, and after Pierre's death she received the Nobel Prize for Chemistry in 1911 for isolating pure radium. She developed X-radiography during World War I and from 1918 until her death was director of the Radium Institute in Paris.

NAZI SUPREMACY

Adolf Hitler takes power after the German government collapses in January and street warfare breaks out between the Nazis and Communist party members. Apart from Hitler, there are only two Nazis in the 11-member cabinet; the rest are right-wing Nationalists who believe they can curb the excesses of the Nazi Party.

OPPOSITE ABOVE LEFT: Nazism looks to the glorious past when the Knights Templar were the military ideal.

OPPOSITE ABOVE RIGHT: Hitler's desire for a powerful empire is reflected in the legionary-style standards of his troops.

OPPOSITE BELOW: The Nazi ideology is forcefully directed at women and young people as well as the military.

ABOVE: Hitler and his mistress Eva Braun. They will marry in a Berlin bunker on April 29, 1945.

BELOW: Hitler understands the power of public appearances and how crowds behave under a charismatic leader.

GERMANY REARMS AND ITALY GOES TO WAR

War clouds begin to drift together over Europe. France and Russia ally in unexpressed apprehension at German expansionism. Hitler makes his intentions clear by creating the German Air Force (Luftwaffe) and reintroducing conscription. He also proves himself to be a master media manipulator with a sound grip on the usefulness of propaganda. Spectacular rallies in Nuremberg, filmed by Leni Riefenstahl, bedazzle the world as anti-Semitism is enshrined in German law. Not to be outdone, Mussolini foments war in Ethiopia. As if anticipating the world-shattering events to come, Charles Richter devises the scale named after him for measuring the force of earthquakes.

1935

Feb	27	Shirley Temple is the youngest person ever to win an Oscar	**June**	28	Roosevelt orders the building of Fort Knox
Mar	16	Germany introduces conscription	**Sep**	8	Alexis Stakhanov, a prodigiously productive Russian coalminer, is established by Stalin as the heroic ideal of the Soviet Worker.
	21	Persia renames itself Iran			
Apr	11	Dust storms sweeps across the American Midwest		10	U.S. senator Huey Long dies after being shot two days earlier by Dr. Carl Weiss
May	19	T.E. Lawrence dies after a motor-cycling accident five days earlier		15	Hitler introduces laws to exclude German Jews from public life
	25	Jesse Owens breaks five world records in one day	**Oct**	2	Italy invades Ethiopia

SAARLAND GOES HOME
Separated from Germany by the Treaty of Versailles, the coal-rich region of Saarland votes overwhelmingly to return to German control.

FRANCE AND RUSSIA ALLY
The U.S.S.R. and France sign a mutual assistance pact pledging assistance if either is attacked. The pact reveals fears in both countries about the intentions of the Nazi government in Germany.

INDIA SCENTS FREEDOM
The British Parliament passes the Government of India Act, which creates a central legislature in Delhi, grants greater self-government to provincial governments, and separates Burma and Aden from India. The Act goes some way to granting India full self-government.

ABOVE: One of the many rallies held by Hitler and the Nazis. The Führer's emotional speeches were heard by thousands of Germans.

INSTITUTIONALIZED ANTI-SEMITISM
Hitler announces new anti-Jewish laws at a mass rally in Nuremberg. Marriage between Jews and non-Jews is banned, and Jews are excluded from working in public services. The new laws are the latest in a long line of anti-Jewish measures in Germany.

GERMANY CALLING UP
Hitler introduces the Luftwaffe (Air Force) and announces that he is reintroducing conscription, and plans an army of 50,000. Both acts make nonsense of the Treaty of Versailles, which was designed to curb German military expansion.

UNIVERSAL TURING MACHINE

British mathematician Alan Turing (1912–54) devises a theoretical machine — the Universal Turing Machine — for solving mathematical problems; it is never built, but leads to many aspects of modern computers.

PORGY AND BESS

George Gershwin (1898–1927) wanted to create an American opera, and this is the result, his last major work. Its use of a black American cast, its tunes, and its ability to close the gap between classical and popular music have kept it in the repertoire ever since.

ONE DAY AT A TIME

Alcoholics Anonymous is founded anonymously in New York City by ex-alcoholics Bill Wilson and Dr Robert H. Smith as a self-help and support group for alcoholics.

BERG'S VIOLIN CONCERTO

Alban Berg's concerto is famous for combining modern musical techniques (a 12-note row) with quotations from a Lutheran chorale (*Es ist genug*), finally played in Bach's harmonization at the end of the piece. The work is a memorial to Manon Gropius, who died at the age of 18.

EARTHQUAKE SCALE

U.S. seismologist Charles F. Richter devises a scale — the Richter Scale — for measuring the magnitude of earthquakes. Each number on the scale equals ten times the force of the number below it.

FIRST SUCCESSFUL RADAR

In great secrecy Scottish physicist Robert Watson-Watt builds the first effective radar equipment for detecting aircraft; he is subsidized by the British government.

NYLON INVENTED

U.S. chemist Wallace H. Carothers, working for the Du Pont Company, invents nylon by polymerizing (making large molecules) of two substances called adipic acid and hexamethylene adipamide; large-scale production begins in 1938.

WAR BETWEEN ITALY AND ETHIOPIA

Italian forces under Fascist leader Benito Mussolini invade the independent African nation of Ethiopia using aircraft, chemical weapons, and armor. The ill-equipped Ethiopians are forced back and Emperor Haile Selassie flees the capital, Addis Ababa. League of Nations sanctions against Italy are ineffective, and Italy eventually leaves the League in 1937. The Italian king is proclaimed emperor of Abyssinia, as the Italians call their new acquisition. Ethiopia remains under Italian control until 1941 when British, French, and Ethiopian forces reinstate the emperor.

THE TRIUMPH OF THE WILL

Shot at the Nuremberg Nazi Party Conference the previous year, this film by Leni Riefenstahl is one of the most effective pieces of Nazi propaganda. She makes it after impressing Hitler with a short film of the previous rally. Her work is a key plank in Hitler's propaganda platform.

FAST WORK

In his car Bluebird, British driver Malcolm Campbell advances the land speed record past the 300 mile per hour barrier. He records a speed of 301.129 miles per hour at the Bonneville Salt Flats in America.

FIRST WONDER DRUGS

The first sulphonamide drugs are introduced when German bacteriologist Gerhard Domagk discovers that the red dye prontosil rubra is an active antibacterial agent. Prontosil itself is no longer used.

OPINION POLLS

George Gallup, an Iowa statistician, is asked to gauge reader reaction to newspaper features and founds the American Institute of Public Opinion to carry out market and political research.

CENTRAL PARK

The first Dutch national park, De Hoge Veluwe, is founded in central Holland. It is the gift of Anthony George Kroller.

WORKING LIGHT

The Anglepoise lamp, a pivoting desk lamp with a jointed arm designed by a British designer, George Carwardine, is produced in the U.K.

BEER TO GO

Beer in easy-carry, throwaway metal cans is marketed by Kreuger in New Jersey, and launched in New York City.

PAYING TO PARK

The first parking meters appear in the streets of Oklahoma City. They were designed and patented in 1932 by the editor of the town's newspaper, Charles Magee.

CAN YOU HEAR ME?

The first wearable hearing aid, with an electric valve and a battery-operated amplifier weighing 2.25 pounds is introduced by its British inventor, A. Edwin Stevens, who founds a company, Amplivox, to market it.

COLOR PICTURES

The Kodak Company introduces Kodachrome film for taking color transparencies.

ABOVE: An early type of mobile radar detector. Radar, first developed in the U.K., will be an important defensive advantage in World War II.

ALFRED DREYFUS
(c.1859–1935)

The French army officer and subject of a *cause célèbre* has died. Dreyfus, born c.1859 of Jewish family, was falsely accused of treason in 1893–94 and sent for life imprisonment to Devil's Island. France was strongly divided over the case, and through the active support of many people in political and intellectual life, including the writer Emile Zola and the statesman Clemenceau, he was eventually reinstated in 1906. He went on to fight in World War I and was awarded the Légion d'honneur.

THOMAS EDWARD (TE) LAWRENCE
(LAWRENCE OF ARABIA)
(1888–1935)

The author of *Seven Pillars of Wisdom*, Col. T.E. Lawrence (Lawrence of Arabia) has been killed in a motorcycling accident near his home in Dorset. Born in 1888 of Anglo-Irish stock, he encountered the Bedouin people when working on an archaeological dig on the Euphrates as a young man, and became a fervent admirer of their character and way of life. He was an Arab guerrilla leader in the Arab struggle against the Turks (1916) and was a delegate at the Paris Peace Conference in 1919. Later, to escape his own fame, he enlisted in the Royal Air Force under the name J.H. Ross.

WAR IN SPAIN AND THE BIRTH OF THE AXIS POWERS

Spain becomes the theater of European war as General Franco, supported by Nazi Germany and Fascist Italy, fights against Republican Spain (supported by Communists and Socialists from all over Europe and Russia). In Germany, Jesse Owens, the black American superathlete, confounds Hitler by sweeping the board at the Olympic Games in Berlin. Germany, Italy, and Japan join up to become the Axis Powers. In Britain, the prototype of the Spitfire, the fighter plane that will win the Battle of Britain, takes a test flight. The British Broadcasting Corporation transmits the first television programs.

1936

Feb	**26**	Volkswagen factory opens in Germany
Mar	**7**	German troops march into the Rhineland in defiance of the Treaty of Versailles
July	**19**	Spanish Civil War breaks out
Oct	**5**	In England, unemployed workers march from Jarrow to London in protest at unemployment
Dec	**11**	Edward VIII abdicates the British throne

ABOVE: The British film actor and director Charlie Chaplin charms cinema audiences with his comedic but endearing performances.

SPEND, SPEND, SPEND

The British economist John Maynard Keynes (1883–1946) publishes *The General Theory of Employment, Interest, and Money*, which advocates public spending to cure unemployment. Keynesian economic theories become widely accepted within a few years, and form the basis of the postwar economic boom.

FALSE DAWN IN SPAIN

The Popular Front of left-wing parties wins the general election in Spain. Manuel Azaña becomes prime minister and restores the 1931 Republican constitution. Anticlerical and antilandlord sentiments explode throughout Spain, and churches are attacked and land seized.

UNEASE OVER GERMANY

German troops occupy the Rhineland, demilitarized since 1919. The move alarms France, but Britain makes no protest.

BRITAIN IN THE MIDDLE IN PALESTINE

A revolt against British rule in Palestine breaks out among the Arab population. Jews are murdered and Jewish property is attacked. The revolt leads to the intervention of the British army, which is attacked by both Arabs and Jews.

BRITAIN AND EGYPT

Britain ends its protectorate over Egypt, with the exception the Suez Canal Zone, entering into an alliance with Egypt which lasts for 20 years.

LIFE MAGAZINE

Life Magazine, one of the first magazines to take photojournalism to new heights, is launched in the United States by Henry Luce. It influences America's understanding of world events in a way previously unknown.

ANYTHING FOR LOVE

King Edward VIII abdicates because he wishes to marry a divorcee, the American Wallis Simpson. He is succeeded by his younger brother, George VI. Edward goes into exile, marrying Wallis in France the following June.

IVAN PETROVICH PAVLOV
(1849–1936)

The Russian physiologist, whose laboratory experiments with dogs established the theory of conditioned reflex or conditioned response (applicable also to human beings), has died. He won the Nobel Prize for his work in 1904,

---

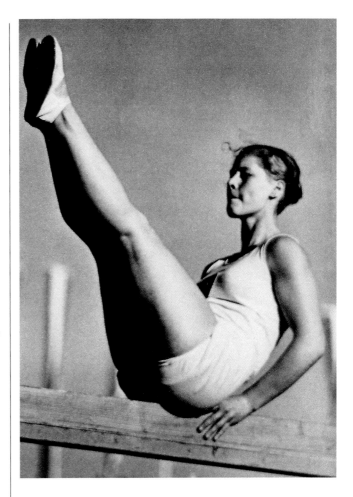

ABOVE: A shot by photographer Leni Riefenstahl of a gymnast taken at the 1936 Olympic Games held in Berlin.

GREAT SHADES

Polaroid lens antiglare sunglasses, developed by U.S. physicist Edwin Land, are introduced by Land-Wheelwight Laboratories.

AXIS POWERS LINE UP

The Italian and German governments sign the anti-Communist Axis Pact; later in the month, Germany signs the Anti-Comintern Pact with Japan.

MODERN TIMES

One of a number of (virtually) silent feature-length films that Charlie Chaplin (1889–1977) produces with his company United Artists, this example brings his brand of serious clowning (tramp as everyman) to bear on a satire of the mechanization of modern life and work. Chaplin is writer, director, producer, and actor (with Paulette Goddard).

OL' MAN RIVER

Black actor and singer Paul Robeson (1898–1976) plays Joe in the film version of *Show Boat*, and turns this song into a personal signature tune and symbol of a black American artist's success and role as social conscience.

MIGRANT MOTHER

Working, like several other great American photographers, for the Farm Security Administration, Dorothea Lange (1895–1965) documents rural America during the Depression — the poverty of the people, the erosion of the land. Lange's photograph, "Migrant Mother," sticks in the public mind more than any other and helps win support for federal aid.

SAFETY IRON

The first electric hand iron with a thermostat goes on sale in the United States. Electric irons first appeared in 1920, but their temperature could not be controlled.

THE PEOPLE'S PORSCHE

The first prototypes of the Volkswagen "Beetle" are displayed at the Berlin Motor Show, designed by Ferdinand Porsche and praised by Adolf Hitler.

MAXIM GORKY
(ALEKSEI MAKSIMOVICH PESHKOV)
(1868–1936)

The Russian writer has died. A largely self-educated peasant who worked in many lowly occupations and described in his writings the life of peasants and outcasts, he was a valiant supporter of the Russian Revolution and had become a national hero.

ABOVE: The dirigible *Hindenburg* and a passenger aircraft in the States.

FALLINGWATER (AKA THE KAUFMANN HOUSE)

Frank Lloyd Wright's most famous house is built over a waterfall at Bear Run, Pennsylvania. It is a daring design, both for the way it seems precariously balanced above the water and for the way it mixes old and new materials (concrete with stone and wood).

MUSIC FOR STRINGS, PERCUSSION, AND CELESTA

One of the major works of Béla Bartók's fruitful period in the 1930s, this piece shows his flair for combining different instrumental colors and for handling rhythm.

SANITARY TOWELS

Kotex sanitary napkins are introduced by Kimberley & Clark Co. of Wisconsin, using a wood-cellulose cotton substitute developed for World War battlefield dressings by German chemist Ernst Mahler. Tampax Inc. is founded in New Brunswick, New Jersey, to produce cotton tampons.

FIRST PUBLIC TV SERVICE

The first regular public electronic TV service is started in Britain by the British Broadcasting Corporation.

ACHTUNG! SPITFIRE!

The first prototype of the British Spitfire fighter plane, designed by Reginald J Mitchell, makes its test flight.

ABOVE: Young German female athletes display the body beautiful. Germany takes gold for the discus and javelin events but does not manage to outpace the athletes from the United States on the track.

ABOVE: Riefenstahl's stylized images, such as this discus thrower, are very powerful. In the real world, the United States takes gold and silver in the discus event and Italy takes bronze.

LEFT: Star of the Olympics is the black American athlete Jesse Owens, who confounds Hitler's "Aryan" expectations, winning gold in four events.

ATROCITIES AND DISASTERS, SHOW TRIALS, AND SNOW WHITE

Japan bombs Shanghai in China and Germany bombs Guernica, in the Basque region of Spain. Both atrocities shock the world. In the Soviet Union, Stalin continues his horrific show trials, an excuse to eliminate his enemies. In the United States, the Golden Gate Bridge opens up California to all comers, but in New Jersey the airship Hindenburg explodes while trying to land. The principle of photocopying is established, but no one can think of how to apply it. Walt Disney cheers a gloomy world with the first full-length animated cartoon, *Snow White and the Seven Dwarfs*.

1937

Apr	**26**	Guernica bombed by Germany at the request of Franco
May	**6**	The airship *Hindenburg* explodes on landing
May	**27**	Golden Gate Bridge opens in San Francisco
Aug	**13**	Japan invades China, attacking Shanghai
Sep	**28**	Hitler and Mussolini stage a joint "Peace Rally" in Berlin

ABOVE: German ground crew help to steady the *Hindenburg*.

232

HINDENBURG DISASTER

On May 6 the German airship Hindenburg is destroyed in a fire while landing at Lakehurst, New Jersey, killing 33 of its 97 occupants; this halts worldwide rigid airship development for generations.

FLOATING ON WATER

The first commercial hydrofoil goes into service on the Rhine River in Germany.

JEAN HARLOW
(HARLEAN CARPENTIER)
(1911–1937)

The American film actress Jean Harlow has died of a brain swelling. Although she was only 26 she had already made a name for herself as a witty and talented screen star. Her films include *Hell's Angels* (1930), *Platinum Blonde* (1931), *Dinner at Eight* (1933), and *Libelled Lady* (1936).

ABOVE: May 6, Lakehurst, New Jersey, the hydrogen-fuelled *Hindenburg* is consumed by fire while docking.

ATROCITY FOR THE BASQUES

Guernica, Spain. German aircraft bomb the Basque town of Guernica in northern Spain, killing many inhabitants. The German Air Force supports the Nationalist forces across Spain, giving them air superiority. Pablo Picasso's response to the bombing of the Basque city, with its images of suffering, is one of his best-known works. It becomes an emblem of the destructiveness and brutality of Fascism. The work creates a powerful visual language through the combination of elements from surrealism and symbolism.

CONTRACEPTION GAINS ACCEPTANCE

Contraception is endorsed by the American Medical Association's Committee on Birth Control, and by Islam's Grand Mufti, who issues a fatwa permitting Muslims to take any measure to avoid conception if both man and woman agree.

ABOVE: Shipping passes under the San Francisco–Oakland Bay Bridge and the new Golden Gate Bridge beyond to reach the Pacific.

MARCHESE GUGLIELMO MARCONI
(1874–1937)

Italian physicist and inventor Guglielmo Marconi, famous for sending the first radio signals across the Atlantic in 1901, has died. His experiments with the newly discovered electromagnetic waves led to the invention of wireless telegraphy. Marconi developed short-wave radio equipment in England, setting up a worldwide radio telegraph network for the British government.

SNOW WHITE AND THE SEVEN DWARFS
Walt Disney's first full-length animated feature film quickly becomes a hit. It paves the way for countless others, both from Disney and from other studios.

SHOW TRIALS
Stalin continues his plan to silence all opposition by putting various opponents "on trial" and shooting them afterwards.

OF MICE AND MEN
John Steinbeck's novel is valued for its sympathetic portrayal of Lennie, the childlike giant who does not know his own strength.

LA GRANDE ILLUSION
This antiwar film, directed by Jean Renoir, son of the impressionist painter Pierre-Auguste Renoir, tells the story of French prisoners of war who plot their escape from a prison camp during World War I. It explores the crosscurrents of values during the war (patriotism versus class ties, for example) and comes out on the side of humanitarianism.

JET ENGINES BUILT
In England, Frank Whittle at last builds his jet aircraft engine (patented in 1930); at the same time, German engineers also build one.

LEFT: King George VI and his family pose after his coronation on May 12.

BARON PIERRE DE COUBERTIN (1863–1937)

The founder of the present-day Olympic Games has died. The modern version of the games held in honor of Zeus at Olympia in Ancient Greece began in Athens in 1896.

XEROGRAPHY INVENTED

American law student Chester Carlson demonstrates a form of copying which can give unlimited numbers of copies. He calls it "dry copying" or xerography. It does not come into use for many years.

GOLDEN GATE BRIDGE

The Golden Gate Bridge spanning the entrance to San Francisco Bay, California, is opened, becoming the world's longest suspension bridge.

RADIO TELESCOPE

The world's first radio telescope is built by a radio amateur, Grote Reber of Illinois, in his back yard; he uses a disc reflector 30 feet across.

CARTS IN THE AISLES

The supermarket cart introduced by Sylvan N. Goldman, owner of Standard Food Markets in Oklahoma City, demonstrates the fast evolution of shopping since 1930, when Harry Socoloff opened the first modern supermarket, the King Kullen Grocery in Queens, New York.

JAVA MAN

Parts of the skull of a one million-year-old hominid are discovered on the island of Java. It is the earliest known evidence of the "missing link" between apes and humans.

CHEAP LIGHT

Energy-efficient fluorescent lighting, developed with help from University of Chicago physicist Arthur Holly Compton, is introduced in the United States by GEC & Westinghouse Electric Corporation.

SHAVE IN THE ROUND

Philips, a Dutch company, produces the Philishave electric razor with circular cutting blades.

SMART MACHINES

The first machine that can learn from experience appears when U.S. engineer Thos Ross makes a mechanical mouse that runs on toy train tracks and learns to find its way through mazes.

ERNEST RUTHERFORD, 1ST BARON RUTHERFORD (1871–1937)

The New Zealand-born British physicist has died. His research into and discoveries concerning the structure and behavior of atoms have earned him the title "father of nuclear physics."

❖ UPDATE ❖
ON THE SINO-JAPANESE WAR

Japanese forces begin a full-scale invasion of China, seizing Beijing and bombing Shanghai in August. Firebombs are used to level Shanghai before the Japanese retake the city they first captured in 1932.

In December, the Japanese capture the city of Nanking: Two hundred fifty thousand people are killed and many raped. Japanese forces continue to press south and west throughout China.

KRISTALLNACHT AND PEACE IN OUR TIME

Germany violates the Treaty of Versailles and grabs the Sudetenland. Hitler himself leads the invading army. At a peace conference in Munich in September, appeasement buys a year of peace and British prime minister Neville Chamberlain brings back the infamous "piece of paper." *Kristallnacht*, a night of looting and wrecking of Jewish shops by uniformed Nazis, shows Hitler's contempt for world opinion. Ballpoint pens and instant coffee come to the aid of hard-pressed journalists and nylon stockings are on sale.

1938

Jan	6	Sigmund Freud and some of his students leave Vienna to work in London
Mar	12	Germany annexes Austria
June	30	The first Superman comic appears
Sep	27	QEI launched
	30	The Munich Peace Agreement is drawn up
Oct	5	Germany occupies Czech Sudetenland
	21	Japan occupies Canton
Nov	10	*Kristallnacht* in Germany; Jewish shops and businesses attacked.
Dec	25	Coelacanth fished up from deep

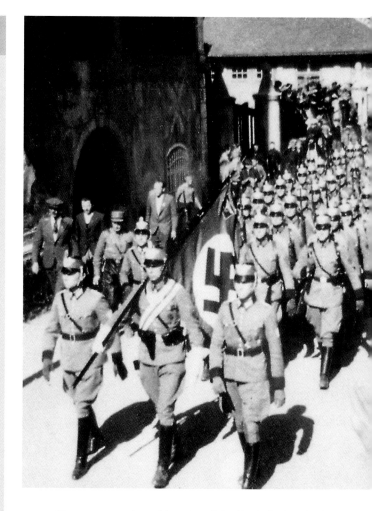

ABOVE: German annexation of Austria and the Czech Sudetenland occurs prior to the outbreak of war in 1939.

ANSCHLUSS

German troops enter Austria and unite the country with Germany. The *Anschluss* (unification) between the two countries is forbidden by the Treaty of Versailles, and alarms the rest of Europe.

GERMANY TAKES SUDETENLAND

Sudeten Germans living on the border with Germany demand autonomy from Czechoslovakia. They are prompted by Hitler, who uses this as an excuse to increase pressure on the Czech government.

PEACE IN OUR TIME?

At a conference in Munich between Britain, France, Italy, and Germany to end the Sudeten crisis, the four powers agree that Czechoslovakia must give up the Sudetenland to Germany. The following month, German troops occupy the territory while Poland seizes the Teschen region. Eduard Benes resigns as president of Czechoslovakia. In November, Hungary occupies southern Slovakia. Czechoslovakia is now effectively dismembered.

THE SOUND OF BREAKING GLASS

In a night of looting and violence, more than 7,000 Jewish shops are attacked and many Jews beaten up. Hundreds of synagogues are burned down. *Kristallnacht*, or the Night of Broken Glass, marks a major attack on the Jewish community in Germany.

HOOVER BUILDING, PERIVALE

Strong geometric forms and sparing use of striking color and pattern mark Wallis Gilbert's factory for Hoover on the outskirts of London as one of the most notable art deco (or Moderne) buildings of its time.

WAR OF THE WORLDS

The power of the mass media is brought home dramatically when thousands panic during this broadcast version of H.G. Wells' science fiction novel *War of the Worlds*, which describes what happens when Martians land on earth. The actor Orson Welles of the Mercury Radio Theatre reads out the lines that scare so many listeners.

PICTURE POST

Not the first picture magazine, but one of the most influential, *Picture Post* brings the news and contemporary events to life with pictures and telling captions to Britain as *Life* is doing for the United States.

BILLY THE KID

Aaron Copland's music brings the hero to life in *Billy the Kid*, his American folk ballet version of an enduring legend, choreographed by Eugene Loring, who also dances the lead role. This is the first of several notable Copland ballet scores based on American folklore.

ABOVE: Orson Welles' radio production of *War of the Worlds* convinces many of his audience that an alien invasion is taking place. His fascination with the power of radio continued throughout his life.

ROCKET DEVELOPMENT

A German team led by engineer Wernher von Braun (1912–27) builds a liquid-fuel rocket that travels about 60 feet, the longest flight yet.

ENTER THE BALLPOINT PEN

Ladislao Biró, a Hungarian journalist, patents the ballpoint pen; it will go into production in 1940 but he makes very little money from it.

SUZANNE LENGLEN
(1899–1938)

The French tennis idol, who was many times a Wimbledon champion, has died. She won her first major championship (women's world hard-court singles in Paris) at the age of 15. She retired in 1927, founded her own tennis school in Paris, and wrote a book on tennis, *Lawn Tennis, the Game of Nations* and a novel, *The Love Game* (both in 1925).

NUCLEAR FISSION DISCOVERED
German radio chemists Otto Hahn and Fritz Strassmann discover nuclear fission by bombarding uranium with neutrons, leading to the development of nuclear power and atomic bombs.

NO MORE BURNT SAUCEPANS
Du Pont engineer Roy Plunkett in the States accidentally discovers polytetrafluroethylene, a plastic better known as Teflon™ or Fluon™; it is used in astronauts' spacesuits and as a nonstick coating for saucepans.

LIVING FOSSIL
In December a South African fisherman hauls up a "living fossil": a coelacanth, a primitive type of fish that scientists hitherto knew only from fossils and believed to have been extinct for 70 million years.

NO MORE DRINKING AND DRIVING
The Drunkometer — the first breathalyzer to test for alcohol in drivers' breath, designed by R.N. Harger — is tested in Indiana, and finds that of 1,750 drivers tested, 250 are drunk.

ABOVE: A parade through Paris to mark the signing of the Entente Cordiale between France and Britain.

ABOVE: Nylon stockings bring smiles of sheer delight and prove popular throughout the world.

ENCORA ITALIA
The Italians repeat their World Cup victory in Paris, France, by beating Hungary 4-2 in the final.

MRS MOODY TAKES WIMBLEDON
American tennis star Helen Wills Moody collects her eighth and final Wimbledon singles crown. With ruthless efficiency, the wins were collected in just nine attempts between 1927 and 1938 and complemented seven US Open titles and six French triumphs.

SAVING THE WHALE
The International Convention for the Regulation of Whaling introduces voluntary quotas for whaling nations, but the Japanese, Russians, and Norwegians ignore the agreement.

AN AWFUL LOT OF COFFEE
Instant coffee is marketed by Nestlé of Switzerland after a request from the Brazilian government to find a use for Brazil's coffee surpluses. Eight years' research have produced a freeze-dried coffee powder that is reconstituted by adding water.

AIR-CONDITIONED JEWELRY
Tiffany & Co.'s new store on Fifth Avenue, New York City, is the first fully air-conditioned store. Invented by W.H. Carrier in 1902, airconditioning has up to now been used for cooling factories.

VICTORY AND FREEDOM
A "V for Victory" campaign is started by two Belgians working for the BBC in London, who realize that "V" stands for *vrijheid* (freedom) in Flemish and Dutch, and *victoire* (victory) in French. The first Vs appear later on walls in occupied Belgium.

SILK STOCKINGS?
Nylon, invented in the United States by Wallace Hume Carothers, who patented it in 1934, is produced commercially by Du Pont in the United States and used to make women's stockings.

GAS IN CHINA
Lewisite poison gas is used by the Japanese against the Chinese during a series of incursions into China via Manchuria, as well as during amphibious landings to seize parts of the hinterland and major ports.

ABOVE: The Duke of Windsor and Wallis Simpson, for whom he gave up the throne.

BELOW: Street fighting in Manchuria as Japan invades the Chinese mainland.

WAR ENGULFS THE WORLD ONCE MORE

A war-torn decade ends with the greatest conflict of them all so far. By the end of the year, most of Europe is at war. Allies and Axis Powers line up on opposite sides and America stays out of the fight. On the silver screen, Dorothy and her three eccentric musketeers make a stand against evil in *The Wizard of Oz* and Scarlett O' Hara endures the Civil War on the losing side in *Gone with the Wind*. Meanwhile, scientists are unlocking the secrets of nuclear fission that will lead to the atomic bomb.

1939

Apr	**7**	Italy invades Albania
May	**22**	Germany and Italy form alliance
July	**20**	New Dalai Lama is discovered in Tibet
Aug	**23**	Hitler and Stalin sign a nonaggression pact
Sep	**1**	Germany invades Poland
	3	Germany and England officially at war
Nov	**8**	Bomb wrecks Munich beer hall where Hitler has been speaking
Dec	**18**	German pocket battleship *Graf Spee* scuttled by her crew

ABOVE: Polish troops mobilize to face the might of the invading German war machine.

WAR AT LAST

German armies invade Poland from the west, with Russian armies later invading from the east. Britain and France declare war on Germany. British children are evacuated from the cities because of fears of air attacks and the British army lands in France to protect it against a possible German attack. A phony war begins as both sides increase war production, but no fighting takes place.

FRANCO VICTORIOUS

The Spanish Civil War ends with victory for the Nationalist forces of General Franco. Britain and France recognize the new government, which represses all dissent and becomes increasingly Fascist in nature. In April, Spain joins Italy, Germany, and Japan in the Anti-Comintern Pact.

SEPTEMBER 1, 1939

This is English poet Auden's poem mourning for a Europe slipping towards war. It confirms his role as leading poet of the prewar period, and social commentator.

BELOW: The New York Giants and the Brooklyn Dodgers open the 1939 season at Ebbets Field, Brooklyn.

OVERTURES TO WAR

In January, Slovakia declares its independence from Czechoslovakia and becomes a German protectorate. Germany annexes the western Czech provinces of Bohemia and Moravia and the eastern province of Ruthenia is seized by Hungary. Hitler enters Prague in triumph. In the same month, Germany seizes the Baltic region of Memel from Lithuania.

In March, following the German takeover of Czechoslovakia, Hitler denounces the German non-aggression pact with Poland, signed in 1934, and demands the Free City of Danzig, on the Baltic, and routes to eastern Prussia through the Baltic corridor, which gives Poland access to the sea. Britain and France pledge to defend Poland from attack. In April, they extend this guarantee to Romania and Greece.

In April, the Soviet Union proposes an alliance with Britain and France against Germany and Italy. Britain refuses, but takes urgent steps to rearm; conscription is introduced and arms production is stepped up. France steps up its war effort.

In August, Stalin and German foreign minister Joachim von Ribbentrop sign the Nazi-Soviet Non-Aggression Pact in Moscow, allowing Germany a free hand in western Poland.

ABOVE: German soldiers advance through the rubble-strewn streets of Warsaw.

ITALY EXPANDS
Italy invades and conquers the Adriatic state of Albania, increasing its empire in the Mediterranean.

FINNEGANS WAKE
James Joyce's *Ulysses* had explored the events of a single day; in *Finnegan's Wake*, Joyce turns to the upside-down, inside-out world of night, sleep, and dreams. He creates his own language (involving multi-linguistic wordplay), to write a book which, because of its difficulty, becomes more talked about than read.

EASTER SUNDAY CONCERT
The Daughters of the American Revolution refuse black singer Marian Anderson's request to sing in Constitution Hall, Washington, D.C., because of her race. Eleanor Roosevelt sponsors an outdoor concert at the Lincoln Memorial instead, and around 100,000 people attend.

PHOTOCOMPOSITION
American inventor William C. Hueber introduces the first photocomposition system, replacing metal type.

THE WIZARD OF OZ
The musical film of the novel by L. Frank Baum stars Judy Garland. She wins a special Academy Award for singing "Somewhere over the Rainbow", and is launched on a series of starring roles in major American films.

GONE WITH THE WIND
The film of Margaret Mitchell's novel quickly becomes a worldwide success. Vivien Leigh stars as Scarlett O'Hara and Clark Gable does not give a damn as Rhett Butler.

STAGECOACH
John Ford's classic western stars the "cowboy's cowboy" John "The Duke" Wayne. This is the film that makes Ford's name synonymous with the western and with films looking back on America's past. It is also Wayne's first major role in a big film, and so establishes him as a major star.

FIRST JET AIRCRAFT
The German Heinkel He 178, the world's first jet-propelled aircraft, makes its test flight, with an engine designed by Dr Hans von Ohain; it reaches 313 miles per hour.

SIKORSKY HELICOPTER
Russian-born U.S. engineer Igor Sikorsky designs his first helicopter, the VS-300; it makes a tethered flight in September, but is not suitable for mass production.

NUCLEAR FISSION

Austrian-born physicists Otto Frisch and his aunt Lise Meitner continue the work started by Meitner and Otto Hahn. They realize that the production of barium atoms after the bombardment of uranium nuclei with neutrons means that the nucleus has been split, and call the process "nuclear fission;" this leads to atomic power.

DDT COMES INTO ITS OWN

Swiss chemist Paul Hermann Müller finds that dichlorodiphenyltrichloroethane — DDT, discovered in 1874 — is a powerful insecticide; it is successfully tested against the Colorado beetle, a potato pest.

THE HEAT OF THE SUN

The first solar-powered house is built as an experiment at the Massachusetts Institute of Technology. A solar panel on the roof heats water stored in a tank.

AN EARLY ANTIBIOTIC

French scientist René Dubos, working in New York City, discovers the antibiotic tyrothricin, but it proves too poisonous for use on humans.

LITTLE LEAGUE

Carl Stotz and George and Bert Bebble form Little League Baseball in Williamsport, Pennsylvania. The format for youth baseball has since spread across America and the world, and the Little League season now culminates in the Little League World Series between an American team and a foreign side.

THE WORLD'S FAIR

New York's World's Fair focuses on Trylon and Perisphere, a 728-foot-high pyramidal tower and a gigantic globe that exhibit futuristic films. Innovative exhibits from 60 nations include a pressure cooker; Electro, a robot who speaks; and Sparks, a dog who barks and wags his tail.

ABOVE: On April 26, 1939, Captain Wendel of the German Luftwaffe sets a world air speed record of 468.9 miles per hour.

FINNS WRESTLE WITH THE BEAR

The Soviet Union invades Finland in November, but the attack is thwarted by the Finnish army used to fighting in winter conditions. The Soviet Union has demanded that Finland demilitarize its border defenses and cede islands and a base to the U.S.S.R. Finland has refused and in November the U.S.S.R. sends in an estimated 1 million men against 300,000 Finnish troops. Defending the Mannerheim line and using their skills as ski troops they inflict heavy losses on the Soviets.

❖KEY DATES❖
IN THE RUSSO-FINNISH WAR

Dec 11, 1939–Jan 8, 1940 SUOMUSSALMI: Two Soviet divisions are annihilated in the woods of eastern Finland in a succession of ambushes and running battles.

Feb 1940 MANNERHEIM LINE: The defenses across the Karelian Isthmus are subject to intense air and artillery bombardment and heavy attacks and in February, despite heavy losses, the Soviet forces break through. This forces the Finns, who had 25,000 killed and 44,000 wounded, to accept Soviet terms. Soviet casualties are estimated at 200,000 dead.

THE POWER OF THE MOVIES

ABOVE LEFT: Barbara Stanwyck, star of many a Hollywood *film noir* and always the most fatale of femmes.

ABOVE: Joan Crawford, undisputed queen of the 1930s genre known as women's pictures.

LEFT: Dashing screen hero Clark Gable will enlist and train as an aerial gunner when the United States enters the war.

ABOVE: Hollywood hoofer Fred Astaire swings a mean shoe on a wartime fundraising tour.

ABOVE: The Hollywood Bond
Cavalcade, galaxy of movie
stars touring the United States
to raise money for War Bonds.

RIGHT: Sound stages at the
Warner Brothers Studios in
Burbank, California.

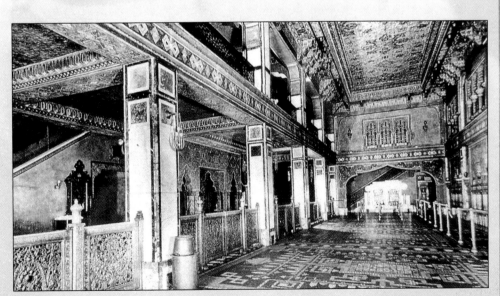

BACKGROUND: The Bay Shore –
Sunrise Drive-In Theater, which
has room for 1,900 cars.

WAR AND PEACE

America joins in the war after Pearl Harbor is attacked and warfare goes global, dominating the first half of the decade. The dropping of the atomic bomb on Hiroshima ends the war in the East but the power unleashed frightens enough people to lead to the Campaign for Nuclear Disarmament. The Iron Curtain descends, separating East from West, and NATO is set up in an effort to avoid further conflict. A spontaneous, life-affirming "baby boom" brightens the immediate post-war period as people look forward in optimism.

RIGHT: Men dwarfed by weaponry, a key image for the decade of the nuclear bomb.

1940-1949

KEY EVENTS OF THE DECADE

- PENICILLIN DEVELOPED
- PEARL HARBOR
- COLOR TELEVISION
- ARAB LEAGUE
- WORLD WAR II ENDS
- UNITED NATIONS
- HIROSHIMA
- IRON CURTAIN
- ATOMIC POWER

- THE NEW LOOK
- THE BABY BOOM
- MARSHALL AID
- PARTITION OF INDIA
- GANDHI ASSASSINATED
- STATE OF ISRAEL FOUNDED
- NATO FORMED
- PEOPLE'S REPUBLIC OF CHINA FOUNDED

WORLD POPULATION: 2,295 MILLION

THE DARKEST HOUR FOR THE ALLIES

A desperate year; as the war escalates, Holland, Belgium, and France fall in rapid succession and Britain stands temporarily alone. Allied troops are snatched from death on the beaches of Dunkirk. Winston Churchill takes over as prime minister and the Battle of Britain is fought between the Luftwaffe and the RAF in the skies over England. General de Gaulle escapes to England to rally French resistance. In Poland, the Warsaw Ghetto is forced on the Jewish population. Leo Trotsky is assassinated. One of the few gleams of light relief is Charlie Chaplin's portrayal of an absurd mustachioed megalomaniac in his film *The Great Dictator*.

1940

Mar	12	War between Finland and Russia ends
Apr	9	Denmark falls to Germany
May	13	Winston Churchill becomes prime minister of Great Britain
	28	Belgium falls to Hitler
June	4	Allied troops evacuated from Dunkirk
	18	Charles de Gaulle escapes to England
	19	Italy declares war on the Allies
	23	France surrenders
Aug	21	Leon Trotsky assassinated in Mexico
Sep	27	Japan makes formal alliance with Italy and Germany
Oct	15	Chaplin's film *The Great Dictator* released

ABOVE: The U.S. base at Pearl Harbor is attacked unexpectedly and at dawn by some 360 Japanese aircraft.

PEARL HARBOR

Following the Japanese attack on the U.S. fleet in Pearl Harbor in the Pacific Ocean, the United States enters the war. The U.S. economy is put on a war footing, with factories turned over to war production and thousands of women pressed into factory work.

YELLOW STAR

The infamous yellow Star of David is imposed on German Jews over the age of six to make them easily recognizable. Jews in Poland already wear such a star.

AMY JOHNSON
(1903–1941)

The English pioneer aviator has been lost in a plane accident while on active service in the British Air Transport Auxiliary. She was the first woman to fly solo from England to Australia in 1930, and made several record solo flights, as well as flying across the Atlantic with her husband, James Mollison, in 1933 and with him to India in 1934.

CITIZEN KANE

A triumph for Orson Welles (although to begin with it does not do well at the box office), this film charts the life of a newspaper magnate (based on William Randolph Hearst). Welles cowrites, produces, directs, and stars. He is established as a Hollywood prodigy, combining camerawork, music, narrative technique, and lighting to produce one of the most impressive films ever.

ATLANTIC CHARTER

British prime minister Winston Churchill and President Franklin D. Roosevelt meet on board a warship off the Newfoundland coast and agree the Atlantic Charter, which ties the two countries closely together.

TWIN-ENGINED JET FIGHTER . . .

The world's first twin-engined fighter aircraft, the German Heinkel He 280, makes its first flight in April, but does not go into production.

. . . AND FIRST BRITISH JET

In May the Gloster E-28/3 experimental aircraft, using one of Frank Whittle's jet engines, makes its maiden flight; it goes into production in 1944 as the Gloster Meteor.

JAMES AUGUSTINE ALOYSIUS JOYCE
(1882–1941)

The influential Irish writer has died in Zurich after an operation for a duodenal ulcer. Since 1902 he has lived mainly in Europe, principally in Paris, where the "stream of consciousness" novel *Ulysses* was published in 1922. *The Dubliners* (1914), *A Portrait of the Artist as a Young Man* (1914-15), and *Finnegans Wake* (1939) are among his other works.

SYMPHONY FOR LENINGRAD

The first three movements of Dmitri Shostakovich's Symphony No. 7 are written while the city is being bombarded. The music is performed with the echoes of bombs in the background. It becomes a work that is closely identified with the heroic Russian role in World War II.

LET US NOW PRAISE FAMOUS MEN

American photographer Walker Evans (1903–75) had worked with writer and journalist James Agee (1909–65) in the late 1930s, taking photographs in Alabama to go with Agee's text about the Depression in the South. The intention was to produce an article for *Fortune* magazine, but it was not used, so Agee expanded the text and the result is this landmark book.

MOTHER COURAGE

German dramatist Bertolt Brecht's great play is first performed in Zurich. It is a complex play, in which Brecht tries to show that war makes us, including Mother Courage herself, inhuman. But audiences respond positively to the vitality of the main character, and Brecht changes the text after this performance.

BUG SPRAYS

Insecticides in aerosols are supplied to U.S. troops in the Pacific. These "bug bombs," using freon gas, were developed by research chemist L.D. Goodhue and entomologist W.N. Sullivan as a protection against insect-borne diseases. The aerosol can was invented in Norway in 1926.

SPAM, SPAM, SPAM, SPAM, SPAM, SPAM, SPAM

Spam, a tinned processed meat made mainly from pork, becomes a wartime staple for troops and civilians.

BELOW: In the New York Yankees squad are (left to right) Joe DiMaggio, Charles (King Kong) Keller, and Bill Dickey.

ABOVE: The powerful beams of antiaircraft lights lace the night sky.

(ADELINE) VIRGINIA WOOLF
(née STEPHEN)
(1882–1941)

The English experimental writer and modernist has committed suicide. Having long suffered from bouts of depression, she was found drowned in the Ouse River near her home in Sussex. Her works include *Mrs Dalloway* (1925), *To the Lighthouse* (1927), and the feminist essay *A Room of One's Own* (1929). She and her husband Leonard Woolf founded the Hogarth Press, publisher of T.S. Eliot, in 1917 and her name is synonymous with the Bloomsbury Group.

FIRST POLYESTER FIBRE
J.R. Whitfield and J.T. Dickson, scientists working for the British Calico Printers' Association, make the first polyester textile fiber, later marketed under the names of Terylene™ and Dacron™.

COLD COMFORT
Freeze-dried orange juice is supplied to the U.S. army after freeze-drying is adapted for the preservation of foods and drinks in the United States. Frozen food or drink, dried in a heated chamber, can be reconstituted quickly without loss of flavor.

DIGNIFIED IN STONE
The Mount Rushmore National Memorial is unveiled. The granite faces of presidents Lincoln, Washington, Jefferson, and Roosevelt survey the Black Hills of Dakota. The work was begun 15 years previously by sculptor Gutzon Borglum, who did not live to see his masterpiece.

WORLD WAR II

The greatest conflict of the twentieth century, World War II touches every continent and devastates some. The best estimate for casualties is 15 million military dead and 25 million military wounded. Civilian deaths are about 38 million. Huge parts of the European and Russian infrastructure are destroyed and the populations of Eastern European states displaced as national borders are adjusted.

❖KEY DATES❖
WORLD WAR II

March 12, 1938 AUSTRIA ANNEXED German troops enter Austria to ensure *Anschluss* (union) with Germany.

March 15, 1939 CZECHOSLOVAKIA German troops enter Prague, Czechoslovakia dismantled.

Sept 1–Oct 7, 1939 POLAND Poland is crushed by armored and mechanized forces backed by bombers and fighter ground attack aircraft. German casualties are 14,000 killed and 30,300 wounded, Polish casualties are believed to exceed 120,000 plus 450,000 prisoners.

Sept 3, 1939 BRITAIN Britain declares war on Germany.

April 9, 1940 DENMARK The tiny country is seized by the Germans to give them airfields for the attack on Norway.

April 8–9–June 8, 1940 NORWAY The German invasion of Norway, intended to protect supplies of iron ore from Sweden, cost the Germans 5,300 killed and wounded, three cruisers, ten destroyers, eight submarines, 11 transports and 11 other ships.

May 10–June 25, 1940 HOLLAND The Germans attack in the west, which draws British and French troops into Holland before the Germans break through at Sedan and in a drive to the channel cut the British off from France. Holland falls on May 15 and Belgium on May 27, France capitulates on June 22 and hostilities end on June 25. On the ground, Germany suffers 27,000 killed, 110,000 wounded and 18,000 missing. France loses 90,000 dead and 200,000 wounded and 1.9 million are either taken prisoner or missing. The Belgians have 23,000 casualties and the Dutch 10,000. Britain loses 68,000 casualties. In the air, the Luftwaffe lose 1,284 aircraft, the RAF 931, and the French 560.

ABOVE: A mass roll-call of SA, SS, and NSKK troops in Nuremberg. During the first year of the war, Germany has the manpower, equipment, and will to win that gives her a great advantage.

DUNKIRK EVACUATION

German tank divisions trap British, French, and Belgian troops around the port of Dunkirk on the north coast of France. Between May 26 and June 4, 1940, in one of the most dramatic events of the war, 338,000 soldiers are rescued by the Royal Navy with assistance from the French and many civilian vessels from England.

ABOVE: Nazis rally in Nuremberg.

BELOW: Hitler announces the annexation of Austria to an ecstatic Reichstag.

RIGHT: A Czech woman's grief-stricken submission as Germany annexes Czechoslovakia, in one of many expansionist actions towards the east.

THEATERS OF WAR

NORTH AFRICA AND THE MEDITERRANEAN 1940–43

The campaign in North Africa fought by the British with United States' assistance in late 1942 against the Italians and Germans (Axis Powers) is unique in World War II. The theater has few civilians so casualties are confined to the armies and the tactics developed for the desert are similar to those employed in naval warfare.

TOBRUK
Jan 22–Nov, 1941 and June 18–June 20, 1942

The former Italian port is held by British and Commonwealth forces behind German lines from January to November 1941. However, when it is again besieged by the Germans in June 1942, they press their attacks home and this time the port is captured with valuable supplies and 33,000 prisoners.

EL ALAMEIN Oct 23–Nov 4, 1942

The British and Commonwealth attack the Axis forces, who are well dug in. The British losses are 2,350 killed and 8,950 wounded, with 2,260 missing. The Axis losses are 10,000 killed, 15,000 wounded, and 30,000 captured.

TORCH LANDINGS
Nov 8, 1942

Some 36,000 British and American forces land in two locations in French Northwest Africa, in effect squeezing Axis forces from the west.

YUGOSLAVIA AND GREECE
April 6–April 23, 1941

After the Italian Army becomes embroiled in Greece and Yugoslavia launches a coup against its pro-Axis government, Hitler decides to invade Yugoslavia and Greece. German casualties in Yugoslavia are 558 while 345,000 Yugoslavian soldiers are captured. In Greece the Germans have 4,500 casualties. Greek losses are 70,000 killed or wounded and 270,000 captured. British forces assisting the Greeks suffer 12,000 casualties.

OPERATION "MERCURY" May 20, 1941

German airborne assault on Crete. The Luftwaffe lands 22,750 men using 493 Ju 52 transport aircraft and about 80 gliders. Though it is a German victory, 4,500 of their men are killed and 150 transport aircraft lost.

ABOVE: General Montgomery's determination overcame Field Marshal Rommel's Afrika Korps.

LEFT: Russians break through German defenses outside Leningrad.

SOVIET UNION AND EASTERN FRONT 1941–44

Hitler boasts that the Soviet Union is so decrepit that "We have only to kick in the door and the whole rotten structure will come crashing down." Invading the U.S.S.R. is the logical outcome of the Nazi doctrine.

SIEGE OF LENINGRAD
Sept 1, 1941–Jan 27, 1944

Besieged for almost the duration of the war, Leningrad withstands German attacks. By 1944 nearly one million of its inhabitants have been killed or starved to death.

MINSK June–July, 1941

A battle of encirclement in which 15 Soviet divisions are destroyed.

SEVASTOPOL Nov 1941–July 3, 1942

The Black Sea port and Soviet naval base is besieged by ten German infantry divisions with 120 batteries of artillery. The Soviet forces number 106,000 men with 700 guns and mortars. Though the port is captured some defenders are evacuated by small boat.

KHARKOV Oct 24, 1941–Aug 22, 1943

The scene of heavy fighting in 1942 and 1943, Kharkov is the location for a major battle of encirclement in which 250,000 Soviet prisoners are taken in 1942.

STALINGRAD Aug 19, 1942–Jan 31, 1943

The attack on the Russian city is a disaster for Hitler, leading to the defeat of the German 6th Army and the loss of 1.5 million men, 3,500 tanks, 12,000 guns and mortars, 75,000 vehicles, and 3,000 aircraft.

KURSK July 5–July 17, 1943

This is the German counteroffensive, of which the Russians are well aware through signals intelligence. In the fighting both sides lose over 1,500 tanks, but the Russians swing on to the offensive and the Germans lose the initiative for good.

BERLIN April 16–May 2, 1945

The final battle for the German capital costs the Russians 100,000 killed, while 136,000 prisoners are taken. It is estimated that 100,000 civilians are killed in the fighting.

WARSAW UPRISING

Between August 1 and October 2, 1944 Polish patriots rise to liberate their city from German occupation as the Soviet army approaches. However, on Stalin's orders they halt until the Poles have been defeated.

ABOVE: A massive bombardment is launched at Monte Cassino.

SICILY AND ITALY 1943–45

Churchill proposes that Italy should be attacked since he describes it as "the soft underbelly" of the Axis. It proves to be a much tougher undertaking than imagined, involving amphibious operations and fighting in mountains in bitter winter weather.

SICILY July 10–Aug 18, 1943

Landings by British and American forces push the Axis towards the Strait of Messina. They are able to evacuate 40,000 Germans and 60,000 Italians but suffer 178,000 casualties and captured. Allied casualties are 31,158 including 11,923 Americans.

SALERNO Sept 9, 1943

The landing on the mainland of Italy by U.S. and British forces is vigorously counterattacked by the Germans. Only after reinforcements have been rushed in does it become secure, and on September 15 the Germans begin to pull back.

MONTE CASSINO Feb 15–May 18, 1944

This strong defensive position costs the Allies 21,000 casualties including 4,100 killed in action. When Cassino falls the Allies take 20,000 prisoners and open the road to Rome.

ANZIO Jan 22–May 25, 1944

An amphibious operation intended to outflank Cassino, the Anzio attack becomes in effect stuck on the beaches where the U.S. forces suffer 21,000 casualties and the Germans about 11,000.

ROME June 5, 1944

Liberated by the Americans, the drive on the Italian capital city actually allows the German 10th Army to escape as a formed unit.

THE FIGHT FOR EUROPE

NORMANDY AND NORTHWEST EUROPE 1942–45

BRUNEVAL Feb 27–28, 1942

In a combined operation, a company of British paratroops launches a raid against a German radar station and an RAF technician removes key components before the force is evacuated by the Royal Navy.

DIEPPE Aug 19, 1942

A large-scale raid against the French port of Dieppe by 5,000 Canadians and 1,000 Commandos is almost a complete disaster. The Canadians lose 215 officers and 3,164 men, the Commandos 24 officers and 223 men, while German losses are 345 killed and 268 wounded.

COUTANCES
July 17, 1944

USAF P-38 Lightnings are involved in the first napalm attack in Normandy launched against a fuel depot at Coutances.

BELOW: The Allied raid on Dieppe costs the lives of thousands of Canadian troops.

D-DAY JUNE 6, 1944

The Anglo-American landings on the Normandy coast turn the tide of the war in Europe. They involve 1,213 warships, 4,126 landing ships, 736 ancillary vessels, and 864 merchant vessels. By midnight on June 6, 57,500 American and 75,000 British and Canadian forces are ashore. The Allied casualties are 2,500 killed and 8,500 wounded.

FALAISE POCKET
Aug 13–21, 1944

The German forces trapped by the United States break out at St. Lo and are pounded from the air. When the pocket closes only 20,000 out of the 80,000 trapped Germans escape. They leave behind vast amounts of weapons and equipment.

ARNHEM
Sept 17–25, 1944

The Arnhem operation is part of an airborne attack to capture bridges across the lower Rhine. British forces from the 1st Airborne Division are forced to withdraw after heavy German attacks. British losses are 1,130 killed and 6,000 captured, of whom half are wounded.

ABOVE: Normandy, June 6, as American soldiers leave their landing craft and plunge toward the shore.

RIGHT: Arnhem's sky blossoms with British paratroopers as the disastrous Operation Market Garden begins.

ARDENNES
Dec 16,1944–Jan 16, 1945

The last great German offensive in the West has initial successes against the U.S. Army but is halted and destroyed by U.S. forces with some British help. Losses are 100,000 German casualties, 81,000 American and 1,400 British.

REMAGEN
March 7, 1945

The Ludendorf railroad bridge across the Rhine is captured intact by men of the U.S. 9th Armored Division.

RHINE CROSSINGS
March 23, 1945

Full-scale amphibious crossings and airborne landings put British and U.S. forces in a position to capture the industrial heartland of the Ruhr.

WAR IN THE EAST 1941–45

Although Japan has been involved in China, its war with the United States and Britain does not begin until December 1941. The Japanese hope that through tactical success at Pearl Harbor they will be able to access oil, raw material supplies, and territorial assets.

HONG KONG Dec 8–25, 1941

Despite being outnumbered and outgunned, the British put up a stout defense. Casualties are 2,000 with 11,000 prisoners; the Japanese lose 2,745 killed.

MALAYSIA AND SINGAPORE
Dec 8, 1941–Feb 15, 1942

The British fight a series of delaying actions down the Malay Peninsula, suffering 5,000 casualties following Japanese landings in three locations. The Japanese capture Singapore for 9,800 casualties. They take 32,000 Indian, 16,000 British, and 14,000 Australian prisoners, more than 50 percent of whom are to die in captivity.

PHILIPPINES Dec 10, 1941–May 6–7, 1942

Japanese troops land on the Philippines and push the American and Filipino soldiers back to the Bataan Peninsula, which they hold until April 9. Some 76,000 men surrender; however, at least 10,000 die during their march to prison. The last defenses to fall are those of Corregidor, where the garrison suffers 2,000 casualties.

BELOW: Japanese forces land on the island fortress of Corregidor, overcoming a valiant stand by U.S. and Filipino troops.

NEW GUINEA 1942–Aug 26, 1944

Following Japanese landings, Australian and U.S. forces counterattack and, over a long campaign, defeat Japan. The cost is 57,046 Australian casualties, of whom 12,161 are killed. U.S. casualties are 19,000, while the Japanese lose 13,000 in Papua and 35,000 in New Guinea.

TARAWA Nov 20–23, 1943

Defended by 4,800 Japanese marines, Tarawa costs the U.S. Marine Corps 1,500 killed or wounded.

KOHIMA/IMPHAL, BURMA April 4–18, 1944

About 13,000 Japanese are killed in the siege of Kohima and at Imphal 53,000 perish from a combination of disease and combat. These two victories are the turning point for the British in Burma.

SAIPAN June 15–July 9, 1944

Out of a garrison of 30,000 only 1,000 Japanese prisoners are taken. U.S. casualties are 1,037 marines and 3,674 soldiers including 3,426 dead.

GUAM July 21–Aug 10, 1944

Defended by 20,000 men, the island falls for the loss of 6,716 marines, 839 soldiers, and 245 sailors including 1,023 dead. Its capture gives the USAF a base for heavy bomber raids on Japan.

THE PHILIPPINE CAMPAIGN

This lasts from October 17, 1944 to July 4, 1945. The liberation of the Philippine Island group is a particular concern for the U.S. commander in the Far East. General Douglas MacArthur, who has spent much of his career in the area.

LEYTE Oct 17–Dec 25, 1944

The American casualties are 15,584 including 3,584 killed, Japanese figures are not known but are believed to be 70,000 killed.

LUZON Dec 15–July 4, 1945

Heavy fighting leads to the liberation of the island which contains the capital of the Philippines, Manila. The Americans suffer 37,854 killed or wounded, in Manila alone. Japanese losses are 16,000 killed.

CORREGIDOR Feb 16–21, 1945

The Americans launch a combined sea and airborne attack on the fortified island, where at least 3,300 Japanese perish.

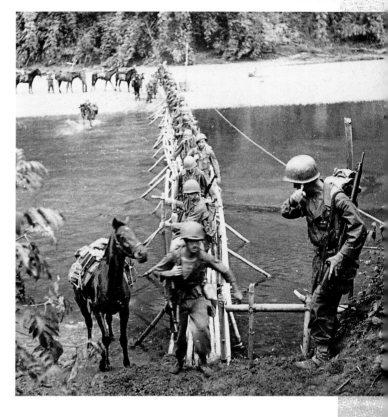

ABOVE: U.S. soldiers cross Burma's Chindwin River.

IWO JIMA Feb 16–March 26, 1945

Fighting for a tiny island of eight square miles defended by 21,000 troops, the Americans suffer 6,821 dead and 18,200 wounded. There are few Japanese survivors. Iwo Jima is strategically important; it had been used as an airstrip for Japanese fighter planes, making it easy for them to attack U.S. bombers.

OKINAWA April 1–July 2, 1945

The casualties in the fighting for this 794 square mile island are 2,938 marines and 4,675 soldiers dead, 31,807 wounded. The Japanese lose 100,000 killed and 10,000 captured.

BELOW: U.S. marines race for the beaches of Iwo Jima.

AIR WAR IN THE WEST

THE BATTLE OF BRITAIN July 10–Oct 12, 1940
With the fall of France, Britain has no allies left in Western Europe. Hitler's plan is to launch air attacks against Britain as a preliminary for an invasion by German ground forces. The Luftwaffe strength is 2,800 aircraft, the RAF has 700. Nearly 500 RAF pilots are killed and 400 are wounded. Even so, Britain holds off the Luftwaffe and prevents invasion.

BLITZKRIEG Sept 7 1940–May 10 1941
After failure in the Battle of Britain, Hermann Goering, commander of the Luftwaffe, turns to flying by night and dropping bombs on civilian targets. Ports and big cities get the worst of it. London is hit almost every night. On November 14/15, 1940, the Midlands city of Coventry is devastated when some 449 German bombers drop 503 tons of high explosive and 881 canisters of incendiaries, killing 550 and injuring 1,200.

FIRST FLIGHT OF TWIN-ENGINED JET AIRCRAFT April 2, 1941
The German He 280 goes into action. The maximum level speed is 510 miles per hour.

THE DAMBUSTERS May 16–17 1943
Attacks by RAF bombers using specialized "bouncing" bombs against the Sorpe, Mohne, and Eder dams are launched. Though the Mohne and Eder are breached the Sorpe is only damaged.

PEENEMUNDE 17–18 August, 1943
Following intelligence that Peenemunde on the Baltic is a rocket research center, it is attacked by RAF Lancaster bombers.

JET FIGHTERS IN ACTION Oct, 1944
Me 262 jet fighters engage the USAAF and RAF. The first aerial victory is a B-17 shot down by a pilot of Kommando Nowotny.

**V-WEAPON CAMPAIGN
June 13, 1944–March 29, 1945**
The *Vergeltungswaffen* or vengeance weapons are the V-1 (the ZZG-76 flying bomb) and the V-2 (the A-4 ballistic missile). About 35,000 V-1s are produced, 9,521 are fired at Britain of which 4,621 are destroyed. About 5,000 V-2s are launched against London, Antwerp, and Liège. On August 4, 1944, a Gloster Meteor jet fighter downs a V-1. The pilot, Flying Officer Dean, tips the missile into the ground with his wing.

OPPOSITE: The V-2 rocket, Hitler's vengeance weapon.

RAF AND USAF BOMBING CAMPAIGN

The Royal Air Force (RAF) opens the war by dropping leaflets over Germany. By the close of the war the United States Air Force (USAF) is attacking enemy targets by day while the RAF flies by night. Though military and economic targets are hit, the RAF also destroy huge areas of housing.

• On May 30–31, 1942, the RAF flies 1,046 bombers over Cologne where it drops 1,455 tons of bombs killing 486 people, injuring 5,027, and destroying 18,440 buildings. Between 1943 and 1944, the Ruhr, Germany's industrial heartland, is attacked by the RAF and USAF. By the end of 1943 the Allied Air Forces have dropped 200,000 tons of bombs on Germany and much of that on the Ruhr.

• On July 24, 27, 29, and August 2, 1943 incendiary attacks create a firestorm that destroys 8.5 square miles of Hamburg and kills 44,600 civilians and 800 servicemen. Between August 23, 1943 and March 1944, a series of 16 heavy raids by the RAF on Berlin damages the city, but does not prevent it working as a capital. Out of 9,111 sorties, the RAF loses 492 bombers.

• On August 17 and October 14, 1943, the USAF stages raids on the German ballbearing plants at Schweinfurt, which, though of considerable strategic value, are very costly: 36 bombers are lost in the first and 60 in the second raid.

• On February 13–14, 1945, RAF and USAF bombers kill between 30,000 and 60,000 civilians in Dresden, many of them refugees, in day and night attacks.

AIR WAR IN THE EAST

PEARL HARBOR, HAWAII Dec 7, 1941
This is the event that brings the United States into the war. In a surprise early-morning attack by the Japanese, lasting no more than two hours, 135 Japanese dive bombers, 104 high-level bombers, and 81 fighter aircraft flying from carriers sink or damage 18 warships, destroy 187 aircraft, and kill 2,400 U.S. servicemen. The U.S. carriers are at sea, escape, and become the main warships in the Pacific. The Japanese lose 29 aircraft and five midget submarines.

DOOLITLE TOKYO RAID April 18, 1942
Sixteen North American B-25 Mitchells commanded by Lt. Col. James Doolittle, flying from the USS *Hornet*, attack Tokyo, Nagoya, Kobe, and Yokohama and then fly on to China.

KAMIKAZE ATTACKS Oct 19, 1944–April 1945
Attacks by about 5,000 suicide aircraft sink or damage about six major Allied ships including an escort carrier at Leyte Gulf in the Philippines.

TOKYO FIRE RAIDS March 9–10, 1945
The first incendiary attack against the Japanese capital devastates the city center and kills 100,000 people.

HIROSHIMA 08.15, Aug 6, 1945
Atomic bomb nicknamed "Little Boy" is dropped on the Japanese city by a B-29 piloted by Colonel Paul Tibbets, and initiates nuclear warfare. The bomb destroys 47 square miles and kills 70,000 people.

NAGASAKI Aug 9, 1945
Atomic bomb nicknamed "Fat Man" is dropped by a B-29 piloted by Major Charles Sweeney, killing 24,000 people.

LEFT: Lt. Col. James Doolittle with one of his B-25 Mitchell bombers that carried out the Tokyo raid. He is to become the commander of the 8th Air Force in 1944 and 1945.

NAVAL WAR IN THE WEST

THE ADMIRAL GRAF SPEE
Dec 13–17, 1939

After a running battle with three British cruisers, the German pocket battleship *Admiral Graf Spee* is scuttled by her captain in the River Plate, on orders from Berlin.

TARANTO Nov 11, 1940

In this naval air action, 27 Swordfish torpedo bombers from the carrier HMS *Illustrious* attack the Italian fleet, safe in its base at Taranto. They cripple three battleships and two cruisers, and sink two other ships. The British lose two aircraft.

CAPE MATAPAN
Mar 27–28, 1941

Using signal intercepts, three British battleships are able to close with three Italian 8-inch cruisers, two smaller cruisers, and two destroyers, and sink them as well as damaging a battleship. The British lose two naval aircraft.

ABOVE: The *Graf Spee*, severely damaged during the Battle of the River Plate, is scuttled by its captain.

HMS HOOD AND BISMARCK May 24–27, 1941

The *Bismarck* is one of the most powerful battleships of the war, used to attack Atlantic shipping. On May 24, 1941 it sinks the British battle cruiser HMS *Hood* off the Greenland coast. Almost the entire British Navy sets out to hunt the *Bismarck* down and finally catches her off the coast of France on May 26. It takes the combined firepower of five destroyers, two battleships, and a cruiser to sink her.

OPERATION CERBERUS, THE "CHANNEL DASH"
Feb 12, 1942

The German battle cruisers *Gneisenau* and *Scharnhorst* and heavy cruiser *Prinz Eugen* make a daylight run up the Channel from Brest, France, to Germany. Both battle cruisers are damaged by British mines.

FIRST NUCLEAR REACTOR
Italian-born physicist Enrico Fermi (1901–1954) starts up the first nuclear reactor, built on the squash court of Chicago University; it demonstrates the first controlled chain reaction.

VICHY FALLS
German troops occupy Vichy France, ending the semi-independence of the country. The French fleet is scuttled in Toulon harbour to prevent it falling into German hands.

MILITARY CHOPPERS
The Sikorsky XR-2 becomes the first helicopter designed and built for military service, and is tested by the U.S. Army.

FIRST V-2 ROCKET
On October 2 the Germans make the first successful launch of their V-2 rocket; it flies for about 12 miles; V-2s go into active service in 1944.

FAMINE RELIEF
The charity Oxfam is founded in the U.K. as the Oxford Committee for Famine Relief, to fight world famine.

THE WARSAW GHETTO
The Germans storm the Warsaw Ghetto in September, killing its 50,000 Jewish inhabitants. The population of Polish Jews, which numbered 2.5 million in 1939, is steadily reduced as the Germans kill or transport all Jews to death camps.

OF ALL THE BARS IN ALL THE TOWNS ...
Humphrey Bogart stars as Rick, Ingrid Bergman as Ilsa, in *Casablanca*, the anti-Nazi film directed by Hungarian-born Michael Curtiz which becomes an instant classic and combines the tension of a thriller with the element of romance.

ABOVE: Bing Crosby (left) and Bob Hope (above) continue their popular road movies; this year Morocco is the destination.

THE OUTSIDER
French novelist Albert Camus's novel about a man who cannot respond to normal conventions and social rituals becomes emblematic of a modern dilemma — how to find our own values when we reject those of the society around us. This first novel puts its author at the forefront of modern debate. His book of essays *The Myth of Sisyphus*, introducing the idea of "the Absurd", also appears this year.

ANTIGONE: A MYTH FOR TODAY
French dramatist Jean Anouilh's updating of the Greek myth enacts the troubles of contemporary France. The oppressive Creon becomes symbolic of the Vichy compromise, the idealistic Antigone with the values of freedom.

CORE SET UP
The Congress of Racial Equality (CORE) is founded by University of Chicago students led by James Farmer, to end racial segregation and discrimination in the United States by nonviolent means. John Harold Johnson begins publication of the *Negro Digest* in Chicago.

FIRST SIGHT OF A FASHION BASIC
The T-shirt appears as regulation U.S. Navy outerwear, specified as a "T-type" knitted cotton shirt, with a round neck and short sleeves set at right angles for maximum underarm sweat absorption. T-type shirts were formerly worn only as underwear.

HOT STUFF
The self-heating can is produced by Heinz to sustain hungry troops when cooking is impossible. When the cap is peeled back, a fuse ignites a heating mixture stored in a tube running through the center of the can.

THE TIDE TURNS AS THE ALLIES FIGHT BACK

The Allies get a grip on their strategy and plan to knock Italy out of the war, then to turn their attention to Germany, and finally Japan. Sicily is first to fall and Italy eventually surrenders. Meanwhile, the arrival of aircraft carriers in the North Atlantic decimates the German submarines that have been preying on the convoy ships, and so food and supplies get through once again. The first electromechanical computer grinds into action in the U.K., decoding German messages. In a Swiss laboratory, Albert Hofmann stumbles into LSD. In New York, the young Francis Albert Sinatra croons his way to stardom.

1943

Jan	3	Siege of Leningrad comes to an end
May	18	The Dambusters raid
Apr	18	Uprising by the inhabitants of the Warsaw Ghetto
July	10	Allies invade Sicily
Sep	8	Axis Powers broken as Italy surrenders
Nov	28	Churchill, Roosevelt, and Stalin meet in Tehran

ABOVE: Increasing numbers of women go to work in factories to replace the men who have gone to war.

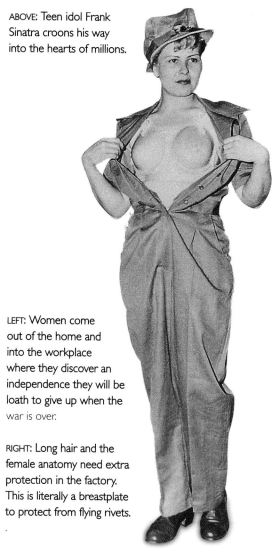

ABOVE: Teen idol Frank Sinatra croons his way into the hearts of millions.

LEFT: Women come out of the home and into the workplace where they discover an independence they will be loath to give up when the war is over.

RIGHT: Long hair and the female anatomy need extra protection in the factory. This is literally a breastplate to protect from flying rivets.

ABOVE: In Katyn Forest, the bodies of 4,000 Polish officers, identifiable only by their army papers, are uncovered.

BELOW: President Roosevelt cuts his birthday cake while returning from the Casablanca Conference.

THE CASABLANCA AGREEMENT

Churchill and Roosevelt meet in Casablanca, Morocco, and agree to fight for the unconditional surrender of Germany, Italy, and Japan. The Allies agree to invade Italy to force it out of the war.

HORROR IN KATYN FOREST

German forces discover the bodies of more than 4,000 Polish Army officers in a mass grave in the Katyn Forest at Smolensk, U.S.S.R.. Germany accuses the U.S.S.R. of their deaths. The murders cause considerable tension between the U.S.S.R. and the Polish government in exile in London.

VICTORY IN THE NORTH ATLANTIC

The campaign by German U-boats against Allied shipping begins to falter as Allied planes flying from aircraft carriers released from the campaign in North Africa are able to hunt down the U-boats at sea. Throughout 1942, more than 650,000 tons of shipping is lost each month, but by May 1943 the figure drops to 18,000 tons in a month, with 17 U-boats sunk. Success in the North Atlantic increases supplies of food and vital war materials to Britain.

SICILY FALLS

The Allies invade Sicily. Mussolini is dismissed by King Victor Emmanuel, and the new government surrenders unconditionally in September. As a result, German troops pour into Italy to defend its former ally, while Mussolini proclaims a new Italian republic from the northern town of Salò, on Lake Garda.

SEYFERT GALAXIES

American astronomer Carl K. Seyfert discovers that a small number of galaxies contain unusually bright nuclei, and emit radio waves and infrared energy; they are now called Seyfert Galaxies.

THE ACCIDENTAL TRIPPER

LSD (lysurgic acid diethylamide) is accidentally discovered by a Swiss chemist, Albert Hofmann of Sandoz AG, whose description of a "trip" inspires further research.

THE TEHRAN STRATEGY

The three leaders of Russia, United States, and Britain meet together for the first time in the Iranian capital Tehran to discuss the war. Churchill and Roosevelt outline their plans to invade France.

BOUNCING BOMBS

Flying Lancaster bombers, the RAF's 617 Squadron, led by Guy Gibson, successfully use specially designed bombs to blow up the Mohne and Eder dams at Mulheim and Dortmund in Germany. The bombs, which bounce along the water like stones skipping on a pond, have been designed by English aero-engineer Barnes Wallis (1887–1979).

STOP PRESS

The *Frankfurter Zeitung*, a highly respected newspaper, is suppressed by Hitler. After the war it is replaced by the *Algemeine Zeitung*, and then by the *Frankfurter Algemeine Zeitung*, which pledges to uphold its predecessor's fairness and objectivity.

BEING AND NOTHINGNESS

Existentialist Jean-Paul Sartre's greatest contribution to philosophy is expressed in this book, which explores the opposition between objective things and human consciousness. It sums up the alienation of the intellectual in the postwar era in such phrases as "Man is condemned to be free."

THE QUEBEC PLAN

British and American leaders meeting in Quebec, Canada, agree to the defeat of Germany before Japan, and plan to invade France in May 1944.

O WHAT A BEAUTIFUL MORNING

Richard Rogers and Oscar Hammerstein bring cheer to a world at war with their musical about life and love among the ranchers and farmers in Oklahoma.

KIDNEY DIALYSIS

Working in secret during German occupation of the Netherlands, physician Willem J. Kolff builds the first artificial kidney machine, which temporarily enables waste products to be eliminated from the bloodstream while damaged kidneys recover.

UNDERSEA ADVENTURE

SCUBA (self-contained underwater breathing apparatus) diving equipment, invented by French naval divers Jacques-Yves Cousteau and Emile Gagnan, is tested successfully. Marketed as the Aqualung, it consists of a steel bottle of compressed air and a control valve to supply air at normal pressure while the diver swims freely.

RACE IN THE UNITED STATES

Gunnar Myrdal, a Swedish sociologist commissioned by the Carnegie Foundation, publishes *The American Dilemma*, an exhaustive study of race relations in the United States and their relationship to the democratic process.

ZOOT RIOTS

In Los Angeles and Detroit black and Hispanic youths dressed in flamboyant long and baggy suits clash with white servicemen. Many are injured and 35 people are killed.

GIANT BRAIN

Colossus, the world's first electromechanical computer, goes into service at Bletchley Park, Buckinghamshire, England, to help decode German messages during World War II.

INVASION, LIBERATION, AND RETALIATION

German war hero Colonel von Stauffenberg fails in his assassination attempt on Hitler. The massive operation of the D-Day landings on the Normandy coast leads to success for the Allies and Paris is liberated in August. In retaliation, Hitler sends V-1 and V-2 rockets to bomb London. Away from the war, the World Bank and the International Monetary Fund are set up, as is the Arab League. Franklin D. Roosevelt is returned for an unprecedented fourth term in office as president of the United States.

1944

June	**4**	Allies and U.S. troops take Rome
	6	D-Day landings; the Allies take France
	17	Iceland becomes a republic
Aug	**25**	Paris liberated
Sep	**2**	Brussels liberated
	9	London hit by V-2 rockets

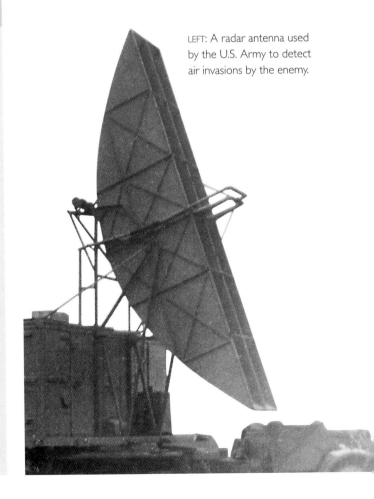

LEFT: A radar antenna used by the U.S. Army to detect air invasions by the enemy.

DEATH CAMPS LIBERATED

In January, Soviet troops are the first to liberate a death camp when they enter Auschwitz, in Poland, finding just 7,000 inmates alive. Over the next five months, Allied troops liberate all the death and concentration camps in occupied Europe, revealing thousands of badly malnourished and ill-treated inmates. U.S. troops entering Dachau are so appalled at the state of the 33,000 survivors and the piled-up bodies of the dead that they shoot all 500 SS guards within the hour. The exact number who died in the camps is not known, but is thought to total more than six million. Most are Jews, although gypsies, gays, and others defined by the Nazis as "undesirable" have also been killed.

ABOVE AND RIGHT: The horrors of Germany's "final solution" are slowly revealed as the concentration camps are opened up.

BELOW: One of the few survivors of Japan's bombing of Shanghai.

ABOVE: Churchill, Roosevelt, and Stalin, allied in the fight against Germany, meet at Yalta to discuss the future.

ABOVE: Grand Admiral Karl Doenitz, Germany's new political leader, is arrested by Allied forces acting on Eisenhower's orders.

ABOVE: Churchill, Roosevelt, and Stalin, allied in the fight against Germany, meet at Yalta to discuss the future.

YALTA CONFERENCE

The three Allied leaders — U.S. president Roosevelt, Soviet premier Joseph Stalin, and British prime minister Winston Churchill — meet at Yalta in the Crimea to plan Germany's unconditional surrender and its division into four parts after the war. They also agree the fate of Berlin and Poland, and make arrangements for the first United Nations conference, to be held in San Francisco. Stalin also agrees to enter the war against Japan when the war in Europe is finished; in return, the Soviet Union will gain control over the north of Korea.

DRESDEN BOMBED

In order to prevent supplies reaching the Eastern Front against Russia, British and U.S. bombers reduce the industrial city of Dresden to ruins, killing between 30,000 and 60,000 civilians. The bombing causes widespread condemnation in Britain. Some attack it for humanitarian reasons, others because it diverts bombers from attacking vital communications and oil supplies.

TOKYO FIRE RAIDS

The first incendiary attack against the Japanese capital devastates the city center and kills 100,000 people.

FIGHTING IN THE PHILIPPINES
The Americans launch a combined sea and air attack on the island of Corregidor to liberate Okinawa, Manila, and the tiny island of Iwo Jima. Casualties on both sides are enormous. The capture of the heavily fortified island of Iwo Jima in particular provides the Americans with a jumping-off point for bombing raids against Japan.

DEATH OF WAR LEADERS
Three war leaders die within days of each other: Franklin Roosevelt dies of a cerebral hemorrhage and is succeeded by Vice President Harry Truman (1884–1972), Benito Mussolini is shot by Italian partisans, and Adolf Hitler takes his own life.

UNITED NATIONS FOUNDED
The founding conference of the United Nations (UN) begins in April in San Francisco. In June, 51 member nations sign the United Nations Charter. Like the League of Nations, which it supersedes, the aim of the UN is to maintain international peace and security. An International Court of Justice is set up in The Hague, Netherlands.

BLACK BOY
In his autobiography, *Black Boy*, black American writer Richard Wright (1908–60) is eloquent about the plight of black people.

ABOVE: After Japan's surrender, Lt. Gen. Torashiro Kawabe boards a plane for a conference in Manila.

VE DAY
War in Europe comes to an end in May with the unconditional surrender of Germany. Throughout the continent, people celebrate Victory in Europe (VE) Day on May 8, even though many of its cities are in ruins and food is in scarce supply.

SIGNALING THE MOON
American and Hungarian experts simultaneously reflect radar signals from the Moon back to Earth.

DAVID LLOYD GEORGE
(1863–1945)
The British Liberal prime minister, who presided over the coalition government during and immediately after World War I (1916–22), has died. He was in Parliament until the year of his death. Of Welsh parentage and upbringing, he was a fine and fiery orator. As chancellor of the exchequer, from 1908 to 1915, he was responsible for the radical "people's budget" of 1909, and introduced pensions, sick pay, and the social insurance system.

ABOVE: Clement Attlee (second from left) becomes Britain's prime minister.

HIROSHIMA AND NAGASAKI

In August, U.S. bombers drop atomic bombs on the Japanese cities of Hiroshima and Nagasaki, so initiating the age of nuclear warfare. The atomic bomb on Hiroshima is nicknamed "Little Boy." Dropped by a B-29, piloted by Col. Paul Tibbets, it destroys 47 square miles and kills 70,000 people. The one dropped on Nagasaki is nicknamed "Fat Man"; it kills 24,000 people.

CHINESE CIVIL WAR

Civil war resumes between the nationalists or Kuomintang, under Chiang Kai-shek (1887–1975), and the Communists, under Mao Zedong (1893–1976), for control of the former Japanese-run province of Manchuria. The war spreads throughout China the following year.

FRANKLIN D(ELANO) ROOSEVELT (1882–1945)

The American Democratic president Franklin D. Roosevelt, who has seen the United States almost through to the end of World War II, has died. He had been president since 1932, winning four successive elections. He introduced the New Deal that helped the United States out of the Great Depression, devised the Lend-Lease deal of 1940–41, whereby the United States supplied arms to Britain, and was instrumental in sorting out postwar Europe at Yalta shortly before his death.

INDONESIA PROCLAIMS INDEPENDENCE

On the surrender of Japan, which was ocupying the archipelago, the Indonesian Nationalist Party proclaims independence from the Netherlands, which refuses to recognize the new government. Fighting soon breaks out between the Nationalist Indonesian People's Army and British (and later Dutch) forces. A truce is declared in November 1946 and again in January 1948.

JAPAN SURRENDERS

The Soviet Union declares war on Japan and invades Manchuria, occupying northern Korea and the northern islands of Japan. Japan surrenders unconditionally, ending the war in the Pacific.

FIRST ATOM BOMB TESTED

U.S. scientists led by American nuclear physicist Professor Robert Oppenheimer (1904–67) test the first atomic bomb in the desert at Alamogordo, New Mexico; It produces a 4,000-foot-high mushroom cloud.

POTSDAM CONFERENCE

Stalin, Churchill, and Truman meet in Potstdam, eastern Germany, to organize the occupation of Germany. German land east of the Oder-Neisse rivers is to be under Polish jurisdiction, with Austria under four-power control.

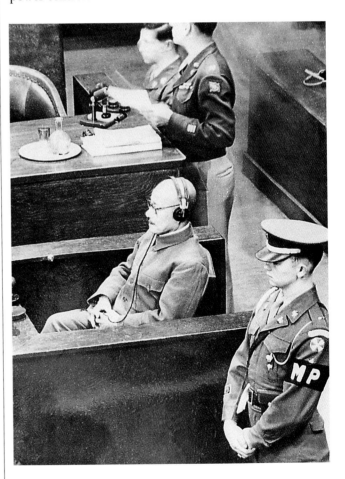

ABOVE: The Nuremberg trials hears evidence of the appalling war crimes ordered by Germany's leaders.

ABOVE: Sir Alexander Fleming, who discovered penicillin, explains some of its properties to a grateful former patient.

ABOVE: Frozen food becomes popular in the United States, and many Americans freeze and pack their own at home.

VIETNAM DECLARES REPUBLIC

Nationalist and Communist Vietminh forces under Ho Chi Minh (1890–1969) enter Hanoi and force the emperor to abdicate. The following month they declare Vietnam a republic, which the former colonial ruler, France, refuses to recognize.

WAR CRIMES

The Allied International Military Tribunal opens the trial of former Nazi leaders at Nuremberg in Germany. At its conclusion in September 1946, 12 Nazis are sentenced to death, three to life imprisonment, four receive long sentences, and three are acquitted.

BUCHENWALD PHOTOGRAPHS

American photographer Margaret Bourke-White (1906–71) shows photographs of the concentration camp at Buchenwald, taken when the camp was liberated by the Allies. For the first time people see the truth about the Nazi atrocities.

ANIMAL SATIRE

English author George Orwell (1903–50) publishes his novel *Animal Farm.* A satire on revolutions, the novel describes how a new tyranny replaces the old when pigs drive out their human masters from the farm, only to turn into something like humans themselves.

HENRY V

British actor Laurence Olivier's film version of Shakespeare's play, *Henry V,* has a special resonance for its British audience. Portraying an England in the grip of a long war in Europe, it reflects Britain's contemporary position and inspires patriotism.

HUIS-CLOS

French existentialist Jean-Paul Sartre (1905–80) has written a new play, which will become his most famous. Entitled *Huis-Clos* (In Camera), it shows three people trapped in a room in hell.

ABSTRACT EXPRESSIONISM

American painter Jackson Pollock (1912–56) is one of the leaders of this rising art movement. His technique of drip-painting seems random, but enables him to create works of striking beauty and energy.

LES ENFANTS DU PARADIS

French actor Jean-Louis Barrault (1910–94) plays the mime Deburau in the film version of Marcel Carné's romantic theatre drama, *Les Enfants du Paradis.* The film becomes an instant classic.

ENTER ENIAC . . .

The first completely electronic computer, ENIAC (Electronic Numerical Integrator And Calculator) is built at the University of Pennsylvania; it weighs more than 27 tons and has 18,000 valves.

. . . AND THE COMPUTER BUG

Mathematician Grace Murray Hopper, working on a new computer, finds a moth has stopped a relay working. This is the first actual computer bug.

"MISSING" ELEMENT FOUND

Element 61, the rare-earth metal promethium, is found by three U.S. chemists, Charles D. Coryell, Lawrence E. Glendenin and J. A. Marinsky; this fills the last gap in the table of the elements.

THE ATOMIC BOMB

ABOVE: The Enola Gay in a dispersal area after its mission against Hiroshima.

ABOVE: The plutonium "Fat Man" bomb is used against Nagasaki.

ABOVE: The Enola Gay's crew receive their final preflight instructions.

RIGHT: The awesome cloud billows above Nagasaki.

INSET: This victim's burns have etched her skin with the pattern of her kimono.

ABOVE AND BELOW: Evidence of the dreadful destructive power of the world's first atomic weapons.

THE IRON CURTAIN COMES DOWN

The United Nations holds its opening session but the first signs of the Cold War appear as former British prime minister, Winston Churchill, warns of an "Iron Curtain" dividing Communist countries from non-Communist countries in Europe. The word "bikini" enters the language, partly after American atomic testing at Bikini Atoll, and partly after a new and "explosive" swimsuit. Paris becomes a center for bohemian writers and artists, and espresso coffee is the new craze from Italy.

1946

Jan	**10**	First session of United Nations opens in London
	20	General de Gaulle resigns as president of France
Feb	**1**	Norwegian Trygve Lie is elected president of the UN
	4	Juan Perón is elected president of Argentina
Mar	**5**	Churchill makes "Iron Curtain" speech in Fulton, Missouri
	6	France recognizes the Democratic Republic of Vietnam
May		Civil war breaks out in Greece
June	**2**	Italy votes for a republic
July	**4**	Philippines becomes independent of U.S. rule
	5	Bikini swimsuit displayed in Paris
Oct	**3**	United Nations General Assembly meets in New York
Nov	**23**	French troops bomb Haiphong, Vietnam, killing around 20,000. The French Indochinese War begins.
Dec	**20**	French troops occupy Hanoi, capital of Vietnam. Ho Chi Minh calls for resistance to the French

OPPOSITE: An atomic, or "mushroom" cloud, rising from Bikini Atoll in the Marshall Islands, the site of nuclear weapon testing by the United States in the 1940s and 1950s.

ABOVE: General Charles De Gaulle resigns as head of France's provisional postwar government after only two months in the post. More than ten years later he is once again elected president by the people of France, a position he holds for over a decade.

DE GAULLE RESIGNS

In France, General de Gaulle (1890–1970) resigns as French president because of continued Communist opposition to his rule.

PERON ELECTED PRESIDENT

Juan Perón (1895–1974) is elected president of Argentina. He first came to power as one of the leading officers who took over the government in 1943, and consolidated his power among both the army and the workers. In October 1945, he briefly lost power in a US-sponsored coup, but was quickly returned to power. Much of his popularity is due to his wife, Eva.

GREEK WAR

Civil war breaks out in Greece between the monarchist Democratic Army of Greece (DSE) backed by Britain, and the Communist National Popular Liberation Army (ELAS) backed by Albania, Bulgaria, and Yugoslavia. In September, a plebiscite agrees to restore the monarchy. Fighting continues until the defeat of the Communists in October 1949.

IRON CURTAIN

Making a speech in Fulton, Missouri, British wartime leader Winston Churchill (1874–1964) warns that an "Iron Curtain" is descending in Europe from the Baltic to the Adriatic, as the U.S.S.R. strengthens its grip on Eastern Europe. For many people, this speech marks the beginning of what becomes known as the Cold War.

FRENCH INDOCHINESE WAR

France recognizes the creation of the Democratic Republic of Vietnam, headed by the Communist leader Ho Chi Minh, as part of a French-led Indochinese Federation. Relations between France and Ho Chi Minh break down, and in November, the French bomb the northern port of Haiphong, killing around 20,000 people, as they seek to maintain control of Vietnam. This marks the start of a war which lasts until 1954.

ZORBA THE GREEK

The novel Zorba the Greek by Nikos Kazantzakis (1883–1957) is published. His portrayal of Zorba and his passionate love of life is a success in Greece and will soon be widely translated.

ITALIAN REPUBLIC

A referendum in Italy produces a huge majority for a republic. King Umberto II (1904–83) goes into exile; the prime minister, Alcide de Gasperi (1881–1954), becomes provisional head of state. The Allies agree to transfer the Italian-owned Dodecanese Islands to Greece, some lands to Yugoslavia, and parts of northern Italy to France.

ITALIAN WOMEN GAIN THE VOTE

In June, Italian women gain the right to vote in national elections for the first time.

RIOTS IN INDIA

More than 3,000 people die as Muslims and Hindus clash in Calcutta, India. The riots are the culmination of unrest caused by British proposals for Indian independence.

PHILIPPINES INDEPENDENT

In July, the Philippines become independent of U.S. rule.

THE HOUSE OF BERNARDO ALBA

This year sees the publication of The House of Bernardo Alba, the last tragedy to have been written by Spanish poet Federico Garcia Lorca (1899–1936). Performed in 1945, nine years after the writer's death, it confirms his stature as Spain's greatest modern dramatist.

ATOMIC TESTING

Americans explode the first of several atomic bombs over Bikini Atoll in the Marshall Islands of the Pacific Ocean; the purpose is to test the effects on warships and animals.

JOHN MAYNARD KEYNES
(1883–1946)

The English economist and patron of the arts John Maynard Keynes has died. He was a Treasury advisor during both World War I and World War II, and put forward the theory of the planned economy. He greatly influenced Franklin D. Roosevelt's New Deal and helped set up the International Monetary Fund. His two major works, *A Treatise on Money* (1930) and *General Theory of Employment, Interest and Money* (1936), were written in response to the unemployment crisis.

ABOVE: Renowned American art collector and politician Nelson A. Rockefeller. He goes on to become the 41st vice president of the United States.

ESPRESSO COFFEE
The Gaggia coffee machine is invented in Italy; it uses steam to produce espresso coffee, which rapidly becomes popular.

EXPLOSIVE BIKINI
French fashion designer Louis Réard displays an abbreviated two-piece bathing costume for women in Paris; he calls it a "bikini" because he thinks its effect is as explosive as the bomb just tested.

PATERSON
American poet William Carlos Williams begins to publish his long poem, *Paterson*; he will add to it for the rest of his life. Using a collage of anecdotes, letters, reports, conversations, and more traditional "poetic" passages, the poem attempts to create a typically American work of art by describing the everyday life of ordinary Americans.

EJECTOR SEAT
British aeronautical engineer James Martin, using dummies, makes the first tests of an ejector seat to enable pilots to escape from crashing aircraft.

MEMOIRS OF HECATE COUNTRY
American writer and critic Edmund Wilson (1895–1972) publishes this collection of short stories. It is accused of obscenity and banned in some jurisdictions, so becoming a bestseller in others.

ZOOM LENS
U.S. scientist Frank Back of the Zoomar Corporation develops the first zoom lens for cameras.

BOHEMIAN QUARTIER
The Paris quarter of St. Germain-des-Prés becomes the focus of writers, artists, and musicians, including the existentialist Jean-Paul Sartre, feminist Simone de Beauvoir, and sculptor Alberto Giacometti.

BELOW: East meets West as Allies (pictured in 1945). This year, rifts emerge and the alliance shows signs of disintegration.

NEW COUNTRIES AND A BABY BOOM

India is partitioned into two separate, independent countries: India and Pakistan. The partition causes conflict. The UN votes to divide Palestine, a decision that also leads to conflict. Marshall Aid is provided to rebuild Europe and a U.S. pilot breaks the sound barrier. Women's fashion adopts a "New Look" and Method acting takes to the stage. This year also sees the start of the "baby boom" and a liberal approach to childrearing.

1947

Jan	25	Chicago gangster Al "Scarface" Capone dies	**June**	5	U.S. Secretary of State George Marshall calls for aid for Europe
				15	Anne Frank's diary is published
Feb	12	French designer Christian Dior launches the "New Look"	**Aug**	15	India becomes independent
				15	Pakistan is created
Mar	12	U.S. President Truman outlines "Truman Doctrine"	**Oct**	14	U.S. pilot Chuck Yeager breaks the sound barrier
	19	Chinese Nationalists capture Communist capital, Yan'an		29	Benelux customs union is formed
Apr	7	Automobile manufacturer Henry Ford dies	**Nov**	29	United Nations announces plan for partition of Palestine
	15	Jackie Robinson is first black American in major league baseball			

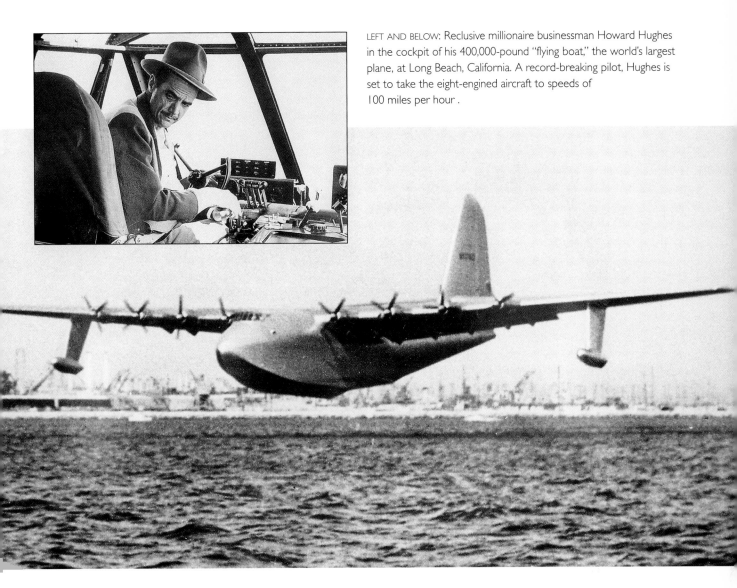

LEFT AND BELOW: Reclusive millionaire businessman Howard Hughes in the cockpit of his 400,000-pound "flying boat," the world's largest plane, at Long Beach, California. A record-breaking pilot, Hughes is set to take the eight-engined aircraft to speeds of 100 miles per hour .

TRUMAN DOCTRINE

In response to Britain's announcement that it can no longer afford to keep troops in Greece to fight the Communists in the civil war, President Truman plans to give aid to both the Greek and Turkish governments to protect them from Communism. This becomes the Truman Doctrine, under which the United States offers to support "free peoples who are resisting attempted subjugation by armed minorities or by outside pressures."

MARSHALL AID

U.S. Secretary of State George Marshall (1880–1959) announces massive financial aid for European nations to enable them to rebuild their economies after the war. Marshall Aid, as it is known, is accepted in Western Europe but rejected by those Eastern European nations occupied by the U.S.S.R.

CARBON-14 DATING

U.S. chemist Willard F. Libby (1908–80) and coworkers perfect carbon-14 dating, by which the amount of this decaying radioactive material left in organic remains shows how long they have been dead.

INDIA PARTITIONED

Britain partitions the Indian Empire, granting India and Pakistan independence, with Burma and Ceylon to follow the following year. Partition brings to an end more than 160 years of British rule. Fighting breaks out between India and Pakistan over the state of Kashmir, whose Muslim population riots in favor of joining, but whose Hindu leader wishes to join India. Many millions die across the subcontinent in inter-communal fighting.

THE NEW LOOK

French fashion designer Christian Dior launches a sensational "New Look". After the austerity of the war years, Dior's look, with its generous use of material, nipped-in waist, soft shoulders and billowing skirts, is welcomed with enthusiasm by women.

FIGHTING IN PALESTINE

Britain hands back the mandate for Palestine to the UN because it is unable to control the country. The UN votes to partition Palestine with separate homelands for Jews and Palestinians. Both sides disagree, and fighting soon breaks out.

ABOVE: Record snowfalls hit New York City in December 1947, making it necessary to shift as much of the snow as possible into the East River at Manhattan.

BELOW: American pilot Captain Charles "Chuck" Yeager becomes the first person to break the sound barrier, in his rocket-propelled Bell X-1 aircraft.

HIGHER EDUCATION BOOMS

Colleges and universities everywhere are swamped by applications for places. In the United States, where many colleges closed down or were almost bankrupted during the war, applications reach an all-time high of more than two million.

UFOS

Unidentified Flying Objects (UFOs) are reported in Washington State, first by a pilot, Kenneth Arnold, and later by members of the public. The many reports of flying saucer-shaped objects illuminating the night sky are ridiculed by the United States Air Force.

BRANDO STARS IN STREETCAR

Tennessee Williams' play, *A Streetcar Named Desire*, opens with Marlon Brando (b. 1924) in the role of Stanley Kowalski. Brando uses the Stanislavski Method of acting, which emphasizes realism and an understanding of the psychology of the character, rather than a declamatory approach.

ACTOR'S STUDIO

Founded by Elia Kazan, Robert Lewis, and Cheryl Crawford, the Actor's Studio in New York City propounds and popularizes the Stanislavski Method in the United States. Many well-known American actors will be trained here, especially during the 1950s.

ABOVE: American Method actor Marlon Brando makes his stage breakthrough in the Tennessee Williams play *A Streetcar Named Desire*. Brando goes on to star in the film version of the play and to become one of the most famous screen actors in the world.

ABOVE: The great baseball player Jackie Robinson becomes the first black player to play outside the Negro Leagues when he joins the Brooklyn Dodgers. Robinson's outstanding performances are a major step in overcoming racial bigotry in sport in the United States.

THE "HOLLYWOOD TEN"
Ten American directors and screenwriters refuse to testify before the House Un-American Activities Committee, which is obsessed with hunting out alleged Communists. The "ten" are given one-year jail sentences, signalling the beginning of "witch hunting" in the cinema world and elsewhere.

ANNE FRANK'S DIARY
The diary of a young Jewish girl, Anne Frank, who died in 1945 in a concentration camp, is published, providing a remarkable insight into the Holocaust. The story of her family's concealment from, and eventual discovery by, the Nazis in Amsterdam becomes known all over the world.

BENELUX FORMED
A customs union is formed by Belgium, the Netherlands and Luxembourg. It is known as the Benelux customs union, an acronym of Belgium, Netherlands, and Luxembourg.

SUPERSONIC FLIGHT
In October Charles "Chuck" Yeager, a U.S. Army pilot, becomes the first man to fly faster than the speed of sound (1,125 feet per second), flying a Bell X1 rocket plane.

CHLORAMPHENICOL DISCOVERED
Scientists discover chloramphenicol, a broad-spectrum antibiotic; in some patients it causes damage to the bone marrow, so its use is confined to severe infections that safer drugs cannot touch.

STRONG FORCE FOUND
British chemist Cecil F. Powell discovers the pion, a sub-atomic particle that produces a "strong force" that holds an atom's nucleus together.

ALPHONSE (AL) CAPONE
(1899–1947)

American gangster Al Capone, sometimes known as Scarface, has died. He joined a street gang as a boy and during the prohibition era amassed profits and notoriety. The infamous St. Valentine's Day Massacre of 1929 was fought between his and a rival gang. Sent to jail in 1931 on tax fraud charges, Capone was released early on health grounds and spent the remainder of his life in his Florida estate.

CRAB NEBULA

Australian radio astronomers discover that the Crab Nebula is a strong radio source; the nebula is the gaseous remains of a supernova, a star which exploded in 1054.

TRANSISTOR INVENTED

U.S. physicists John Bardeen, Walter Brattain, and William Schockley invent the transistor, a tiny electronic device that controls electric current; it revolutionizes all electronic apparatus.

POLAROID CAMERA

U.S. scientist Edwin H Land (1909–91) invents and demonstrates the Polaroid Land Camera™, which can produce a print seconds after a picture is taken.

HELL'S ANGELS ARRIVE

The Hell's Angels — Harley-Davidson biker gangs — cause a riot when they converge on the town of Hollister, California. Dressed in leather, bikers in their thousands roam Califorinia breaking the law in a quest for thrills.

BABY BOOM

A baby boom begins, with 3,411,000 births recorded in the United States, and 20.5 births per 1,000 — one-fifth more than the 1939 figure — in the U.K.

MICROWAVE OVENS

The first microwave ovens are sold in the United States. Invented in 1945 by Percy LeBaron Spencer after a factory radar power tube melted a chocolate bar in his pocket, they are bulky and designed for use in commercial food preparation.

JACKIE ROBINSON

Jackie Robinson becomes the first African-American to play baseball in the major leagues. He plays for the Brooklyn Dodgers and paves the way for the racial integration of the American pastime.

DEAD SEA SCROLLS

The Dead Sea Scrolls are discovered when a Bedouin boy, Muhammad ad-Dibh, explores a cave at Qumran in Jordan and finds an earthenware jar containing leather and parchment scrolls. They were written by the Essenes, a Jewish sect of the 1st century B.C.

PERSONALITY DIMENSIONS

Hans Eysenck (1916–97), a British psychologist, publishes *Dimensions of Personality*, a study of neuroticism and extrovert behavior. He argues that personality is biologically determined and criticizes psychoanalysis because it does not increase the likelihood of recovery from the disorder being treated.

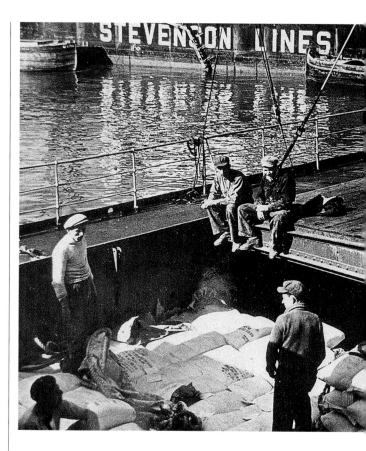

LIBERAL CHILD CARE

American pediatrician Benjamin Spock (1903–98) publishes *The Common Sense Book of Baby and Child Care*, the first practical manual of childcare, which he wrote while serving in the army. He rejects authoritative child-raising methods and advocates a liberal upbringing.

DOMESTIC ELECTRIC BLENDER

An electric blender is produced for home use in the United States. Invented in 1919, it was used only in commercial kitchens until Frederick J. Ossius introduces the Waring Blender, named after band leader Fred Waring.

HENRY FORD
(1863–1947)

American car manufacturer Henry Ford, who founded the Ford Motor Company in 1903, has died. He introduced the assembly line technique, which allowed cars to be produced with great efficiency "on the line." While refusing to accept unionization, he paid unusually high wages, even when this was in opposition to government policy under the New Deal. He set up the Ford Foundation. Always eccentric, at the age of 82 shortly before his death, he attempted to regain control of the Ford Motor Company from his grandson.

MAHATMA ("GREAT SOUL") GANDHI
(1869–1948)

Indian leader Mahatma Gandhi has been assassinated. Venerated as a great pacifist leader, patriot, and social reformer, Gandhi trained as a lawyer. He gave up a lucrative practice to live in South Africa, where he spent 20 years opposing discrimination. In 1914, he returned to India and, although an ardent supporter of Britain, spearheaded the campaign for Indian independence. He was committed to nonviolent civil disobedience but his various campaigns, including the salt march of the 1930s, brought him several terms of imprisonment.
In 1946, he negotiated independence with the British Cabinet Mission. His last months were clouded by Muslim-Hindu strife.

CHRISTINA'S WORLD

U.S. artist Andrew Wyeth paints his paralyzed neighbor, Anna Christina Olson, against a background of an open horizon and a house. The painting, which becomes one of the artist's best known, shows Wyeth's ability to suggest the limited world of the disabled woman, as well as reflecting his love of the scenery around his Maine summer home.

NATIONAL HEALTH

In Britain, the National Health Service is formed. It is one of the first comprehensive health services in the world. The service provides free healthcare to all, "from the cradle to the grave."

LONG-PLAYING RECORDS

By using plastics instead of shellac, American record companies are able to introduce long-playing records, at two speeds, 33.5 rpm and 45 rpm.

MARTIAN ATMOSPHERE

Dutch-born U.S. astronomer Gerard P. Kuiper (1905–73) predicts that the atmosphere of Mars is mostly carbon dioxide, a fact later proved by space probes. He also discovers Miranda, the fifth moon of the planet Uranus.

FIRST ATOMIC CLOCK

The first atomic clock is built at the U.S. National Bureau of Standards, in Washington, D.C.; it is accurate to one second in 300 years. Later, atomic clocks are accurate to one second in 200,000 years.

BATHYSCAPHE INVENTED

Swiss physicist Auguste Piccard (1884–1962) invents the bathyscaphe, a deep-sea diving craft, and tests it o a depth of 4,495 feet. Its development makes possible the exploration of the deepest parts of the oceans.

NUCLEAR STRUCTURE

Physicists Hans Jensen of Germany and German-born Maria Goeppert Mayer of the United States independently discover the structure of atomic nuclei.

DELVING INTO THE ATOM

U.S. physicist Richard Feynman (1918–88) develops the theory of quantum electrodynamics, the interaction between the subatomic particles, electrons, photons, and positrons.

TUBELESS TYRES

The American Goodyear Company introduces the tubeless tire for motor vehicles.

CYBERNETICS INVENTED

U.S. statistician Norbert Wiener invents and names a new branch of science: cybernetics, the study of information control in animals and machines.

RECREATING EARLY NAVIGATION

Thor Heyerdahl (b. 1914), a Norwegian ethnographer, sails from Peru with a Scandinavian crew on a balsawood raft built using techniques known to the Incas. After sailing and drifting more than 5,000 miles, he has reached the Tuamotu archipelago, proving that Precolumbian people could have crossed the Pacific and colonized Polynesia.

FIRST SNEAKERS

Adidas of Germany, a sportswear manufacturer, develops sneakers from war-surplus canvas and fuel-tank rubber. Their first shoe, designed by Adolf Dassler, is decorated with three white stripes.

VELCRO DEVELOPED

Velcro fastening is invented by a Swiss engineer, George de Mestral, inspired by spiny burrs found sticking to his clothing and his dog's coat after a walk.

BRADMAN BOWLED OUT

Australian hero Don Bradman needed just four runs in his last innings in a cricket test match to score 7,000 test runs and record an incomparable average of 100. To the disbelief of all, he is out for nought but still cheered back to the pavilion.

GEORGE HERMAN (BABE) RUTH
(1895–1948)

The American baseball player and coach "Babe" Ruth has died. He played in ten World Series and has set a record for home runs that will not be broken until 1974. During his career he played for the Boston Red Socks (1914–19), the New York Yankees (1920–34), and the Boston Braves (1935–38).

PLANNED PARENTHOOD

The International Planned Parenthood Federation is founded by American social reformer and founder of the birth control movement, Margaret Sanger.

ABORTION ON DEMAND

As the population of Japan approaches 80 million, and in response to increased fetal abnormalities resulting from the 1945 nuclear explosions, the Eugenic Protection Law authorizes abortion on demand.

WINTER GAMES

The Fifth Winter Games are held in St. Moritz, Switzerland, where the facilities have survived World War II unscathed. However, postwar shortages mean hardship for athletes and few visitors. Downhill races for men and women are added to the events, indicating the growing importance of alpine events.

AUSTERE OLYMPICS

The Olympic games are held in London, England, which was the proposed site for the cancelled 1944 games. Events are beset by scarcity and competitors live in army barracks, but crowds flock to Wembley for the games. Athlete Fanny Blankers-Koen, a mother of two, and nicknamed the "flying housewife," takes four gold medals back to Holland.

SKYDIVING

Frenchman Leo Valentin develops the modern sport of skydiving by discovering that arching the back is the way to control free fall before opening the parachute.

ABOVE: U.S. President Harry S. Truman (rear left) enjoys a Welcome Home parade in Washington after his reelection to office in November. The dome of the Capitol is seen in the background.

ABOVE LEFT: American Flying Wing aircraft, notable for the absence of tails and fuselages, which shortens their overall length to about a third of other planes. These superefficient new bombers are pictured at Hawthorne, California.

ABOVE RIGHT: The house of American architect and designer Charles Eames in Santa Monica, California. Eames is especially famous for his innovative chairs, which become collectors' items.

LEFT: California has proved to be an important oil-producing area in the United States, and this oilfield in Long Beach, with its many derricks, is typical of those found in the state. Oil has played an important part in the wealth of the United States.

MAKING MOVIES

ABOVE LEFT: The British-born director and producer Alfred Hitchcock (center) is one of early Hollywood's most important figures.

ABOVE RIGHT: Backstage in Hollywood; the romance of a film is created by unsung craftsmen.

RIGHT: The splendor of Hollywood, illuminated by searchlights as a new film is premièred.

ABOVE: The director surveys the scene from the platform of a movable crane. The use of the crane increases the number of angles from which a shot can be taken on a film set, and improves the overall fluidity of movement.

ABOVE: On location for the film version of Ernest Hemingway's novel *For Whom the Bell Tolls*. The director explains to the actors exactly what he has in mind.

RIGHT: The Austrian-born director Fritz Lang (center) is seen explaining a scene of the film *Woman in the Window* to actress Joan Bennett (left). Lang is one of the many European film directors who went to Hollywood when the Nazis came to power.

BELOW: The western is the film genre that distinguishes American movies from those of other cultures. Irish-American John Ford is the maker of many seminal westerns, including *Stagecoach*.

NATO AND THE PEOPLE'S REPUBLIC

Chinese Communists defeat the Kuomintang and set up the People's Republic of China, headed by Mao Zedong. NATO is formed to provide mutual support for Western nations and the division of the world into Communist and non-Communist blocs is emphasized by the separation of Germany into East and West. Architecture features glass and steel, a Soviet-US arms race begins, and the novel *1984* warns of a bleak future.

1949

Jan	1	Ceasefire ends India-Pakistan war over Kashmir
	10	Communists capture Xuzhou, China
Apr	4	North Atlantic Treaty Organization (NATO) is formed
	16	Western Allies fly 1,398 sorties in 24 hours, delivering 12,937 tons of supplies to Berlin in the greatest number of sorties during the Berlin Airlift
	24	Communist forces advance on Shanghai, China
May	12	Berlin blockade ends
	23	Federal Republic of Germany (West Germany) comes into being
	26	Shanghai falls to Communists, China

July	20	Ceasefire declared in Arab-Israeli war
Sep	23	Soviet Union tests atomic bomb
	30	Berlin Airlift ends
Oct	1	Mao Zedong proclaims establishment of People's Republic of China
	7	Communist Democratic Republic established in East Germany
	16	Greek Civil War ends, with defeat of rebels
Dec	8	Kuomintang (Chinese Nationalists) leave mainland China for Formosa (later Taiwan)
	27	Netherlands transfers sovereignty of Indonesia

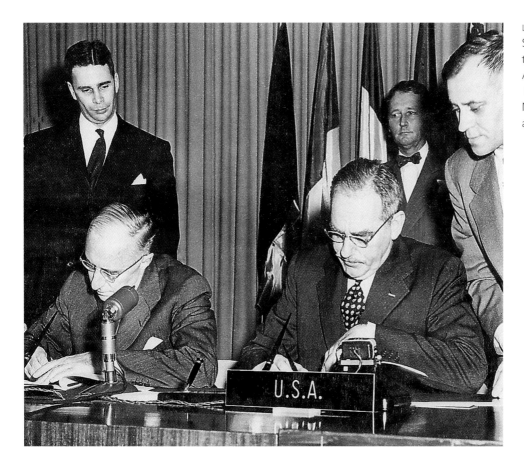

LEFT: Delegates for the United States and the Netherlands add their signatures to the North Atlantic Treaty. The original 12 members include the Netherlands, Britain, France, and the United States.

NATO AND COUNCIL OF EUROPE

Ten European nations, including the Netherlands and Britain, join with the United States and Canada to form the North Atlantic Treaty Organization (NATO), providing mutual support for each other against aggression. In May, ten Western European nations, including the formerly neutral nations of Sweden and Ireland, set up the Council of Europe to support freedom and the rule of law. The Council meets in Strasbourg and includes a European Court of Human Rights.

WEST AND EAST GERMANY

The United States, Britain, and France merge their three zones in West Germany to create the Federal Republic, which comes into being in May with its capital in Bonn. In September, the Christian Democrat, Konrad Adenauer (1876–1967), becomes chancellor. The following month, the Soviet Union establishes the German Democratic Republic in East Germany.

ARMS RACE BEGINS

The Soviet Union carries out its first atom bomb test, exploding it at a site in Kazakhstan. This marks the start of an arms race with the United States.

PEOPLE'S REPUBLIC OF CHINA

Following their victory in the civil war, the Chinese Communist Party establishes the People's Republic under the leadership of Mao Zedong (1893–1976). The Kuomintang Nationalists retreat to the offshore island of Taiwan under the leadership of Chang Kai-shek.

INDONESIA

After lengthy and complex UN-sponsored peace talks, the Netherlands transfers sovereignty to Indonesia under the leadership of President Sukarno (1902–70). Indonesia therefore becomes independent of its former colonial masters, the Dutch. The costs of four years' war include some 25,000 Dutch and 75,000 Indonesian casualties.

THE THIRD MAN

U.S. actor and director Orson Welles (1915–85) gives a brilliant performance as Harry Lime in Carol Reed's film *The Third Man*, with a screenplay by Graham Greene. The "Harry Lime Theme" by Anton Karas becomes almost as famous as the film itself.

DEATH OF A SALESMAN

One of the most successful American plays of all time, *Death of a Salesman* establishes Arthur Miller as a leading American dramatist. It tells the story of the salesman Willy Loman, who disintegrates because he relies too heavily on the hollow values of modern society.

1984

English author George Orwell's seminal dystopia, *1984*, is published and immediately engages the interest of readers in the English-speaking world and beyond. Many phrases from the book, such as "doublethink", and "Big Brother", find a permanent place in the language.

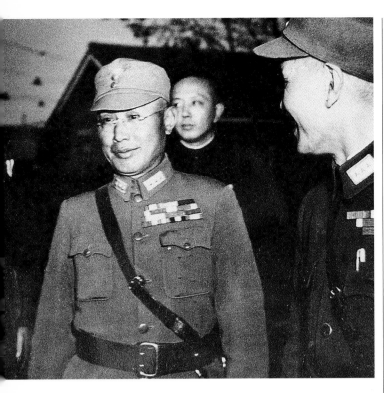

ABOVE: Chiang Kai-shek moves Nationalist Chinese government to Taiwan.

ABOVE: United Nations officials distribute clothing made from cotton supplied by the UN International Children's Emergency Fund to needy Japanese people at the Reikan Building in Tokyo.

THE SECOND SEX

French feminist Simone de Beauvoir (1908–86) publishes *The Second Sex*, which draws on art, literature, and philosophy to describe how men have consistently denied the right of humanity to women, and calls for the abolition of the myth of "the eternal feminine." A significant and groundbreaking work, it will later become a key text of the Women's Liberation Movement and a global bestseller.

CONVENIENT CAKES

Cake mixes prepared by General Mills and Pillsbury in the United States increase the range of convenience foods available in the United States.

GLASS HOUSE

Philip Johnson's Glass House in New Canaan, Connecticut, essentially consists of a glass box with a steel frame, typical of a number of modernist houses currently being designed. Influenced strongly by architect Mies van der Rohe, this house is the perfect example of the tenet "less is more."

NEPTUNE'S MOON

Dutch-born U.S. astronomer Gerard P. Kuiper (1905–73) discovers the second moon of the planet Neptune, now named Nereid.

ROCKET RECORD

Americans launch the WAC Corporal, a research rocket which reaches the record height of 250 miles; it is launched as a second stage from a V-2 rocket.

MORE ELEMENTS FOUND

American chemists headed by Glenn T. Seaborg create and discover two more elements: numbers 97, berkelium, and 98, californium. They are radioactive rare earths.

SICKLE-CELL DISEASE

American biological chemist Linus C. Pauling (1901–94) discovers that the inherited sickle-cell disease is caused by differences in the blood: People with this trait are also found to have immunity from malaria.

INDO-PAKISTAN WAR

Fighting between India and Pakistan ends and Indian troops control Kashmir.

U.S. BASKETBALL ASSOCIATION

Rivals the National Basketball League and the Basketball Association of America merge to create the National Basketball Association in America.

RIGHT: A nighttime game of baseball in the small American town of Mount Vernon.

ABOVE: The new transatlantic flights mean sleeping during the trip. Beds are made up for the passengers of this Constellation aircraft.

ABOVE: The world's oldest airline, KLM, introduces the "Flying Dutchman," which flies between New York and Amsterdam.

ABOVE: Front view of a mechanical calculator that is able to add numbers running into their billions in less than one-fifth of a second.

ABOVE: After the war, even neutral Switzerland finds the going tough. The U.S. supplies aid in the form of food.

BERLIN AIRLIFT

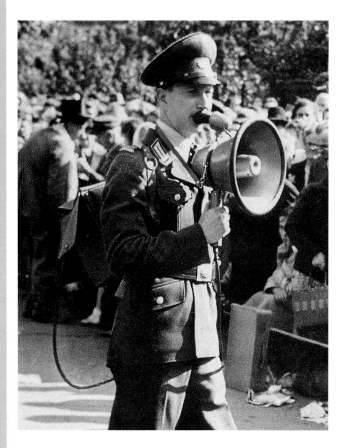

Western Allies begin running an airlift to carry supplies into Berlin. Land access to the western sector of Berlin, which is administered by France, Berlin and the United States, has been blocked off by the Soviet Union. The airlift continues until May 1949, when the Soviet Union relaxes its grip on the city, allowing convoys to use the autobahns across East Germany. A total of 277,264 flights are made, lifting 2,343,315 tons of cargo.

ABOVE: A West German policeman shouts instructions to waiting crowds of East Germans in Berlin as food parcels are distributed in the second joint American-West German food relief program.

ABOVE: Mini-parachutes drop sweets and chewing gum for German children.

BELOW: C-54 Skymasters unload their cargoes at Templehof Air Force Base.

ABOVE: A C-74 Globemaster airplane arrives at Gatow airfield with a supply of flour to help blockaded Berlin.

RIGHT: The baby's carriage seems an ideal place to secrete tins of food received as part of the joint American-West German food relief program.

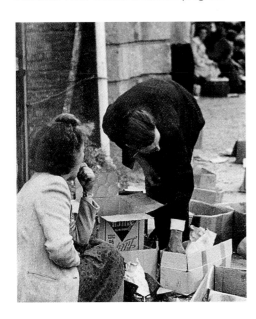

ABOVE: For these East Berliners the trip to West Berlin to collect their food parcels has been a tiring one.

THE NUCLEAR AGE

Postwar paranoia flavors the decade: Espionage, Cold War, and witch-hunts preoccupy the military and political classes. Unfinished business in the East leads to war in Korea and there are uprisings in Africa and Cuba. The babies who "boomed" in the 1940s grow up into a new phenomenon known as a teenager. Rock and roll is born: Elvis Presley thrusts his pelvis into the face of the Establishment and the Beat Generation try to articulate the joys of existential freedom. The space race begins, with the U.S.S.R. launching the satellite *Sputnik*.

BACKGROUND: The handwriting of Albert Einstein, describing his theory of relativity.

1950–1959

KEY EVENTS OF THE DECADE

- KOREAN WAR
- COMMUNIST WITCH-HUNTS
- CHINA INVADES TIBET
- ROCK AND ROLL
- CIVIL WAR IN CUBA
- MT. EVEREST CLIMBED
- DNA STRUCTURE DISCOVERED
- HYDROGEN BOMB
- BEAT
- THE WARSAW PACT

- POLIO VACCINE DEVELOPED
- HUNGARIAN UPRISING
- SUEZ CRISIS
- EEC SET UP
- RUSSIAN SPUTNIK IN SPACE
- CND FOUNDED
- ELVIS PRESLEY
- CASTRO TAKES CUBA

WORLD POPULATION 2,516 MILLION

elle – wie dieselbe gegenwär[tig]
in ihrer Anwendung auf beweg[te]
welche den Phänomenen nicht
t. Man denke z. B. an die elektr[o]
schen einem Magneten und
nomen hängt hier nur ab von
[der] Magnet, während nach
[der] üblichen, dass der eine oder der
sei; streng voneinander zu
ich der Magnet und ruht der
das Magneten ein elektrisches
welches an den Orten, wo sich
erzeugt. Ruht aber der Magnet
[ruh]t in der Umgebung des Magnet[en]
[Lei]ter eine elektromotorische
entspricht, die aber – [bei] Gleichheit
ins Auge gefassten Fällen vera[n]

WAR AND WITCH-HUNTS

The Korean War breaks out when Communist North Korea invades South Korea. UN forces, headed by the United States, side with South Korea. Later in the year, China invades Tibet. The fight against Communism in the Western world becomes an obsession with a witch-hunt in the United States and a spate of notorious spy trials. European countries make plans for a common trading market and a Dutch-born astronomer measures the planet Pluto.

1950

Jan	9	U.S. senator McCarthy alleges that Communists are working in the U.S. State Department
Mar	1	Atomic scientist Klaus Fuchs sentenced to 14 years' imprisonment for betraying secrets to the U.S.S.R.
May	1	Marriage Law passed in China gives women full equality in marriage and divorce
	9	Schuman Plan proposed to create single European authority for German and French coal production
June	25	North Korean forces invade Republic of South Korea Korean War breaks out
	28	North Korean forces capture Seoul, South Korea

July	1	First UN forces, most from United States, arrive in Korea
	16	World Cup takes place in Brazil
Aug	1	King Leopold III of Belgium abdicates.
Sep	11	South African statesman Jan Smuts dies
	16	U.S. marines make amphibious landings at Inchon, Korea
	26	UN forces recapture Seoul, South Korea
Oct	1	South Korean and UN troops cross 38th parallel, border between North and South Korea
	21	Chinese forces occupy Tibet
Nov	24	UN forces launch offensive into North Korea
	26	Chinese forces enter Korean War

COMMUNIST WITCH-HUNT

U.S. senator Joe McCarthy (1909–57) alleges that 57 Communists and 205 Communist sympathizers are working in the State Department. The Senate Foreign Relations Committee is given the job of investigating the charges, beginning an anti-Communist witch-hunt in the United States which lasts, with McCarthy in the lead, until he attacks the U.S. Army in October 1953, leading to his censure in October 1954 and rapid downfall.

SPY-FEVER

In Britain, atomic scientist Dr Klaus Fuchs (1911–88) is arrested and jailed for 14 years for giving nuclear secrets to the Russians. The information he passed on enables Soviet scientists to advance their nuclear plans by many years. The following year, American Communists Julius and Ethel Rosenberg are tried and executed in the United States for similar crimes. In June 1951, two British diplomats, Guy Burgess and Donald MacLean, defect to the U.S.S.R. These and other cases lead to a spate of spy fever in the Western world.

COMMON ECONOMIC POLICY

French foreign minister Robert Schuman (1886–1963) puts forward a plan for pooling the French and German coal and steel industries under a joint authority, to which other nations might join. The plan, worked out by French economist Jean Monnet, leads to the formation of the European Coal and Steel Community (ECSC), set up in Paris in April 1951 and joined by France, West Germany, Italy, and the three Benelux countries. The ECSC starts functioning in July 1952.

PHILIPPINES HUK REBELLION

The Hukbalahap or People's Anti-Japanese Army, a Communist resistance group in Luzon, which has adopted guerrilla tactics against the newly independent Republic of the Philippines, attacks Manila. However, its secret HQ in the capital is raided and the attack is called off. With U.S. military help and a program of reforms initiated by President Magsaysay, the popularity of the Huks wanes and the surviving leader surrenders in 1954.

MILLIONS WATCH TELEVISION

More than 75 million people watch the first transcontinental American television broadcast, marking the growing popularity of commercial network services since 1946. Color broadcasts are now transmitted by CBS. In the U.K., almost half a million television sets now tune into one BBC channel.

FOURTH WORLD CUP

The winner of the fourth soccer World Cup, hosted by Brazil, is decided by matches in a final pool of four teams. Uruguay wins for the second time but the pool system is never used again. England, the nation which invented the game, plays in the World Cup for the first time, but is beaten 1–0 by the United States.

ABOVE: Television becomes one of the most sought-after consumer products in the early 1950s.

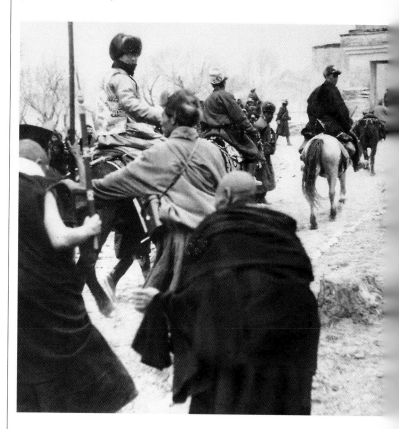

ABOVE: The Dalai Lama is forced into exile and flees to Dharamsala in Punjab, India, where he is to set up an alternative government.

CHINESE INVADE TIBET

The Chinese invade Tibet and although the Tibetans appeal to the UN, their country is quickly overrun. The youthful Dalai Lama remains as a figurehead but finally escapes to India.

LEOPOLD ABDICATES

King Leopold III returns to Belgium after six years' exile, and abdicates in favor of his son, Baudouin.

ABOVE: Motion pictures enter a new golden age in the early 1950s. *All The King's Men*, based on a Pulitzer Prize-winning novel by Robert Penn Warren, stars Broderick Crawford, Jeanne Dru, John Ireland, John Derek, and Mercedes McCambridge.

KURT WEILL
(1900–1950)

German-born American composer Kurt Weill has died. The composer of "Mack the Knife" and "September Song" worked with Bertolt Brecht on *The Rise and Fall of the City of Mahagonny* (1927–29) and the outstandingly successful *The Threepenny Opera* (1928). He left Nazi Germany in 1933 with his wife, the singer Lotte Lenya, and settled in the United States in 1935, where he composed several Broadway musicals.

JAN CHRISTIAN SMUTS
(1870–1950)

South African elder statesman and former prime minister Jan Christian Smuts has died. He helped to create the Union of South Africa (1910), was a member of the Imperial War Cabinet during World War l, and acted as counsel to the British War Cabinet during World War ll.

UNIVERSITY CITY

Modernist architects Mario Pani and Enrique del Moral design this Central American complex, the campus of the Autonomous National University of Mexico.

HOW BIG IS PLUTO?

In March Dutch-born U.S. astronomer Gerard P. Kuiper measures the planet Pluto, and finds it is tiny; its diameter is finally determined by the Hubble Space Telescope in the late 1990s as 1,453 miles.

THE OORT CLOUD

Dutch astrophysicist Jan Oort (1900–92) suggests that there is a huge reservoir of comets at a great distance from the Sun; it is later known as the Oort Cloud.

ENTER CYCLAMATES

Cyclamates, artificial sweeteners much used in food and drinks as an alternative to saccharin, are introduced; some countries ban them.

CHINESE WOMEN EQUAL

Mao Zedong's Communist government passes a new marriage law, which recognizes the role women played in the Communist victory. Chinese women now have full legal equality in marriage, divorce, and the ownership of property. Forced arranged marriages, polygamy, child marriage, and infanticide are forbidden.

INSIDE THE CELL

Using an electron microscope, Belgian cytologist (cell specialist) Albert Claude (1899–1983) discovers the endoplasmic reticulum, a network of space inside a living cell that holds things together.

DINER'S CREDIT CARD

Diner's Club is founded by Ralph Schneider, who issues the first charge card, a prototype credit card (it is paid off every month). Two hundred cardholders pay an annual fee for credit at 27 New York restaurants.

2,000-YEAR-OLD DEATH

Tollund Man, a 2,000-year-old corpse, is found preserved in a bog near Jutland, Denmark. Aged between 30 and 40, the man was killed by hanging or strangling — a leather rope is still around his neck.

OFF ON PACKAGE HOLIDAYS

Package holidays are launched by European entrepreneurs Gerard Blitz, a Belgian, and Vladimir Raitz, who advertise inexpensive campsite accommodation in "holiday villages" on the islands of Majorca and Corsica.

COMPUTER CHESS

U.S. mathematician Claude E. Shannon designs the first chess-playing computer.

VASLAV NIJINSKY
(1890–1950)

The great Russian dancer and choreographer Vaslav Nijinsky has died. Trained at the Imperial Ballet School at St. Petersburg, he became the leading dancer with Diaghilev's Ballets Russes. Sadly, after a period of internment in World War 1. he was diagnosed schizophrenic in 1917, and his life has been a struggle.

THE PLASTIC AGE

ABOVE: Newly invented nylon zippers are light enough for sheer fabrics and resistant to cleaning compounds.

ABOVE: A tough, moisture-resistant plastic called Tenite covers this portable radio case.

ABOVE: A clock encased in transparent plastic, a popular ornament.

ABOVE: A telephone handset made of Bakelite, an early plastic.

ABOVE: Plastics are easily molded, so can be used to make intricate shapes such as this record rack.

FIRST JET AIRLINER SERVICE

The first jet airliner service is inaugurated with a flight from London to Paris in the Vickers Viscount 630 four-engined turboprop aircraft.

YOUTH FASHION

Bobbysoxers, so called because of the knee-length socks they wear, emerge as a new youth group in the United States. They are teenage girl fans of the new singing sensation Frank Sinatra (1915–98), and they follow him wherever he performs.

RASHOMON

Japanese director Akira Kurosawa's film *Rashomon* is premièred, establishing his worldwide reputation. It is a study of a violent crime from four different points of view. Kurosawa will later become famous for the epic Samurai movie *The Seven Samurai* (1954).

STONE AGE NORTH POLE

The Danes complete a three-year expedition to Greenland in which they find traces of a Stone Age culture 470 miles from the North Pole.

KOREAN WAR

North Korean forces invade South Korea, leading to three years of bitter conflict. United Nations troops, led by the United States, aid South Korea, while China joins in on the North Korean side in November. North Korean forces push South Korean and U.S. forces down to a small perimeter at Pusan. In September 1950, U.S. marines land at Inchon, the port serving Seoul, the South Korean capital, as part of the UN breakout operation from Pusan. The landings, which are a success, lead to a counteroffensive up to the Chinese border. With a combined strength of 485,000, Chinese and North Korean troops drive the 365,000-strong United Nations forces south. A UN counterattack stabilizes the line; by June 1951 the two sides face each other across the 38th parallel. Negotiations and prisoner exchanges take place in 1953. By the end of the war, UN casualties are 118,515 killed, 264,591 wounded, and 92,987 captured. The Communist armies suffer 1,600,000 battle casualties, with 171,000 taken prisoner.

The Korean War sees the first-ever jet-versus-jet victory when in November 1950 an American USAF F-80C shoots down a Chinese MiG-15 fighter over Sinuiju on the Yalu River.

ABOVE: A soldier stands guard in a machine-gun nest.

ABOVE: U.S. Navy Sky Raiders fire rockets at North Korean positions.

ABOVE: A U.S. soldier comforts a fellow infantryman, while another writes casualty tags.

ABOVE: A 75mm recoilless rifle is fired in support of infantry units near Oetlook-tong.

LEFT: U.S. marines use scaling ladders to storm ashore during the amphibious landings at Inchon.

RIGHT: A Korean delegate to the Kaesong Conference.

BELOW: Images from the conflict. Top left, U.S. marines advancing under close air support. Top right, United Nations troops fighting in the streets of Seoul. Bottom left, bombardment of warehouses in Wonsan, North Korea. Bottom right, the USS *Missouri* fires a 16-inch salvo to disrupt communications in the north of the peninsula.

SPIES, PACTS, AND BEATNIKS

War continues in Korea and French Indochina. Libya gains independence. A new and most advanced digital computer — UNIVAC 1 — is developed. It uses magnetic tape to input and output information and will have a revolutionary impact on business. American author J.D. Salinger's novel *The Catcher in the Rye* creates a hero whose alienation is understood by adolescents everywhere. Italian-American composer Menotti creates an opera specifically for television.

1951

Jan	**1**	North Koreans and Chinese take Seoul
	26	UN launches counteroffensive against Chinese and Korean forces
Mar	**30**	Julius and Ethel Rosenberg found guilty of espionage
Apr	**22**	Battle of Imjin River, Korea. UN defensive action against Chinese and Korean troops
May	**25**	British diplomats Burgess and Maclean warned they are under suspicion of spying and leave Britain
Sep	**1**	United States, Australia, and New Zealand sign Pacific Security Agreement.
	8	Peace treaty signed with Japan
Dec	**13**	French National Assembly ratifies Schuman Plan
	24	Libya becomes independent

ABOVE: President Harry S. Truman addresses the American people. Television broadcasts are a common feature of the time.

OPPOSITE: Dramatic changes in aircraft design are represented by the 1912 "pusher" biplane, which can fly at 60 miles per hour, and the North American F-86 Sabre jet, which holds the world speed record of 670 miles per hour in 1951.

ABOVE: In Saudi Arabia, American experts advise on the use of scientific farming techniques to help grow crops such as watermelons in the desert soil.

ABOVE: South Korean refugees, fleeing from fighting in their home area, follow a railroad track to what they hope will be a safer place.

THE CATCHER IN THE RYE
American writer J.D. Salinger (b. 1919) publishes a short novel, *The Catcher in the Rye*. It portrays the adolescent Holden Caulfield, who runs away from boarding school. Holden's attacks on the "phony" nature of adult attitudes make the novel an instant hit with teenagers.

THE DESTROYED CITY
This work by Russian sculptor Ossip Zadkine (1890–1967) is a memorial to the (predominantly civilian) victims of the Nazi bombing of Rotterdam in 1940. It is subsequently placed at the entrance to Rotterdam harbor.

AMAHL AND THE NIGHT VISITORS
U.S. composer Gian Carlo Menotti composes this work specifically for the increasingly popular medium of television. A Christmas work, it is premièred on Christmas Eve and is his most famous work.

BILLY BUDD
The opera *Billy Budd* by English composer Benjamin Britten (1913–76) is performed. It is based on Herman Melville's novel *Billy Budd*. Novelist E.M. Forster collaborates with Eric Crozier on the libretto, and English tenor Peter Pears creates the lead role.

UNIVAC 1 ARRIVES
The first mass-produced computer goes into production; it is the UNIVAC 1 (Universal Automatic Computer). It is the first computer to store its data on magnetic tape.

STICKY SUBJECT
U.S. scientist Fred Joyner accidentally discovers an adhesive that sticks to everything it touches; it turns out to be the first of the superglues, which harden in seconds in the absence of air.

FESTIVAL OF BRITAIN
The Festival of Britain opens in London around Robert Matthew's Royal Festival Hall and a Dome of Discovery. Exhibitions display new textiles, minimalist furniture of metal and plastic, and modern art and design. Telekinema, the star attraction, shows stereoscopic movies watched through polarizing spectacles.

PEACE AT LAST
Representatives of 49 nations meet in San Francisco and sign the peace treaty with Japan, formally bringing World War II hostilities to an end.

LIBYA INDEPENDENT
The former Italian colony of Libya becomes independent. Occupied by the British during the war, Libya becomes the first independent state created by resolution of the UN, and the first former European colony in North Africa to gain independence.

FRENCH INDOCHINESE WAR
War continues in Indochina. The Vietminh establish a common front with Communist groups in Laos and Cambodia and move to conventional tactics.

PEST CONTROL
Biological pest control is tried out in Australia, when myxomatosis from Brazil is introduced by sheep farmers to kill rabbits, introduced by settlers in 1859 and now numbering about 500 million and consuming the grazing. In the United States, entomologist Edward F. Knipling of the Department of Agriculture introduces sterilization of female insects, which die without reproducing.

ABOVE: The 35th annual Memorial Day 500-mile race at Indianapolis (the Indy 500) is won by Lee Wallard in a record time of 3 hours 57 minutes and 38 seconds, at an average speed of 126.25 miles per hour.

THE MILKY WAY

U.S. astronomer William Morgan confirms that our own galaxy, the Milky Way, has a spiral structure; the solar system is on one arm of the spiral.

FLUORIDATION

Fluoride naturally present in some drinking water is discovered to prevent tooth decay; work begins to add fluoride to water supplies elsewhere.

LUDWIG JOSEF JOHANN WITTGENSTEIN (1899–1951)

Austrian-born British philosopher Ludwig Wittgenstein has died of cancer in Cambridge. His early work, *Tractatus Logico-Philosophicus* (1921), was highly influential among contemporary philosophers and he immediately had a great personal following when, in 1945, he finally took up a post at Cambridge, although nothing further was published. His second major work, *Philosophical Investigations* (1953), and other writings will be published after his death.

ROCK AND ROLL IS HERE TO STAY

The United States tests an H-bomb in the Pacific Ocean as the U.S.–Soviet Union rivalry steps up. Mau Mau disturbances break out in Kenya against British colonial rule and a state of emergency is declared. Transistors are applied to a variety of uses from telephones to radios and rock and roll bursts onto the popular music scene. Cold War rivalry is reflected at the Olympic Games where Czech Zatopek runs off with three golds.

1952

Feb	**6**	The British king George VI dies Queen Elizabeth II succeeds him
	14	Winter Olympics open in Oslo, Norway
Mar	**1**	India holds first national elections. Pandit Nehru's Congress Party wins 364 out of 489 seats in the National Assembly
July	**19**	Olympic Games open in Finland
	25	European Steel and Coal Community comes into being
	26	Eva ("Evita") Perón dies of cancer
	27	Emil Zatopek wins three gold medals for Czechoslovakia
Sep	**11**	Eritrea federated with Ethiopia, East Africa
Oct	**20**	Mau Mau disturbances begin. A state of emergency is declared in Kenya
Nov	**1**	U.S. scientists test hydrogen bomb in the South Pacific
	5	Dwight D. Einsenhower wins U.S. presidential election
	9	Chaim Weizmann, first Israeli president, dies

ABOVE: The California wine districts of Napa, Sonoma, and Mendocino produce fine varieties of New World wines.

U.S. TESTS H-BOMB

American scientists test a hydrogen bomb at Eniwetk Atoll in the Marshall Islands of the Pacific. According to observers, a small island is completely obliterated in the blast. Radioactive dust rises some 25 miles high and spreads some 100 miles. The hydrogen bomb is a thermonuclear weapon, which works by nuclear fission.

"IKE" WINS PRESIDENTIAL ELECTION

In November, former U.S. general Dwight D. Eisenhower (1890–1969) wins the presidential election for the Republicans with a landslide over his Democratic opponent, Adlai Stevenson. His vice president is Richard Nixon.

MAU MAU CAMPAIGN

A revolt against British colonial rule in Kenya breaks out, headed largely by the Kikuyu and Meru tribes. The British declare a state of emergency and commit 50,000 troops. Trouble continues until 1960.

NEW BRITISH QUEEN

George VI dies and Princess Elizabeth (b. 1926) becomes queen as Elizabeth II. Many heads of state attend the state funeral in London.

ERITREA FEDERATED WITH ETHIOPIA

In East Africa, the former Italian colony Eritrea is federated by the UN with Ethiopia.

DEATH OF EVITA

Eva Perón (Evita), much-loved and popular wife of President Juan Perón, dies from cancer. Her death starts the gradual erosion of his appeal.

ROCK AND ROLL ARRIVES

In the United States, rock and roll is launched with Alan Freed's Moondog's Rock'n'Roll Party on the WJW radio station in Cleveland, Ohio. The teen style movement has also reached the U.K., where Teddy boys dress in updated Edwardian fashions.

THE COMET FLIES

The world's first all-jet airliner, Britain's De Havilland DH 106 Comet 1, inaugurates a regular passenger service between London and Johannesburg.

ELEMENTS DISCOVERED

Elements 99 and 100, einsteinium and fermium, are discovered — after a hydrogen bomb explosion — by U.S. scientists working at the University of California and two national laboratories.

WAITING FOR GODOT

Irish writer Samuel Beckett's most famous play, *Waiting for Godot*, is performed and becomes a theatrical landmark. It portrays two tramps who wait for the mysterious Godot, who never comes. Their predicament seems to reflect the hopelessness of the modern world.

UNITE D'HABITATION,

French architect Le Corbusier (1887–1965) creates a remarkable housing development in Marseilles. It incorporates facilities such as shops, a swimming pool, a gym, and a childcare center, as well as apartments, and meets the architect's aim of housing an entire community in a vast modernist block.

MULTIPLE-USE TRANSISTORS

In Japan the first pocket-sized transistor radio is produced by Masaru Ibuka, who improves the technology of the USA's Western Electric Co. division of AT&T and launches it under the Sony name. The first transistorized hearing aids are produced in the United States, and in the U.K. transistors are applied to central telephone dialing apparatus to provide automatic dialing.

WRECK INVESTIGATION BY SCUBA

The first archaeological investigation of a wreck using scuba-diving equipment is carried out by French diver and marine archaeologist Jacques Cousteau, who discovers an ancient Greek ship off the coast of Marseilles, which contains wine urns.

ANTABUSE

Antabuse™, a drug which helps alcoholics to stop drinking, is introduced; its generic name is disulphiram.

GAS CHROMATOGRAPHY

British biochemists Archer Martin and A.T. James invent gas chromatography, a method of separating chemical vapors.

4'33"

American composer John Cage (1912–92) has "written" a piano piece containing four minutes and 33 seconds of silence. The audience is encouraged to listen to the noises in the environment around them.

DREAMING SLEEP

Biologists studying sleep patterns discover a period in which a sleeper's eyes move rapidly; this is known as dreaming sleep or rapid eye movement (REM) sleep.

INSULIN ANALYZED

British biochemist Frederick Sanger (b. 1918) discovers that insulin is a protein and works out its structure.

MARIA MONTESSORI
(1870–1952)

Italian educational pioneer and physician Maria Montessori has died. Her teaching methods, which include learning through play, were developed from her early experiences in her school for children with learning disabilities, and Montessori schools have become established as a leading method of teaching nursery and primary school children throughout the world.

CHAIM AZRIEL WEIZMANN
(1874–1952)

Israel's first president, Dr. Chaim Weizmann, has died. An eminent chemist of Russian birth, as a young man he worked in Switzerland where he became a leading Zionist. In Great Britain, where he lived from 1904 until 1934, he discovered the bacterium *Clostridium acetobutylium*, which is active in producing acetone from carbohydrate.

RIGHT: Television studios boom in response to the huge popularity of the new medium.

FLOAT GLASS
English glassmaker Arthur Pilkington invents float glass, in which liquid glass is floated on a bath of molten tin, producing a completely flat and shiny sheet.

AMNIOCENTESIS
Doctors develop amniocentesis, a procedure during pregnancy by which some of the amniotic fluid in a woman's womb can be examined to see if the baby she is carrying is healthy; it is used only in high-risk cases.

ACRYLIC GOES ON THE MARKET
New acrylic fibers such as Orlon, discovered by Du Pont, and Acrilan, produced by the Chemstrand Corporation, are marketed in the United States. They are soft and when spun into yarn can be knitted like wool.

ANTARCTIC MAPPED
The Antarctic is mapped by air and major glaciers are explored by a Norwegian-Swedish-British expedition organized by H.V. Sverdrup, former director of the Scripps Institution in the United States, and professor of Oceanography at the University of California.

AUSTRALIAN DISCOVERS ORE MOUNTAIN
An iron ore mountain is discovered in the Hammersley Range by Australian prospector Langley Hancock, who spots rust-colored outcroppings when his aircraft is blown off course. He keeps it secret, awaiting a change in mining laws before staking his claim.

FIRST SUGARLESS SOFT DRINK
No-Cal Ginger Ale, the first sugar-free soft drink, uses the new cyclamate sweeteners instead of sugar. It is also salt-free, so suitable for people with obesity, diabetes, and high blood pressure.

SCANDINAVIAN OLYMPICS
Mammoth crowds in Oslo, Norway, welcome the Winter Olympics to Scandinavia for the first time. Spectators on skis encourage cross-country competitors, 150,000 set an Olympic record to watch the ski jumping, and home cheers ring out for speed skater Hjalmar "Hjallis" Andersen's three golds. Athletes from the U.S.S.R. take part for the first time in the Summer Olympics held in Helsinki. Emil Zatopek (b. 1922), the "Czech Express," thrills Finnish spectators and takes golds in the 5,000m, 10,000m, and marathon.

> ### MARIA EVA (EVITA) DUARTE DE PERON (1919–1952)
>
> Eva Perón, the immensely popular second wife of the Argentine populist right-wing president Juan Perón, has died from cancer at the age of 33. She had a strong influence on her husband and pursued the cause of women's suffrage and social and healthcare reform. Her death is greatly mourned by the Argentine people.

DOUBLE HELIX DECODED

Soviet ruler Joseph Stalin dies and is succeeded by Nikita Khrushchev. The Korean War comes to an end. British scientists begin to unlock life's secrets by discovering the structure of DNA and the world's highest mountain — Mt. Everest — is finally climbed. The Netherlands experiences severe flooding and an American conservationist warns of the dangers of misusing the Earth's natural resources.

1953

Jan	20	Dwight Eisenhower inaugurated as 34th president of the United States
Feb	10	Common market for coal and steel begins among various European nations
Mar	5	Joseph Stalin, leader of the Soviet Union, dies (b. 1879)
Apr	25	British scientists discover the structure of DNA
May	29	Mountaineers Hillary and Tensing reach the peak of Mt. Everest; the news is received on June 1
June	17	Workers' strike turns into uprising against Communist government, East Germany
July	5	Imre Nagy becomes prime minister of Hungary
	26	Fidel Castro leads attempt to overthrow Batista government, Cuba
	27	Armistice is signed ending the Korean War
Sep	12	Nikita Khrushchev appointed first secretary of the Central Committee of the Communist party, Soviet Union
Nov	23	Hungarian soccer team beats the English at Wembley

STALIN DIES

Joseph Stalin, leader of the U.S.S.R. for nearly 30 years, dies at the age of 73. He is succeeded by Georgi Malenkov as prime minister, but in September Nikita Khrushchev (1894–1971) becomes Communist party first secretary.

KOREAN WAR ENDS

An armistice is signed in Panmunjon, Korea, bringing to an end the three-year-old Korean War. Prisoners are exchanged and both sides withdraw from occupied areas. Under the agreement, Korea remains divided into North and South Korea.

UPRISING CRUSHED

In East Berlin, a workers' uprising against the partition of the city and the harsh Soviet rule is put down by Soviet tanks.

REGIME RELAXES IN HUNGARY

Imre Nagy (1895–1958) becomes the new prime minister of Hungary. He announces an end to enforced collectivization of agriculture and begins to relax Communist rule.

SHELLFISH POISONING

Environmental poisoning is identified as the cause of deaths from eating fish and shellfish caught in Minamata Bay in Kyushu and Niigata in Honshu, Japan. The waters are found to be contaminated with lead, a byproduct of industrial processes.

BELOW: After the armistice is signed in July 1953, peace negotiations to end the Korean War continue and prisoner exchanges are completed in September.

ABOVE: Czech refugees make a dramatic escape to the West by crashing through the Czech-German border in a stolen tank.

ABOVE: A miniature weapon used by East German secret agents in the continuing conflict with the West. It is a standard cigarette case concealing cyanide-coated bullets.

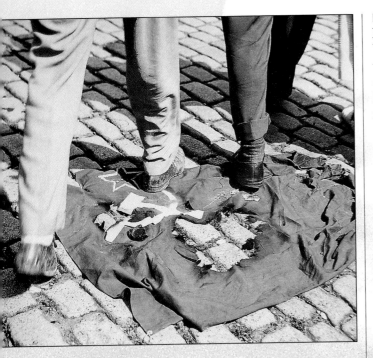

ABOVE: East Germans burn and trample Soviet flags during riots in the divided city of Berlin.

DOUBLE HELIX

British scientists Francis Crick, James Watson, Maurice Wilkins, and Rosalind Franklin discover the structure of the complex molecule DNA (deoxyribonucleic acid), the chemical that forms the basis of genes, which pass on hereditary characteristics. The structure of DNA is made up of two strands that intertwine to form a double helix. With this discovery, scientists can now establish how living things reproduce themselves.

NETHERLANDS FLOODS

Hurricane winds and abnormally high tides cause heavy flooding in the Netherlands and hundreds of people are drowned. Work immediately begins on the 30-year Delta Project to build dams across coastal estuaries and inlets, a pioneering storm surge barrier across the Oosterschelde Estuary, and the world's longest bridge across the Scheldt River.

UNDER MILK WOOD

Welsh poet Dylan Thomas (1914–53) puts his vivid language and humor to use to create a play for voices. *Under Milk Wood* is set in a Welsh seaside town and deals with the daily lives, loves, and dreams of the inhabitants. Thomas takes a lead role in the play, which is performed in New York City, but dies later in the year.

CUBAN CIVIL WAR

Communist rebel leader Fidel Castro (b. 1927) leads an attack on army barracks in Cuba in an unsuccessful attempt to overthrow Cuban premier Batista. Some rebels are killed; Castro and others are imprisoned.

COMMON COAL AND STEEL

The countries involved in the European Coal and Steel Community — France, Italy, Luxembourg, Belgium, the Netherlands, and West Germany — begin operating a common market for coal, iron ore, and steel.

BACKGROUND: Atomic bomb tests are conducted at Bikini Atoll in the Pacific Ocean.

EARTH'S LIMITS

American zoologist and conservationist Fairfield Osborne publishes *The Limits of Our Earth*, warning of the consequences of misusing available natural resources and the dangers of overpopulation. In *Our Plundered Planet*, published in 1948, he had explained the dangers of using DDT.

THE CRUCIBLE

American playwright Arthur Miller's play *The Crucible* is performed. It takes as its subject the 17th-century witchcraft trials in Salem, Massachusetts, using them as a metaphor for the McCarthyite hunting and trial of "communists" in contemporary America.

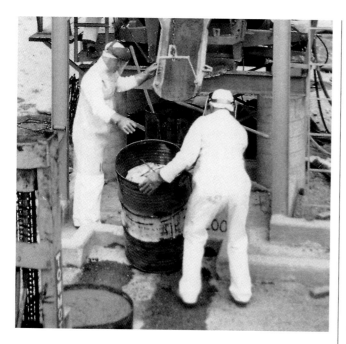

ABOVE: Methods of disposing of nuclear waste include burying it deep underground.

HEART-LUNG MACHINE

U.S. surgeon John H. Gibbon develops a heart-lung machine and uses it to keep a patient alive while performing heart surgery.

GEODESIC DOME

Geodisic domes appear at Ford's HQ at Dearborn, Michigan. They are the invention of designer and writer Richard Buckminster Fuller (1895–1983), who developed them in the 1930s and 1940s. Based on polyhedra, geodisic domes are designed to allow the maximum space to be covered with the most lightweight structure. They are also cheap to make, and easy to prefabricate and assemble.

MICROWAVE OVEN

Percy L. Spencer, working for a firm in Massachusetts, patents the microwave oven. Used initially for commercial catering, it is later manufactured for domestic use.

EVEREST CONQUERED

New Zealander Edmund Hillary, and Tibetan sherpa Tenzing Norgay, become the first climbers to reach the 29,039-foot summit of Mt. Everest, the world's highest mountain.

STRANGENESS

U.S. physicist Murray Gell-Mann introduces the term "strangeness" to classify subatomic particles.

RIGHT: Joseph Stalin, real name Iosif Vissarionovich Dzugashvili, dies. Expelled from a seminary in his youth for his Marxist evangelism, he rose through the ranks to lead the U.S.S.R.

MASER

U.S. physicist Charles Townes invents a device for generating high-intensity microwaves; he calls it a maser, short for Microwave Amplification by Stimulated Emission of Radiation.

CREAM IN YOUR COFFEE?

Powdered cream for coffee, produced by M&R Dietetic Laboratories of Ohio in 1950, is followed by the production of dried milk by American dairy scientist David D. Peebles.

SCIENTOLOGY FOUNDED

The Church of Scientology is founded in Washington, D.C., by a former seaman, Lafayette Ronald Hubbard. His science of Dianetics is a form of psychotherapy designed to eliminate neuroses and offer a spiritual alternative to personal problems.

GO TELL IT ON THE MOUNTAIN

African-American writer James Baldwin (1924–87) publishes his first novel, *Go Tell it on the Mountain*. Set in Harlem, and based on his own life, it establishes him on the literary scene as a writer who will portray the lives and plights of black Americans.

SOCCER SHOCK

The Hungarian soccer team, captained by Ferenc Puskas, defeats the English team by 6–3 at the English home ground at Wembley, so becoming the first overseas team to defeat England at home.

DISPOSABLE BIC

The Bic, a disposable ballpoint pen devised by Baron Bich, is sold in Paris.

JOSEPH STALIN
(1879–1953)

The Soviet ruler, Joseph Stalin, has died. Born in Georgia, the son of a shoemaker, Stalin became a Bolshevik and in 1922 was appointed General Secretary to the Central Committee. He began to build a power base and, after Lenin died in 1924, succeeded him as leader of the Soviet Union, ruthlessly crushing all opposition to his leadership. Through collectivization and a series of five-year plans, he transformed the Soviet economy and established it as a world power.

TROUBLE IN ALGERIA AND VIETNAM

Anti-French violence flares in Algeria as a war for independence begins. Vietnam, Laos, and Cambodia gain independence and Vietnam is divided into two. The arrival of the nuclear age is underpinned by the launch of the world's first nuclear-powered submarine and the opening of the world's first nuclear reactor. An English athlete runs a mile in less than four minutes, Marlon Brando becomes a cult figure, and the world's first successful kidney transplant is carried out.

1954

Jan	21	First nuclear-powered submarine launched, United States
Mar	1	United States tests H-bomb in the Marshall Islands, causing widespread concern
Apr	9	Comet jet airliner crashes north of Messina, Sicily
	24	Mau Mau rounded up in Kenya
May	6	Roger Bannister breaks the four-minute mile record
	7	French troops forced to surrender in Dien Bien Phu, Vietnam
	17	U.S. Supreme Court rules that racial segregation in schools is unconstitutional
June	27	World's first nuclear power station opens, U.S.S.R.
July	15	Boeing 707 makes maiden flight, Seattle
	20	Armistice signed in Geneva ends French Indochinese War. Cambodia, Laos, and Vietnam independent. Vietnam is divided along the 79th parallel
Sep	8	Southeast Asia Treaty Organization (SEATO) established
Oct	8	Communist forces occupy Hanoi, North Vietnam
Nov	1	Violence breaks out in Algeria. Algerian War of Independence begins
Dec	2	U.S. Senate censures Senator Joseph McCarthy

ABOVE: Vietnamese civilians in Hanoi set up informal street markets while waiting to be evacuated to the south.

RIGHT: An anti-Communist former prisoner of war jubilantly waves the South Korean flag on reaching Seoul.

VIETMINH TAKE DIEN BIEN PHU

In Vietnam, some 10,000 French troops are surrounded at Dien Bien Phu by the 50,000-strong Vietminh Army led by General Giap and forced to surrender after a savage 56-day siege. This defeat leads to a series of agreements signed between France and other powers. France recognizes the independence of Cambodia and Laos and agrees to the independence and partition of Vietnam: the Communist-led north under Ho Chi Minh (1890–1969) and the pro-Western south, a republic under Ngo Dinh Diem (1901–63).

FIRST NUCLEAR SUBMARINE

The world's first nuclear-powered submarine, the *Nautilus*, begins service with the U.S. Navy; she is powered by two steam turbines, with the heat for the steam provided by a nuclear reactor.

LEFT: The opening ceremony of a stadium and sports complex in Bucharest, Romania.

ABOVE: The crashed remains of a Czech airplane flown across the Iron Curtain to West Germany by Karel Cihak.

SEGREGATION UNCONSTITUTIONAL

The U.S. Supreme Court rules in the Brown v. Board of Education case that racial segregation in schools is unconstitutional. The judgement leads to considerable racial tension throughout the American South.

BIKINI ATOLL

The United States tests its second H-bomb at Bikini Atoll in the Marshall Islands. It is more than 500 times as powerful as the A-bomb dropped on Hiroshima and its effects cause considerable concern. Nearby Japanese fishermen suffer radiation burns and sickness.

NUCLEAR POWER PLANT

The first nuclear power plant to produce electricity is built in the Soviet Union, near Moscow. It is capable of generating 5 megawatts of electricity, enough for a small town.

SEATO FORMED

Eight nations — the United States, Australia, New Zealand, Pakistan, Thailand, the Philippines, Britain, and France — sign a defence treaty in Manila, establishing the Southeast Asian Treaty Organization (SEATO) as a defense against Communist power in the region.

ROCKING AROUND THE CLOCK

Bill Haley and the Comets release their latest record "Rock Around the Clock." It rapidly sells a million copies and within a year has become a youth anthem, establishing the new sound of rock and roll. And in Memphis, Tennessee, Elvis Presley (1935–77) records "That's All Right Momma" for Sun Records.

SOLAR BATTERY

The solar battery is developed by Bell Laboratories of AT&T, making it possible to convert sunlight to electric power. The Association for Applied Solar Energy is founded and a periodical launched, *The Sun at Work*.

LEFT: On a state visit to Turkey, Marshal Tito of Yugoslavia, accompanied by President Bayar of Turkey, reviews a guard of honor on his arrival.

DUTCH AUTONOMY FOR TERRITORIES

The Dutch government grants full domestic autonomy to its territories in South America and the West Indies.

ALGERIAN WAR OF INDEPENDENCE

An insurrection breaks out against French rule in the North African colony of Algeria, which France regards not as a colony, but rather as mainland France. The rebels call themselves the Algerian National Liberation Front (FLN) and launch what is to be a long and bloody struggle for independence that continues until 1962. The French win the military campaign but lose the political battle in the UN. When General de Gaulle becomes president in 1958, he pulls out of Algeria.

LORD OF THE FLIES

English novelist William Golding (1911–93) publishes *Lord of the Flies*. The novel describes what happens when, after a plane crash on a desert island, a group of schoolboys try to create a democratic society. The social order rapidly degenerates and reverts to savagery.

LIJNBAAN, ROTTERDAM

This long pedestrian shopping way, stretching some 656 yards from Rotterdam's commercial center to the railroad station, becomes highly influential in town planning. Many other pedestrian precincts will soon follow all over Europe.

LA STRADA

The poetic, tragicomic movie *La Strada* by Italian film director Federico Fellini (1920–93) is premièred. It portrays the lives of two wandering mountebanks, stars Fellini's wife, Giulietta Masina, and has a memorable score by Nino Rota.

BRANDO ON THE WATERFRONT

Starring Marlon Brando as an ex-prizefighter, *On the Waterfront* is the latest film directed by Elia Kazan. Brando's performance will gain him an Oscar, and follows his powerful performance as a leather-clad motorbike gang leader in *The Wild One*.

COMETS CRASH

Following a Comet airliner crash — one of a series — north of Messina, Sicily, all Comets are grounded and one is tested to destruction. Metal fatigue in the cabin is found to be the cause of the disasters.

GERMANY BEATS HUNGARY

The talented Hungarian soccer team is beaten by Germany in the final of the 1954 World Cup in Switzerland. Hungarian star player Ferenc Puskas scores a goal but the final score is 3–2 to Germany.

RIGHT: Yugoslav troops parade in honor of the visit to Belgrade of President Bayar of Turkey, to sign the tripartite alliance between Yugoslavia, Turkey, and Greece.

TABLE TENNIS CHAMPIONS

The Table Tennis World Championships take place in London. China and Japan are confirmed as new powers in the sport when they displace previous leaders Hungary and Czechoslovakia.

MOONIES

The Unification Church is founded by Korean evangelist Reverend Sun Myung Moon. His acolytes are dubbed "Moonies." Moon becomes notorious for arranging mass marriages between members of the church who do not meet until the day of their wedding.

A MILE IN UNDER FOUR MINUTES

English athlete Roger Bannister achieves the holy grail of middle-distance running and runs a mile in under four minutes. Bannister, a 25-year-old medical student, breaks the four-minute barrier at the Oxford University running track, running the mile in 3 mins 59.4 seconds.

BIRTH PILL TESTED

The first oral contraceptive, a pill for women containing a synthetic hormone, is developed by U.S. physiologist Gregory Pincus. It is successfully tested in Puerto Rico the following year.

EATING IN FRONT OF THE TV
TV dinners, a new convenience food, are introduced in the United States by Omaha's C.A. Swanson & Sons.

VTOL AIRCRAFT
The U.S. Navy's Convair XFY-1 fighter aircraft makes its first test flight; it is a VTOL (Vertical Take-Off and Landing) aircraft, nicknamed the "flying pogo stick."

SUCCESSFUL KIDNEY TRANSPLANT
U.S. surgeons J. Hartwell Harrison and Joseph Murray carry out the first successful kidney transplant, the donor being the recipient's identical twin brother.

PLASTIC LENSES
Contact lenses, known since 1887, are now available in plastic, and are lighter and more comfortable to wear.

ENRICO FERMI
(1901–1954)

The eminent nuclear physicist Enrico Fermi has died. Born in 1901 in Italy, where he was educated, and where he worked until 1938, he and his colleagues were the first to split uranium atoms by bombarding them with neutrons, contributing to the development of nuclear power and nuclear weapons. He was awarded the Nobel Prize for Physics in 1938, and left for the United States, where he became naturalized, because of Italian anti-Semitism. He was responsible for the world's first nuclear reactor, built in Chicago in 1942.

ABOVE: Leaders of the three nations occupying West Germany — Pierre Mendes-France of France, Anthony Eden of Great Britain, and John Foster Dulles of the United States — meet with Germany's Chancellor Konrad Adenauer in Paris to end postwar occupation.

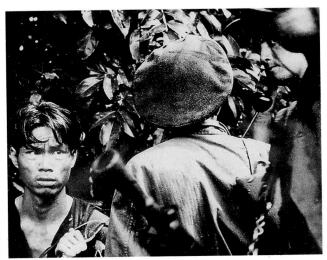

HENRI EMILE BENOIT MATISSE
(1869–1954)

The great French painter, stained-glass artist, and sculptor Henri Matisse has died in his 80s. Even as an old man he continued to work, most recently on making pictures from cutout paper (*L'Escargot*, 1953). As a young man Matisse was one of the group known, from 1905, as the fauves (wild ones). Although he was influenced by cubism (and gave the movement its name), his painting was more representational; he is admired for his flow of line and use of pure color.

ABOVE: The French Foreign Legion questions a Vietminh soldier in the Indochinese War.

TOP: The Dalai Lama and Chairman Mao Zedong at the First National People's Congress in Beijing.

RIGHT: Workers parade in Moscow's Red Square to celebrate the 37th anniversary of the Great October Revolution.

BELOW: Rocky Marciano delivers the winning punch that ends the challenge of Ez Charles.

AN END TO SEGREGATION

An amnesty in Kenya ends the Mau Mau rebellion. Countries in Africa and Asia join together to form a nonaligned bloc, separate from both superpowers. Eastern European nations form the Warsaw Pact as a counter to NATO. Polio vaccine goes on trial and a new vehicle — the hovercraft — is patented. The Beat Generation finds its voice. Jazzman Charlie Parker dies, as does the great scientist Albert Einstein. Rosa Parks won't move.

1955

Jan	18	Amnesty declared in Kenya to calm Mau Mau rebellion
Mar	12	U.S. jazzman Charlie Parker dies
Apr	18	Afro-Asian Conference is held in Bandung, Indonesia, to form "nonaligned" bloc. It lasts until April 24
	18	German-born scientist Albert Einstein dies
May	14	Warsaw Pact is set up
	15	Austria's independence is restored
June	11	More than 80 spectators and one driver are killed during the Le Mans car race
July	18	Disneyland theme park opens, California
Aug	30	Greek, Turkish, and British foreign ministers meet in London to discuss Cyprus. The meeting lasts until September 7
Sep	30	U.S. film star 23-year-old James Dean dies in car crash

ABOVE: Prime Minister Nehru of India discusses policy with Richard Nixon on the latter's visit to India.

ABOVE RIGHT: Rosa Parks is arrested for violating the segregation laws in Montgomery, Alabama.

MAU MAU REBELLION ENDS

In Kenya, an amnesty by the British government calms the Mau Mau rebellion against British rule. The Mau Mau, a secret society of the Kikuyu tribe, was formed in 1948 and in 1952 began a campaign of arson and killings to drive whites off Kikuyu land and force the British to leave Kenya. Their leader, Jomo Kenyatta (1889–1978), was imprisoned, but the Mau Mau lost much ground after a massacre at Lari in the Rift Valley in March 1953 killed more than 80 people, mostly African. In total, more than 11,000 Mau Mau members have been killed in the uprising, mainly by fellow Africans.

WARSAW PACT

In response to West Germany joining NATO in October 1954, seven Eastern European nations — Albania, Bulgaria, Czechoslovakia, East Germany, Hungary, Poland, and Romania — plus the U.S.S.R. establish the Warsaw Pact. This provides for a unified military structure with its headquarters in Moscow and the stationing of Soviet armed forces in member countries.

MENDELEVIUM

Element 101 is produced artificially by a U.S. team headed by Glenn T. Seaborg. It is named mendelevium.

THE FAMILY OF MAN

Photographer Edward Steichen (1879–1973) mounts a notable exhibition at New York's Museum of Modern Art. A showcase of photography, it contains just over 500 photographs selected from more than two million.

ABOVE: President Ngo Dinh Diem of South Vietnam, in discussion with Buddhist priests.

BLACK WOMAN ARRESTED

In Montgomery, Alabama, American civil rights campaigner Rosa Parks is arrested for sitting in the front of the bus in seats reserved for white people after the Interstate Commerce Commission orders the desegregation of transport. Her arrest leads to a mass boycott of all buses in Montgomery, led by Martin Luther King Jr. (1929–68).

ABOVE: Dizzy Gillespie, the originator of bebop jazz, hits a high note for New York Democrat Adam Clayton Powell Jr.

NONALIGNED BLOC

Leaders of 29 African and Asian countries meet in Bandung, Indonesia, at the invitation of President Sukharno (1902–70) and form a "nonaligned bloc" of countries opposed to the "imperialism and colonialism" of the superpowers, the United States and the U.S.S.R.

AUSTRIAN INDEPENDENCE RESTORED

The four occupying powers — United States, Soviet Union, Britain, and France — agree to restore Austrian independence within its 1937 frontiers in return for its neutrality, a ban on any *Anschluss* or unity with Germany, and a ban on any return of the Hapsburg monarchy. The treaty removes one of the major irritants in relations between East and West in Europe.

ABOVE: The jazz clarinetist Benny Goodman.

ABOVE: Television becomes the focal point of home entertainment for most Western families.

LEFT: The newly developed vaccine against poliomyelitis is expected to prevent death and disablement from the disease that causes infantile paralysis (above).

CYPRUS WAR OF INDEPENDENCE

Greek Cypriots begin a guerrilla war of independence against Britain. Their leading organization is the National Organization of Cypriot Combatants (EOKA) and their aim is unification or enosis with Greece. Their leaders include Cypriot Archbishop Makarios.

POLIO VACCINES

U.S. physician and microbiologist Jonas Salk (1914–95) announces the development of a vaccine against poliomyelitis, which is rife in the United States. It is an injectible vaccine and is given a large clinical trial. U.S. virologist Albert Sabin (1906–93) has also developed a vaccine against poliomyelitis. It is an oral vaccine, which can be taken on a sugar lump.

HOWL: ANTHEM OF THE BEAT GENERATION

American beat poet Allen Ginsberg (1926–97) has published *Howl*. A long poem, it is a rejection of material values and an elegy for the American dream. With its publication, a group of young writers known as the Beat Generation now become widely known.

ANTIPROTONS

Scientists detect antiprotons, short-lived subatomic particles identical to protons but with negative electrical charges.

MODERN-STYLE CHAPEL

French architect Le Corbusier completes his chapel of Notre Dame du Haut in Ronchamp, France. With its curved walls clad in white concrete and its great billowing roof, it brings a new, plastic language to modern architecture.

LOLITA

Russian-born U.S. novelist Vladimir Nabokov (1899–1977) publishes *Lolita*. A novel about the infatuation of a middle-aged writer with a young girl, it provokes a storm of controversy — and increases Nabokov's reading audience.

ABOVE: Berlin students hold torches in memory of the Germans who lost their lives in the uprising of June 17, 1953.

JAMES BYRON DEAN
(1931–1955)

The young American actor James Dean has been killed in a car crash. He made his name with the film *East of Eden* (1955), which was swiftly followed by *Rebel Without a Cause*. He began his acting career while studying at California University, and trained at the Actors' Studio. His last film *Giant* will be released next year.

ALBERT EINSTEIN
(1879–1955)

Almost certainly the greatest scientist of our age, Albert Einstein. has died. His work on the theory of relativity (published in 1905 and 1916) explained problems that had been waiting to be solved since Newton and gained him the Nobel Prize in 1921. German-born, he eventually became a citizen of the United States.

CHARLES "BIRD" PARKER
(1920–1955)

The great Kansas-born tenor and alto sax player, Charlie Parker, has died, partly as a result of lifelong addiction to heroin and alcohol. A much-admired improviser, he was one of the pioneers of the bebop style, and had a strong influence on the development of jazz in the 1940s. He played in quintets with musicians such as trumpeters Dizzy Gillespie and Miles Davis, and pianists Al Haig and Duke Jordan.

ABOVE: The USS *Nautilus* is the American Navy's first submarine to be driven by nuclear power.

HELP IN THE KITCHEN
French engineer Mark Grégoire begins producing and marketing nonstick frying pans coated with polytetrafluoroethylene (PTFE), a slippery plastic material discovered in 1938.

SYNTHETIC DIAMONDS
The General Electric Research Laboratory in the United States makes the first synthetic diamonds by treating carbon at very high temperature and pressure; the first products are small diamonds of industrial quality.

HOVERCRAFT PATENTED
English radio engineer and boat designer Christopher Cockerell (1910–99) patents the hovercraft, also known as an air-cushion vehicle or ACV.

KILLER SMOG
In the U.K., a new Clean Air Act attempts to control city air pollution by banning the burning of soft, smog-producing coal. Smogs in London and other major British cities, as well as in the United States, have killed more than 9,000 people since 1950.

DISNEYLAND OPENS
U.S. film director Walt Disney (1901–66) and creator of world-famous cartoon character Mickey Mouse, has opened a fantastic Disneyland amusement theme park at Anaheim, California. It features a whole host of rides and attractions based on the Disney cartoons.

BELOW: The ultramodern St. Louis Airport Terminal designed by the Missouri-based architects Hellmuth, Yamasaki, and Leinweber.

FIFTIES FASHION

The Fifties see an explosion of new fashion ideas, celebrating Western women's growing independence and freedom of choice, as well as reflecting increasing affluence.

LEFT: Casual elegance is the of keynote of Fifties fashion.

ABOVE: Postwar women are entering the workforce and smart clothes for the office are in demand.

ABOVE: Free and easy wear for the holidays more can now afford.

ABOVE AND RIGHT: After the war decade, fashion reflects the desire for luxury without sacrificing women's newfound independence.

CRISIS IN SUEZ, REVOLT IN HUNGARY

Soviet tanks put down a prodemocracy uprising in Hungary, despite appeals by Hungary to the United Nations. World political tensions rise during the Suez Crisis and Israel attacks Egypt. Fidel Castro and his followers begin guerrilla warfare against the Batista regime in Cuba. In the field of medicine, kidney dialysis begins, and astronomers measure the surface temperature of the planet Venus. Popular music includes hits from *My Fair Lady* and Elvis Presley's "Heartbreak Hotel."

1956

Jan	1	Sudan is declared an independent republic
	26	Winter Games televised, Italy
Feb	29	Soviet premier Nikita Khrushchev denounces Stalin's policies
Mar	2	Morocco becomes independent from France
	9	Archbishop Makarios deported from Cyprus
	20	Tunisia becomes independent from France
July	26	President Nasser of Egypt nationalizes the Suez Canal
Aug	14	German playwright and director Bertolt Brecht dies

Oct	23	Demonstrations in Hungary call for democratic government
	24	Imre Nagy appointed Hungarian prime minister
	29	Israeli forces invade Sinai Peninsula
Nov	1	Emergency session of United Nations to discuss Suez Crisis
	2	Hungarian government appeals to UN for assistance against Soviet invasion
	5	British paratroopers land in Port Said, Egypt
	20	Castro and followers land in Cuba to begin guerrilla war against Batista
	22	Olympic Games open in Melbourne, Australia
Dec	5	British and French forces begin to withdraw from Egypt

ABOVE: Antigovernment demonstrators in Salonika, Greece, use rolls of newsprint as roadblocks against the Army's armored cars.

STALIN DENOUNCED

Nikita Khrushchev, now in firm control of the Soviet Union, denounces Stalin at a closed session of the Communist Party Congress. The break with Stalinism leads to a relaxation of state control and terror in the Soviet Union, and leads some Eastern European nations to loosen their ties with the Soviet Union.

MAKARIOS DEPORTED

Britain deports Archbishop Makarios and other Greek Cypriot leaders to the Seychelles on suspicion of involvement with EOKA terrorists fighting to unite Cyprus, a British colony, with Greece. Conflict between Greeks and Turks on the island has been growing for some years as the Greeks seek union with Greece and the Turks seek to protect their rights.

ARAB-ISRAELI WAR

In October, in a prearranged secret move with the British and French governments, the small but well-equipped and well-trained Israeli army attacks Egyptian forces in the Sinai who have been threatening Israel's access to the Red Sea from Eilat. In a lightning campaign they capture the Sinai Peninsula plus huge quantities of Egyptian military equipment and large numbers of prisoners. The Franco-British intervention at Suez was ostensibly a peacekeeping operation to separate the Israeli and Egyptian forces.

CUBAN REBELS

Having reassembled, Fidel Castro and his followers, who include Castro's brother Raul and Che Guevara (1928–67), land in Cuba, from the yacht *Gramma*. They begin a campaign of guerrilla war to overthrow the dictatorial government of President Batista. As volunteers join Castro's group in the Sierra Maestra, he is able to go on the offensive.

FORMER COLONIES INDEPENDENT

The former Anglo-Egyptian colony of Sudan becomes independent from Britain in January. Morocco and Tunisia receive their independence from France in March.

KITCHEN SINK DRAMA

The play *Look Back in Anger* by British writer John Osborne (1929–94) is performed. It centers on an "angry young man," Jimmy Porter, who becomes the archetype of a generation. The play is typical of so-called British "kitchen sink dramas" which feature working-class or lower middle-class domestic settings.

THE SEVENTH SEAL

Starring actor Max von Sydow, *The Seventh Seal* is the latest film by Swedish film director Ingmar Bergman (b. 1918). Including a game of chess between Death and a knight, who argues the goodness of humanity, the film establishes Bergman's reputation as a major force in the cinema.

HEARTBREAK HOTEL

Rock star Elvis Presley records bestselling "Heartbreak Hotel" and makes his film début in *Love Me Tender*. In the United States, he appears live on T.V. on the Ed Sullivan Show. His fans adore him but some criticize his "provocative" movements.

MY FAIR LADY

Alan Jay Lerner and Frederick Loewe's musical *My Fair Lady* opens on Broadway. Based on George Bernard Shaw's play *Pygmalion*, it is a smash success.

SUEZ CRISIS

In July Egyptian President Nasser (1918–70) nationalizes the Anglo-French Suez Canal Company, which controls the vital waterway between the Mediterranean and Red Sea. The move is strongly opposed by Britain. Nasser makes the move after Britain and the United States refused to provide funds to build the Aswan Dam across the Nile, which is designed to increase Egypt's cultivable land by more than half and to provide hydroelectricity. The dam is later built with Soviet aid. In November, in collusion with the Israelis, the British and French launch an airborne and amphibious attack to seize the Suez Canal. Operationally, the landings are a complete success, but politically they are a disaster. The UN votes for a ceasefire after international condemnation of the Anglo-French invasion, led by the United States. Britain and France are obliged to halt their attacks and withdraw in December. As a result of the débâcle, the British prime minister, Anthony Eden, resigns the following year, and both Britain and France lose considerable prestige.

LONG DAY'S JOURNEY

U.S. playwright Eugene O'Neill's play *Long Day's Journey into Night* is performed. A family tragedy, partly based on the writer's own life, it depicts the disintegration of the relationships between the ex-actor James Tyrone, his drug-addict wife Mary, and their two sons.

ABOVE: Demonstrators fill the streets of Polish cities, reflecting growing unrest that culminates in the Poznan riots.

TRANSATLANTIC PHONE CABLE
The first cable, called TAT 1, to carry telephone calls is laid across the Atlantic between Scotland and Newfoundland; it contains 51 repeaters along its 2,263-mile length to boost the signal.

NEUTRINOS DETECTED
U.S. physicists Frederick Reines and Clyde Lorrain detect the subatomic particles neutrinos and antineutrinos.

VIDEOTAPE BEGINS
The Ampex Company of California builds the first commercial videotape machine; it uses 2.5-inch tape.

KIDNEY DIALYSIS BEGINS
The kidney dialysis machine, which was invented by Dutch physician Willem J. Kolff (b. 1911) in 1943, comes into general use in America. The machine uses a membrane to filter out impurities from the blood.

VENUS IS HOT STUFF
American astronomers studying the microwaves emitted from the planet Venus discover its surface temperature is far above boiling point (in 1962, a space probe measures it at 900°F).

CELL MESSENGERS FOUND
Scientists studying cells discover messenger RNA (ribonucleic acid). This makes a reverse copy of the plans for making a protein from the DNA of that protein, and serves as a mold for making a new one.

INTERFERON
British virologist Alick Isaacs and a Swiss colleague, Jean Lindenmann, discover interferon, a protective substance produced in cells when they are infected by viruses.

TELEVISED GAMES
The first televised Winter Games sees action broadcast from Cortina d'Ampezzo in Italy. The Seventh Olympiad is rescued by heavy snow on the opening day. On the rink, the Soviets end Canadian domination of ice hockey.

BREASTFEEDING ENCOURAGED
The La Lèche League is founded at Franklin Park, Illinois, to encourage breastfeeding, since breast milk has been found to give babies additional protection against disease.

TIPPEX
Bette Nesmith, an American housewife, converts her cottage industry selling Mistake Out (a white paint preparation to blank out typing errors) to local typists, into a national corporation, Liquid Paper Inc.

LEFT: The Melbourne Olympic Games attract huge crowds from all over the world.

Highlights include the U.K.'s Chris Brasher winning the 3,000m steeplechase (top) and American Milt Campbell (above) taking the decathlon gold. Australia dominates the women's track events.

MELBOURNE GAMES

This year's Olympic Games are in Melbourne, Australia, the first to be held in the southern hemisphere. They are affected by a series of political boycotts, in the wake of the Suez crisis and the Soviet invasion of Hungary. Soviet gymnast Larissa Latynina wins four golds, a silver, and a bronze. The hosts sweep the board in the swimming events.

LEFT: Preparations for the American expedition to the South Pole, as the advance survey party leaves the supply ship anchored at McMurdo Sound.

BERTOLT EUGEN FRIEDRICH BRECHT
(1898–1956)

The German-born playwright and theater director Bertolt Brecht has died. Having settled in Hollywood after his retreat from Nazi Germany, he had returned to his native Germany to found the radical theater company the Berliner Ensemble. Always mindful of his Marxist political beliefs, he introduced a revolutionary approach to theater, which demanded the audience's detachment. His plays include *Mother Courage* (1941) and *The Resistible Rise of Arturo Ui* (1957). He also collaborated with the composer Kurt Weill on *The Threepenny Opera* (1928) and other musical works.

THE HUNGARIAN UPRISING

Demonstrations break out in Budapest against Soviet domination — Hungary has been part of the Communist bloc since 1946. The former Hungarian prime minister, Imre Nagy, who was forced out of office in February 1955, returns to power promising reform after demonstrators call for democratic government and the withdrawal of Soviet troops. However, demonstrations lead to a wider uprising against the Soviet Union. Nagy forms a government including non-Communists and takes Hungary out of the Warsaw Pact, appealing for Western aid against any Soviet invasion. However, in November, Moscow sends 2,500 tanks and armored vehicles and 200,000 troops into Hungary. Street fighting erupts in Budapest but the Hungarians are crushed, suffering 12,000 killed. Nagy is deposed in favor of János Kádár, who changes sides to head the new government. Nagy is executed after a secret trial in June 1958.

ABOVE: Students pose in front of Budapest University with their machine guns during the October Revolution, having taken up arms against the threat of Soviet domination.

RIGHT: In Mexico, workers demonstrate in support of the Hungarian revolutionaries.

ABOVE: A huge statue of Stalin is pulled down and dragged through the streets of Budapest during the anti-Soviet riots.

ABOVE: The Hungarian flag is draped over the body of a freedom fighter.

RIGHT: A Hungarian resistance fighter explains how to use a Molotov cocktail.

SPUTNIKS ORBIT THE EARTH

The Space Race gets under way as the Russians launch the world's first artificial satellites: *Sputnik I* and *Sputnik II*. *Sputnik II* carries a little dog, Laika, and captures the imagination of the world. Free trade comes closer in Europe as various countries form the European Common Market. U.S. troops are sent to Little Rock, Arkansas, to enforce racial integration in the schools. *West Side Story* opens on Broadway.

1957

Jan	21	Fashion designer Christian Dior dies (b. 1905)
	22	Israeli forces make complete withdrawal from Sinai Peninsula but remain in Gaza Strip
Feb	6	Gold Coast becomes independent as Ghana
Mar	25	Treaty of Rome sets up European Common Market
	28	Britain releases Archbishop Makarios
July	6	Althea Gibson, U.S. tennis player, becomes first black player to win Wimbledon singles
Aug	4	Argentinian racing driver, Fangio, wins 24th Grand Prix
	31	Malaya gains independence from Britain
Sep	25	Schools desegregate in Little Rock, Arkansas, after U.S. troops are sent in
	26	The musical *West Side Story* opens on Broadway
Oct	4	Russians launch the world's first artificial satellite, Sputnik I
Nov	3	Russians launch Sputnik II, carrying an animal
	25	Diego Rivera dies (b. 1884)

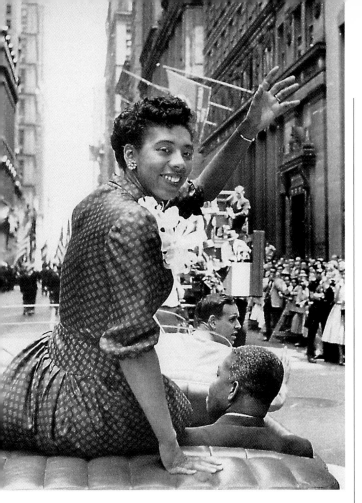

ABOVE: Althea Gibson receives a rapturous welcome on her return from winning the Women's Tennis Championship at Wimbledon.

EUROPEAN COMMON MARKET
France, West Germany, Netherlands, Belgium, Luxembourg, and Italy sign the Treaty of Rome, setting up the European Common Market, later the European Economic Union (EEC). Its aim is the free movement of goods, money, and people through its member nations. The Treaty also sets up the European Atomic Energy Authority (Euratom).

FIRST SPUTNIKS
Sputnik I, the world's first artifical Earth satellite, is successfully launched by the Soviet Union on the 50th anniversary of the Russian Revolution. A month later they launch Sputnik II, which carries the first animal to go into space, a female dog called Laika. This is in preparation for sending humans into space.

LITTLE ROCK
U.S. federal paratroopers are sent in to enforce integration in local schools in Little Rock, Arkansas, after black pupils are refused admission to the Central High School. Arkansas governor Orval Faubus uses the state militia to bar their entry. The action causes outrage in the southern states against the federal government.

MALAYA INDEPENDENT
The Federation of Malaya gains its independence from Britain, the last major British Asian colony to do so.

GOLD COAST INDEPENDENT
The British colony of the Gold Coast becomes the first black African state to win its independence from European rule as Ghana, under the charismatic leadership of Kwame Nkrumah (1909–72).

DOCTOR ZHIVAGO
Russian author Boris Pasternak (1890–1960) publishes his novel *Doctor Zhivago* — in Italy because it will not be published in his native U.S.S.R. An account of Russia and its intelligentsia during the revolutionary period, the novel is a rapid success. The following year, Pasternak is awarded the Nobel Prize for Literature.

ON THE ROAD
American author Jack Kerouac (1922–69) publishes his partly autobiographical novel *On the Road*. Fast-moving and loosely structured, the style of the novel reflects the travels and life of the central character, writer Sal Paradise. It puts Kerouac on the literary map and makes him, together with writers Alan Ginsberg and William Burroughs, a leading figure of the Beat Generation. Followers of Beat Generation philosophy reject social and artistic conventions, favor progressive jazz, and explore mystical experiences offered by Eastern religions.

PALAZETTO DEL SPORT
Italian architect Pier Luigi Nervi (1891–1979) designs the Palazetto del Sport for the 1960 Olympic Games to be held in Rome. The stadium is made of prefabricated parts (including striking concrete Y-frames) enabling construction of the main dome 200 feet in diameter to be completed in a staggering 40 days.

WEST SIDE STORY
American conductor and composer Leonard Bernstein's musical *West Side Story* has opened on Broadway. An adaptation of *Romeo and Juliet*, the exciting musical is set among the street gangs of New York City. U.S. composer Stephen Sondheim has written the lyrics, including popular favorites "America" and "Maria."

VOSS
The Australian novelist Patrick White (1912–90) publishes *Voss*, a novel about a German explorer's bid to lead an expedition across Australia. It brings him international recognition.

VELCRO PATENTED
Swiss inventor Georges de Mestral patents Velcro™, the cling fabric fastener based on the cocklebur principle; he has taken 17 years to perfect it.

RADIO TELESCOPE
A radio telescope with a steerable dish 249 feet across comes into operation at Jodrell Bank, Cheshire, England, for use by astronomers at the University of Manchester.

ABOVE: Screen icons Elizabeth Taylor and James Dean in *Giant*, a story of lust and oil in Texas, released the year after Dean's death.

ABOVE: In the People's Republic of China, the Cultural Revolution means that everyone does hard physical work.

PACEMAKER
U.S. physician Clarence Lillehei devises a pacemaker small enough to be inserted in a patient's body and control a heart that is beating irregularly.

NUCLEAR ACCIDENTS
Two nuclear accidents release radioactivity into the atmosphere. One occurs at Windscale nuclear power plant in the U.K.; the other in a Russian nuclear waste store in the Ural Mountains.

PSYCHOLINGUISTICS
The psychology of language, or psycholinguistics, is galvanized by the publication of *Syntactic Structures* by Noam Chomsky (b. 1928). He theorizes that language began — and begins in children — not with sounds but with rudimentary sentences whose structure follows rules common to all languages.

GRAND PRIX WINNER
At the age of 46, Juan Manuel Fangio (1911–95) wins a record fifth Grand Prix World Championship with a stunning victory in the German Grand Prix. The Argentinian, driving a Maserati, smashes the lap record ten times during the race.

FATS CAUSE HEART DISEASE
A paper by University of Minnesota nutritionist Ancel Keys, published in the *Journal of the American Medical Association*, establishes a connection between diets high in animal fats and heart disease.

WOLFENDEN REPORT
In the U.K., the Report of the Home Office Committee on Homosexual Offenses and Prostitution by Sir John Wolfenden, chancellor of Reading University, unexpectedly recommends an end to punitive laws against homosexual acts between consenting adults.

DODGERS TO MOVE
Walter O'Malley, president of the Brooklyn Dodgers, announces the team is moving from New York City to Los Angeles. The news outrages Dodgers fans but is the first of many such transfers as baseball expands.

OPPOSITE: Archaeologists in Iraq unearth one of the biggest finds of inscribed Sumerian clay tablets ever discovered.

CHRISTIAN DIOR
(1905–1957)

Christian Dior, the French couturier who launched the postwar "New Look" in Paris in 1947, has died. The House of Dior also introduced the A-line and the sack dress, and created several well-known perfumes, including "Miss Dior."

JOSEPH RAYMOND MCCARTHY
(1909–1957)

The fanatical anti-Communist American Republican, Senator Joseph (Joe) McCarthy, has died. Since 1950 he had been conducting a witch-hunt among citizens and officials, becoming chairman of the so-called House Committee on Un-American Activities in 1953. Many prominent intellectuals and actors have been among those accused of being Communists. In 1954, McCarthy was censured by the Senate for his methods but he remained rabidly anti-Communist to the end.

ABOVE: U.S. President Eisenhower, reelected in 1956, is pictured here talking to Lyndon Johnson.

ABOVE: Future astronaut John H. Glenn celebrates a nonstop flight round the world in a B52 bomber.

MARCHING AGAINST THE BOMB

The United States launches *Explorer I* into space, the first of a series of science satellites. Antinuclear feeling finds a voice as the Campaign for Nuclear Disarmament is formed. In the face of continuing Algerian problems, Charles de Gaulle becomes president of France. The new contraceptive pill goes on sale in the United States with the potential for transforming women's lives. The Netherlands hosts a conference on sexual equality and Barbie is born.

1958

Jan	3	New Zealand expedition reaches the South Pole
	20	British expedition reaches the South Pole
	31	United States launches *Explorer I*
Feb	3	Benelux economic union formed
	6	Manchester United footballers killed in major air crash
	17	CND formed in London with the slogan "Ban the Bomb"
Mar	24	Elvis Presley begins two years' military service
Apr	7	CND holds first "Aldermaston March" from London to Aldermaston nuclear research station
May	29	Algerian crisis forces recall of Charles de Gaulle
June	29	Brazil wins soccer's World Cup
July	14	Army mounts coup against King Faisal II of Iraq
	14	King Hussein of Jordan assumes power as head of Arab Federation
	15	United States sends troops to Lebanon
Sep	9	Race riots flare in Notting Hill district, London
Oct	2	Guinea declared an independent republic
Dec	21	Charles de Gaulle is elected president of France

CND FORMED

Antinuclear protesters form the Campaign for Nuclear Disarmament (CND) at a rally in London, addressed by the philosopher Bertrand Russell (1872–1970). They march from London to the nuclear research establishment at Aldermaston to protest against Britain's nuclear capacity. Other CND-type organizations are formed elsewhere.

BENELUX ESTABLISHED

Belgium, the Netherlands, and Luxembourg meet at The Hague in the Netherlands and establish the Benelux economic union, which provides for the free movement of capital, goods, and people between the three states.

DE GAULLE COMES TO POWER

Trouble continues in Algeria. After a revolt by French settlers in Algeria against moves by the French government to negotiate with the Algerian Nationalist forces, the French government falls and Charles de Gaulle (1890–1970) takes power. He takes emergency powers for six months and draws up a new constitution, which ends the unstable Fourth Republic and establishes the Fifth Republic with strong presidential powers. In December, de Gaulle becomes president of France, and promises talks with the Algerian rebels.

KING FAISAL OVERTHROWN

In Iraq, the army overthrows the pro-Western monarchy of King Faisal, destabilizing the region. In response, U.S. troops land in Lebanon and British troops land in Jordan to support these governments against possible coup attempts.

ABOVE LEFT: Jerry Lee Lewis, a charismatic singer and pianist who outrages the Establishment.

ABOVE: Teenagers, with their own music, style, crazes, and language, are the phenomenon of the 1950s in America and all over Europe.

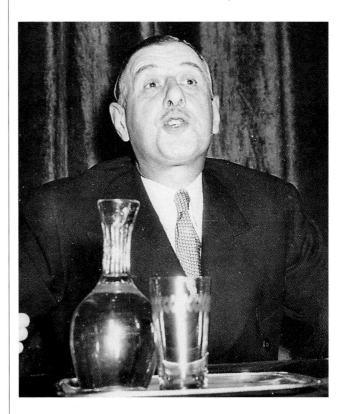

ABOVE: Charles de Gaulle is elected first president of the Fifth Republic this year. He will remain in power until his resignation in 1969.

ABOVE: Marian Anderson, American contralto, is accompanied by the Bombay City Orchestra, in a scene from *The Lady from Philadelphia*.

ABOVE: Composer and conductor Leonard Bernstein conducting a rehearsal of the New York Philharmonic Symphony Orchestra.

GUINEA INDEPENDENT
Prime Minister Sekou Toure (1922–84) declares Guinea an independent republic in the French West African colony and leaves the new French community. Other French colonies remain tied to France.

THE LEOPARD
The only novel by Sicilian prince Giuseppe di Lampedusa (1896–1957) is published posthumously. Entitled *The Leopard*, it describes how a noble family in Sicily respond to changes after Italy annexes the island in 1860.

THE FIRE RAISERS
A play, *The Fire Raisers*, by architect and writer Max Frisch, is performed. It targets the complacency of the middle classes in the person of a man who will tolerate even the burning down of his own home.

NOBELIUM PRODUCED
Element 102, nobelium, is artificially created by American scientists. It is the ninth and last with which Glenn T. Seaborg is involved.

LYCRA LAUNCHED
In the United States, Du Pont launches Lycra, the first of the Spandex fibers or manmade elastics.

ABOVE AND RIGHT: The *Vanguard* satellite (above) was sent into orbit successfully by the *Vanguard* rocket (right), at 72 feet the largest of its kind at the time.

SEAGRAM BUILDING

A new office building, the Seagram Building in New York City, is the ultimate modern tower — restrained in its details, well-proportioned, based on a glass-and-metal structure. Designed by Mies van der Rohe (1886–1969) and Philip Johnson (b. 1906), the building's detail and high-quality material make it extremely distinctive.

EXPLORER I

The United States follows the Soviet Union and sends its first artificial satellite, *Explorer I*, into space. The launch rocket has been developed by Werner von Braun, previously head of Germany's V-2 program. *Explorer I* is the first in a series of U.S. scientific satellites.

VAN ALLEN BELTS

At the suggestion of physicist James Van Allen (b. 1914), U.S. satellite Explorer 4 carries radiation counters heavily shielded with lead. They register cosmic rays, showing that there are belts of very high radiation, later called the Van Allen Belts.

SUB UNDER ARCTIC OCEAN

U.S. nuclear submarine *Nautilus*, launched in 1955, sails under the Arctic Ocean ice cap, the first-ever underwater voyage from the Pacific to the Atlantic beneath the North Polar ice cap.

NEW ZEALAND ARRIVES FIRST

Edmund Hillary's New Zealand team beats Vivian Fuchs's British team overland to the South Pole. Hillary's party sets out from McMurdo Sound and the British from the Vansee Sea. As a contribution to the International Geophysical Year, Britain's team goes on to make the first transantarctic crossing.

BIRTH PILL

The Pill, the first oral contraceptive for women, is marketed in the United States. Containing artificial hormones estrogen and progesterone, it prevents conception by simulating pregnancy. The pill has been developed by Gregory Pincus, who in 1951 was visited by the feminist Margaret Sanger. Pincus produced the Pill in association with Hudson Hoagland and Min-Cheh Chang in 1954.

SEXUAL EQUALITY

The Netherlands COC (Cultuur-en-Ontspannings Centrum) sponsors the fifth International Conference on Sexual Equality; the first was in 1951. The Conference offers a beacon of rational support for lesbian and gay organizations elsewhere in Europe, where they are suppressed and persecuted.

BARBIE IS BORN

The Barbie doll is created in the United States by Mattel. A madeover version of an earlier doll, she is given a teenage fashion model look and a complete, up-to-date wardrobe is designed for her 1959 launch.

ABOVE: Robots seize the imagination: American Sherwood Fuehrer, age fourteen, invents a person-sized robot called Gizmo, which he can manoeuvre from a remote-control box.

AMERICAN EXPRESS

The Bank of America launches American Express, the first-ever credit card. By December, it is being used by some 500,000 people.

HULA HOOP AND SKATEBOARD CRAZE

New crazes sweep the United States when the hula hoop, launched by Arthur Melin and Richard Knerr, and the skateboard, invented by Bill and Mark Richards, appear in California.

XEROX GOES COMMERCIAL

The first commercial Xerox copier goes on sale. Invented in 1947, it makes dry copies of documents.

STEREO RECORDING

Record companies in the United States and Britain issue the first stereophonic records.

UNDERSTANDING SOCIAL BEHAVIOR

Claude Levi-Strauss, Belgian-born anthropologist and professor of ethnology at the University of Paris, publishes *Structural Anthropology*. He theorizes that societies have a similar structure that reflects the way myths are created, and these, when accurately understood, will enable us to understand their behavior.

BRILLIANT BRAZIL

The World Cup takes place in Sweden and marks the arrival of Brazilian player Pelé, the world's greatest exponent of the beautiful game. He scores six goals in the tournament and Brazil takes home the title, beating the hosts 5–2 in the final.

POLYGAMY RESTRICTED

The government of newly independent Morocco liberalizes the law in favor of women, granting women the right to choose their own husbands and restricting polygamy.

CASTRO TAKES CONTROL IN CUBA

In Cuba, Fidel Castro succeeds in toppling Batista to take over the Cuban government. The Dalai Lama, Tibet's spiritual leader, flees Chinese-occupied Tibet. The oldest known hominid remains are found in Africa. The new Guggenheim Museum in New York City is opened but its brilliant architect, Frank Lloyd Wright, dies just before completion. Soviet spacecraft crash-land on the Moon and send back the first photographs of its dark side.

1959

Jan	1	Batista resigns and then flees Cuba, following guerrilla campaign
	3	Castro enters Havana and sets up provisional government
Mar	17	Tibetan uprising against Chinese. Dalai Lama is smuggled out of Tibet
Apr	3	Dalai Lama reaches India from Chinese-occupied Tibet
	9	Frank Lloyd Wright dies (b. 1867)
June	26	St. Lawrence Seaway opens
July	17	British anthropologists discover *Homo habilis*
Aug	7	Chinese forces enter northeast India
Oct	26	Soviet spacecraft films dark side of the Moon

Nov	10	United Nations condemns apartheid in South Africa
	20	The "Seven" set up European Free Trade Agreement (EFTA)
Dec	1	Antarctic Treaty signed by 12 nations keeps Antarctic free of territorial or military claims

ABOVE: Emperor penguins and the USS *Glacier* in Antarctica.

BELOW: Astronaut monkeys provide important information about the biomedical factors affecting manned space flight.

ABOVE: Self-propelled anti-aircraft guns pass the reviewing stand at the May Day parade in East Berlin.

ABOVE: An East German bread vendor stands beside a poster of Soviet premier Nikita Khrushchev shaking hands with East Germany's Communist leader Walter Ulbricht.

LEFT: A new type of radio telescope built by Australian astronomer Dr. Ronald Bracewell.

ABOVE: The bows of the cruiser USS Long Beach, the U.S. Navy's first nuclear-powered surface ship, stand tall in the naval shipyard at Quincy, Massachusetts.

BUDDY (CHARLES HARDIN) HOLLY
(1936–1959)

Charles Hardin, the singer better known as Buddy Holly, has died in a plane crash. The fans of the American rock and roller will be devastated. He and his band the Crickets set up the new standard lineup of two guitars, bass, and drums, and were innovative in their recording techniques. A body of recordings is the legacy of Buddy Holly's brief career.

JOHN FOSTER DULLES
(1888–1959)

American Republican politician John Foster Dulles has died of cancer. As secretary of state in the 1950s, he devoted his energies to alerting the world to the threat of Communism, and at the same time contributing to the rise of Cold War tension.

CASTRO IN POWER

Fidel Castro takes power in Cuba after Batista flees into exile in the Dominican Republic. The takeover comes at the end of an insurrection that has lasted for more than two years. Dr. Manuel Urratia is proclaimed provisional president of Cuba with Castro as prime minister.

DALAI LAMA FLEES

A rising against Chinese rule is repressed by the Chinese army and the Dalai Lama, Tibet's Buddhist spiritual leader, is smuggled out of Tibet and flees into exile in India, where he appeals for UN intervention to secure the independence of Tibet.

RWANDAN CIVIL WAR

Civil war breaks out in Rwanda, which has recently been granted self-government by Belgium, the colonial power. The ruling Tutsi people, who make up only a small percentage of the population, have been attacked by the Hutu, who make up 85 per cent of the population. A Hutu-dominated republic is proclaimed following a UN-supervised vote but when armed Tutsi *emigrés* attack the new nation they are driven off and many Tutsi are massacred in reprisal.

DISPUTE OVER INDIA/CHINA BORDER

A border dispute breaks out in the Himalayas between India and China, prompted by China's belief that the British-designated border is no longer valid.

ABOVE: India's Prime Minister Jawaharlal Nehru at the inauguration of the Hirakud Dam, one of several projects designed to boost food production through irrigation and to provide hydroelectric power for India's developing industry.

RIGHT: Dog models in Soviet rocket chambers designed to carry real canines on short space flights. Two dogs do in fact make the trip and return safely to earth.

EFTA

Seven European countries — Sweden, Norway, Denmark, Britain, Portugal, Austria, and Switzerland — set up the European Free Trade Area (EFTA) to rival the EEC.

FIRST TRIP TO THE MOON

Lunar II, an uncrewed Soviet spacecraft, becomes the first space probe to crash-land on the Moon. On the way it confirms the existence of the solar wind, a flow of gases from the Sun. Later this year, *Lunar III* orbits the Moon and transmits pictures of its dark side — the side never seen from Earth.

GUGGENHEIM MUSEUM

With its unique spiral design, the new Guggenheim Museum in New York City is one of the most striking modern buildings. The paintings are hung beside a continuous spiral ramp; visitors take the elevator to the top and walk down, thereby, in theory at least, minimizing "museum fatigue."

RHINOCEROS

Romanian-born dramatist Eugène Ionesco (1912–94) creates "anti-plays," in which a world of nightmare fuses with farce. His latest is *Rhinoceros*, in which the cast turn one by one into rhinoceroses, interpreted by most critics as the image of a totalitarian takeover.

HANDY MAN FOUND

British anthropologists Louis and Mary Leakey discover in Olduvai Gorge, Tanzania, fossils of the earliest human species. The species is named *Homo habilis*, "Handy Man," and lived two million years ago. Stone tools found on the site are the earliest so far discovered.

THE TIN DRUM

German novelist Günter Grass (b. 1927) publishes *The Tin Drum*. The novel, which features the hunchback Oskar who decides to stop growing in infancy, becomes a bestseller in Germany. Its narrative seems to sum up the history of Germany during the twentieth century.

SYNTHESIZER

The Radio Corporation of America invent the synthesizer, an electronic instrument which can imitate the sounds of many traditional instruments and also make new sounds.

SWISS WOMEN REJECTED

The Swiss electorate votes to reject a proposed amendment to the constitution to permit women to vote in national elections and run for national office.

SOME LIKE IT HOT

U.S. film actress Marilyn Monroe (1926–62) stars as singer Sugar Kane in a new Billy Wilder film, *Some Like it Hot*. The film, which is a lively comedy, confirms her status as an international star.

BILLIE (ELEANOR FAGANA) HOLIDAY (1915–1959)

American jazz singer Billie Holiday, also known as Lady Day, has died. She sang with leading jazz artists such as Benny Goodman, Lester Young, Count Basie, and Louis Armstrong, and leaves the world recordings of songs such as "Easy Living" (1937) which are bound to endure.

NOUVELLE VAGUE

French film director Alain Resnais (b. 1922) premières his first full-length film, *Hiroshima Mon Amour*. Set in Hiroshima, it establishes Resnais as a leading member of the *Nouvelle Vague* (New Wave). This year too, French film director Jean Luc Godard (b. 1930) releases his first full-length film, *A Bout de Souffle*. The film is shot without a script, indicating Godard's emphasis on improvisatory techniques.

ANTARCTICA

The Antarctic Treaty signed by 12 nations, including the U.S., Britain and the U.S.S.R., suspends all territorial and military claims, restricts exploration of the Antarctic to peaceful purposes only, and establishes the continent south of 60° as a preserve for scientific research. The treaty lasts until 1989, then is renewed.

STOCK CAR RACING

The most prestigious race in American stock car racing is born at Daytona International Speedway in Florida. Lee Petty wins the first Daytona 500 in an Oldsmobile.

ST. LAWRENCE SEAWAY

The St. Lawrence Seaway, a system of rivers, lakes, and canals that enables oceangoing ships to carry cargoes to and from the Great Lakes of North America, opens.

BULGING EARTH

The U.S. satellite *Vanguard 1* makes thousands of orbits of the Earth and shows that the planet is about 25 feet fatter in the south than in the north.

FRANK LLOYD WRIGHT (1867–1959)

The outstanding modern architect, the American Frank Lloyd Wright, has died in his 90s. He had been designing arresting buildings during the whole of this century, including domestic works such as the Prairie-style Robie House (1908) and the international modernist-style Fallingwater (1937), and offices such as the Johnson Wax Office Building (1936). He has almost completed the Guggenheim Museum in New York City when he dies.

THE SWINGING SIXTIES

The 1960s witness a creative explosion of popular culture, a major shift in attitudes to personal and public morality. In the United States, there is a new Camelot with President Kennedy in the royal role. For a decade in pursuit of peace, love, and understanding, there is a remarkable amount of violence: Revolutions, riots, protests, assassinations, and demonstrations abound. In America and Africa, black people assert their rights. Energy and optimism are directed upwards as the Soviet Union and the United States race each other to conquer space.

OPPOSITE: Civil rights protests and demonstrations characterize the decade.

1960–1969

KEY EVENTS OF THE DECADE

- SHARPEVILLE MASSACRE
- JOHN F. KENNEDY ASSASSINATED
- CONTRACEPTIVE PILL
- HUMANITY IN SPACE
- THE CUBAN CRISIS
- THE BERLIN WALL
- BLACK CIVIL RIGHTS
- VIETNAM WAR
- THE BEATLES
- MINISKIRTS

- BLACK POWER
- UDI IN RHODESIA
- POLIO VACCINE
- PRAGUE SPRING
- SUMMER OF LOVE
- THE SIX-DAY WAR
- STUDENT PROTEST
- MEN ON THE MOON

WORLD POPULATION 3,109 MILLION

WINDS OF CHANGE START TO BLOW

The decade starts as it means to go on, as liberation of all kinds scents the breeze. In Africa, European colonial power evaporates as more countries gain independence. Only South Africa bucks the trend, with white minority rule cracking down on the black populace. In the United States, a dynamic young president is elected. Italian director Federico Fellini anticipates the sexual revolution with his film *La Dolce Vita*, while in Britain, D.H. Lawrence's *Lady Chatterley's Lover* is declared a good (and legal) read.

1 9 6 0

Jan	**4**	French author Albert Camus dies in car crash, aged 46
	8	Kenneth Kaunda freed from jail in Northern Rhodesia (Zambia); he later becomes president
	23	Bathyscaphe *Trieste* makes record dive of some 30,000 feet in Marianas Trench
Feb	**18**	Eighth Winter Olympics open at Squaw Valley, California
Mar	**21**	Sharpeville Massacre: South African police panic and kill 56 black protesters
Apr	**1**	First weather satellite, *Tiros 1*, is launched
May	**1**	Soviets shoot down US U-2 spy plane over the Ural Mountains
	30	Russian author Boris Pasternak dies

June	**30**	Belgian Congo becomes independent as Congo Republic
Aug	**16**	British colony of Cyprus becomes an independent republic
Nov	**8**	John F. Kennedy is elected 35th U.S. president

ABOVE: Democratic Senator John F. Kennedy is president-elect.

RUNNING THE SPACE RACE

There is crisis in Cuba after a botched U.S.-backed invasion. The United States sends an unlikely number of military observers to Vietnam, taking the first step on a path paved with good intentions that will lead to all-out conflict. The big story of the year is the race to put a man in space, which is won by the Russians as cosmonaut Yuri Gagarin orbits the Earth in triumph. American Alan B. Shepard gets there second in a spacecraft that can be controlled by its pilot.

BELOW: The Moon becomes the focus for the rivalry between the United States and the U.S.S.R.

1961

Jan	**20**	John F. Kennedy is inaugurated as U.S. president
	14	South Africa introduces new decimal currency
Apr	**12**	Soviet cosmonaut Yuri Gagarin becomes the first man in space
	17	Cuban exiles land at Bay of Pigs, Cuba, but are routed
May	**5**	U.S. astronaut Alan B. Shepard becomes the second man in space
	31	South Africa leaves the Commonwealth as an independent republic
Aug	**17**	East Germans build Berlin Wall to separate East and West Berlin
Sep	**17**	UN Secretary-General Dag Hammarskjöld is killed in plane crash over Congo

BAY OF PIGS INCIDENT
In April, 1,500 Cuban exiles, trained by U.S. military instructors, land in the Bay of Pigs (Bahia de Cochinos) in Cuba. The expected revolt against Fidel Castro fails to materialize and the invaders are killed or captured. The U.S. government faces considerable criticism for its action.

ALGERIAN COUP FAILS
The French Army revolts against de Gaulle's government over its policy for independence in Algeria. De Gaulle declares a state of emergency and the coup collapses. The rebel leaders are tried for treason and eight are sentenced to death.

TOP LEFT AND RIGHT: Automobiles begin to take over; production rises and road systems become more complicated.

ABOVE: Cuban leader Fidel Castro plans battle strategy on the hoof during the Bay of Pigs invasion by the United States.

RIGHT: Cuban troops launch a counterattack at Playa Larga.

INDEPENDENCE IN AFRICA

Sierra Leone (in May) and Tanganyika (in December) both gain independence from British rule.

THE WALL GOES UP

The East German authorities seal off West Berlin and erect a wall across the city, thus preventing the escape of East Germans to the West.

BABI YAR

The poem by Russian poet Yevgeny Yevtushenko (b. 1933) commemorates Jews massacred at Babi Yar, near Kiev, during World War II. His stand is against Soviet as well as Nazi anti-Semitism.

TRAGEDY FOR UN

UN Secretary-General, Dag Hammarskjöld is killed in a plane crash while trying to obtain peace in the Congo. His successor at the helm of the UN is a Burmese diplomat, U Thant.

A DANCER DEFECTS

Touring with the Kirov Ballet, Russian dancer Rudolf Nureyev (1938–93) leaps to freedom over an airport barrier while the company is in Paris. His defection brings a new star to Western ballet, and brings dance into the news. From 1962 on, he will regularly and memorably partner Margot Fonteyn.

MORE MILITARY HELP

The United States increases the number of military advisers in South Vietnam to defend the government against Communist incursions from the north.

CATCH-22

American writer Joseph Heller's huge first novel, about life in the American Air Force during World War II, enjoys great commercial success. The title, *Catch 22*, adds a new phrase to the language. The book hits out at bureaucracy as well as war.

A NEW CONTRACEPTIVE

The loop, an IUD (intrauterine device) contraceptive, is introduced by an American, Jack Lippes. Made of inert plastic, it is less likely to irritate the body or to be rejected than Ernest Grafenburg's simple silver ring, introduced in the 1930s.

FIRST MAN IN SPACE

The Soviet Union beats the United States to win the space race. On April 12, cosmonaut Yuri Gagarin (1934–68) of the Soviet Union becomes the first man to orbit the Earth in a spacecraft launched from aboard *Vostok 1* from Kazakhstan. He completes a single orbit of the Earth at a maximum altitude of 204 miles and a maximum speed of 1,746 miles per hour. His craft parachutes down safely after 88 minutes near the village of Smelovka in Saratov, U.S.S.R.

FIRST AMERICAN IN SPACE

On May 5, astronaut Alan Bartlett Shepard, Jr., of the United States makes the world's second space flight, a "hop" of just 15 minutes in the *Freedom 7* capsule.

SECOND RUSSIAN IN SPACE

On August 6, cosmonaut Gherman Titov of the Soviet Union makes 17 orbits of the Earth, a day-long space flight.

MOON PLEDGE

On May 25, U.S. president John F. Kennedy says the United States will aim to put the first man on the Moon.

THE HUNTING OF THE QUARK

American theoretical physicist Murray Gell-Mann introduces the quark theory to account for the strange behavior of particles. It will win him the Nobel Prize for Physics in 1969.

MEGACITY

In December, Tokyo becomes the world's first city to have a population of ten million.

ERNEST MILLAR HEMINGWAY (1899–1961)

The American writer and Nobel Prize-winner has died by his own hand at his home in Idaho from a bullet in the mouth. After World War I (in which he worked as an ambulance driver for the Red Cross) he returned to journalism as a roving correspondent in Paris and began his career as a hard-living, hard-drinking, and later bull-fighting, writer. He was four times married and lived in Europe and Florida before settling in Cuba. Among his best-known works are *The Sun Also Rises* (1926), *A Farewell to Arms* (1929), *Death In the Afternoon* (1932), *For Whom the Bell Tolls* (1940, about the Spanish Civil War) and *The Old Man and the Sea* (1952).

ATMOSPHERES

Hungarian composer György Ligeti creates *Atmosphères*, a shimmering orchestral work in which every musician plays a separate part, the whole weaving together to create a floating, atmospheric texture. Ligeti himself describes it as one of his most radical works.

BEATING THE BABE

Roger Maris passes the supposedly unbreakable record of fellow Yankee, Babe Ruth, by hitting his 61st home run of the year. Maris has the advantage of a longer baseball season but the media attention is intense and the stress is so great that his hair starts to fall out.

BATTLE OF THE BULGE

Weight Watchers is founded by American housewife Jean Nidetch. Her weight-loss program combines a high-protein diet (devised by Norman Joliffe of the New York Department of Health) with the proscription of certain foods and the use of group therapy methods.

LAWRENCIUM CREATED

The artificially created element 103, lawrencium, is synthesized by four U.S. scientists, Albert Ghiorso, Torbjørn Sikkeland, Almon E. Larsh, and Robert M. Latimer. It is named after Ernest Lawrence, the American inventor of the cyclotron.

BELOW: Oil derricks at Baytown, Texas. The oil from these rigs is used to make gasoline for the growing number of automobiles.

GOLFBALL TYPEWRITER

International Business Machines introduces the "golfball" typewriter. The characters are mounted on a rotating sphere instead of on separate type bars. The typeface can be changed by changing the golfball.

STREET-FIGHTING MEN

In the Netherlands, youth groups, or the *nozems* (rowdies), clash with police on the streets of The Hague, marking the beginning of the 1960s youth protest movements in Europe.

EXPANDING CAMPUSES

Three new universities are to be built in Britain, marking the start of a huge worldwide expansion in university education, designed to accommodate the postwar baby boom.

FREEDOM FIGHTERS

Amnesty International, a nonpolitical organization to help prisoners of conscience anywhere in the world, is founded in Britain.

TIME TO CHANGE

Electronic watches are introduced to the market. Winding becomes a thing of the past as the watches are battery-driven.

BELOW: Missiles being transported to Cuba soon trigger the Cuban Missile Crisis.

SAVING THE ANIMALS

The World Wildlife Fund, an international organization to raise funds for wildlife conservation by public appeal, is founded. Its headquarters are in Switzerland. It will later become the World Wide Fund for Nature.

THE END OF COLONIALISM IN INDIA

Indian forces invade Portuguese Goa and other enclaves in India, removing the last European colonies.

ABOVE: Number 57 comes to grief spectacularly after losing a wheel in the Daytona 500 race held at Daytona International Speedway, Daytona Beach, Florida. Note the rocket in the background; the Kennedy Space Center is a close neighbor.

PATRICE LUMUMBA
(1925–1961)

Patrice Lumumba (born Katako Kombe), who became the first prime minister of the Democratic Republic of the Congo when the country gained independence from Belgium last year, has been arrested by his own army and murdered by the Katangese.

CARL GUSTAV JUNG
(1875–1961)

Carl Jung, the Swiss psychiatrist who has given us the concepts of the collective unconscious, introvert and extrovert, and the school of analytical psychology, has died. Early in the century Jung worked in Vienna with Sigmund Freud, but they parted company over the latter's overinsistence (in Jung's view) on the psychosexual nature of neurosis. Among Jung's works are *The Psychology of the Unconscious* (1911–12), *Psychology and Religion* (1937), and *The Undiscovered Self* (1957). He had just completed his autobiography, *Memories, Dreams, Reflections*, to be published in 1962.

FIRST AMERICAN IN SPACE

ABOVE: Astronaut Alan Shepard suits up for his space trip.

BELOW: Safe splashdown and rescue from the Atlantic.

BELOW: The president congratulates America's first space hero.

ABOVE: *Freedom 7* blasts off from Cape Canaveral.

THE WORLD ON THE BRINK

The Soviet Union and the United States confront each other in Cuba and the world holds its breath as nuclear war seems to be imminent. Diplomacy saves the day. The space race continues. U.S. astronaut John Glenn orbits the Earth three times and *Telstar*, the first communications satellite, is launched into permanent orbit and so catches the public imagination that a song is written for it. An unmanned space probe, complete with camera, is despatched to photograph the planet Venus. James Bond, superspy, makes his first appearance on the world's cinema screen and beautiful Marilyn Monroe is dead.

1962

Jan	1	Western Samoa becomes the first independent Pacific state
Feb	20	Astronaut John Glenn makes the first true U.S. space flight with three orbits of the Earth
July	3	Algeria wins independence from France
	10	*Telstar*, first telecommunications satellite, is launched
Aug	5	Marilyn Monroe, American glamour star, is found dead
Oct	9	Uganda becomes independent within the Commonwealth
	22	U.S. president John F. Kennedy announces that the Soviet Union has established missile bases in Cuba
Nov	28	Wilhelmina, Queen of the Netherlands from 1890 to 1948, dies aged 82
Dec	14	Space probe *Mariner 2* makes the first flight to another planet, passing close to Venus

ABOVE LEFT: A U.S. sentry keeps watch during the Cuban crisis.

ABOVE: Anti-tank crew play pinochle as they wait in Cuba.

MORE INDEPENDENCE

Western Samoa becomes the first Pacific island state to gain its independence from Britain. During the year, Jamaica, Trinidad and Tobago, and Uganda all become independent from Britain, and Burundi and Rwanda gain their independence from Belgium.

LAWRENCE OF ARABIA

British director David Lean's sprawling epic brings together all the elements of film — camerawork, acting, settings, music, and so on — to make a notable whole, one of the masterpieces of British cinema. The film also makes Peter O'Toole an international star and introduces Omar Sharif to the anglophone world.

ABOVE: Costa Rican students protest against the Soviet Union's intervention in Cuba.

LEFT: Marilyn Monroe, who dies this year, entertaining the troops.

MARILYN MONROE (NORMA JEAN MORTENSON) (1926–1962)

American movie star Marilyn Monroe is found dead, apparently after taking an overdose of sleeping pills. After working as a model and bit-part Hollywood actress, she made her name with *How to Marry a Millionaire* and *Gentlemen Prefer Blondes* (both 1953) and went on to make the comedies *The Seven-Year Itch* (1955) and *Some Like it Hot* (1959). She then took acting lessons at the Actors' Studio and married playwright Arthur Miller, who wrote *The Misfits* (1961) for her, and from whom she was divorced last year. Her name has been linked with those of both the president of the United States, John F. Kennedy, and his brother Robert.

ABOVE: *Telstar* is assembled in Bell Telephone Laboratories. The signals it sends from space will be picked up by the tracker (right).

TWA BUILDING, KENNEDY AIRPORT
Finnish-born architect Eero Saarinen (1910–61) designed the dramatic shell-concrete roof of the terminal, which is completed this year. It reminds many observers of a soaring bird. Although the architect denied that this was what he had in mind, the building shows that, for many, modern architecture can hold symbolic meanings.

TELSTAR LAUNCHED
America launches the first telecommunications satellite, *Telstar 1*. It makes possible transatlantic TV pictures, but only in 20-minute sessions. This marks the beginning of global telecommunications.

CUBAN CRISIS
After the Soviet Union places nuclear missiles on Cuba, the United States blockades the island. The United States and Soviet Union confront each other, bringing the world to the brink of nuclear warfare, before the Soviet missiles are removed.

FIRST TRUE U.S. SPACE FLIGHT
U.S. astronaut John Glenn, Jr., makes America's first true space flight, three orbits of the Earth in the spacecraft *Friendship 7*. He remains in space for five hours.

TWO CHEESEBURGERS WITH EVERYTHING
American sculptor Claes Oldenburg, one of the leaders of the pop art movement, is famed for his off-beat, surreal interpretations of everyday items (plaster models magnified many times). Now he turns to soft sculpture, in which a subject is modelled in soft materials and stuffed with kapok. *Soft Typewriter* (1963) and *Soft Toilet* (1966) will follow.

DR. NO
The first of the perennial series of movies featuring British agent James Bond, based on the creation of novelist Ian Fleming, is made. This one stars Scottish actor Sean Connery, who becomes identified with the part and will star in six further Bond films.

TAPE CASSETTES
Dutch electronics firm Philips introduces the compact tape recorder cassette. These can be played on portable tape machines. This will lead to music cassettes and talking newspapers for the blind.

ONE DAY IN THE LIFE OF IVAN DENISOVICH
Russian novelist Alexander Solzhenitsyn's novel of the Soviet Gulag describes the prisoner's world in the most vivid terms. For many in the West, it is the first such account to reach them.

THALIDOMIDE TRAGEDY
Thalidomide, introduced in 1958 as a safe sleeping tablet and remedy for morning sickness during pregnancy, is withdrawn after it is found that some women who take it give birth to children with serious abnormalities.

MARINER 2 LAUNCHED
U.S. space probe *Mariner 2* sets out on a voyage to inspect Venus, the first such trip to another planet. It measures the planet's temperature and confirms the existence of solar wind.

VIVE ALGERIE

After eight years of warfare, Algeria wins its independence from France. Ben Bella becomes president of the new republic.

EQUAL EDUCATION

Black student and Air Force veteran James Howard Meredith enrolls at the University of Mississippi, which is ordered to admit him by a court order upheld by the Supreme Court. Rioting breaks out on campus when he makes his first attempt to enter on September 30, and he is escorted by federal marshals and troops.

SILENT SPRING

American marine biologist Rachel Carson writes this chastening book warning of the indiscriminate use of pesticides. Her success in alarming the public begins a new era in environmental awareness.

BEER IN CANS

Beer is marketed in aluminium cans that open with pull-off tabs by the Aluminum Corporation of America. First produced in 1958, aluminium cans replace the traditional steel can plated with tin.

WORLD BEATERS

Brazil retains the soccer World Cup in a bad-tempered competition in Chile.

ABOVE: Crossing point in the "Bamboo Curtain" which divides the People's Republic of China from the city of Hong Kong.

LEFT: The *NS Savannah*, the first nuclear-powered merchant ship, sails the Panama Canal.

ABOVE: The launch of the nuclear-powered U.S. polaris submarine *Alexander Hamilton*.

THE BERLIN WALL GOES UP

LEFT: East Berliners carry red flags on the first May Day parade after the Wall goes up.

BELOW LEFT: Willy Brandt, the mayor of West Berlin, and his sons look at the Soviet sector.

BELOW: East Berlin troops display military might and weaponry, although a number of soldiers defect to the West.

BOTTOM: President Kennedy visits the Berlin Wall.

A DREAM AND AN ASSASSINATION

Valentina Tereshkova scores a first for Russia and for women as she becomes the first female astronaut. A hotline telephone link is established between the White House and the Kremlin. President de Gaulle keeps the U.K. out of the EEC, Indonesia and Malaya seize independence, and African nations unite under the umbrella of the Organization of African Unity. Black civil rights leader Martin Luther King leads a march on Washington, D.C., and delivers a speech that will become famous. The year ends in tragedy and shock as President Kennedy is assassinated.

1963

Jan 28 American poet Robert Frost dies aged 89

29 The European Economic Community rejects Britain's request to join

Jun 3 Pope John XXIII dies after four years in office

16 First woman in space, U.S.S.R.'s Valentina Tereshkova, begins her three-day flight

20 The United States and U.S.S.R. agree to set up a "hotline" between the White House in Washington, D.C., and the Kremlin in Moscow

Jul 31 In Britain, the Peerage Act allows hereditary peers to disclaim their titles; Viscount Stansgate (Tony Benn) is the first

Aug 5 The United States, Soviet Union, and Britain sign the Nuclear Test-Ban Treaty

28 Black leader Martin Luther King, Jr., makes his "I have a dream" speech in Washington, D.C.

Oct 18 U.K. premier Harold Macmillan resigns; he is succeeded by the earl of Home (who will later renounce his title)

Sep 15 Confrontation begins between Malaysia and Indonesia

Nov 22 President John F. Kennedy is assassinated in Dallas; he is succeeded by Vice President Lyndon B. Johnson

24 Jack Ruby kills Lee Harvey Oswald, who had been accused of Kennedy's murder

ABOVE: The Texas School Book Depository, allegedly the place from which President Kennedy was shot. Possible positions for the killer are marked.

RIGHT: Alleged killer Lee Harvey Oswald in custody for the murder of the president. Before he can stand trial he is shot dead by Jack Ruby.

INDEPENDENCE FOR THE EAST INDIES

The final Dutch East Indies colony, West Irian, becomes part of Indonesia. In September, the British colonies of Singapore, Sarawak, and Sabah join Malaya in the Federation of Malaysia. Conflict begins as Indonesian forces infiltrate Malaysia in an attempt to gain control over the whole of Borneo. British, Commonwealth, and Malaysian forces counterattack. The Commonwealth military and civilian services suffered 150 dead and 234 wounded, with four captured; the Indonesians count 590 dead, 222 wounded and 771 captured. Conflict continues until a peace agreement is finally signed in August 1966.

AFRICA UNITES

The Organization of African Unity (OAU) is formed in Addis Ababa, the Ethiopian capital, by African leaders to increase cooperation and remove colonialism from the continent.

KENNEDY IN BERLIN

President Kennedy visits West Berlin to support freedom, stating that "Ich bin ein Berliner" (I am a Berliner). In the same month, a "hotline" telephone link is established between Washington, D.C., and Moscow.

BANNING THE BOMB

Britain, the United States, and the Soviet Union sign the Nuclear Test-Ban Treaty, prohibiting weapon tests in outer space, the atmosphere, and under water. Many other nations sign the treaty later.

I HAVE A DREAM

More than 200,000 civil rights protesters, led by Martin Luther King, Jr., march on Washington, D.C. In his "I have a dream" speech, King states that one day African-Americans will gain true equality.

DEATH IN TEXAS

President Kennedy is assassinated in Dallas, apparently by a lone gunman. Vice President Lyndon Johnson takes over. A loner named Lee Harvey Oswald is quickly arrested but is himself assassinated before he gets to trial. The Kennedy assassination will engender countless conspiracy theories for the rest of the century.

FIRST WOMAN IN SPACE

Russian cosmonaut Valentina Tereshkova becomes the first woman in space when she makes 45 orbits of the Earth piloting *Vostok 6*.

QUASARS IDENTIFIED

Quasars — Quasi-Stellar Objects — are identified by American astronomer Allan Rex Sandage and the Australian astronomer Cyril Hazard. Quasars are objects in deep space, possibly galaxies, that may be as far as 16 billion light years away.

ENTER THE MOUSE

U.S. scientist Douglas Engelbart invents the computer mouse, a device for controlling an on-screen pointer.

ABOVE: Joan Baez and Bob Dylan, princess and prince of the protest song, at the civil rights demonstration led by Martin Luther King, Jr.

DUTCH PROTEST
In the Netherlands the Provos (young "provocateurs") agitate vigorously for the liberation of repressed minority groups such as homosexuals, the introduction of antipollution laws, and the preservation of inner-city areas from property development.

SCORPIO RISING
Kenneth Anger, doyen of underground, independent filmmaking, makes *Scorpio Rising*, a documentary about motorcyclists in New York. Although made outside the normal film creation and distribution channels, it will be seen by millions of viewers over the years.

NEW ALLIANCES IN AFRICA
Kenya and Zanzibar become independent nations in the British Commonwealth. Zanzibar joins with Tanganyika to form the new nation of Tanzania in April 1964.

LEDS INVENTED
U.S. scientist Nick Holonyak invents the Light-Emitting Diode (LED), a semiconductor device that glows when a current passes through it; they are used for clocks, calculators, and other display lights.

CARBON FIBER
Engineers at England's Royal Aircraft Establishment invent carbon fiber, a thin, tough fiber of nearly pure carbon combined with plastics. It is used in spacecraft because it is light yet strong.

FIRST HOLOGRAPHS
U.S. scientists Emmett Leith and Juris Upatnieks give the first demonstration of holography, using the recently invented laser to project light to form three-dimensional images.

DE GAULLE A DIT NON
General de Gaulle forcefully vetoes Great Britain's attempt to join the Common Market.

THE FEMININE MYSTIQUE
Betty Friedan publishes *The Feminine Mystique*, a study of the social conditioning that shapes women's lives. She argues that women are victimized by false values and delusions that lead them to find fulfillment in husbands and children.

BUNKER MENTALITY
Nuclear bomb shelters are built in the cellars of houses and other private buildings across the United States and stocked with the necessities of life by citizens fearful of a nuclear war.

FLOATING BLADES
The Hover lawnmower is produced by Flymo, a British company. It works on the same principle as the hovercraft, which floats on a cushion of air just above the ground, so is easy to push across grassy gardens.

DEATHS IN THE FRENCH ARTS
Poet and writer Jean Cocteau, composer François Poulenc, and artist Georges Braque all die this year.

OPPOSITE: President Kennedy's family at his funeral in Washington, D.C.

EDITH PIAF (EDITH GIOVANNA GASSION) (1915–1963)

French chanteuse Edith Piaf has died after a long period of ill-health. The "little sparrow," whose father was a well-known acrobat and who began her career singing in the streets of Paris, became famous for songs such as "La Vie en Rose" and "Non, je ne regrette rien."

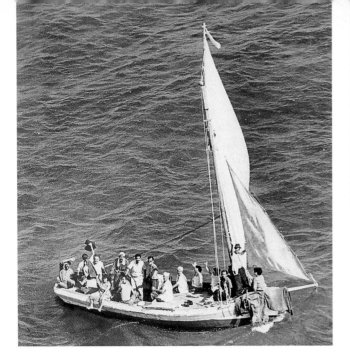

ABOVE: Refugees from Cuba adrift off the coast of Miami.

ABOVE: Engineers work on a Mariner spacecraft at Cape Canaveral, fixing solar panels to harness the power of the Sun.

BLACK CIVIL RIGHTS MOVEMENT

ABOVE: The charismatic Martin Luther King, Jr., leads the march.

ABOVE: Many black celebrities such as actor Sidney Poiter and singer Harry Belafonte join the protest.

BELOW: What started as a peaceful demonstration turns to violence as protestors make the strength of their feelings known.

BELOW: Entertainer Sammy Davis, Jr., joins the cause.

OPPOSITE: The 20,000 marchers reach the Mall in Washington, D.C.

ABOVE: Tension between white and black youths can be felt on the streets.

THE SIXTIES START TO SWING

Tension rises in southern Africa as Nelson Mandela, leader of the African National Congress, is jailed for life in South Africa and Ian Smith plans a unilateral declaration of independence on behalf of the whites in Southern Rhodesia. Things are looking better in the United States, when Martin Luther King, Jr., receives the Nobel Peace Prize and the Civil Rights Act becomes law. Three Russian cosmonauts orbit the Earth together and the U.S. probe *Ranger* takes the first photographs of the Moon's hidden dark side.

1964

Jan	29	Ninth Winter Olympics open at Innsbruck, Austria
Apr	5	U.S. general MacArthur dies aged 84
May	27	India's Prime Minister Jawaharlal Nehru dies aged 74
June	11	In South Africa, African National Congress leader Nelson Mandela is jailed for life for trying to overthrow the government
July	6	British territory Nyasaland becomes independent as Malawi
	31	Space probe *Ranger* photographs the Moon
Oct	10	Eighteenth Olympic Games open in Tokyo
	12–13	First three-man space flight by Soviet crew
	14	Martin Luther King, Jr., is awarded the Nobel Peace Prize
	15	Soviet leader Nikita Khrushchev is deposed. He is replaced by Leonid Brezhnev and Alexei Kosygin
	16	Harold Wilson forms Labour government in Britain
	24	Northern Rhodesia becomes independent as Zambia

LEFT: British pop combo the Beatles take America by storm. Their fans (above) display all the symptoms of Beatlemania.

MANDELA JAILED
Nelson Mandela, leader of the African National Congress, is sentenced to life imprisonment for sabotage and attempting to overthrow the government after the Rivona trial. He is sent to Robben Island in Table Bay, Cape Town.

MORE FREEDOM FOR AFRICA
Malawi gains its independence from Britain, followed by Northern Rhodesia, to be known as Zambia, in October, thus ending the British attempt to construct a Central African Federation. Only white-dominated southern Africa, plus a few small British, Spanish, and Portuguese colonies in West Africa, still remain in European hands.

AMERICAN CIVIL RIGHTS
The Civil Rights Act becomes law in the United States. It prohibits racial discrimination in employment, public accommodation, union membership, and federally funded programs. The act is the biggest single civil rights law in U.S. history.

KHRUSHCHEV OUSTED
Russian premier Nikita Khrushchev is deposed while on holiday at his country *dacha* and replaced by Leonid Brezhnev as Communist party leader and Alexei Kosygin as prime minister.

HOUSE FOR VANNA VENTURI
American architect Robert Venturi designs a proto-postmodern house for his mother in Chestnut Hill, Pennsylvania. Some of the features of the building (for example, the broken line of the entrance façade) look forward to the postmodern style, reflecting the fact that Venturi was writing his book *Complexity and Contradiction in Architecture* while the house was being built. This and other of his writings argue for the importance both of historical links and the inspiration of popular culture in architecture.

MARAT/SADE
The Persecution and Assassination of Marat as Performed by the Inmates of the Asylum of Charenton under the Direction of the Marquis de Sade (aka *Marat/Sade*) will be Peter Weiss's most famous play. It becomes the archetype of the Theater of Cruelty. In it, Sade directs his play depicting the murder of Marat while lunatics murmur in the background.

FOR THE UNION DEAD
In this and other volumes, American poet Robert Lowell stands up against the deadening, depersonalizing influence of war and violence. His concern for America and its traditions sets him apart from his contemporary "confessional" poets and marks him out as perhaps America's most powerful poet.

ABOVE: Black voters exercise their rights in Baton Rouge.

BELOW: Brazilians celebrate a successful revolution in Rio.

MR. SMITH TAKES CHARGE

Ian Smith becomes prime minister of Southern Rhodesia. He disagrees with the British plan to give democratic rights to the African majority and plans to go for unilateral independence.

DEATHS IN THE ENTERTAINMENT WORLD

Silent brother Adolph "Harpo" Marx (b. 1884) dies, as does writer Ian Fleming (b. 1908), the creator of James Bond. Irish playwrights Brendan Behan (b. 1925) and Sean O'Casey (b. 1884) also die.

DR. STRANGELOVE, OR HOW I LEARNED TO STOP WORRYING AND LOVE THE BOMB

Stanley Kubrick (1928–99) directs this antiwar comedy, which stars Peter Sellers in three roles. It becomes popular all over a world sensitized to the nuclear question by the recent Cuban Missile Crisis.

REQUIEM

Russian poet Anna Akhmatova's elegiac tribute to those who perished under Stalin is published, after being suppressed since Akhmatova wrote it in the 1940s. Its appearance confirms her status as Russia's greatest and most courageous 20th-century poet.

FAB FOUR IN AMERICA

English pop group the Beatles, already legends in their own land, conquer America. Beatlemania grips American teenagers.

SHOT RED MARILYN

Andy Warhol produces one of his most famous pop art images, in which subject matter from popular culture is depicted, and the modern reproduction methods (using the silkscreen technique, which Warhol was one of the first to exploit) is utilized.

JAWAHARLAL (PANDIT) NEHRU
(1889–1964)

The Harrow- and Cambridge-educated Indian leader and statesman Jawaharlal Nehru, known as Pandit or "teacher," has died. He spent a total of 18 years in prison under British rule, during which time he was elected president of the Indian National Congress (1928). He became his country's first prime minister on the gaining of independence in 1947, and was responsible for India's nonalignment policy and the development of an industrial base.

Douglas MacArthur, the American general and larger-than-life character, has died in his 80s. The much decorated veteran of World War 1 became commanding general of U.S. forces in the Far East in 1941, and later supreme commander of the Pacific Area. As supreme commander of the Allied forces he took control of the Allied occupation of Japan after the Japanese surrender (1945–51). In 1950 he was appointed United Nations Commander in Chief in Korea, but was relieved of his duties by President Truman when they differed over the handling of the Chinese intervention.

IN C

American composer Terry Riley is one of the originators of minimalism, and this work brings the movement fame. The work consists of a repeated high C on the piano, which forms a backdrop to a series of 53 short fragments, which the players may repeat any number of times (but they have to do all 53 in a set order). There can be any number of players.

BULLET TRAIN

Japan's "Bullet Train" service between Tokyo and Osaka opens, with speeds up to 125 miles per hour.

MULTIPERSON SPACE FLIGHT

In October the Soviet spacecraft *Voshkod I* carries three cosmonauts on a 16-orbit mission, the first multiperson spaceflight.

BELOW: Finnish troops serving with the UN force help to keep the peace during unrest on the island of Cyprus.

ABOVE: Funded by the U.S. AID program, the first stages of the Sharavathi Hydroelectric Project near Mysore, India, approach completion.

BELOW: The Cleveland Browns battle with the Baltimore Colts for the 1964 NFL title game. Jim Brown helps Cleveland to win the championship.

ABOVE: The cameras used on board the unmanned *Ranger II* spacecraft send back over 4,000 pictures of the cosmos.

ABOVE: Brigitte Bardot, international sex symbol and actress, is later to champion animal welfare rights and the cause of endangered species.

ELEMENT 104

Scientists in Russia and the United States both claim to have artificially created element 104; the names kurchatovium, rutherfordium, and unnilquadium are all proposed for it.

BOYS' TOYS

Action Man (in the U.K. and Europe) and G.I. Joe (in the United States) — a toy soldier doll aimed at boys — is launched by Hasbro and is as big a hit as Barbie has been with girls. Combat accessories and a wardrobe of uniforms are also provided.

BELOW: The Warren Commission, set up to investigate the Kennedy assassination. Its findings will not satisfy everybody.

ENGLAND SWINGS

Time magazine announces Swinging London, where a consumer boom rages, clothes designed to outrage are sold in diminutive boutiques instead of department stores or couture houses, discothèques are new-style nightclubs with lights flashing in time to amplified pop music, and homes will be transformed by designer Terence Conran's style ideas at Habitat, his furniture and interiors shop.

DISASTER IN ALASKA

An earthquake in Alaska measuring 8.4 on the Richter scale (later upgraded to 9.2) kills 110 people and sets off a 220-foot *tsunami* (tidal wave), the largest ever recorded.

ABOVE: The Unisphere, symbol of the New York World's Fair. Over 200,000 people visit on the first Sunday of its opening.

BACKGROUND RADIATION

American scientists Arno Allen Prenzias and Robert Woodrow Wilson discover background microwave radiation coming from all directions in space; it is thought to be an "echo" of the Big Bang with which it is believed that the universe started.

DARK GLASSES

Photochromic spectacles are invented by Dr. Stookey at the Corning Glass Works, New York. They are made from silica glass embedded with silver compound crystals. These absorb light, so the glasses darken rapidly when exposed to the sun, clearing again when light levels fall.

WINTER OLYMPICS

Thousands of tons of snow are moved to Innsbruck by the Austrian Army to permit the Ninth Winter Games to take place. Eleven hundred competitors take part in 34 events; both figures are records. Soviet Lidia Skoblikova wins all four speed-skating golds and Sjoukje Dijkstra wins the figure-skating for Holland. Lugeing, in which athletes slide down an ice course on their backs on a toboggan, makes its Olympic début.

MOON SHOTS

U.S. Ranger spacecraft takes the first close-up television pictures of the Moon.

HE'S THE GREATEST

Cassius Clay beats champion Sonny Liston to take the heavyweight boxing championship at age 22. Clay had embraced the Black Muslim faith in 1962 and as champion uses his position to challenge racism in America. He changes his name to Muhammad Ali and refuses to be drafted for the Vietnam War. For that he is stripped of his title. He does not fight between June 1967 and February 1970 but will return to win the heavyweight crown twice more.

SOUTH AFRICAN SPORT BOYCOTT

The International Olympic Committee bans South Africa over apartheid. The international community later institutes a ban on all sporting links with South Africa.

JAPANESE OLYMPICS

The 18th Games in Tokyo, 24 years after war robbed the city of the Olympics, are the first in Asia and see many world records set. Judo and volleyball are added and athletes from a record 93 nations take part.

RIGHT: Cassius Clay, soon to be Muhammad Ali, dances like a butterfly and stings like a bee.

RACE RIOTS AND THE LITTLE RED BOOK

In the United States, Black Muslim leader Malcolm X is assassinated, Nobel Prize-winner Martin Luther King is arrested marching in Alabama, and riots flare in Watts, Los Angeles. Meanwhile, in China the Cultural Revolution is under way, instigated by Mao Zedong and codified in his *Little Red Book*. In space, the first space walks take place and *Mariner 4* sends back pictures of the craters on Mars. War breaks out between India and Pakistan. Britain declares Rhodesia's UDI illegal and the country plunges into conflict.

1 9 6 5

Jan	24	Britain's wartime leader Sir Winston Churchill dies aged 90
Feb	1	Martin Luther King arrested after leading civil rights march in Alabama
	21	U.S. black leader Malcolm X is assassinated in New York
Mar	18	Soviet cosmonaut Alexei Leonov performs the first space walk
Apr	6	*Early Bird*, the first geostationary telecommunications satellite, is launched
	9	Conflict breaks out between India and Pakistan
July	14	U.S. space probe *Mariner 4* photographs Mars
Aug	15	Race riots break out in the Watts area of Los Angeles

Sep	1	War breaks out between India and Pakistan over Kashmir
	4	Franco-German missionary Albert Schweitzer dies in Africa aged 90
Nov	11	White government of Rhodesia makes illegal unilateral declaration of independence

LEFT: Malcolm X, the black American civil rights leader, is assassinated in New York.

MALCOLM X KILLED

Malcolm X, a prominent Black Muslim, is assassinated by his former colleagues in New York. Malcolm X had opposed the nonviolent civil rights movement of Martin Luther King, Jr., and supported black separatism, but in recent years had favored cooperation rather than confrontation between the races.

MARCHING IN ALABAMA

Martin Luther King, Jr., leads a march from Selma to Montgomery in Alabama to protest against the lack of civil rights in the southern state. In August, race riots break out in the Watts district of Los Angeles as racial tension rises throughout the United States.

WAR BETWEEN INDIA AND PAKISTAN

Border clashes break out between India and Pakistan on the Kutch–Sind border in April. In September, Pakistani forces cross the cease-fire line in Kashmir, leading to war. India moves 900,000 troops into West Pakistan. In fighting near Lahore the Pakistanis lose 450 tanks. Indian casualties are 2,212 dead, 7,636 wounded, and 1,500 missing. Pakistan estimates over 5,800 dead. Peace is agreed at talks in Tashkent in the Soviet Union in January 1966.

CRATERS ON MARS

The U.S. space probe *Mariner 4* photographs Mars from only 6,063 miles away, and transmits 21 pictures showing that the surface is pitted with craters like the Moon but revealing no signs of life.

THE TERRACOTTA ARMY

The tomb of a Chinese Han Dynasty king, Liu Sheng, King of Zhongshan (near Beijing) 154–112 B.C., is found to contain 3,000 miniature representations of cavalry and foot soldiers. The king is covered with 2,156 jade wafers sewn together with gold thread.

ABOVE: Eero Saarinen's eagle-shaped terminal for TWA at Kennedy Airport, New York City.

CULTURAL REVOLUTION IN CHINA

Chinese leader Lin Piao urges a Cultural Revolution to renew revolutionary zeal and root out those opposed to the revolution. The Red Guards, who are leading the new revolution, target intellectuals and party officials, and many schools are shut down. The Cultural Revolution introduces the cult of Mao Zedong, and continues until the dismissal of the president, Liu Shaoqi, in October 1968.

IN THE HEAT OF THE NIGHT

Rioting erupts in Watts, a district of Los Angeles, after a black man is arrested for drunken driving.

ARIEL

American poet Sylvia Plath's most famous book of poems impresses readers with a voice in which tight verbal and poetic control is used to describe extreme situations and unstable mental states.

ALBERT SCHWEITZER
(1875–1965)

Alsace-born Franco-German missionary, musicologist, and theologian, Dr. Albert Schweitzer, has died. In 1913, having qualified as a doctor, he went with his wife to set up a medical mission in French Equatorial Africa, where leprosy and sleeping sickness were rife. He was known in Europe for the organ recitals he gave to fund his missionary project, and for his many writings on religion, culture, and music. In 1952 he was awarded the Nobel Peace Prize.

UDI IN RHODESIA

The minority white government of Southern Rhodesia, led by Ian Smith, makes a unilateral declaration of independence (UDI) from Britain. Britain declares the regime illegal and imposes sanctions. In December 1972 the black independence movements ZANU and ZAPU will launch a concerted campaign against Rhodesia with Soviet and Chinese support. The war will end with ZANU, under Robert Mugabe, gaining power. Rhodesia will become Zimbabwe.

WAR IN THE DESERT

War breaks out in Dhofar and Oman between the Sultan's armed forces, with British assistance, and the Communist Dhofar Liberation Front which later becomes part of the People's Front for the Liberation of the Occupied Arabian Gulf (PFLOAG). Between 1971 and 1975 the Sultan of Oman's forces will lose 187 killed and 559 wounded

CLOSELY OBSERVED TRAINS

Czech writer Bohumil Hrabal becomes famous for this short novel, about Milos Hrma, a railroad worker who watches as the Nazis transport troops through Czechoslovakia to the Eastern Front. It will be made into a film directed by Jiri Menzel in 1966.

SALK INSTITUTE LABORATORIES

The handling of concrete masses marks this building in La Jolla, California, as one of American architect Louis Kahn's major achievements. The planning, with mechanical services on their own lower floors to give uninterrupted floor space in the labs, is also important.

OLD MAP OF A NEW CONTINENT

A parchment map drawn in 1440 — 52 years before Columbus reached America — is found, showing a large island west of Greenland called "Vinland." This is Newfoundland, the land discovered by Norse explorers Bjarni and Leif Eriksson, who crossed the Western Ocean in the 11th century.

ABOVE: Drugs of all kinds become available, although illegal in the decade that turns on, tunes in, and drops out.

FIRST SPACE WALKS

On March 18, Soviet cosmonaut Aleksei Leonov makes the first "space walk," floating free while tethered to his spaceship *Voskhod II*. He stays outside the spaceship for ten minutes. U.S. astronaut Edward H. White makes a space walk on June 3 which lasts four minutes longer.

EARLY BIRD FLIES

On April 6, Early Bird (later called *Intelsat 1*), the first geostationary communications satellite, is launched from the United States. It provides a constant communications link between Europe and North America.

COMPUTERS SHRINK

The first so-called "mini-computer" is introduced in the United States; it has 4k of memory and costs a mere $18,000.

TURN ON, TUNE IN ...

Timothy Leary, former professor of Psychology at Harvard University, publishes *The Psychedelic Reader*, urging readers to "turn on"— to narcotic and psychedelic drugs — "tune in, and drop out." He had been dismissed in 1963 for experimenting with the hallucinogen LSD.

ABOVE: Julie Andrews stars in the blockbuster *The Sound of Music*.

CHARLES-EDOUARD JEANNERET (LE CORBUSIER) (1887–1965)

Swiss-born French architect and town planner Charles-Edouard Jeanneret, better known as Le Corbusier, has died. He was one of the most influential architects of the modern movement, dedicated to developing architectural forms for the machine age, and deviser of the modular system (which uses standard units in building). His buildings include the Unité d'Habitation at Marseilles (1945–50), and he worked on the town plan and the Law Court and Secretariat buildings at Chandigarh, India (1951–56). His writings include *Towards a New Architecture* (1923).

ABOVE: Open-heart surgery being performed in Houston, Texas, can be seen live in Geneva, Switzerland, thanks to transmission via the U.S. Early Bird communications satellite.

LEFT: During the Cultural Revolution in China the population suffers intimidation at the hands of the Red Guard under the direction of Chairman Mao.

SURFING THE SLOPES

An engineer in Michigan takes his daughter's sled and adds "footstops" to create a sled you can stand on. He christens it the "Snurfer." Unwittingly, Sherman Poppen has created the snowboard, which now challenges traditional skis on slopes around the world.

HARE KRISHNA

The International Society of Krishna Consciousness is founded in New York City by A.C. Bhaktivedanta, a Sanskrit scholar and chemist who arrived from Calcutta with $50 in rupees and a pair of cymbals to spread Lord Krishna's word. His young followers shave their heads, wear saffron-colored robes, and chant.

BABY RACERS

The lightweight, collapsible McLaren baby buggy appears.

SOFT FOCUS

Soft contact lenses are added to improvements in vision correction recently introduced. They include the omnifocal lens, developed in 1963, which allows close-up and distant vision without disruption.

ASTROTURF

Baseball's Houston Astros become the first team to play on Astroturf. Their ground, the Astrodome in Houston, is enclosed. Clear glass panels in the roof are supposed to allow natural grass to grow. Fielders, however, are blinded by the glare of the sun when trying to catch high balls and so the panels have to be painted, killing the grass. A new artificial surface, named after the building and team, is used instead.

WINSTON LEONARD SPENCER CHURCHILL (1874–1965)

The venerable English statesman and wartime leader Sir Winston Leonard Spencer Churchill has died. Crowds line the streets to witness his funeral procession. He began his parliamentary career in 1900, was Conservative chancellor of the exchequer in 1924–29, and on the stepping-down of Neville Chamberlain, formed the wartime Coalition Government. As British prime minister from 1940–45, he used his powers of oratory to make morale-boosting broadcasts to the nation. He served again as prime minister during the days of postwar recovery, from 1951 until 1955.

FLOODS AND HAPPENINGS

Indira Gandhi takes the helm of the Indian government and Prime Minister Hendrik Verwoerd of South Africa is assassinated. Civil war breaks out in the Dominican Republic and the Marines are sent in. Priceless Italian art treasures are lost or damaged in floods that devastate Venice and Florence. Russian and American unmanned space probes land on the Moon at last. Back on earth, an H-bomb is lost at sea (but recovered), fiber optics are introduced, and the art world unveils the Happening.

1 9 6 6

Jan	11	Indira Gandhi becomes India's prime minister following the death of Lal Bahandra Shastri
Feb	3	Soviet space probe makes a soft landing on the Moon
	14	Australia adopts decimal currency
Mar	10	Princess Beatrix of the Netherlands marries Claus von Amsberg, a German diplomat
	31	Labour wins decisive victory in U.K. general election with majority of 96
Apr	24	Civil war breaks out in the Dominican Republic

May	26	British Guiana becomes independent as Guyana
June	3	U.S. space probe makes a soft landing on the Moon
July	30	England wins soccer World Cup
Sep	6	South African prime minister Hendrik Verwoerd is assassinated in parliament
	13	B.J. Vorster becomes South African prime minister
Dec	15	Cartoon king Walt Disney dies aged 65

GANDHI BECOMES PRIME MINISTER

Indira Gandhi, daughter of Nehru, becomes prime minister of India after the unexpected death of Lal Shastri.

INDEPENDENCE IN AFRICA AND THE CARIBBEAN

Guyana gains its independence from Britain, followed by Botswana, Lesotho, and Barbados. Seven other Caribbean islands, plus Belize, will gain their independence from Britain by 1983.

DOMINICAN REPUBLIC CIVIL WAR

Some 20,000 U.S. forces intervene in the civil war to restore peace following a coup that overthrows President Juan Bosch. In the fighting more than 2,000 Dominicans are killed but by October 1966 new elections will bring stability and U.S. forces withdraw.

VERWOERD ASSASSINATED

South African prime minister Hendrik Verwoerd, a firm supporter of apartheid, is stabbed to death in Cape Town's parliament by a lone assassin. He is succeeded by Balthasar Johannes Vorster.

MOON PICTURES

Within months of each other, Soviet and American space probes make soft landings on the Moon. Both take photographs of the surface, enabling both sides of the Moon to be mapped for the first time.

YAMANASHI CENTER

Japanese architect Kenzo Tange designs this center in Kofu, Japan, for press and broadcasting. It uses an innovative structure in which office spaces are supported by 16 massive concrete tubes, each some 16 feet wide. The structure gives the building a unique appearance and character.

DOCKING IN SPACE

Aboard the *Gemini 8*, U.S. astronauts Neil Armstrong and David Scott dock with the final stage of their rocket, but a technical error means the docking is not entirely successful. The ability to dock in orbit is essential to any attempt to land on the Moon.

THE BASSARIDS

German composer Hans Werner Henze reworks Euripides' ancient drama *The Bacchae* in what he feels to be his finest opera. Rational, disciplined King Pentheus (possibly an emblem of Nazism) is overcome by irrational Dionysus.

COOKING ON CHINA

The ceramic stove, a flat surface consisting of hotplates and cool surrounding areas, is introduced by an American glassworks. It is patterned to indicate the position of the hotplates, and heated by electric elements beneath.

ABOVE: A cable-controlled underwater research vehicle (top) and *Alvin* the midget sub find and recover an H-bomb lost at sea.

AGAINST INTERPRETATION

In this, the first of several influential books of essays, American writer Susan Sontag ranges over many subjects — art, film, music, politics — and confirms her stature as one of America's new intellectuals.

PHONING BY GLASS

British scientists Charles Kao and George Hockham invent telephone cables made of glass optical fibers. Fiber optics make it possible for many more calls to be transmitted along one cable than before.

FLOODS IN ITALY

Venice is flooded when high waters affecting the Adriatic cause the Venetian Lagoon to rise above its normal level. Storms in northern Italy cause the Arno River to burst its banks, flooding the city of Florence. Ancient buildings, frescoes, paintings, sculptures, and books are damaged.

IT'S ALL HAPPENING

The "Happening," a form of performance art, is introduced by American painter Robert Rauschenberg at the New York Armory Show. It is the first of many.

LOST H-BOMB FOUND

A hydrogen bomb inadvertently falls off a U.S. bomber in February. Fortunately for all concerned, it is found intact on the Atlantic seabed two months later, and is carefully recovered.

DEATHS IN THE PERFORMING ARTS

American comic genius of the silent screen Buster Keaton (b. 1886) dies, as does poet André Breton (also born in 1886), founder of the surrealist movement.

ON AGGRESSION

Austrian biologist Konrad Lorenz publishes this controversial book. His pioneering studies in ethology (animals in their environment) lead him to conclude that some aspects of animal and human aggression are innate. In *King Solomon's Ring*, published in 1963, he had argued controversially that Darwinian natural selection determines behavioral characteristics of animals.

WALTER ELIAS (WALT) DISNEY (1901–1966)

The death of Walt Disney is announced. The American cartoon filmmaker has given us such characters as Donald Duck and Mickey Mouse, and the first color animated film, *Snow White and the Seven Dwarfs* (1937). This was followed by *Pinocchio* (1940) and *Bambi* (1943), and later *Lady and the Tramp* (1956), and many more. He opened his theme park, Disneyland, in California in 1955.

LEFT: Walt Disney dies aged 65. In addition to his well-known cartoon characters, he also produced colored nature and adventure films.

BELOW: A model of Boeing's version of a supersonic aircraft. It does not take off from the drawing board.

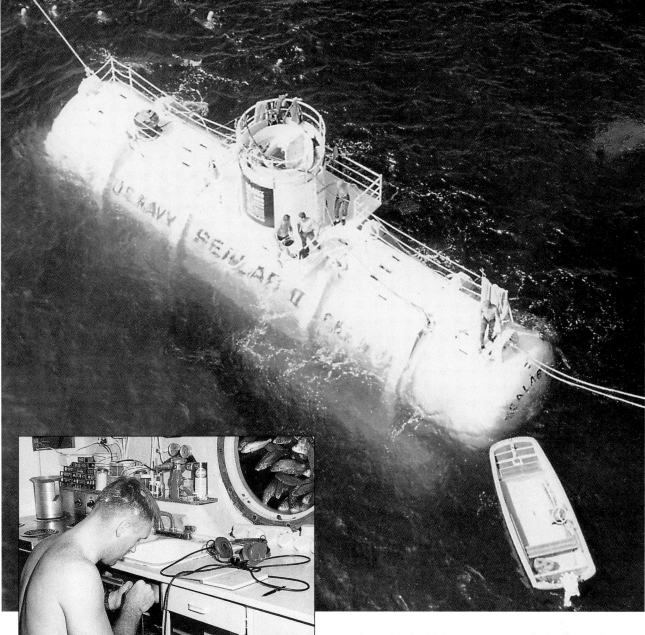

LEFT: At work in *Sealab II*. The fish find it fascinating.

ABOVE: *Sealab II*, the U.S. Navy's underwater research station.

CLEAN AND GREEN
Biodegradable liquid detergents are introduced. They are considered to be better for the environment.

THEY THINK IT'S ALL OVER
England uses home advantage to win the soccer World Cup for the first time. A thrilling final goes into overtime before England beats the Germans 4–2, thanks to a hat-trick from Geoff Hurst.

FOOD CRISIS
A world food crisis has resulted from prolonged drought in Asia and the Sahel, harvest failures in the Soviet Union and rapid world population growth. High-yielding dwarf indica rice is introduced into Asian countries where there is widespread starvation.

BELOW: Cuban refugees are picked up off the coast of Florida.

THE SUMMER OF LOVE

The Monterey Pop Festival inaugurates the summer of love. In the United States and Europe the air is alive with the scent of flowers and the tinkle of bells. Civil war tears Nigeria apart and Israel fights and wins the Six-Day War. America's Vietnam involvement attracts escalating protest in the United States and elsewhere, and there are marches and demonstrations. The military takes over Greece and both competitors in the space race suffer their first tragedies. Handsome, charismatic revolutionary Che Guevara is killed and his image becomes a poster icon for the age.

1967

Jan	27	Three U.S. astronauts die when their spacecraft catches fire during test
Apr	19	Former German chancellor Konrad Adenauer dies aged 91
	21	Junta of colonels takes over Greece following a military coup
	24	Soviet cosmonaut Vladimir Komorov dies when his spacecraft's parachute fails on landing
May	26	Civil war starts in Nigeria after Biafra breaks away
	28	U.K. yachtsman Francis Chichester completes the first solo round-the-world voyage
Jun	5–10	Six-Day War: Israel defeats coalition of five Arab states
Jul	1	EEC, European Coal and Steel Community, and Euratom merge to form the European Community (EC)
	24	President Charles de Gaulle of France angers Canada during visit by supporting independence for Quebec
Oct	9	Revolutionary guerrilla leader Che Guevara is killed in Bolivia
Dec	3	First human heart transplant performed in South Africa; patient lives only 18 days
	31	To celebrate Canada's centenary, Expo 67 opens in Montreal

SPACE TEST-BAN
The treaty banning nuclear weapons from outer space is signed by the United States, the Soviet Union, and 60 other nations.

GREECE UNDER MILITARY RULE
A junta of right-wing colonels, led by Colonel Georges Papadopoulos, takes military power in Greece and overthrows the civilian government.

CIVIL WAR IN NIGERIA
Following a military coup and tribal discord, the predominantly Ibo eastern region of Nigeria declares unilateral independence as the Republic of Biafra, under Lieutenant Colonel Odemegu Ojukwu. The Nigerian Federal government launches ground and air attacks. Many refugees flee the fighting, and starvation causes many deaths, until the rebellion collapses in January 1970 with the fall of Owerri and the victory of the Nigerian Army. Biafra loses 200,000 dead from starvation and fighting, and Nigerian casualties are estimated at 10,000 dead.

THE SIX-DAY WAR
In a preemptive strike against its Arab neighbors, which had been threatening its borders, Israel invades Egypt, Jordan, and Syria in a rapid six-day war, establishing new borders on the Suez Canal and in Jordan, gaining the strategic Golan Heights, and re-uniting the city of Jerusalem. The Israelis lose 679 killed; the Arabs lose 3,000 dead, 6,000 wounded, and 12,000 prisoners. Refugees from the West Bank territories of Jordan form the basis for the Palestine Liberation Organization (PLO) which becomes the umbrella organization for attacks on Israel.

EUROPE UNITES
The European Community (EC) is formed out of the European Economic Community (EEC), the European Coal and Steel Community (ECSC), and Euratom. In December, France vetoes the second application for membership by Britain.

ANTI-VIETNAM RALLY
In Washington, antiwar protesters, novelist Norman Mailer and poet Robert Lowell among them, surround the Pentagon. Soldiers and police drive them back with nightsticks and rifle butts and 250 people are arrested. Anti-Vietnam marches and rallies will proliferate all over America and Europe until the war ends.

QUEBEC LIBRE
French president Charles de Gaulle stirs up Quebec nationalism on a visit to Canada by supporting a free Quebec.

CHE KILLED
Argentinian-born Marxist and co-architect of the Cuban Revolution, Ernesto "Che" Guevara is killed in Bolivia, trying to start a revolution against the government. He becomes an icon of student revolutionaries everywhere.

LOST LEADER
Australian prime minister Harold Holt is missing, presumed drowned, after swimming off the coast at Portsea in Victoria.

ONE HUNDRED YEARS OF SOLITUDE
Colombian writer Gabriel García Márquez's novel depicts a decaying village from the viewpoint of seven generations of one family. In the novel, the magical and fantastic can happen alongside real, everyday events, and every detail glows with significance. This makes the book the key text in the style known as "magic realism".

BLUEBIRD OF TRAGEDY
British racer Donald Campbell is killed on Coniston Water in the Lake District in an attempt to break the world water speed record in his jet-powered vehicle.

HOMOSEXUALITY LEGALIZED
Homosexuality is decriminalized in Britain by the Sexual Offenses Act, which legalizes sex between consenting adult men aged 21 or over.

DEATH OF A PHYSICIST
J. Robert Oppenheimer (b. 1904) dies. A nuclear physicist, he was part of the team that developed and built the atom bomb, but resigned in 1945 protesting against its use on Hiroshima and Nagasaki.

THE MEDIUM IS THE MESSAGE
In the sociological-philosophical tract, *The Medium is the Message,* Canadians Marshall McLuhan and Quentin Fiore analyze popular culture, media, and the impact of printing on civilization. The work has a strong influence on thinking about everything from advertising to literature. The book's title introduces a new buzzword into the language. McLuhan is also responsible for the concept of the "global village," referring to the proliferation of communication methods.

ROSENCRANTZ AND GUILDENSTERN ARE DEAD
Czech-born playwright Tom Stoppard's second play brings him fame and critical attention. Centered on the off-stage lives of two minor characters in Shakespeare's *Hamlet*, it shows the writer's talent for taking an idea and running with it, as well as his resourcefulness with language.

SPACE TRAGEDIES
Three U.S. astronauts — Roger B. Chaffee, Virgil I. Grissom, and Edward H. White — are killed during a ground test of an Apollo spacecraft, which catches fire. The Soviet spacecraft *Soyuz I* crashes to the ground when its parachute tangles on reentry. Cosmonaut Vladimir M. Komarov is killed.

ANOTHER NEW ELEMENT
The artificial radioactive element 105 is produced by Russian scientists; they propose the name nielsbohrium for it; American scientists also produce it and call it hahnium. Neither name has been accepted.

DEATHS IN THE ARTS
British actress Vivien Leigh (b. 1913), American jazzman John Coltrane (b. 1926), writer and critic Dorothy Parker (b. 1893), actress Jayne Mansfield (b. 1932), actor Spencer Tracy (b. 1900), and French writer André Maurois (b. 1885) all die in this year.

THE FASHION FOR JOGGING
The book *Jogging*, by University of Oregon athletics coach Bill Bowerman, helps create the jogging and running craze. Bowerman had observed jogging programs for health and fitness in New Zealand and uses the ideas in his book.

PULSARS DISCOVERED

British astronomer Jocelyn Bell Burnell discovers pulsating stars (later called pulsars), using a multidish radio telescope she helped to build at Cambridge University, England.

NOVEMBER STEPS

Japanese composer Toru Takemitsu's *November Steps* is performed for the first time. Written for a Western orchestra and two Japanese instruments, the *biwa* and *shakuhachi*, it brings together Japanese and Western classical musical traditions and is regarded as his most important work.

EXPO 67

Expo 67 opens in Montreal to celebrate Canada's centenary on December 31, 1966. The Canadian pavilion is an inverted pyramid named Katimavik, the Inuit word for "meeting place." America displays contemporary art in a geodesic dome. Israeli-born Canadian architect Moshe Safde celebrates "a sense of house" in an imaginative apartment house with private outdoor space. This apartment house is made up of hundreds of prefabricated containers, held together by steel cables. The design allows other containers to be added at later dates. The house shows the scope of prefabrication.

ADEN INDEPENDENT

Britain grants independence to Aden, in Yemen, its last Middle East colony, after many years of local revolt.

FIRST HUMAN HEART TRANSPLANT

South African surgeon Christiaan Barnard performs the first human heart transplant at Grote Schuur hospital. However, the patient, Louis Washkansky, dies from pneumonia 18 days later.

THE SUMMER OF LOVE

The Monterey Pop Festival in San Francisco marks the beginning of the hippie "Summer of Love," which spreads to London, where pop festivals are held in Hyde Park, and to Amsterdam, Europe's capital of alternative culture.

ABORTION REFORM

Abortion is legalized in Britain under medical supervision and subject to specified criteria. Sweden, Denmark, and Iceland legalized abortion on several grounds before World War II, but Britain is the first Western European country to do so. Colorado also legalizes abortion this year.

THE NAKED APE

Published by British zoologist Desmond Morris, this book interprets aspects of human behavior, such as hunting instincts, pair-bonding, mutual grooming, and territoriality, with the behavior of animals, especially that of apes.

KONRAD ADENAUER
(1876–1967)

German elder statesman Konrad Adenauer has died. Adenauer, whose political career began as Lord Mayor of Cologne in 1917, was dismissed from office and imprisoned by the Nazis, but reinstated by the Allies in 1945, when he founded the Christian Democratic Union. He was chancellor of the Federal Republic of Germany from 1949 to 1963.

SUPERBOWL

The Green Bay Packers of the National Football League rout the Kansas City Chiefs of the American Football League 35–10 in Superbowl I. The Superbowl matches the champions of the two leagues after the merger of the bodies in 1966. The concept is not an immediate success and the game is not a sellout.

COGNITIVE PSYCHOLOGY

In the theory put forward in this book, American psychologist Ulric Neisser focuses on analyzing mental processes such as memory and perception, through which we acquire knowledge, rather than observing human behavior. Neisser believes we use our experience to build models (called "schemas"), which we use to analyze impressions and anticipate what might happen.

ELEMENTS OF SEMIOLOGY

French philosopher Roland Barthes (1915–80) develops the idea that any product of culture, from language and literature to dress and children's toys, is a system of signs which together provide a means of interpreting and understanding the culture.

NUCLEAR FOOD

The U.S. Department of Agriculture begins a test project of irradiating wheat and other foods to kill insects.

SAILING ROUND THE WORLD

British yachtsman Francis Chichester completes a solo circumnavigation of the world in *Gypsy Moth IV.*

RENE FRANÇOIS GHISLAIN MAGRITTE
(1898–1967)

Belgian surrealist painter René Magritte has died. In 1924 he became a member of the newly founded Belgian Surrealist Group and then continued to produce bizarre but meticulously painted works depicting incongruously juxtaposed objects, such as the neat bowler-hatted men dripping from the sky in *Golconda* (1953).

VIETNAM WAR

With the exception of the Civil War, the Vietnam War is the most divisive war ever fought by the United States. Under four presidents, the United States is drawn into the war between North and South Vietnam and then struggles to withdraw with dignity. It begins on July 8, 1959, when unprecedented numbers of "military observers" are sent into South Vietnam by the United States, and escalates into full-scale war in 1964. During the war the South Vietnamese suffer 150,000 killed and 400,000 wounded while the North Vietnamese and Vietcong suffer 100,000 killed and 300,000 wounded. Between January 1, 1961, and January 27, 1972, the United States suffers 45,941 killed and 300,635 wounded. The war lasts until April 30, 1975, and is very unpopular with the American people

LEFT: American troops from a reconnaissance patrol discover part of the network of tunnels the Vietcong use as a strategic base.

❖ KEY DATES ❖
IN THE VIETNAM WAR

U.S. ATTACKS Aug 5, 1964
Aircraft from the USS *Constellation* and *Ticonderoga* attack North Vietnamese torpedo boat bases.

"ROLLING THUNDER" Mar 2, 1965
This operation is the first of major USAF and USN air attacks on North Vietnam. On 8 March, 1965, the first U.S. Marines arrive in South Vietnam.

KHE SANH Jan 22–Apr 14, 1968
Some 6,000 U.S. Marines and South Vietnamese troops with 46 guns held a mountain base against 15,000 men in three North Vietnamese divisions.

TET OFFENSIVE Jan 30–31, 1968
The attempt by the Vietcong and North Vietnamese to score a major victory over the United States and South Vietnam cost them 46,000 dead and 9,000 wounded, while South Vietnam suffer 2,788 killed and 8,886 wounded and the U.S. forces 1,536 killed and 7,775 wounded. It is a military defeat for the North, but a political victory.

LAM SON 719 Feb 8–Apr 9, 1971
The South Vietnamese unsuccessfully thrust into Laos to disrupt supplies down the Ho Chi Minh Trail. U.S. forces suffer 176 killed and 1,942 wounded. South Vietnam 1,483 killed, 5,420 wounded, and 691 missing, and North Vietnam 13,636 killed and 69 captured.

ABOVE: Fighting takes place on the streets and is equally as dangerous as jungle warfare.

ABOVE: The chop of helicopter rotor blades is the defining soundtrack to the war in Vietnam.

ABOVE: South Vietnamese civilians run from the scene of a skirmish in which three Vietcong soldiers have been killed.

ABOVE: U.S. Marines move cautiously through flooded rice paddies on a search and clear mission, Operation Deckhouse.

FIGHTING IN THE STREETS

A year of violence and confrontation as the Prague Spring in Czechoslovakia is stifled by Soviet tanks, Martin Luther King, Jr., and Senator Robert Kennedy are gunned down, and student revolutionaries take to the streets of Paris. In Vietnam the Vietcong throw all their energy and fire power into the Tet Offensive. The American retaliation causes protest at home. In Northern Ireland, civil disobedience initiates what will be decades of troubles. The Olympic Games are held in Mexico and are memorable for the Black Power salute given defiantly by black athletes.

1 9 6 8

Jan	5	Reformer Alexander Dubcek becomes head of the Czech Communist party
	30	Vietcong launch Tet Offensive on South Vietnam
Feb	6	The 10th Winter Olympics open in Grenoble, France
Apr	4	U.S. black leader Martin Luther King, Jr., is assassinated in Memphis, Tennessee
May	2	Demonstrating students in Paris begin series of clashes with police
June	5	U.S. senator Robert F. Kennedy is shot in Los Angeles; he dies the next day

July	6	Sixty-one nations sign a treaty on the nonproliferation of nuclear weapons
	31	First regular cross-Channel hovercraft service begins
Aug	20	Soviet and allied troops invade Czechoslovakia to stop Dubcek's reforms
Oct	5-6	Civil rights demonstrators in Londonderry, Northern Ireland, clash with police
	12	The 19th Olympic Games open in Mexico City
Nov	5	Republican Richard M. Nixon is elected U.S. president

LEEFT: Civil rights leader Martin Luther King, Jr., is assassinated this year, provoking an outbreak of angry scenes and rioting (above).

SPRINGTIME IN PRAGUE
Alexander Dubcek becomes first secretary of the Czechoslovak Communist Party in January and begins the reforms known as the Prague Spring. Seven months later, Soviet and allied troops invade the country to stop reform. The reforms are abandoned, but Dubcek retains power until he is deposed in April 1969. He later becomes ambassador to Turkey.

DEATH OF A DREAM
Civil rights leader Martin Luther King, Jr., is shot in a motel by an unknown gunman in Memphis, Tennessee. His death leads to major race riots across America.

ANOTHER KENNEDY SHOT
Leading Democratic politician, and brother of the former president, Robert Kennedy is shot and killed after winning the primary election in California. His death leads to widespread disillusionment in the United States, and results in the victory of the Republican candidate Richard Nixon in November's presidential election.

TET OFFENSIVE

The Vietcong use the lull of the Tet (New Year) holiday to launch a multitargeted offensive on Saigon and other strategic ares of the country. They occupy the U.S. embasssy in Saigon and capture Hue. The United States and South Vietnam fight back and retake Hue in February, but the retaliation, which is televised and involves civilian executions, has a disastrous effect on U.S. morale at home.

SINFONIA

Italian composer Luciano Berio writes *Sinfonia* for the virtuoso vocal group the Swingle Singers. Full of quotations, both musical and verbal, and references to recent events (the student unrest in Paris), the work finally comes to rest in a meditation on the life and death of Martin Luther King, Jr.

LEFT: "Earthrise," as seen and photographed by the U.S. astronauts who orbit the Moon in *Apollo 8* in December of this year.

BELOW: Plastic research balloons are sent up into the stratosphere to collect data for the National Center for Atmospheric Research.

LEFT: Robert F. Kennedy is assassinated this year by a Jordanian student, Sirhan Bissara Sirhan.

LES EVENEMENTS

French students protesting against the Vietnam War and other grievances occupy their universities and take their protests to the streets. Barricades are erected in Paris, and the government almost falls. The protests are copied by students throughout Europe and the United States. Violent demonstrations take place against the autocratic structure of universities across Europe, from Britain to West Germany. The French universities close after demonstrations at the University of Nanterre spread to the Sorbonne in Paris. In the Netherlands, the Maris Report, calling for extensive centralization of university resources, leads to demonstrations in Utrecht, Delft, Wageningen, Groningen, and, later, Amsterdam.

NONPROLIFERATION PACT

In London, 61 nations, including Britain, the U.S.S.R., and the United States, sign the Nuclear Nonproliferation Treaty, which prohibits the spread of nuclear weapons.

TROUBLE IN IRELAND

Disturbances break out as civil rights demonstrators protesting against anti-Catholic discrimination by the Protestant majority government clash with police. In the next few months, civil rights demonstrators increase their agitation across the province. The minority Catholic population has not enjoyed full civil rights following the 1922 partition of Ireland. Rioting in Londonderry cannot be contained by the Royal Ulster Constabulary (RUC) and the British government sends in troops to regain control.

MILE-LONG DRAWING

Two parallel lines on the desert floor make up Walter de Maria's Mile-Long Drawing. It is an early work of conceptual art, and also an early example of making art on and out of the land.

POWER FROM THE TIDES

The first successful tidal power station goes into operation on the Rance River, in Brittany, France.

ASTRONAUTS ORBIT THE MOON

In December the U.S. spacecraft Apollo 8 orbits the Moon for 20 hours, carrying astronauts Frank Borman, James A. Lovell, and William A. Anders, and returns safely to Earth.

ABOVE: Day-to-day images such as this wounded American soldier appear daily on television and help to bring an end to the war.

PULSARS IDENTIFIED

U.S. astronomer Thomas Gold discovers that pulsars, first observed in 1967, are actually neutron stars. These are formed of closely packed neutrons and are the densest known stars.

MARCEL DUCHAMP
(1887–1968)

French-born American artist Marcel Duchamp, pioneer of dadaism and surrealism, has died. He moved to the United States in 1915 and shocked the art world with "ready-made" works such as his urinal, entitled Fountain, of 1917. His work includes The Large Glass: The Bride Stripped Bare by Her Bachelors Even, a construction of lead, wire, and tinfoil on a large piece of sheet glass, which he abandoned as uncompleted in 1923 after eight years' work. After this he concentrated on playing chess.

REGULAR HOVERCRAFT SERVICE

The first regular hovercraft service across the English Channel, from Dover to Boulogne, begins. The N4 hovercraft carries 254 passengers and 30 cars.

OIL IN ALASKA

U.S. petroleum companies discover a huge oilfield at Prudhoe Bay, on the Arctic Sea coast of north Alaska.

CLEANER WALLS

Washable wallpaper is manufactured by Du Pont in the United States. It is made from polythene and resists tearing. A flexible fabric version is used to make disposable underwear and uniforms.

WIMBLEDON OPENS TO PROFESSIONALS

Rod Laver takes the inaugural Open Wimbledon. After a long struggle in the face of rising professionalism, the tournament allows professional tennis players to participate for the first time.

ABOVE: Mrs. Coretta King speaking in front of the Lincoln Memorial in Washington, D.C., after the assassination of her husband.

WINTER OLYMPICS IN FRANCE

Events at the 10th Winter Olympics center on Grenoble in France, but events are spread over the surrounding area and seven "villages" host competitors. Drug tests after each event make an appearance. French skier Jean-Claude Killy makes home crowds happy with three skiing golds.

SUPERTANKERS

The first supertankers, giant oceangoing ships for carrying petroleum, come into general use.

BLACK POWER OLYMPICS

The 19th Olympics in Mexico are filled with stunning performances and powerful protest. The altitude of Mexico City gives an advantage in sprint events and 34 world records and 38 Olympic records are set. American Bob Beamon smashes the long jump record by 55cm and his compatriot Jim Hines wins the 100m in 9.95 seconds. Fellow sprinters Tommie Smith and John Carlos create the image of the games, however, when they raise gloved fists on the medal podium in a salute to black power. The U.S. team sends the 200m medal winners home, but the world sees their protest. Dick Fosbury of America transforms the high jump with the technique that becomes known as the "Fosbury Flop."

LEFT: Led by his eldest son Joseph, the friends and family of Senator Robert F. Kennedy carry his coffin to its burial site at Arlington National Cemetery, Virginia.

ABOVE: President Lyndon B. Johnson is made to feel at home in El Salvador, where he has been on a goodwill mission.

ABOVE: Senator Richard M. Nixon hits the campaign trail in Oregon hoping to take another step towards the presidency.

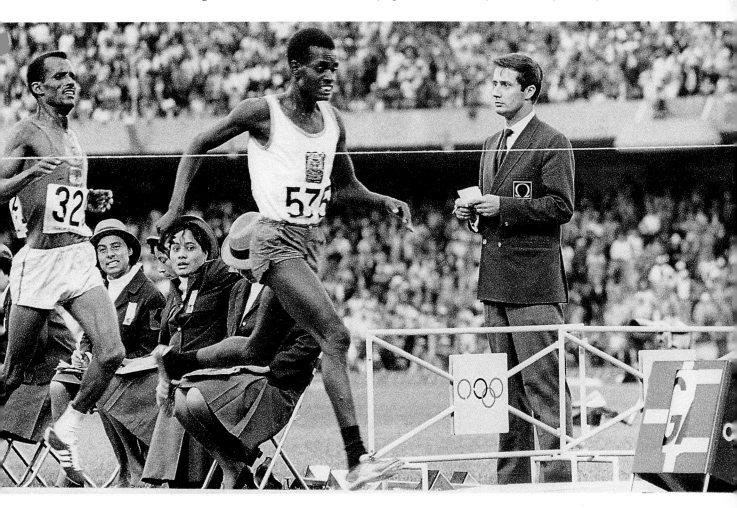

ABOVE: Neftali Temo wins gold for Kenya in the 10,000m men's event; it is the first gold medal of the Mexican Olympic Games.

MOON LANDING AND FLOWER POWER

The year is dominated by the successful U.S. Moon landing and the world watches in awe as astronaut Neil Armstrong takes a giant step on our behalf. President Nixon initiates the long withdrawal of U.S. troops from Vietnam but in South America, Honduras and El Salvador have a short, fierce war about football. Biafra starves as Nigeria blocks aid flights. The open-air rock festival at Woodstock, three days of music, mud, and love, stamps its image on the hearts and minds of a generation.

OPPOSITE: U.S. astronaut Neil Armstrong fulfills President Kennedy's 1961 promise to put an American on the Moon.

1969

Feb	3	Yasser Arafat is appointed head of the Palestine Liberation Organization
	9	The American Boeing 747, the world's largest airliner, makes its first flight
Mar	2	Anglo-French Concorde, the first supersonic airliner, makes its trial flight
Apr	28	President Charles de Gaulle of France resigns
May	14	President Richard Nixon proposes withdrawal of U.S., Allied, and North Vietnamese troops from South Vietnam
July	1	In Britain, Prince Charles is invested as Prince of Wales
	13	Dispute over football match leads to war between Honduras and El Salvador
	20	U.S. astronaut Neil Armstrong becomes the first man to set foot on the Moon
Aug	19	British troops take over security duty in Northern Ireland
Sep	1	In Libya, Colonel Gaddaffi overthrows King Idris and becomes head of state
	3	President Ho Chi Minh of North Vietnam dies aged 79

ABOVE: President Nixon greets the press in the Socialist Rebubalic of Romania. He is the first U.S. president to visit the country.

TROOPS IN NORTHERN IRELAND

British troops patrol the streets to protect Catholics from attack by Protestant gangs. The troops are sent in as a temporary measure to keep the two communities apart, but are forced to remain for longer as the security situation deteriorates.

LIBYAN COUP

King Idris of Libya is toppled in a coup and replaced as head of state by Colonel Muammar Gaddafi, a follower of the political theories of Mao Zedong.

OSTPOLITIK IN GERMANY

The Social Democrats win the general election and Willy Brandt, former mayor of West Berlin, becomes chancellor, the first Social Democrat to lead West Germany. He begins a policy of *Ostpolitik*, or reconciliation with the Eastern bloc.

ISRAEL'S NEW LEADER

Seventy-year-old Golda Meir becomes the first woman prime minister of Israel.

MANSON FAMILY MURDERS

American actress Sharon Tate (wife of film director Roman Polanski) is found brutally murdered, along with four friends, at her Beverly Hills home. Another couple, Leno Lo Bianca and his wife, are also found dead in the same fashionable district. Eventually Charles Manson, a charismatic ex-convict, and four members of his desert-dwelling hippie family are arrested, tried, and found guilty of the crimes.

SLAUGHTERHOUSE FIVE

Set partly during the bombing of Dresden, American writer Kurt Vonnegut's cult novel cuts through genres. Part science fiction, part antiwar tract, part autobiography, its slangy, surreal approach makes it popular. It remains the best known of Vonnegut's many books.

PALACH'S PROTEST

Jan Palach, Czech philosophy student, sets light to himself and dies in protest against the Soviet occupation of his country.

THE GENERAL STEPS DOWN

General de Gaulle resigns as president of France after losing a constitutional referendum. The Gaullist Georges Pompidou wins the presidential election in June.

EIGHT SONGS FOR A MAD KING

A key work of "music theater" (not quite opera, not quite concert music), the eight songs by British composer Peter Maxwell Davies are sung by the mad George III, or at least a character who thinks he is the mad George III. The range of musical references (Handel on the honky-tonk piano) and the violence of the emotions (and extremes of vocal technique needed to express them) makes the work notorious.

FLOWER POWER

The free music festival on a muddy farm in Woodstock, New York, brings 400,000 people together for a three-day celebration of peace, love, and understanding. Major music stars include Jimi Hendrix, The Who, The Band, and Janis Joplin.

TRAGEDY IN BIAFRA

Following the Nigerian ban on aid planes, thousands of people in the breakaway province of Biafra are condemned to die of starvation. Television brings horrific pictures of skeletal children into the homes of the world.

OH, CALCUTTA!

English drama producer and critic Kenneth Tynan's famous musical begins its run in New York City. The satirical work will run for years on Broadway. It contains nude scenes and the title is a pun on the racy French phrase, "O, quel cul tu as" (oh, what a great butt you've got).

MONTY PYTHON'S FLYING CIRCUS

English comic John Cleese and company create a new brand of bizarre humor on television. Acting styles, linguistic wit, and groundbreaking animation all push television humor in new, surreal directions and the Pythons gain popular following in Europe and America. The style will later be even more successful worldwide in a series of films.

ARCHITECTS TOP OUT

Influential German architects Ludwig Mies van der Rohe (b. 1886) and Walter Gropius (b. 1883), founder of the Bauhaus, die this year.

STONEWALL RIOTS

In New York City, police raid the Stonewall Bar, popular with lesbians and homosexuals. They meet resistance. This marks the beginning of the fight for gay rights.

SUPERSONIC AIRLINERS

In March, the world's first supersonic airliner, the Anglo-French *Concorde 001*, makes its first flight in France. Not to be outdone, Russia's supersonic airliner, the *TU-144* (called "Concordski" by the English-speaking press) makes its first flight two months later.

ANTIBIOTIC BAN

The British Ministry of Agriculture and the American Food and Drug Administration both ban the addition of penicillin and tetracycline antibiotics to livestock feed because of the danger of an increase in drug-resistant bacteria.

METEORITES FOUND IN ANTARCTICA

Japanese geologists find meteorites on the Antarctic ice cap.

OVER THE RAINBOW

Judy Garland (b. 1922), forever remembered as Dorothy in *The Wizard of Oz*, dies in London.

HO CHI MINH
(BORN NGUYEN THAT THANH)
(1890–1969)

Ho Chi Minh, the Vietnamese leader whose name is a household word around the world thanks to the Vietnam War, has died. The son of a mandarin, between 1912 and 1930 he spent much of his life in Britain, the United States, France, and Russia. Founder of the Indo-Chinese Communist party (1930) and the Vietminh Independence League (1941), he led his country against the French (1946–54), and became prime minister of the newly established North Vietnam in 1954. He led the struggle against the U.S.-aided South Vietnam, which developed into war in 1964 and which still continues.

ABOVE: The King is back — Elvis Presley returns to the public stage this year, performing mainly in Las Vegas.

A GIANT STEP FOR MANKIND

U.S. astronaut Neil A. Armstrong becomes the first man to set foot on the Moon; he is followed by Edwin E. "Buzz" Aldrin 18 minutes later. They become the first people to photograph another planet, using modified Hasselblad cameras. The third astronaut, Michael Collins, orbits the Moon in *Apollo 11*, ready to pick the others up and return them to Earth. The whole mission is televised and viewed across the world.

NORTHWEST PASSAGE VOYAGE

The American icebreaking supertanker *Manhattan* makes the first commercial voyage through the Northwest Passage, the seaway around Canada linking the Pacific and the Atlantic; it takes three months.

SOCCER MAD

El Salvador and Honduras go to war over a soccer game. Honduran citizens attack Salvadorians in Honduras after El Salvador wins a World Cup qualifying game in Mexico. The government of El Salvador retaliates. Fighting lasts a week.

AN ELEPHANT FLIES

The largest commercial jetliner, the Boeing 747, makes its first flight. Popularly known as a jumbo jet, it can carry 362 passengers.

NORTH SEA OIL FOUND

High-grade crude petroleum is found in the northern North Sea between Britain and Norway. The find will mean great prosperity for both countries.

WALKING ON WATER

The British Trans-Arctic Expedition led by Wally Herbert reaches Spitzbergen. Its members become the first people to cross the frozen Arctic Ocean on foot. They have travelled 3,600 miles in 464 days from Point Barrow, Alaska.

OPEN SESAME

Sesame Street begins on American Public Service TV and revolutionizes children's attitudes to learning. Designed by Children's TV Workshop and funded by the Ford Foundation, Carnegie, and the U.S. Office of Education, it uses techniques of commercial television to teach letters and numbers in English and Spanish. Kermit the Frog and other "muppets" make their first appearance.

WORDS OF WARNING

Problems of the Human Environment, commissioned by the United Nations, reports that 1,236 million acres of arable land and two-thirds of the world's original forests have been lost, mainly through poor agricultural management and forest clearances.

OFF THE ROAD

American writer Jack Kerouac (b. 1922), the original "beatnik" and assiduous chronicler of the romance of the road, dies.

POLLUTION SPREADS

Alarm over pollution grows after millions of Rhine fish are killed by leakage from Thiodan 2 insecticide canisters that had been dropped into the river in 1967. In 1968, nerve gas from a U.S. Army site in Utah escapes, killing 6,000 sheep, and now Japan reports cadmium-poisoning, Texas reports mercury-poisoning, and in Arizona DDT is found in mothers' milk.

SUPERBOWL SUCCESS

The upstart New York Jets of the junior American Football League beat the Baltimore Colts of the National Football League 16–7 to take the Superbowl, a win that had been confidently predicted by the Jets' brash quarterback Joe Namath. The Superbowl becomes America's top sporting occasion.

VOYAGE TO THE MOON

ABOVE: Liftoff for *Apollo 11* on its historic mission to the Moon.

LEFT: The command and service module of *Apollo 11* floats above the Sea of Tranquillity, photographed from the orbiting lunar module.

ABOVE: Safe splashdown for the crew of *Apollo 12*, the second team of U.S. astronauts to walk on the Moon. They are (l to r) Charles Conrad, Jr., Richard F. Gordon, Jr., and Alan L. Bean.

ABOVE: Aboard the USS *Hornet* President Nixon hails the *Apollo 11* crew on their safe return from the Moon.

MEN ON THE MOON

The 1960s see human beings on the Moon. From the first short space-hops of 1961 to the full-scale multi-teamed expeditions that characterize this year, the whole Moon mission fits neatly into the decade. Using techniques learned on previous missions, *Apollo 11* at last lands the first men on the Moon as the world watches. The mission is followed up by the exploratory team from *Apollo 12* a few months later.

ABOVE LEFT: *Apollo 12* astronaut unpacks the Apollo lunar surface experiments package in the first EVA (extravehicular activity) period of the mission.

ABOVE RIGHT: The fragile-looking *Apollo 12* lunar module. Astronauts Alan Bean and Charles Conrad land on the Moon in this, while Richard Gordon remains with the command and service module in lunar orbit.

LEFT: *Apollo 11* commander Neil Armstrong, photographed by Edwin "Buzz" Aldrin, takes soil samples from the Moon as his first task, in case the expedition is cut short. Armstrong and Aldrin remain on the Moon for just over 21 hours.

ABOVE: From close up, the Moon's surface appears pock-marked with craters and holes.

INSET: A piece of Moon rock brought back from the *Apollo 12* mission in November. This piece is a form of olivine basalt.

RIGHT: Humanity's first view of its own home, taken from the orbiting lunar module of *Apollo 10*. The blue and green beauty of Earth is a wonderful surprise to many of its inhabitants.

REVOLUTION AND LIBERATION

Against a background of civil war, coups, and oppression, technology moves forward: Commercial flight goes supersonic, computers invade everyday life, and "test-tube" babies are born. Mars is found to be apparently barren; humanity loses interest in space and turns its attention to the pollution of the environment and the impact of technology on the ecological balance. Feminism becomes at once more militant and mainstream. The first signs of religious fundamentalism show themselves in the Middle East.

RIGHT: Demonstrators rally to protest about the war in Vietnam.

1970–1979

KEY EVENTS OF THE DECADE

- IDI AMIN SEIZES POWER IN UGANDA

- GREENPEACE BEGINS ITS PROTESTS

- TROUBLE IN NORTHERN IRELAND

- END OF VIETNAM WAR

- WATERGATE SCANDAL

- BLACK SEPTEMBER OLYMPICS

- PINOCHET COUP IN CHILE

- THE COD WAR

- POL POT REGIME IN CAMBODIA

- CIVIL WAR IN THE LEBANON

- THE STEVE BIKO INCIDENT

- ELVIS PRESLEY DIES

- FIRST TEST-TUBE BABY BORN

- CIVIL WAR IN NICARAGUA

- HOMOSEXUAL RIGHTS

- ISLAMIC REVOLUTION IN IRAN

- THREE MILE ISLAND

- RUSSIA INVADES AFGHANISTAN

WORLD POPULATION **3,693** MILLION

DÉTENTE IN THE EAST AND DEATH ON THE CAMPUS

The new decade sees continued protest over the American involvement in Vietnam, despite promises of withdrawal. Antiwar demonstrations continue and in the United States four students are shot dead on the campus of Kent State University, Ohio, by the National Guard. West Germany's chancellor, Willy Brandt, initiates détente with East Germany. The Palestinian Black September movement is formed and attacks Jordan. *Apollo 13* proves as unlucky as its number and the astronauts in it get back to Earth on a wing and a prayer. Political heavyweights Charles de Gaulle and Gamal Nasser of Egypt leave the world stage.

1 9 7 0

Mar	19	First meeting of East and West German heads of state
Apr	11–13	U.S. *Apollo 13* Moon mission aborted after explosion; crew return safely
Sep	5	In Chile, Marxist Salvador Allende is elected president
	16–27	War in Jordan between Jordanian Army and Palestinian militia
	18	Jimi Hendrix (b. 1943), American guitar ace, dies

	28	In Egypt, President Nasser dies aged 52
	29	Anwar Sadat becomes president of Egypt
Nov	9	Former French president Charles de Gaulle dies aged 79
	17	Soviet space probe *Luna 17* lands on the Moon and deploys an unmanned exploration vehicle
Dec	7	West Germany and Poland sign treaty recognizing Poland's frontier

ABOVE: The staff at Houston Mission Control celebrate the safe return of the *Apollo 13* crew, whose mission went badly wrong.

GERMAN DETENTE
The first meeting between Willy Brandt of West Germany and Willi Stoph of East Germany, at Erfurt in East Germany, starts the process of détente in Europe.

DEATH ON THE CAMPUS
U.S. National Guards shoot dead four antiwar demonstrators on Kent State University campus in Ohio. Antiwar protests continue throughout the United States against U.S. involvement in the Vietnam War.

ALLENDE WINS
Salvador Allende wins the presidential election in Chile. He becomes the first democratically elected Marxist head of state in the world, and begins a program of reform, including the nationalization of copper mines owned by U.S. subsidiaries.

BLACK SEPTEMBER
After militant Palestinians hijack three aircraft to Jordan, the Jordanian government evicts the Palestinians and regains control of the kingdom in a month of struggle which will be known as Black September.

TROUBLED INDEPENDENCE FOR ADEN
After four years, British troops withdraw from Aden as independence approaches. The withdrawal sees conflict with the National Liberation Front (NLF). The British suffer 57 dead and 651 wounded. Local civilian casualties are bad: 280 dead and 922 wounded.

POWER CHANGE IN EGYPT
Egyptian president Gamal Abdel Nasser (b. 1918) dies and is succeeded by Anwar Sadat.

RIGHT: Aquanauts replicate conditions in space, spending 20 days in *Tektite 11*, an underwater habitat designed and funded by NASA.

HIPPIES IN HOLLAND
Hippies are cleared from the Dutch National Monument in Dam Square, Amsterdam. The permissive Dutch capital has become the alternative capital of Europe for the young, called *asfaltjeugd*, or "asphalt youth," in Dutch, because they sleep in the city's parks and squares.

POLISH BORDER ASSURED
West Germany and Poland sign a treaty recognizing the current border between Poland and Germany, thus reassuring Poland about any possible German moves to reacquire land lost after the war.

SPACE DRAMA
U.S. spacecraft *Apollo 13*, on its way to the Moon, is crippled by an explosion. The astronauts on board, James Lovell, John Swigert, and Fred Haise, guided by ground control in Houston and watched by the world, manage to swing the damaged craft round the Moon and return safely to Earth, using the lunar module Aquarius as a "lifeboat."

I KNOW WHY THE CAGED BIRD SINGS

American writer Maya Angelou's autobiography, including her account of sexual and racial oppression (raped at the age of eight, a period of muteness), marks her emergence as a major writer (although she has published poetry before). Further volumes of autobiography will follow.

LUNOKHOD EXPLORES THE MOON

Russian unmanned spacecraft *Luna 17* lands an eight-wheeled vehicle, *Lunokhod 1*, on the Moon; it travels more than ⅔ mile exploring the surface by remote control.

M*A*S*H

Robert Altman makes moving comedy out of events in the Korean War. Two surgeons in a mobile army hospital try to keep themselves sane with joking, womanizing, and subverting authority. Although set in Korea, the parallels with Vietnam are inescapable. The film forms the basis of a popular TV series.

ESCALATION IN IRELAND

In Belfast, the Provisional Irish Republican Army kills a British soldier on October 31. This signals war between the illegal army and the British government.

VENUS PROBE

The Russian space probe *Venera 7* drops a package of instruments on to the surface of the planet Venus; it sends back information for 23 minutes before the fierce heat destroys it.

THE FEMALE EUNUCH

Australian writer, academic, and feminist Germaine Greer argues that characteristics in women traditionally valued by men (delicacy, passivity, etc.) show "castration" of the true female personality, something in which women have colluded. The book becomes a key feminist text.

RIGHT: Burt Bacharach wins an Oscar for his music score for the 1969 movie *Butch Cassidy and the Sundance Kid.*

ENVIRONMENTAL AWARENESS

The first Earth Day is celebrated by 20 million Americans, who attend teach-ins and rallies, and participate in schemes to clean up the environment.

CROW

This collection confirms Ted Hughes' early promise as the major English poet of his generation. The sinister figure of Crow, mythically memorable, surviving through hostility to humankind, is one of the most powerful creations in the literature of the time.

ACCIDENTAL DEATH OF AN ANARCHIST

In this play, Italian Marxist Dario Fo draws influence from traditional European forms (farce, *commedia dell'arte*) to bring a satirical sharpness to the theater.

FLOPPY DISKS

U.S. computer company IBM introduces floppy disks for storing computer information.

CROWDED SKIES

China and Japan launch their first space satellites.

COMPUTERIZED CATALOGUE

The Smithsonian Institution in Washington, D.C., begins to compile a computerized catalogue of all U.S. plants.

EXPLORING EARTH'S CRUST

Russian scientists begin drilling a deep well on the Kola Peninsula, north of the Arctic Circle, to examine the Earth's crust; they plan to drill down 9 miles.

CHARLES ANDRE JOSEPH MARIE DE GAULLE
(1890–1970)

Former French president and founder in exile of the Free French Army (1940), Charles de Gaulle has died. The World War I army officer who headed postwar provisional governments and became president of the Fifth Republic in 1958 is credited with resolving the Algerian crisis and restoring stability to postwar France. His handling of the situation in May 1968 seemed at first to guarantee his continued popularity but he resigned last year after a disastrous referendum vote of no-confidence.

ABOVE: The film version of *One Day in the Life of Ivan Denisovich*, Solzhenitsyn's grim description of life in a Soviet prison gulag.

ECOWARRIORS AND BLACK HOLES

The Canadian pressure group for the environment, Greenpeace, carries out its first act of confrontation in Alaska. In Switzerland, women get the vote at last. East Pakistan declares itself independent and chooses a new name, Bangladesh, while in Uganda, Idi Amin seizes power. U.S. astronauts visit the Moon again, and the U.S.S.R. puts a space station into orbit. Homosexuals assert their rights and the term Gay Pride is coined. In space, black holes, the imprints of collapsed, gravity-sucking stars, are discovered.

1971

Jan	10	French fashion queen Coco Chanel dies aged 87
Feb	7	Swiss women get the vote
	15	U.K. introduces decimal currency
	20	Idi Amin seizes power in Uganda
Mar	26	Awami League declares East Pakistan independent as Bangladesh
Apr	6	Russo-American composer Igor Stravinsky dies aged 88
	19	Soviets put *Salyut 1*, the first space station, into orbit
	25	In the U.S., 200,000 people demonstrate against the Vietnam War in Washington, D.C.
Jun	30	Three Soviet cosmonauts are found dead in their spacecraft after an apparently normal landing
Jul	1	West Indies cricketer and statesman Learie Constantine (Baron Constantine) dies aged 69
Aug	9	Internment without trial introduced in Northern Ireland
Sep	30	Canadian ecowarriors Greenpeace stage their first protest in Alaska
Nov	12	President Nixon ends the U.S. offensive role in Vietnam
Dec	6	India recognizes Bangladesh's independence and goes to war with Pakistan
	17	End of the Indo-Pakistan War

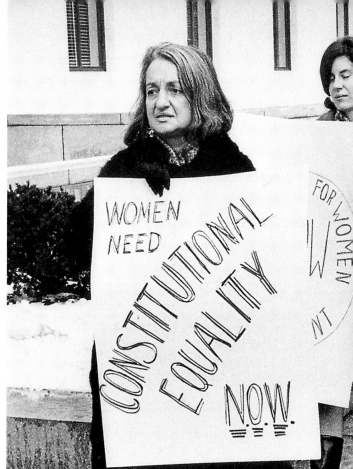

ABOVE: Feminist writer Betty Friedan leads NOW, the National Organization of Women.

ABOVE: Women demonstrate to legalize abortion and for the right to choose what to do with their own bodies.

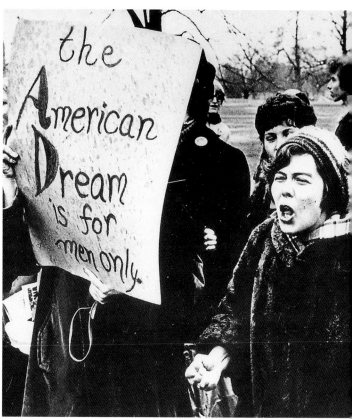

LEFT: Gloria Steinem, former Playboy Bunny, campaigns for women's rights.

ABOVE: Women demonstrate in support of the Equal Rights Amendment to the U.S. Constitution.

■426■

ABOVE: Flags of 126 nations flutter outside the United Nations building in New York City. China joins this year.

BELOW: The *Apollo 14* launch vehicle on the pad. Alan B. Shepard, Stuart A. Roose and Edgar D. Mitchell are the astronauts on this mission.

THE HARDER HOUSE
Eccentric American architect Bruce Goff designs this house for a Minnesota turkey farmer. The building combines natural and "postmodern" materials (stone, wood, and shingle on the one hand, orange roof covering and mirror mosaic on the other) to create a unique synthesis.

MADMEN AND SPECIALISTS
Nigerian writer Wole Soyinka's volume of verse and prose shows his versatility as a writer. His diverse writings stress the need for a distinctively African written culture, crossfertilized by, but independent from, that of Europe.

UNDERNEATH THE ARCHES
London-based artists Gilbert and George impersonate English music-hall artists Bud Flanagan and Chesney Allen (one of whose best-known routines was a song and dance duet called "Underneath the Arches") to create the first "living sculpture." The work causes hilarity and controversy — which is presumably what the artists intend.

DIGITAL WATCH
U.S. engineers George Theiss and Willy Crabtree develop the first digital watch, powered by a vibrating quartz crystal.

UAE FORMED
The United Arab Emirates is formed by six sheikhdoms as Britain leaves the Persian Gulf after 150 years. Bahrain and Qatar become independent in their own right.

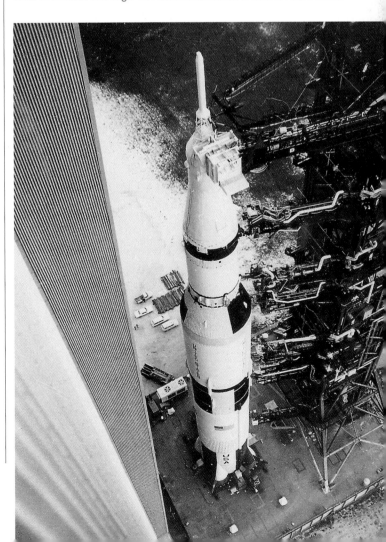

GABRIELLE (COCO) CHANEL (1883–1971)

French couturier Coco Chanel has died. She founded her couture house in Paris in 1924 and created the classic chemise dress and the Chanel suit with its collarless jacket. She was also responsible for the "little black dress" that remains chic cocktail-party wear, and her own perfumes, especially Chanel No. 5. After a long period of retirement she took up her career again during the 1950s.

BANGLADESH GAINS INDEPENDENCE

Led by Sheikh Mujibur Rahman, the Awami League wins all the seats in East Pakistan in the general election in December 1970 and begins talks on a new constitution for the province. As talks break down, Rahman declares independence as Bangladesh, in protest against neglect of the province by West Pakistan, and establishes a government in exile in Calcutta in April. Tension rises during the year, until border clashes between India and East Pakistan lead to a brief war in December. Indian forces defeat the Pakistani Army; as a result, Pakistan is divided and Bangladesh gains its independence.

GAY LIBERATION GROWS

Gay liberation groups emerge in major American cities in North America, Australia, and Western Europe, following the foundation of active American groups who led a successful campaign to challenge injustices perpetrated against homosexuals. Gay Pride marches raise public consciousness of the predicament of gay and lesbian people.

BLACK HOLES FOUND

Astronomers discover black holes in space. These have been predicted by English physicist Stephen Hawking. Black holes are collapsed stars whose gravity is so strong that not even light can escape from them, so they cannot be observed visually.

"POCKET" CALCULATORS

U.S. company Texas Instruments introduces the first pocket calculator, the Pocketronic. It goes into mass production at once, weighing 2 1/2 pounds and costing $150.

ABOVE: Beat poet Alan Ginsberg meets his admirers.

BELOW: Dr. Daniel Ellsberg, the whistleblower of Watergate.

ABOVE: British rock star Rod Stewart performs in the United States.

ORBITING MARS

In November, U.S. space probe *Mariner 9* goes into orbit around Mars, the first planet to be explored in this way; *Mariner 9* sends back 7,329 photographs, allowing scientists to make accurate maps of the planet.

FIRST SPACE STATION

On April 19 the Russians put *Salyut 1*, the first space station, into orbit. The idea is to establish a kind of base camp in space so that teams of cosmonauts can work in shifts.

IGOR FYODOROVICH STRAVINSKY
(1882–1971)

Composer, pianist, and conductor Igor Stravinsky has died in New York. Born in Russia in 1882, he left for France after the revolution and later became an American citizen, having moved to the United States in 1939. He first came to fame with his ballets for Diaghilev's Ballets Russes: *The Firebird* (1910), *Petrushka* (1911), and *The Rite of Spring* (1913). Other works include *Pulcinella* (1919–20) and *The Rake's Progress* (1951), and many orchestral, voice, and chamber compositions. He incorporated such diverse influences as Russian folk music, American jazz, Verdi, Monteverdi, Baroque music, and music of the Viennese school. His burial will be in Venice, in the cemetery of San Michele, close to Diaghilev.

COSMONAUT DEATHS

Three Russian cosmonauts are found dead in their spacecraft *Salyut II* after an apparently normal landing; Loss of air from the cabin is blamed for their deaths.

MOON ROCKS BROUGHT BACK

U.S. spacecraft *Apollo 14* and *Apollo 15* bring back Moon rocks for analysis. Members of the *Apollo 15* crew, David Scott and James Irwin, gather theirs during a drive in a lunar roving vehicle or "Moon buggy."

INTERNMENT IN IRELAND

The British government introduces internment without trial in an attempt to prevent terrorism. It leads to riots and hunger strikes.

HOME VIDEO

Philips launches the first video cassette recorder (VCR) for home use. The ½-inch tape plays for 1 hour.

CHINA IN THE UN

China takes its seat at the UN in place of Taiwan, which has held the seat since 1945.

BLOODY SUNDAY AND BLACK SEPTEMBER

Sunday January 30 in Londonderry, Northern Ireland, sees 13 civilians killed, leading to decades of murders and bombings. President Nixon goes to China to make an alliance with the world's third superpower, while back in the United States, burglars break into the Watergate Building to plant bugs. At the Munich Olympics, Palestinian activists murder 11 Israeli athletes. In Burundi, rival tribes Hutus and Tutsis slaughter each other. FBI chief J. Edgar Hoover dies and some very surprising secrets emerge from his closet.

1972

Jan	30	"Bloody Sunday" in Londonderry, Northern Ireland: British troops fire on demonstrators, killing 13
	30	Pakistan leaves the Commonwealth
Feb	2	Winter Olympics open in Tokyo, Japan
	21	U.S. president Nixon begins visit to China
Mar	2	U.S. launches *Pioneer 10* to photograph Jupiter
	30	Britain suspends Northern Ireland parliament and imposes direct rule
May	28	The Duke of Windsor (ex-King Edward VIII) dies aged 77
Jun	17	Intruders try to bug Democratic Party HQ in the Watergate Building in Washington, D.C.
Jul	23	U.S. launches *Landsat 1*, which orbits Earth taking strips of photographs
	31	Belgian statesman Paul Spaak dies aged 72
Aug	4	President Idi Amin of Uganda orders all Asian citizens to leave
	26	The 20th Olympic Games open in Munich, Germany
Sep	5	Arab terrorists murder 11 members of the Israeli Olympic team
Dec	2	Labour wins Australian general election
	7	Last Apollo mission to the Moon

ABOVE: *Apollo 16's* lunar module, known as *Orion.*

ABOVE: Commander John W. Young salutes the Stars and Stripes planted on the Moon during the *Apollo 16* mission.

BELOW: Commander Gene Cernan test-drives the Moon buggy on the *Apollo 17* mission.

ABOVE: President Nixon goes to China and meets Chou En-Lai, premier of the People's Republic.

WATERGATE

Burglars are arrested breaking into the Democratic Party headquarters in the Watergate Building. Over the next year, it is established that they were working for the U.S. president, Richard Nixon, in his campaign to gain reelection in the 1972 presidential elections, which he wins easily against antiwar campaigner and Democratic candidate George McGovern.

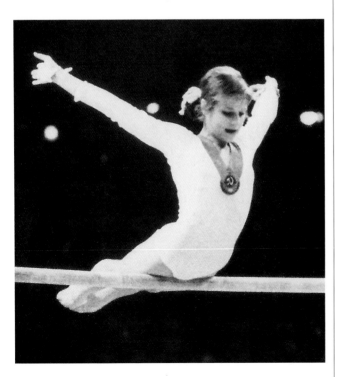

ABOVE: Olga Korbut wins three Olympic golds in Munich.

BLOODY SUNDAY

In Londonderry, Northern Ireland, British paratroopers open fire on unarmed demonstrators protesting against the British policy of interning Irish Republican Army (IRA) members, and kill 13 civilians. Bloody Sunday marks the low point of relations between the Catholic community and the British Army, and leads to a huge increase in violence across the province. In March, as a direct result of the violence, the Northern Irish parliament is suspended and direct rule is imposed from London.

NIXON IN CHINA

In a historic move, U.S. president Richard Nixon visits China and meets the Communist leadership. The visit leads to a thaw in relations between the two superpowers, both of which have reason to work together against the Soviet Union.

UGANDANS EXPELLED

President Idi Amin expels 50,000 Asians with British passports from Uganda, claiming that they are sabotaging the national economy. The Asians all leave within three months, causing economic ruin in Uganda as factories close and vital services stop.

AUSTRALIA TURNS TO THE PACIFIC

Gough Whitlam leads the Labour Party to victory in the general election in Australia. He radically changes Australian foreign policy away from the United States and toward Asia, recognizing China, giving Papua New Guinea its independence, pardoning Vietnam draft dodgers, and ending national service.

GAY MINISTRY

A ministry to the gay community, founded in 1968 in Los Angeles by Troy Perry, an expelled Pentecostal preacher, is expanding across America, and the Evangelical Lutheran Church of the Netherlands declares that there is no obstacle to the appointment of gay ministers.

LASERVISION

The Dutch firm of Philips introduces a system of recording on plastic discs using lasers. The system is later marketed as LaserVision.

WINTER OLYMPICS IN JAPAN

Disputes over amateur status lead to the disqualification of a skier and the withdrawal of the Canadian ice hockey team from the 11th Winter Games in Sapporo, Japan. Revenue from TV rights climbs to $8.47 million, three times the 1968 sum.

SPEED OF LIGHT REMEASURED

U.S. scientist Kenneth M. Evenson produces a more accurate measurement of the speed of light than has been possible hitherto: 186,282.3959 miles per second.

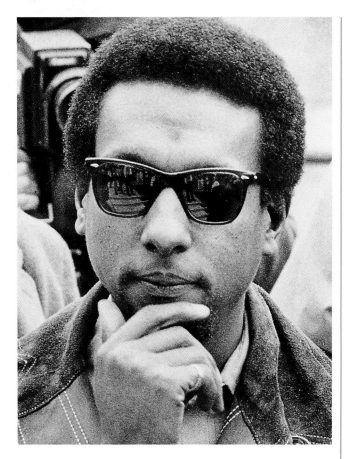

ABOVE: Writer Stokely Carmichael, a prominent activist in the black civil rights movement.

BLACK SEPTEMBER OLYMPICS

Palestinian terrorists hijack the 20th Olympiad in Munich, Germany. Their attack on the Israeli team in the Olympic Village leaves 11 athletes and a policeman dead. German authorities botch a rescue attempt as the terrorists and hostages transfer from helicopters to a plane at a military airfield. Five of the eight Palestinians are killed. The International Olympic Committee refuses to bow to violence and, with the backing of the Israeli government, the games continue with flags at half-mast. In competition, U.S. swimmer Mark Spitz claims an astounding seven golds. Soviet gymnast Olga Korbut is the crowd favorite and wins three golds.

IT'S A WRAP

Bulgarian-born French artist Christo wraps a section of the coastline of Australia. The enormous artwork uses some 1 million square feet of plastic sheeting and attracts publicity all over the world.

EQUIVALENT 8

U.S. sculptor Carl André's *Equivalent 8* is a sculpture consisting of a pile of 120 bricks. It is bought by London's Tate Gallery, to derisive comments from press and public alike. (The sculptor explains his work in terms of making "cuts in space.")

JOHN EDGAR HOOVER
(1895–1972)

The American J. (John) Edgar Hoover, for 48 years director of the Federal Bureau of Investigations, has died. In this role he was responsible for establishing the national fingerprint file and the FBI crime laboratory. He clamped down both on the gangster rackets of the 1920s and 1930s and the postwar spread of Socialist and Communist sympathies, and had been exempted from civil service retirement regulations to allow him to retain his post. Later it will be revealed that he had been a homosexual while publicly demonstrating homophobic tendencies.

ENDGAME

Maverick Bobby Fischer is crowned the first American chess world champion after defeating Russian Boris Spassky in Iceland.

THE UN AND THE ENVIRONMENT

A United Nations Conference on the Human Environment meets in Stockholm to discuss environmental issues.

LANDSAT 1 LAUNCHED

The United States launches *Landsat 1*, otherwise called the Earth Resources Test Satellite, which photographs the Earth's surface in a series of strips and covers all the globe, except the two Poles, every 18 days. The photographs will yield vital information about crop growth, deforestation, floods, and other data.

OFF TO JUPITER

NASA (America's National Aeronautics and Space Administration), launches *Pioneer 10*, a spaceprobe designed to take close-up photographs of the planet Jupiter. It is scheduled to fly past the giant planet in December 1973.

IN A FREE STATE

Trinidadian-born British writer V.S. Naipaul's novel explores identity through three linked narratives of people outside their native territory. Its bleak vision is typical of the author's later work.

CAT SCANNER

British engineer Godfrey Hounsfield and South African physicist Allan Cormack invent the Computerized Axial Tomography scanner (known as CAT). It uses computer technology to produce images of the brain and becomes an important diagnostic tool.

MASSACRES IN BURUNDI

Rebel Hutus massacre thousands of their compatriots from the minority Tutsi tribe who are in government. The Tutsis retaliate and much slaughter ensues.

POLLUTION AND WASTE

ABOVE: Pesticides and agribusiness dominate farming.

BELOW: Wrecked automobiles pile up, a symbol of Western waste.

ABOVE: Dallas, Texas, where the automobiles and the road seem to cover the planet.

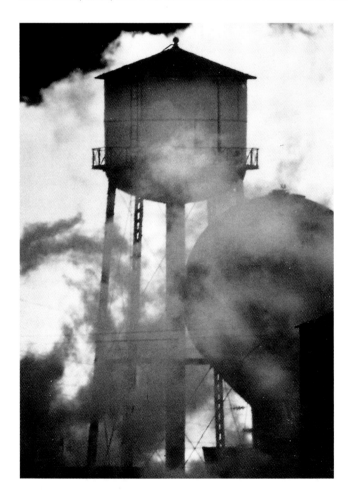

ABOVE: Atmospheric pollution from a steelworks.

ABOVE: Raw sewage discharging into a river.

PEACE IN VIETNAM, WAR IN THE MIDDLE EAST

Peace treaties are signed to end the wars in Vietnam and its neighbor Laos. The United States will take many years to recover from the war it did not win. In Chile, General Pinochet stages a coup and President Allende is murdered. Egypt and Syria attack Israel in the Yom Kippur War. In the North Atlantic, Icelandic fishing trawlers battle with the British fleet over disputed territories. CITES is established to monitor the trade in endangered species and the European Community admits Denmark, the United Kingdom, and Ireland.

1973

Jan	1	Denmark, Ireland, and the United Kingdom join the European Union
	22	Former U.S. president Lyndon B. Johnson dies aged 64
	27	Ceasefire in Vietnam signed by North and South Vietnam, the Vietcong guerrillas, and the United States
Mar	8	United States launches *Pioneer 11* to take close-ups of Jupiter and Saturn
Apr	8	Spanish painter Pablo Picasso dies aged 91
May	25	United States launches *Skylab*, its first space station
Sep	11	Junta headed by General Augusto Pinochet seizes power in Chile; President Allende is killed
Oct	6	Arab countries attack Israel on Yom Kippur, the Jewish Day of Atonement
	10	U.S. Vice-President Spiro T. Agnew resigns after tax evasion scandal
	24	Yom Kippur War ends
Nov	3	United States launches *Mariner 10* to photograph Venus and Mercury
Dec	1	David Ben-Gurion, former Israeli prime minister, dies aged 87
	6	Gerald Ford becomes new U.S. vice-president

PEACE IN VIETNAM

A ceasefire is declared in Vietnam as a peace agreement is signed in Paris between the United States and North and South Vietnam. The United States agrees to withdraw all its troops, and exchange prisoners of war.

COUP IN CHILE

President Allende of Chile is ousted and killed in a coup by General Pinochet. The new military government introduces martial law and imprisons its opponents, driving thousands into exile.

YOM KIPPUR WAR

Egypt and Syria attack Israel during the religious Yom Kippur holiday. Israel fights back, crossing the Suez Canal and threatening to cut off the invading Egyptian Army. A ceasefire is arranged by the UN, but oil-rich Arab nations raise the price of oil by 70 percent in protest against U.S. support for Israel. As a result, fuel shortages and inflation hit all the Western economies.

THE SECOND BATTLE OF WOUNDED KNEE

Members of the American Indian Movement seize Wounded Knee on the Sioux Reservation in South Dakota to protest against Indian treaties broken by the U.S. government. Fighting to end the occupation results in two deaths and many injuries and arrests.

CEASEFIRE IN LAOS

In this former French colony, the Pathet Lao, backed by the North Vietnamese, fight the Royalist Laotian government. Since the Ho Chi Minh trail passes through Laos the United States backs the Royalist forces against the 35,000 strong Pathet Lao. A ceasefire is agreed in 1973 when South Vietnam falls to the North. In 1975 Laos will come under complete Pathet Lao control.

INNER PLANETS

U.S. space probe *Mariner 10* is launched, designed to observe Venus and Mercury, the two planets that orbit between Earth and the Sun.

ABOVE: Former president Lyndon Baines Johnson dies this year.

EC EXPANDS

The United Kingdom, Ireland, and Denmark join the European Community (EC) after the new French government of Georges Pompidou relaxes its veto on British entry. Nine nations are now members of the EC.

OPEN STUDY

The first graduates of the Open University, founded in the U.K. in 1969 for mature students without formal qualifications to gain university-level education, receive their degrees.

CITES ESTABLISHED

A Convention on International Trade in Endangered Species (CITES) is drawn up at a conference to end the trade held in Washington, D.C., and is signed by representatives of 80 countries.

RIDING ROUGH TERRAIN

A mountain bike is designed for riding the slopes of canyons in California, by the Marin County Canyon cycling club.

PABLO CASALS
(1876–1973)

Spanish-born cellist Pablo Casals has died in Puerto Rico, where he has lived since 1956. He gave his first performances in Barcelona cafés, and ever since his first American tour in 1901 has been recognized as the world's leading cellist, playing as a soloist and with the pianist Alfred Cortot and violinist Jacques Thibaut. In exile from Franco's Spain, he founded the Prades Festival in France before settling in Puerto Rico.

ABOVE: Richard M. Nixon is sworn in for his second term in presidential office. It will only last for two years.

ABOVE: John Mitchell and his attorney at the Watergate trial.

ABOVE: Nixon's chief of staff Robert Haldeman testifies at the Watergate trial.

SYDNEY OPERA HOUSE

Jørn Utzon's opera house is finally completed. Its construction has been a saga of bumbles and U-turns; the authorities accepted Utzon's sketches before anyone had worked out how to build the roofs. They have to swap the roles of the two main auditoria and have to start a lottery to pay for it. But they get as great a civic symbol as any in the world.

A LITTLE NIGHT MUSIC

One of the most successful of U.S. composer Stephen Sondheim's early musicals, *Night Music* has a tragicomic plot based on Bergman's film *Smiles on a Summer Night*. The score is notable for its operatic vocal requirements and for being almost entirely in waltz time, and the lyrics demonstrate Sondheim's perennial wit. The whole thing cements Sondheim's reputation for creating grown-up musicals.

DAY FOR NIGHT

French director François Truffaut's film is about filmmaking. The loving depiction of both the pleasures and frustrations of the art explores all aspects from technical details and props to the relationship between actor and director — and between movie and reality.

GRAVITY'S RAINBOW

American writer Thomas Pynchon produces his largest book, set at the end of World War II. Its fantastic take on reality reminds some critics of Latin American magic realism.

MUSIC FOR PIECES OF WOOD

Steve Reich's work is a typical minimalist piece, scored for five tuned claves, which play separate repeated patterns of notes. This is one of the most extreme forms of minimalism.

THE COD WAR

Hostilities break out between Iceland and the U.K. when Icelandic territorial waters are expanded from 50 miles to 200 miles, so encroaching on fishing grounds used by the British. British fishing boats are escorted into the zone by a super-tug and the situation rapidly escalates, involving the Royal Navy and Icelandic gunboats. There are riots outside the British embassy in Reykjavik.

ICELANDIC VOLCANO

A volcano erupts on the island of Heimaey and all 5,000 inhabitants have to leave their homes in the middle of the night.

SKYLAB

America's first space station, *Skylab*, is launched and goes into orbit 270 miles above the Earth; three three-man crews are sent in turn to *Skylab* during the year. It delivers information about Earth's resources and the structure of the Sun.

ABOVE: Almost-normal life is possible for the crew inside the space station *Skylab 3*.

RIGHT: Astronaut Jack Lousma works outside *Skylab 3*. He is one of a three-man team.

JUPITER AND SATURN TO BE EXPLORED
NASA launches *Pioneer 11*, a space probe designed to take close-up pictures of both Jupiter (in 1974) and Saturn (in 1979).

GENETIC ENGINEERING
U.S. chemists Stanley H. Cohen and Herbert W. Boyer use the process of genetic engineering to make bacteria produce small quantities of insulin. This represents the beginning of genetic engineering.

DOLPHIN TRIUMPH
The Miami Dolphins cap a perfect 17-victory season by beating the Washington Redskins in Superbowl VII. The Dolphins are the only team in NFL history to win all their games in a season.

ABOVE: Redford and Newman in the Oscar-winning film *The Sting*.

DEATHS IN THE ARTS
Edward G. Robinson (b. 1893), the screen gangster, U.S. writer and Nobel Prize-winner Pearl S. Buck (b. 1892), French painter Jacques Lipchitz (b. 1891), U.S. Kung Fu star Bruce Lee (b. 1940), English playwright Noel Coward (b. 1899), film director John Ford (b. 1895), author J.R.R. Tolkein (b. 1892), and poet W.H. Auden (b. 1907) all die this year.

POLITICAL DEATHS
Former U.S. President Lyndon Baines Johnson (b. 1908), Jeanette Rankin, the first woman in Congress (b. 1880), and Fulgencio Batista, the Cuban dictator (b. 1901) all die this year.

SMALL IS BEAUTIFUL
American economist E.F. Schumacher introduces the idea of alternative technology in his bestseller *Small is Beautiful: a Study of Economics as if People Mattered*.

TELETEXT DEMONSTRATED
British TV companies demonstrate teletext news and information pages in addition to normal programs.

PABLO PICASSO
(1881–1973)

Pablo Picasso, the prolific painter, sculptor, and ceramic artist, who was born in Spain in 1881 but who has for many years lived and worked in France, has died. Together with Georges Braque he developed cubism and has had a hugely powerful influence on the direction of modern art. He designed costumes and sets for the Ballets Russes from 1917 onwards, and became a Communist during World War ll. His work *Guernica*, painted in 1937 during the Spanish Civil War, has become a byword for antiwar art.

RESIGNATION BEFORE IMPEACHMENT

The fallout from the Watergate scandal forces President Nixon to resign before he is impeached. A military coup in the dictatorship of Portugal leads to democracy and independence for Portuguese colonies Goa, Mozambique, and Portuguese Guinea. In Cyprus, President Makarios is overthrown and Turkey invades. Civilian rule reasserts itself in Greece. In Ethiopia, Haile Selassie is deposed and exiled and the remains of humankind's oldest-known ancestor are found. The propellant in aerosol cans, CFC, is unmasked as the agent that is blowing a hole in the ozone layer. From space, *Mariner 10* sends back images of Mercury and Venus.

1974

Feb	8	Three U.S. astronauts return after a record 84 days aboard *Skylab*		24	Constantine Karamanlis returns from exile to form civilian government in Greece
Apr	25	General Antonio de Spinola seizes power in Portugal	Aug	9	Because of Watergate scandal, Richard M. Nixon becomes the first U.S. president to resign; Vice-President Gerald Ford succeeds him
July	1	Argentine president Juan Perón dies aged 78; succeeded by his wife Isabel			
	15	In Cyprus, the National Guard overthrows President Makarios; former terrorist Nicos Sampson takes over	Sep	12	A military coup overthrows Emperor Haile Selassie of Ethiopia
	20	Turkey invades Cyprus	Nov	12	"Lucy," ancient ancestor of human beings, is found in Ethiopia
	23	Greek military government resigns			

MOZAMBIQUE INDEPENDENT

Since 1962, the Front for the Liberation of
Mozambique (FRELIMO) has been fighting the 40,000-
strong Portuguese Colonial Army. In 350 actions, the
Portuguese inflict 4,000 casualties on FRELIMO.
However, under the Marxist Samora Machel, the 10,000
men of FRELIMO are able to profit from the 1974
military coup in Portugal and seize larger areas of
Mozambique. Machel negotiates from strength with the
Portuguese and is elected the first president of
Mozambique in 1975. Instability will dog the early
years of the new country as Rhodesian-backed members
of the anti-Communist MNR (Mozambican National
Resistance) sabotage oil supplies and communications
and South African forces raid southern Mozambique
attacking African National Congress (ANC) bases.

ABOVE: President Nixon puts a brave face on the Watergate affair as
he addresses a meeting of Young Republicans.

NIXON RESIGNS

President Nixon resigns rather than face impeachment
for his role in the Watergate burglary. He is succeeded
by Vice-President Gerald Ford, who promptly pardons
Nixon for his misdemeanors. Several Nixon aides go to
jail after their trial.

PERON DIES

On the death of President Juan Perón, his wife Isabel
becomes president, the first woman to hold such a job
anywhere in Latin America. She proves to be a weak
leader and is toppled by a military coup in March 1976.

ABOVE: Joint U.S. and Soviet space vehicles on exhibition.

COUP IN PORTUGAL

A military coup led by General de Spinola overthrows the Portuguese government in the "Revolution of Flowers" and begins moves towards democracy. The Socialist leader, Mario Soares, returns from exile, leading his party to victory in the first democratic elections in April 1975. An attempted Communist coup by left-wing soldiers is defeated in November 1975, ensuring the survival of Portuguese democracy.

PARTITION IN CYPRUS

The National Guard overthrows President Makarios and installs former EOKA terrorist Nicos Sampson, who is in favor of union with Greece, in his place. Turkey promptly invades the north of the island and partitions it, setting up a separate state in February 1975.

SPACE MISSION RECORD

On February 8, three U.S. astronauts return to Earth after having spent 84 days in *Skylab*, a space record; this is the last mission to the space station.

GERMAN TRIUMPH

The Dutch, playing freeflowing "total soccer," are everyone's choice to win the World Cup in West Germany, but the hosts take the title. Germany beats Holland 2–1 in the final.

GUINEA-BISSAU INDEPENDENT

Nationalists, the African Party for the Independence of Guinea and Cape Verde (PAIGC), have been fighting for independence from the colonial power Portugal since 1963. By 1973, PAIGC had gained control of two-thirds of Portuguese Guinea and the military coup in Lisbon in 1974 gives the country independence.

INCLUDE ME OUT

Sam Goldwyn, legendary film mogul, dies. Born Samuel Goldfish in Poland in 1882, he began life as a glove salesman. His films were always aimed at the family and he was famous for his "Goldwynisms" (such as, "A verbal contract is not worth the paper it's written on."), not all of which he actually said.

HAILE SELASSIE DEPOSED

Emperor Haile Selassie is deposed in a left-wing military coup after a massive famine in 1973 weakens his rule. The new government introduces massive reforms, executes its enemies, and kills Selassie in August 1975.

TOUR DE FORCE

Belgian cyclist Eddie Merckx crosses the line first in the Tour de France cycling race for the fifth time in six years. In the seven tours Merckx enters he wins 35 stages and wears the leader's yellow jersey for 96 days — both records.

EARLY FOOTPRINTS

At Laetoli, near Olduvai Gorge in Tanzania, fossils of hominids who lived three million years ago, the earliest known hominid footprints, and the oldest human artifacts have been found by British archeologist Richard Leakey and his team.

RUMBLING WITH THE GREATEST

Muhammad Ali regains the heavyweight boxing title in a fight against George Foreman in Kinshasa, Zaire. "The Rumble in the Jungle" goes eight rounds before Foreman is counted out.

ANOTHER MOON FOR JUPITER

U.S. astronomer Charles T. Kowall discovers another satellite of Jupiter, which is subsequently named Leda.

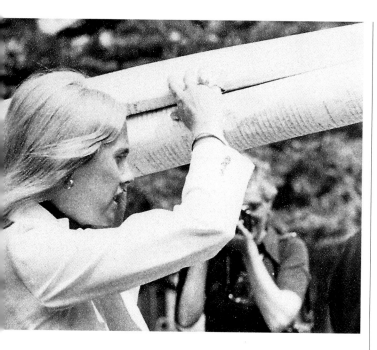

ABOVE: The tree-sized petition carrying signatures of people who believe that President Nixon should be impeached.

MARINER VISITS PLANETS

U.S. space probe *Mariner 10* passes Venus and carries on to pass Mercury on March 29; it swings round the Sun to pass Mercury twice more, on September 21 and on March 16, 1975.

EASY SHAVES

Disposable lightweight plastic razors are developed by Gillette in Boston.

ANCIENT AMERICAN

Anthropologists using new dating techniques discover that a human skull found in Southern California is 48,000 years old, showing that people have lived in North America far longer than previously thought.

THE DUKE BOWS OUT

U.S. jazz pianist Duke (Edward Kennedy) Ellington dies. One of the great men of big band jazz, his career lasted for 55 years.

AEROSOLS ACCUSED

U.S. scientists Sherwood Rowland and Mario Molina point out that the chlorofluorocarbons (CFCs) used as propellants in aerosol cans could damage the ozone layer high above the Earth.

ANOTHER QUARK

U.S. physicist Burton Richter discovers another quark (a subunit of protons and neutrons); this one is given the name of charmed quark.

RIGHT: The fearsome teeth of a shark loom out of the screen to terrify moviegoers in the blockbuster film *Jaws*.

GREEK CIVIL RULE RETURNS

As a result of the débâcle in Cyprus, the Greek military government resigns and civilian rule is restored in mainland Greece. The ex-premier, Constantine Karamanlis, returns from exile in Paris to form a new government, winning elections in November. In December, Greece votes to become a republic, ending any chance of a restoration of the monarchy.

"LUCY" DISCOVERED

U.S. anthropologist Donald C. Johanson discovers in Ethiopia the fossil skeleton of a female *Australopithecus afarensis*, an apelike ancestor of human beings. She is nicknamed "Lucy" after the Beatles song, "Lucy in the Sky with Diamonds."

POMPIDOU DIES

The president of France, Georges Pompidou, dies of an unnamed illness.

STANDING TALL IN CANADA

Toronto's stunning telecommunications tower, the CN tower, becomes the world's tallest freestanding structure. It is 1,815 feet high.

SOLZHENITSYN EXPELLED

The first part of *The Gulag Archipelago* is published and its author Alexander Solzhenitsyn is expelled from the Soviet Union. This marks the height of Solzhenitsyn's fame as Soviet dissident and prophet.

THE WATERGATE SCANDAL

ABOVE: Domestic Council Chief John D. Ehrlichmann confers with his lawyer during his trial for his part in the Watergate affair.

ABOVE: John Ehrlichmann faces the press. Nixon's aides share the blame for the greatest political scandal of the 1970s.

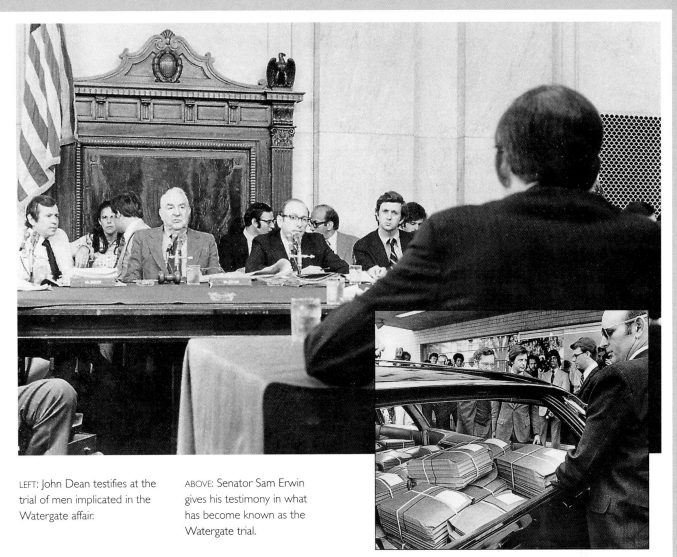

LEFT: John Dean testifies at the trial of men implicated in the Watergate affair.

ABOVE: Senator Sam Erwin gives his testimony in what has become known as the Watergate trial.

ABOVE: Mountains of files and tapes, damning evidence on its way to the Watergate trial.

LEFT: President Nixon is left to face the music alone as even his lawyer testifies against him.

HANDSHAKE IN SPACE

The Vietnam War finally comes to an end. The Khmer Rouge, under Pol Pot, seizes Cambodia and embarks on a bloodbath. Indonesia invades East Timor. The United States and Soviet Union link up in space when two of their spacecraft dock in Earth's orbit. The United States sends out space probes in search of life on Mars while Soviet space probes send back the first-ever pictures from the planet Venus. General Franco dies and archaeologists find a 2,000-year-old "army."

1975

April	5	President of Nationalist China, Chiang Kai-shek, dies aged 88
	17	Khmer Rouge takes control of Cambodia
	31	Vietnam War ends; Saigon surrenders to North Vietnam; mass evacuation of Americans
June	6	Israelis attack Lebanon
	12	Indian prime minister Indira Gandhi found guilty of corruption
	25	Mozambique gains independence
July	11	Archaeologists discover ancient terracotta "army" in China
	17	U.S. astronauts and Soviet cosmonauts meet in space
Aug	1	Helsinki Conference on security and cooperation in Europe
Nov	10	Angola becomes independent of Portugal
	20	General Franco dies in Spain, aged 73
	22	Monarchy is restored to Spain
	24	Civil war begins in Angola
Dec	7	Indonesian troops invade East Timor

KHMER ROUGE SEIZE POWER
In Cambodia, Communist Khmer Rouge forces led by Pol Pot (1926–98) seize power in Cambodia and begin a four-year reign of terror. Within months, thousands of Cambodians are executed. The cities are emptied out and people forced to work on the land as the new government attempts to rebuild Cambodian society from Year Zero. More than 3.5 million people — half the total population — die during famine, fighting, and political killings.

INDONESIA INVADES EAST TIMOR
Indonesian paratroopers invade the former Portuguese colony of East Timor, just before it gains independence. The country is engaged in a civil war between the Timorese Democratic Union (UDT), backed by the Timorese Democratic People's Union (APODETI), and the Communinist-backed Revolutionary Front for Independence (FREITLIN). The Indonesian move halts the fighting but is a land grab on the part of Indonesia. It provokes protests from the East Timorese and leads to violent repression and human rights abuses.

ABOVE: Russian and American astronauts meet in space in the joint U.S.–Soviet mission to dock in Earth's orbit.

VIETNAM WAR ENDS
Communist North Vietnam finally takes over South Vietnam, ending the 15-year Vietnam War. The old southern capital of Saigon is renamed Ho Chi Minh City in honor of the Communist leader.

COLONIES INDEPENDENT
Mozambique gains its independence from Portugal, followed by the Cape Verde Islands, Angola, and São Tomé and Príncipe. In South America, the former Dutch colony of Surinam gains its independence from the Netherlands.

MISSIONS TO MARS AND VENUS
The United States launches two space probes — *Viking 1* and *Viking 2* — to look for signs of life on Mars. And in October, Russian space probes *Venera 9* and *Venera 10* send back the first pictures of the surface of Venus.

ABOVE: The U.S.S.R.'s *Soyuz* spacecraft and launch vehicle on their way to the launch pad.

ABOVE RIGHT: An artist's idea of what the *Soyuz* spacecraft will look like as it orbits the Earth.

CIVIL WAR IN ANGOLA

Within two weeks of gaining independence, civil war intensifies in Angola. Thousands die as rival groups struggle for control of the country. The Soviet Union and Cuba back the Marxist Popular Movement for the Liberation of Angola (MPLA); the United States supports non-Marxist groups — the National Angolan Liberation Front (FNLA) and National Union for the Total Independence of Angola (UNITA).

INDIRA GANDHI FOUND GUILTY

Prime Minister Indira Gandhi (1917–84) is found guilty of electoral corruption. She declares a state of emergency, imposing censorship and imprisoning opposition leaders. The state of emergency lasts until January 1977, when she calls an election, losing heavily to the opposition Janata Party. However, she regains power in 1980.

TERRACOTTA ARMY

In China, archaeologists make a remarkable discovery when they uncover a vast army of 6,000 terracotta soldiers, near the ancient Chinese capital of Xian. The soldiers date back some 2,000 years and were probably made to guard the tomb of the first emperor in 206 B.C. The terracotta soldiers stand in rows; each one is different from the other and was probably modelled on a real person.

NATIONS JOIN FOR HUMAN RIGHTS

In Helsinki, Finland, more than 30 European nations, plus the United States and Canada, join together to sign the Final Act of the Conference on Security and Cooperation, promising to avoid the use of force in disputes and to respect human rights.

DEMOCRATIC SPAIN

General Franco dies and Spain becomes a monarchy once more as he is succeeded by King Juan Carlos. The new king begins moves to introduce democracy, granting an amnesty to all opponents of the previous government.

LEBANON CIVIL WAR

Seeking a pretext to attack the Palestine Liberation Organization (PLO) in southern Lebanon, the Israeli government launches operation "Peace for Galilee" in June. The attack takes them up to Beirut and costs the Israelis 368 killed and 2,388 wounded. Some 17,800 PLO, Syrians, and civilians are killed and more than 30,000 wounded. By 1976, the PLO has evacuated Lebanon and abandoned heavy weapons.

MID-ATLANTIC DIVES

Three research submersibles make a total of 43 dives on the Mid-Atlantic Ridge, taking photographs and collecting rock samples.

BLACK TENNIS SUCCESS

At Wimbledon, Arthur Ashe (1943–93) beats fellow American Jimmy Connors to become the first male black Wimbledon champion.

DISTANT GALAXIES

The enormity of space is emphasized when U.S. astronomer Hyron Spinrad discovers that a faint galaxy he is studying is approximately eight billion light years away from us. In Holland, Dutch astronomers at Leiden University map radio galaxy 3C236, the largest object in the universe, spanning eighteen million light years.

HANDSHAKE IN SPACE

U.S. astronauts in an Apollo spacecraft link up with Soviet cosmonauts in a Soyuz spacecraft some 140 miles above the Atlantic Ocean. One from each of their crew — U.S. captain Tom Stafford and Soviet Alexei Leonov — shake hands through the hatches of their respective spacecraft. While linked together, the crews carry out joint scientific experiments and visit each other's crafts.

HEALTHY EATING

A healthy vegetarian diet becomes popular in the United States and Britain. It is influenced by the macrobiotic diet, based on brown rice, natural salt, and green tea, which was fashionable in the 1960s. Its importance is also reinforced by a report from a British doctor indicating a link between bowel cancer and a low-fiber diet.

THE BOOK OF SAND

This collection of stories by Argentinian writer Jorge Luis Borges (1899–1986) confirms his international stature as a master of serious puzzles, play with truth and identity, and the role of time in fiction. His fiction is newly fashionable for its similarity to magic realism, but truly Borges belongs to no school.

NEW SHOPPING CENTER

SITE Projects Inc. have designed a stunning new shopping center — the Almeda-Genoa — in Houston, which exemplifies their witty style. The façade seems to be crumbling, with holes, piles of bricks, and jagged edges, a witty impersonation of a modern ruin.

RITUEL, IN MEMORIAM BRUNO MADERNA

French modernist composer Pierre Boulez (b. 1925) has created a work in memory of his Italian colleague, Bruno Maderna. The performing ensemble is divided into eight groups, dominated by a group of brass instruments, which play alternate sections. The work impresses with its manipulation of chords and rhythms.

FRANCISCO FRANCO
(1892–1975)

General Franco, leader of the Nationalists during the Spanish Civil War, and dictator of Spain since 1939, has died in Madrid. In 1969, he announced that the monarchy would be restored on his death.

ABOVE: Arthur Ashe is the first black male player to win the singles title at Wimbledon.

GAY COMMERCIALS

In the Netherlands, gays advertise openly as a result of a gay-recognition campaign conducted by COC (an organization for men) and MVM (Man-Vrouw Maatschappij or Man-Woman Society) for lesbians.

STREAKING

A new craze — streaking — has hit both sides of the Atlantic. In both the U.S. and Britain, sports events are being interrupted by the arrival of naked people, both men and women, "streaking" across the playing areas.

PCs ON SALE

In the United States, the Altair, the world's first personal computer (PC), is launched.

ABOVE: A scene from *The Godfather II*, winner of six Oscars.

APARTHEID VIOLENCE AND SUPERSONIC FLIGHT

Chairman Mao, Chinese cult figure and leader of the revolution, dies. Police fire on students in Soweto, South Africa, and African nations boycott the Olympic Games. Israeli commandos carry out a lightning rescue of hostages in Uganda. Concorde, the uniquely designed supersonic jet, begins regular passenger flights. Drug laws are liberalized in Holland.

1976

Jan	21	Concordes fly from Paris to Rio de Janeiro, and London to Bahrain, launching start of regular Concorde passenger flights
Feb	4	Winter Olympics open at Innsbruck, Austria
	27	Polisario Front declares independence of Western Sahara
Mar	24	Military coup in Argentina overthrows President Perón
April	14	Western Sahara partitioned between Morocco and Mauritania
June	16	South African police gun down students in Soweto and other black townships
July	3	Israeli commandos rescue hostages at Entebbe airport, Uganda
	20	U.S. *Viking* space probe lands on Mars
	31	Olympic Games open, Montreal, Canada
Aug	8	Women launch peace movement in Northern Ireland
Sept	9	Chairman Mao Zedong dies in China aged 83
Oct	23	"Gang of Four," including Mao's widow, arrested in China
Nov	2	Democrat Jimmy Carter wins U.S. presidential elections
	15	Parti Québécois wins large victory in Quebec elections, Canada
	27	Northern Irish women lead 30,000-strong peace march through London

ABOVE: Operation Sail brings the tall ships from 28 nations to New York City. This is the Portuguese ship *Sagres*.

ABOVE: Surprise film hit of the year is *Rocky*, written by and starring Sylvester Stallone. It will be followed by a dynasty of *Rockys*.

WESTERN SAHARA DISPUTE

Following Franco's death, the Spanish colony of Western Sahara is divided between Morocco and Mauritania. However, a nationalist pro-independence movement known as Polisario, formed in 1973, rejects the partition and wages a guerrilla war. Mauritania later withdraws, leaving Morocco in sole control of the colony and fighting a lengthy campaign against Polisario, who fight for its independence.

KILLINGS IN SOWETO

Protest breaks out in the black township of Soweto, South Africa. This follows a government decision that secondary-school subjects must be taught in the Afrikaans language, which black South Africans see as the language of oppression. Police open fire; seventy six students are killed and more than 1,000 are injured. Subsequently, the government drops its controversial education plans.

DUTCH LIBERALIZE DRUG LAWS

The drug laws are liberalized in the Netherlands with the revision of the Opium Act of 1928. Possession of soft drugs now has the lowest penalties in a new table of penalties for drug offenses.

ENTEBBE RESCUE

Israeli commandos rescue 110 people held hostage in Entebbe airport, Uganda, after their Air France plane is hijacked by Palestinian guerrillas and flown to Entebbe. All seven hostage-takers and 20 Ugandan soldiers are killed in the raid, with the loss of only three hostages. Most of the Ugandan Air Force is destroyed on the ground by the Israelis.

SUPERSONIC BIRD

Air travel reaches supersonic speeds when two Anglo-French supersonic Concorde turbo jets, one taking off from Paris, one from London, begin a regular passenger service across the Atlantic. With its distinctive drooping nose and looking like a fantastic bird, Concorde cruises at 1,461 miles per hour and can cross the Atlantic in three hours.

QUEBEC VOTES

In Canada, the Parti Québécois, which is seeking an independent Quebec, wins a large majority in the state elections, led by René Levesque, and promises a referendum on independence from Canada. In May 1980 Quebec votes by a large majority to remain in Canada.

ABOVE: American John Naber wins gold in the 100m men's backstroke event at the Montreal Olympics.

ARGENTINA "DIRTY WAR"

In Argentina, a military coup overthrows President Isabel Perón and a three-person junta led by Lt. Gen. Jorge Videla is installed. The constitution is amended and the junta takes action against left-wing activists or those suspected of left-wing sympathies. Political and trade union activity is banned. Between 1976 and 1983, an estimated 10,000 to 15,000 people are murdered or "disappeared" during internal repression.

EINSTEIN ON THE BEACH

American composer Philip Glass (b. 1937) has produced a new opera, *Einstein on the Beach*. In typically minimalist mode, very little happens, although the opera has hypnotic qualities. It cements Glass's position as a major opera composer.

NO LIFE ON MARS

The U.S. space probe *Viking I* lands on Mars and sends close-up pictures of the surface of Mars back to Earth. These reveal a barren surface littered with rocks and no signs of life. But there are signs of dry river beds, showing that water once existed there. The space probes also scoop up soil samples and analyze them for the presence of microorganisms.

ROOTS

American author Alex Haley (1921–92) has published a new book, *Roots*, the saga of a black African sold into slavery in the United States, and of his descendants. In this novel, Haley, who has already published a biography of black American activist Malcolm X, depicts poverty and racial hatred as modern forms of enslavement for black people. It will be a phenomenal success.

WINTER OLYMPICS

The Winter Olympics are held at Innsbruck in Austria, using the facilities from 1968, after Denver withdraws. Austrian hero Franz Klammer takes gold in the men's downhill event while Rosi Mittermaier wins the women's downhill and a further gold and silver for Germany.

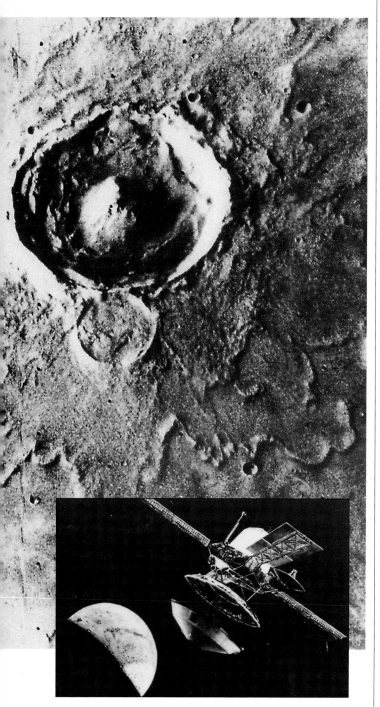

ABOVE: The surface of Mars photographed by *Viking I*. The inset shows a model of the Viking spacecraft in orbit round the red planet.

WOMEN PRIESTS

The Episcopal Church — the American wing of the Anglican church — approves the ordination of women Christian priests. Previously, in July 1974, four American Episcopalian bishops ordained 11 women priests in contravention of Church law.

IRISH WOMEN MARCH FOR PEACE

The women of Belfast, in Northern Ireland, launch a peace campaign. Subsequently, they organize a protest march against continued fighting in Northern Ireland, which is joined by 30,000 people. American folk singer Joan Baez (b. 1941) gives support.

SYMPHONY OF SORROWFUL SONGS

Polish composer Henryk Górecki produces a new symphony — *Symphony No 3* or *Symphony of Sorrowful Songs*. Its use of traditional form (canons) and a tonal idiom mark a turning-away from the harshly modernist style of the composer's earlier works.

GYMNAST SHINES AT BOYCOTTED GAMES

Amid strict security and unfinished building, the Olympic Games open in Montreal, Canada. African nations boycott the games in protest at New Zealand's rugby connection with South Africa. Romanian gymnast Nadia Comaneci, who is aged only 14, gives a dazzling display, winning five medals and the affection of the spectators.

HITE REPORT

U.S. feminist Shere Hite (b. 1943) publishes *The Hite Report: A Nationwide Study of Female Sexuality*. The result of five years' research, it includes information from 3,000 women on all aspects of female sexuality. It challenges many traditional assumptions about women's sexuality and causes a sensation.

MAO ZEDONG (MAO TSE-TUNG) (1893–1976)

Chinese Marxist leader Mao Zedong has died. Mao was one of the founders of the Chinese Communist party when it was founded in 1921, and a leader in the long struggle against the Japanese and then the Kuomintang Nationalists. In 1949, he became first chairman of the new People's Republic of China. In 1958, he launched the disastrous Great Leap Forward of agricultural reforms and resigned as head of state later that year. But he remained party chairman, and in 1962, his *Little Red Book*, containing his many sayings and thoughts, was fervently studied all over China. In 1966, now a cult figure, he set alight the Cultural Revolution with the aim of overthrowing the enemies of Socialism. At the end of this period, 1970, he became supreme commander of the nation.

ABOVE: Computer games make their début with this exciting game of virtual tennis. Over 200 such games are available.

LEGIONNAIRES' DISEASE

The first outbreak of a new type of pneumonia occurs at an American Legion convention in Philadelphia; it is named Legionnaires' Disease.

MOUNTAIN BIKE RACE

The first official mountain bike race takes place on a 2-mile course on Mount Tamalpais, California.

MOON ROCK DATED

Researchers discover that Moon rock sample 76535 is at least 4.54 billion years old.

ABOVE: The Washington Redskins battle with the New York Jets.

ABOVE: Rock fans chill out among the laid-back crowd.

ABOVE: Some fans find inspiration for their own musical efforts.

STADIUM ROCK CONCERTS

ABOVE: Rock legends Lynyrd Skynyrd electrify the audience at an open-air concert.

STAR WARS AND MICROSOFT

Black South African activist Steve Biko is killed in police custody. African nations boycott the Olympic Games. Charter 77 calls for human rights in Czechoslovakia. Nineteen-year-old Bill Gates founds Microsoft. The inside-out Pompidou Center is a dramatic new Paris landmark. A new film, *Star Wars*, opens to rapturous audiences. A new medical development — balloon angioplasty — offers new treatment for heart disease. Elvis Presley, "the King of Rock and Roll," dies.

1977

Jan	**7**	Charter 77 calls for human rights in Czechoslovakia
	17	Gary Gilmore is executed in the United States, the first execution for ten years
Feb	**18**	Archbishop of Uganda murdered by Idi Amin's forces
Mar	**10**	Astronomers discover rings of planet Uranus
	27	Jumbo jets collide in the Canary Islands, killing more than 500 people
June	**15**	First democratic elections in Spain since 1936 lead to victory for center parties

Aug	**16**	King of Rock, Elvis Presley, dies in Memphis, aged 42
Sep	**7**	United States and Panama sign a treaty returning Canal Zone to Panama
	12	Black South African activist Steve Biko is killed in police custody
Nov	**19**	Egyptian President Sadat visits Israel on a peace mission

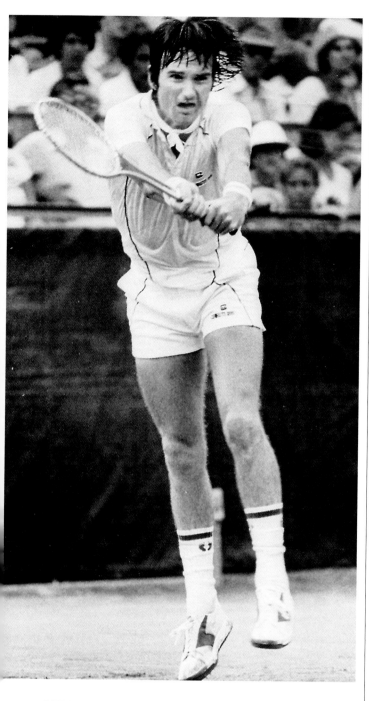

LEFT: American tennis star Jimmy Connors smashes his way to victory in the men's singles at Wimbledon.

AIR DISASTER

Two jumbo jets collide at Tenerife airport, in the Canary Islands. More than 570 people are killed, most of them American holidaymakers. It is the worst disaster in the history of aviation.

CHARTER 77 CALLS FOR HUMAN RIGHTS

In Czechoslovakia, 240 intellectuals and dissidents sign Charter 77, calling for the Czech government to implement the human rights it agreed to support as part of the 1975 Helsinki Declaration. Several of the signatories are arrested, and the leader, Jan Potocka, dies after police interrogation.

POMPIDOU CENTER

Italian Renzo Piano and Englishman Richard Rogers design a revolutionary new-style arts center in Paris — the Pompidou Center. It provokes considerable controversy. All the services (drains, wiring, elevators, heating ducts) are suspended on the outside of the building, making a striking decorative amalgam. This leaves the interior free for broad uninterrupted exhibition spaces.

STAR WARS

A new science fiction film is released and is a smash success. Directed by U.S. filmmaker, George Lucas (b. 1944), it is called *Star Wars*. It features the latest in special effects as well as starring a princess, a dashing hero, and two robots — R2D2 and C-3PO. Two more films will follow, with more in the pipeline.

MICROSOFT FOUNDED

Paul Allen and Bill Gates (b. 1955) set up a new computer software company, Microsoft. Gates is only 19; He will be a millionare within ten years and Microsoft will be the world's largest producer of micro-computer software.

BIKO KILLED

Black consciousness leader Steve Biko is killed in custody by South African police. He was one of a number of black leaders who have been arrested under new security legislation. A postmortem reveals brain injuries. Some 15,000 people attend his funeral. Biko's death causes an international outcry, increasing international pressure on the apartheid National Party government, which wins a record majority in white-only elections in November.

EGYPT TALKS PEACE WITH ISRAEL

President Sadat (1918–81) of Egypt offers peace to Israel, alienating other Arab states. At the end of November, he visits Israel and addresses the Knesset, the Israeli parliament.

SIR CHARLES SPENCER (CHARLIE) CHAPLIN (1889–1977)

English comedian and filmmaker Charlie Chaplin has died. After a tough childhood he became a member of the Fred Karno vaudeville company and went with them to Hollywood, where he was to make a film every two weeks between 1914 and 1916. He created the flat-footed, baggy-trousered, bowler-hatted tramp still regarded with affection today. His comic talent was at its best in the silent cinema, and he will be remembered for classics such as *The Kid* (1920), *The Gold Rush* (1925), and *City Lights* (1931).

TOP AND ABOVE: The Trans-Alaska oil pipeline under construction. It will be 800 miles long.

RIGHT: An earth-moving machine helps to build the 360-mile service road for the Alaska pipeline.

LIFE IN THE OCEAN DEEP

U.S. scientists aboard the submersible *Alvin* discover worms, crabs, and fish living in warm water from vents in the Galápagos Rift near Ecuador, far from sunlight and feeding on bacteria.

DEATH PENALTY BACK

The death penalty returns to the United States when convicted murderer Gary Gilmore is executed by firing squad. This is the first execution to take place for ten years and follows considerable protest and public debate.

CANAL BACK TO PANAMA

U.S. president Jimmy Carter and General Omar Torrijos of Panama sign a treaty to return the Canal Zone to Panamanian control by 2000.

APPLE RIPENS

The Apple II, the first personal computer sold ready assembled, goes on the market.

ARCHBISHOP MURDERED

In Uganda, President Idi Amin's regime becomes increasingly repressive when Amin's forces murder the human-rights advocate, the Most Reverend Janani Luwum, archbishop of Uganda.

DEMOCRATIC SPAIN

The first democratic elections since 1936 are held in Spain. They lead to victory for Adolfo Suárez (b. 1932) and the Democratic Center party.

BALLOON ANGIOPLASTY

Swiss doctor Andreas Grünzig devises balloon angioplasty. This involves inserting a tiny inflatable balloon into a blocked artery to clear it.

ABOVE: Rock music becomes an industry; vinyl is worth money.

BELOW: Greek-born opera diva Maria Callas dies this year.

MARIA MENEGHINI CALLAS
(1923–77)

The great operatic soprano Maria Callas has died in Paris. Born in New York City into a Greek family, she studied at the Athens National Conservatory from the age of about 15. Her début was in Athens in 1940. She sang many roles from Brunnhilde to Violetta, and her prima-donna status was secured by her first performance at La Scala in 1950 in *Aida*. She worked with conductors such as Giulini and Karajan, and with producers such as Visconti and Zeffirelli, drawing recordbreaking audiences. Her last performance was in *Tosca* at Covent Garden in 1965 but she continued to make records and give occasional concerts. Her unsurpassed musicianship was accompanied by great dramatic talent. Her glamour made her the focus of attention in private as well as public life.

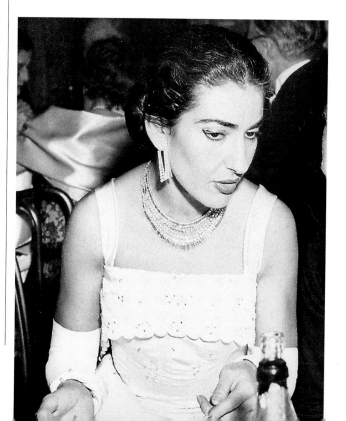

ELVIS AARON PRESLEY
(1935–77)

Elvis Presley, the world's most popular pop star, has died suddenly at his home in Memphis of the accumulated effects of overweight and narcotics. Presley was born in Mississippi and first sang in his local Pentecostal church choir. He came to fame with his first single "That's All Right Mama" in 1954 and will always be remembered for his 1956–58 rock and roll classics such as "Heartbreak Hotel," "Hound Dog," and "Don't be Cruel," and the songs from the 1958 films of the same names, "Jailhouse Rock" and "King Creole." In the 1960s the King of Rock and Roll took to crooning and gave up live performances, but in the 1970s he had again been performing frequently, to huge audiences, in Las Vegas nightclubs.

URANUS RINGS FOUND

Astronomers discover the rings of the planet Uranus, confirmed and counted by *Voyager 2* in 1985.

GOSSAMER CONDOR FLIES

In California, cyclist Bryan Allen pedals an 81-pound aircraft, the *Gossamer Condor*, round a 1.19-mile figure-of-eight course in 6 minutes 22.5 seconds to win an $87,000 prize for human-powered flight.

SMALLPOX ERADICATED

The world's last case of the disease smallpox occurs in Somalia, following a campaign by the World Health Organization to eradicate it. Formal eradication is announced in 1980.

RIGHT: Elvis Presley in the Vegas years that preceded his early death, apparently from an overdose of prescription drugs.

WERNHER VON BRAUN
(1912–1977)

German-born rocket expert Wernher von Braun has died. Having perfected the V-2 rockets used by Germany during World War ll, he and his team surrendered at the end of the war and took up residence in the United States, where he continued his work. An American citizen since 1955, he was responsible for the development of the satellite *Explorer l* (1958). As director of the Marshal Space Flight Center (1960–70), he developed the rocket used in the 1969 *Apollo 8* Moon landing.

TEST-TUBE BABIES BORN

The world's first "test-tube" baby is born, following the development of *in-vitro* fertilization. Astronomers observe a new moon, that of the planet Pluto, and U.S. space probes begin mapping the surface of Venus. Civil war breaks out in Nicaragua. Egypt and Israel make peace at Camp David. The world's worst oil spill to date occurs and environmentalists become increasingly concerned about the impact of CFCs on the ozone layer.

1978

Mar 1 Communist support enables a new Italian government in "Historic Compromise"

8 UN recognizes March 8 as International Women's Day

16 World's worst oil spill occurs off coast of France

May 20 United States launches space probe *Pioneer Venus I*, which goes into orbit around Venus

June 22 Pluto's moon, Charon, is discovered

July 25 World's first "test-tube" baby born

Aug 17 First manned transatlantic crossing in a hot-air balloon

22 Kenyan statesman Jomo Kenyatta dies aged about 89

22 Sandinistas seize control of parliament building, Nicaragua

Sep 5 Peace summit at Camp David between U.S. president Carter, President Sadat of Egypt, and Israeli prime minister Begin

15 U.S. boxer Muhammad Ali beats Leon Spinks

Oct 16 Archbishop of Cracow, Karol Wojtyla, becomes first non-Italian pope for more than 400 years

Nov 29 More than 900 people die in cult mass suicide, Guyana

Dec 25 Vietnam begins full-scale invasion of Cambodia

ABOVE: Women march in Washington to protest against the government's seven-year delay in ratifying the Equal Rights Amendment.

HISTORIC COMPROMISE

A "Historic Compromise" is agreed between Christian Democrats and Communists in Italy, allowing Prime Minister Andreotti (b. 1919) to take power with Communist Party support. The Italian Communist Party is the biggest in Western Europe and the deal gives it influence in government for the first time since the war.

CAMP DAVID PEACE SUMMIT

A summit held at the U.S. presidential retreat at Camp David achieves peace between Egypt and Israel. In the deal, between President Anwar Sadat of Egypt and the Israeli prime minister, Menachem Begin, Israel agrees to give back the Sinai Peninsula to Egypt. The deal is heavily criticized in the Arab world.

POLISH POPE

Polish-born John Paul II (b. 1920) becomes the first non-Italian pope for 435 years after the deaths of both Paul VI and John Paul I. A conservative, John Paul II uses his office to attack Communist control of Eastern Europe and liberal tendencies inside the Church.

VIETNAM INVADES CAMBODIA

Vietnam invades to overthrow the Khmer Rouge government. The Vietnamese seize the capital, Phnom Penh, in January and install the rebel leader, Heng Samrin, in power. The discovery of the killing fields, where the Khmer Rouge disposed of their millions of victims, causes international outrage. Despite their fall from power, Khmer Rouge rebels keep up armed resistance until their leader Pol Pot dies, probably by suicide, in 1998.

NICARAGUAN CIVIL WAR

In August, guerrillas of the Sandinista National Liberation Front fight the government of President Anastasio Somoza in Nicaragua, taking over the parliament building in Managua. By September, the rebellion is suppressed at a cost of 5,000 killed and 10,000 wounded.

TEST-TUBE BABIES

Louise Brown, the world's first "test-tube" baby, is born in the U.K. This follows work by physiologist Robert Edwards and gynecologist Patrick Steptoe, who have devised a method of fertilizing an egg outside the human body. The new technique is known as *in-vitro* and involves fertilizing an ovum in a test-tube. The embryo is then replaced in the mother's uterus where it develops naturally. Some months later, in October, a second "test-tube" baby is born in Calcutta, India, to Bela and Pravat Agarwal.

PLUTO'S MOON OBSERVED

U.S. astronomers James W. Christy and Robert S. Harrington of the U.S. Naval Observatory, Washington, D.C. discover that the planet Pluto has a moon. It is named Charon. Earlier attempts to detect a moon have been unsuccessful because Pluto is so remote.

VENUS SPACE PROBES

The National Aeronautics and Space Administration (NASA) launches two space probes: *Pioneer 1* in May, and *Pioneer 2* in August. They go into orbit around the planet Venus in December, and map the surface using radar.

CFCs BANNED

The use of chlorofluorocarbons (CFCs) is banned in the United States and Sweden because they are thought to be harming the ozone layer. CFCs are synthetic chemicals used as propellants in aerosols, refrigerants in fridges and air conditioners, and in the manufacture of foam boxes used for take-out foods.

GOLDA MEIR
(1898–1978)

Former Israeli prime minister Golda Meir has died. Born in Russia, she lived in the United States before settling in Palestine in 1921. Having been involved in the Labour Movement, she became Israeli ambassador to the Soviet Union on the founding of the new state. In 1949 she became a government minister and in 1969 was elected prime minister. She resigned after the fourth Arab-Israeli war in 1974.

VIRUS GENES EXAMINED

The genome (genetic structure) of Virus SV40 is worked out, the first organism to be examined and mapped in this way.

EVITA

A new musical, composed by Andrew Lloyd Webber with lyrics by Tim Rice, has opened. Called *Evita*, it is based on the life of Argentinian leader Eva Perón and achieves international success.

SUPERMAN THE MOVIE

Starring Christopher Reeve and directed by Richard Donner, a new movie, *Superman*, has opened. Featuring wonderful special effects, it is one of the most expensive films ever made.

MAJOR OIL SPILL

The Amoco Cadiz supertanker runs aground in storms in the Atlantic off the Brittany coast and splits in two. Some 80,000 tons of crude oil devastate French beaches, wildlife habitats, and fishing grounds. It is the worst oil spill to date.

TRANSATLANTIC BALLOON FLIGHT

Three U.S. businessmen complete the first manned transatlantic balloon crossing from the United States to France in 137 hours, 18 minutes.

INTERNATIONAL WOMEN'S DAY

March 8 is officially International Women's Day. Seventy years ago, on March 8, 1908, hundreds of women clothing workers in New York City demanded the vote, and in 1910 the Socialist Women's International led by German feminist Clara Zetkin (1857–1933), named the date International Women's Day. Now the United Nations has made it official.

TALES OF THE CITY

Armistead Maupin publishes *Tales of the City*. Stories of life in San Francisco, they began as a regular feature in the *San Francisco Chronicle*. Now they appear in book form for the first time, bringing Maupin widespread recognition.

MASS SUICIDE

More than 900 members of the People's Temple, a religious cult under the leadership of the Reverend Jim Jones, located in the rainforest of Guyana, commit mass suicide. The dead include adults and children, who have died by drinking cyanide, some under duress.

VERSATILE FOOD PROCESSOR

The Magimix electronic food processor comes on to the market. Designed in France, it combines several functions, such as blending, shredding, chopping, and even kneading, in one operation.

DYSON CLEANER

Centrifugal force is harnessed by British inventor James Dyson to extract dust and dirt from the industrial or household environment. His Dual Cyclone is the only alternative to the vacuum cleaner since Hoover's first suction cleaner appeared in 1908.

SKATEBOARDING CRAZE

Teenagers have taken up a new craze — skateboarding. Sidewalks and parks in both America and Britain are full of young people performing skateboarding stunts.

ARGENTINA BEATS HOLLAND

The Dutch again fall to the home country in the final game of the soccer World Cup. Argentina beats them 3–1 in front of an ecstatic crowd.

ALI VICTORIOUS

U.S. boxing star Muhammad Ali beats Leon Spinks, who had taken the title from him, to regain the heavyweight boxing crown for an unprecedented third time.

IRONMAN RACE

The Ironman race in Hawaii begins when sports enthusiasts combine a 2.4-mile swim, an 112-mile bike race, and a 26-mile marathon to find the best all-round athlete. The race has grown from small beginnings to become a prestige event and has spawned other, shorter triathlons.

JOMO KENYATTA
(c.1889–1978)

Kenyan leader Jomo Kenyatta has died. The former herd boy, who eventually studied at London University, was president of the Pan-African Federation and, from 1946, president of the Kenyan African Union. He was the Kikuyu people's Mau Mau leader during the struggles for repossession of their lands and was imprisoned from 1952–59. He became prime minister in 1963 in the period up to independence and became president in 1964.

REVOLUTION IN IRAN

The Shah of Iran flees into exile. Fundamentalist spiritual leader Ayatollah Khomeini takes over and U.S. hostages are seized. The Sandinistas gain victory in Nicaragua. The U.S.S.R. invades Afghanistan. Idi Amin's rule comes to an end. A potentially catastrophic accident at Three Mile Island draws attention to the dangers of nuclear power. Space probes send back photographs of Venus and Saturn and a tiny personal stereo — the Sony Walkman — goes on sale.

1979

Jan	8	Vietnamese occupy Phnom Penh, Cambodia, overthrowing Khmer Rouge regime
	16	Shah of Iran flees into exile
Mar	26	Israel and Egypt sign peace treaty
	28	Major accident occurs at Three Mile Island nuclear plant
April	2	Mass graves are discovered in northeast Cambodia, evidence of mass murders carried out by Khmer Rouge
	11	Tanzanian forces overthrow Ugandan dictator Idi Amin
May	4	Margaret Thatcher becomes the first British woman prime minister
June	18	U.S.S.R. and U.S. sign Strategic Arms Limitation Treaty (SALT-2)
July	17	General Somoza flees Nicaragua after Sandinista victory
Nov	4	Followers of Ayatollah Khomeini seize U.S. embassy in Tehran and take hostages
Dec	4	First successful launch of European Space Agency's rocket, *Ariane*
	10	Mother Teresa wins Nobel Peace Prize
	27	U.S.S.R. invades Afghanistan

ISLAMIC REVOLUTION IN IRAN

The Shah flees into exile in Egypt as supporters of the fundamentalist religious leader, Ayatollah Khomeini (1900–89), seize power. His flight follows months of demonstrations and unrest and is greeted with enormous celebration. The ayatollah returns from exile in Paris and institutes an Islamic republic. In November, students seize the U.S. embassy in Tehran and take its 63 U.S. staff and 40 other people hostage, demanding the return of the Shah for trial. The crisis leads to a confrontation between Iran and the United States. The hostages are not released until January 1981, after 444 days in captivity.

SANDINISTA VICTORY

Fighting breaks out again in Nicaragua. This time the Marxist Sandinistas are better armed, and equipped by Cuba. By July, they have ousted Nicaraguan dictator General Anastastio Somoza, who flees to the U.S. This brings to an end a cruel and corrupt dictatorship. The Sandinista rebels, named after a revolutionary leader killed in the 1930s, form a provisional government.

EL SALVADOR REBELS

A communist guerrilla movement, the Farabundo Marti Liberation Front (FMLN), is waging war against El Salvador's right-wing government.

THREE MILE ISLAND

A major accident occurs at Three Mile Island nuclear power station in Pennsylvania. Owing to a technical error, a nuclear reactor overheats, causing the release of some radioactive gas. The possibility of a total meltdown causes the evacuation of thousands of people. The crisis is averted but it is the worst nuclear accident in the United States and alerts people to the possible dangers of nuclear power.

THE CHINA SYNDROME

American actress Jane Fonda (b. 1937) stars as the journalist investigating the story of meltdown at a nuclear reactor in a new film, *The China Syndrome*. The title comes from the fire which, it is said, could theoretically burn through the Earth to China. The film gains new topicality after the accident at the power plant at Three Mile Island.

UGANDAN CIVIL WAR

Ugandan dictator Idi Amin (b. 1925) has annexed the Kagera area of northern Tanzania, near the Ugandan border. Tanzanian president Julius Neyere (b. 1922) sends troops to support the Uganda National Liberation Army (UNLA) which has been formed to fight the dictatorial and increasingly bloodthirsty Idi Amin. As they approach Kampala, Libyan troops, who have come to Amin's assistance, attack and halt them briefly, but UNLA takes the capital and Amin is forced to flee. A civilian government returns to power.

CHINA INVADES VIETNAM

Chinese forces invade the Cao Bang area of northern Vietnam to punish the country for its invasion of Cambodia. The Chinese are fought to a standstill and forced to withdraw after suffering 20,000 killed and wounded. Vietnamese casualties are estimated to be 27,000 killed and wounded.

APOCALYPSE NOW

Directed by Francis Ford Coppola (b. 1939), the film *Apocalypse Now* is a loose adaptation of Joseph Conrad's novel *Heart of Darkness*, set in the Vietnam War. The film stuns audiences with its images of helicopters and warfare, and its gripping tale of Captain Benjamin Willard's (Martin Sheen) quest for Kurtz (Marlon Brando).

ABOVE AND LEFT: Gays and lesbians march on Washington to demand human rights.

ABOVE: The mellow proprietor of a real drugstore in Washington, D.C. The shops sells marijuana and the equipment needed to use it.

THATCHER VICTORY
Margaret Thatcher (b. 1925) becomes the first British woman prime minister when her Conservative Party wins the general election. She embarks on a right-wing, free-market policy of privatization of state assets and a tough anti-trade union policy.

SALT-2
U.S. president Carter (b. 1924) and Soviet leader Leonid Brezhnev (1906–82) sign the SALT-2 (Strategic Arms Limitation Talks) Treaty, agreeing to restrict each side to 2,250 strategic nuclear missiles. The deal is never ratified by the U.S. Senate and is abandoned as the arms race intensifies during the early 1980s.

POSTMODERNISM
Jean-François Lyotard publishes a new study summing up a distanced, ironic approach, which comes to be known as postmodernism, a term that will be widely used in the coming decade in fields as diverse as literature and architecture.

SOVIET UNION INVADES AFGHANISTAN
Intending to make a quick change in government, Soviet president Leonid Brezhenev sends 55,000 troops into Afghanistan to oust President Hafizullah Amin and replace him with a new Afghan leader, Babrak Karmal. This leads to a drawn-out guerrilla war. The Communist coup is opposed by fundamentalist Muslim tribal groups, who are assisted by the United States.

PEDALING OVER THE CHANNEL
In June the 77-pound airplane *Gossamer Albatross* flies across the English Channel powered by U.S. biologist Bryan Allen, who drives the propeller using bicycle-type pedals.

THE DINNER PARTY
American feminist and artist Judy Chicago's multimedia creation, *The Dinner Party*, goes on show. A tribute to women's history, it takes the form of a triangular table with 39 symbolic place settings, each representing a key woman. The whole thing is positioned on a floor inscribed with the names of 999 other women of note.

PHOTOGRAPHS FROM SPACE
Photographs of Saturn are transmitted by U.S. space probe *Pioneer 11*, launched in 1973. *Voyager 1*, launched in 1977 to take advantage of an alignment of Jupiter, Saturn, Uranus, and Neptune, transmitted photographs of Jupiter's rings in March. Passing within 3,000 miles of each planet's surface, *Voyager 1* and *2* discover Jupiter's powerful magnetic field, and its continuous thunderstorms. They also photograph the planet's moons.

AIR-CUSHIONED SNEAKERS
The first air-cushioned sneaker is developed by engineer Frank Rudy at Nike. The company was formed in 1967 to market track shoes with nylon uppers developed by William J. Bowerman, the track coach of the University of Oregon. These will become the style statement for young people.

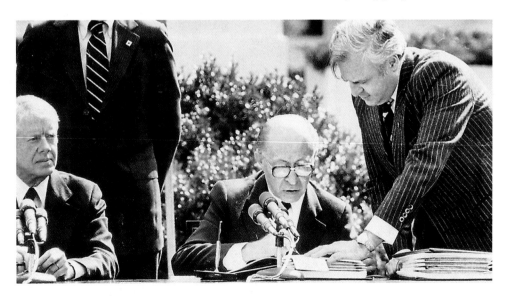

LEFT: Israeli leader Menachem Begin signing the Middle East peace agreement at Camp David. President Jimmy Carter, architect of the agreement, looks on.

RIGHT: The accident at Three Mile Island nuclear reactor polarizes opinion on the usefulness and safety of nuclear power. Thousands take to the streets to protest.

ABOVE: American automobiles line up for gas during the politically inspired oil crisis that slows down the late 1970s.

LEFT: Smart shop owners stockpile cans of gas in anticipation of panic buying by their customers.

SKYLAB CRASHES
The U.S. space station *Skylab I* falls back to Earth. It has traveled 87 million miles in orbit since its launch in 1973.

GLUONS DETECTED
U.S. scientists detect the existence of subatomic particles that hold quarks together. They are called gluons.

PEACE PRIZE
Mother Teresa (1910–97), an Albanian Roman Catholic nun, founder of the Missionaries of Charity religious order who works among the poor in Calcutta, is awarded the Nobel Peace Prize.

WALKMANS
The Japanese company, Sony, has launched the Sony Walkman, a portable personal stereo cassette player with headphones. It is so small that you can listen to music anywhere, even when walking around the streets.

ABOVE AND ABOVE LEFT: Pope John Paul II comes to the United States and celebrates mass on the Mall in Washington, D.C.

NEW DINOSAUR CLUE
U.S. scientists Luis and Walter Alvarez discover traces of a huge meteorite impact some 65 million years ago. They propose that dust from it may have changed the climate and caused the extinction of the dinosaurs.

IRANIAN WOMEN PROTEST
March 8, International Women's Day, is marked by protests by Iranian women against strict Islamic laws introduced under Ayatollah Khomeini.

ROLLERBLADING
Brothers Scott and Brennan Olsen create the first popular Rollerblade or in-line skate in Minneapolis. Keen ice skaters, they wanted to be able to practice in summer.

OPPOSITE ABOVE: Disco fever still rages at the terminally hip New York City night clubs.

OPPOSITE BELOW: Two years after *Saturday Night Fever*, young hopefuls still dance for prizes.

THE GLOBAL VILLAGE

The 1980s see countries of the world coming closer, largely through growing awareness of environmental destruction. Poverty and famine in Africa wake the world's conscience as the gap between rich and poor widens. However, discovery of a hole in the ozone layer and nuclear fallout from Chernobyl prove that pollution affects all equally. Politically, the decade sees monumental change as the INF Treaty is signed, the Berlin Wall comes down, and the Cold War ends.

OPPOSITE: Live Aid, the rock concert that raises over $60 million for famine relief.

1980–1989

KEY EVENTS OF THE DECADE

- IRAN–IRAQ WAR
- THE FALKLANDS CONFLICT
- CIVIL WARS IN CENTRAL AMERICA
- THREE MILE ISLAND AND CHERNOBYL
- LIVE AID AND FAMINE RELIEF
- INF TREATY
- IRANGATE
- SOVIET BLOC BREAKS UP
- COLD WAR ENDS

- ORGAN TRANSPLANTS
- AIDS EPIDEMIC
- SPACE SHUTTLE AND SPACE LAB LAUNCHED
- OZONE HOLE DISCOVERED
- COMPACT DISCS
- POSTMODERNISM

WORLD POPULATION: **4,450** MILLION

SOLIDARITY AND WAR

Independent trade unions are recognized in Poland and begin to change the country. Iraq invades neighboring Iran, sparking off war between the two countries. Former film star Ronald Reagan wins the U.S. presidential election for the Republican party. Princess Beatrix becomes queen of the Netherlands. U.S. attempt to rescue hostages in Tehran fails. A new craze for health and fitness sweeps through the United States and Europe. President Tito of Yugoslavia dies and John Lennon is assassinated by a crazed fan.

1980

Feb	13	Winter Olympics are held at Lake Placid, New York
Apr	18	Rhodesia gains legal independence as Zimbabwe
	25	U.S. attempt to rescue hostages in Tehran ends in disaster
	30	Crown Princess Beatrix becomes queen of the Netherlands
May	4	President Tito of Yugoslavia dies aged 88
	18	Mount St. Helens volcano erupts, Washington
July	19	The 22nd Olympic Games open in Moscow
Aug	31	Independent trade unions are recognized in Poland
Sep	22	Iraq invades Iran

Nov	4	Republican Ronald Reagan wins U.S. presidential election
Dec	8	Former Beatle John Lennon is shot dead outside his home in New York City

ABOVE: Public grief after former Beatle John Lennon is shot dead in New York. City

IRAN–IRAQ WAR

Profiting from disorder in Iran, Iraq invades neighboring Iran in an attempt to gain the strategic Shatt al-Arab waterway to the Persian Gulf. During the eight-year war that follows, Iraq employs chemical weapons and both sides fire ballistic missiles at major cities. Iraq also launches antiship missile attacks against tankers shipping oil from Iran. In 1988, Iran accepts a UN-sponsored ceasefire.

FAILED RESCUE

In a rescue attempt, nicknamed "Operation Eagle Claw," the United States sends men from Delta Force 200 miles into Iran to rescue the hostages being held in the U.S. embassy in Tehran. At a refuelling operation in the desert, there is an equipment failure. The force withdraws but the airplane crashes into a tanker aircraft causing the death of eight Americans and injury to others.

ZIMBABWE

After the collapse of the rebel white-only government in Rhodesia, Britain agrees to a new multiracial constitution for the country and grants its last African colony independence as Zimbabwe. Robert Mugabe (b. 1924) becomes prime minister of the new country.

TITO DIES

Yugoslav president Josip Tito dies. His death leads to an eight-man collective presidency. Tensions soon begin to emerge between Serbs and Croats in the country.

ABOVE: The coronation of Queen Beatrix of the Netherlands in Amsterdam's Nieuwe Kerk; her husband Prince Claus looks on.

BEATRIX BECOMES QUEEN

In the Netherlands, Queen Beatrix (b. 1938) takes the throne after her mother, Queen Juliana, abdicates.

HEALTH — THE NEW FASHION

Health clubs and gyms open all over America, Britain, and Europe, offering electronic running machines, classes in aerobic exercise, and dance-exercise, to cater for the desire for fitness. The trend influences fashions and cosmetic products.

POLISH SOLIDARITY

After two months of strikes and demonstrations against the government, independent trade unions are recognized in Poland in an agreement between Lech Walesa (b. 1943), strike leader in the Lenin shipyard in Gdansk, and the Polish government. The Solidarity union is formally registered in October.

REAGAN ELECTED PRESIDENT

Ronald Reagan (b. 1911) wins the U.S. presidential election for the Republicans, defeating incumbent president Jimmy Carter. He reverses the consensus politics of his predecessor and begins an arms buildup against the Soviets, working closely with the British government led by Margaret Thatcher.

DIFFICULT CUBE

Rubik's cube, a game consisting of 26 small colored cubes rotating on a central axis, becomes Britain's Toy of the Year. It was invented by Erno Rubik, a Hungarian professor of design, who failed to patent his design so did not profit from it.

Rubik's cube.

AMADEUS

A new play by English dramatist Peter Shaffer (b. 1926) has opened. *Amadeus* tells the story of Mozart and his alleged murder by "rival" composer Salieri. The play courts controversy with its frank portrayal of the earthy, scatological side of Mozart's character.

MOUNT ST. HELENS ERUPTS

The volcano Mount St. Helens in Washington erupts, having been inactive since 1857. The explosion measures 4.1 on the Richter scale. It destroys all life in an area of 154 square miles, and kills at least eight people.

BELOW: The force is still with us when *The Empire Strikes Back*, crewed by the same heroes, is released three years after *Star Wars*.

MOSCOW OLYMPICS

Once again politics and sport mix at the Olympic Games. The United States leads a boycott, which includes West Germany and Kenya, in protest at the Soviet Union's invasion of Afghanistan. Competitive highlights include the achievements of British athletes Seb Coe and Steve Ovett on the track, and Soviet gymnast Alexander Ditiatin's perfect 10 in the vault.

SOLAR MAX IS LAUNCHED

Solar Max (the U.S. Solar Maximum Mission Observatory) is launched to record events during a period of sunspot activity.

BYKER DEVELOPMENT

A groundbreaking housing development is created in Newcastle, England. Its importance lies in the fact that it involves the future residents in the design of the building. Members of Ralph Erskine's architectural practice live on site to ensure they are accessible to the future tenants.

SOLAR-POWERED FLIGHT

The *Gossamer Penguin* makes the first flight of a solar-powered aircraft in California. The power is obtained from panels of solar-electric cells.

WINTER OLYMPICS

The 13th Winter Olympics in Lake Placid, witness the first use of artificial snow. American skater Eric Heiden takes five speed-skating golds.

ICELAND GAINS WOMAN PRESIDENT

Vigdís Finnbogadóttir (b. 1930) is elected president of Iceland. She wins a little over a third of the vote, defeating three male rivals to become the world's first democratically elected woman president.

BORG WINS FIFTH TITLE

Swedish tennis star Björn Borg (b. 1956) claims his fifth Wimbledon tennis title in a row, beating John McEnroe in the final.

JEAN-PAUL SARTRE
(1905–1980)

French existentialist philosopher and writer, Jean-Paul Sartre has died. During World War II, he was a member of the Resistance. A Marxist, he founded, with Simone de Beauvoir, the left-wing journal *Les Temps Modernes* and was known as one of the intellectuals of Left Bank Paris café society. His most important philosophical work is *Being and Nothingness* (1943) and his fictional writings include the trilogy *Roads to Freedom* (1945–49). During the events of May 1968 Sartre was once more out on the streets of Paris supporting student and worker rebellion, but of late he has suffered from ill-health and near-blindness.

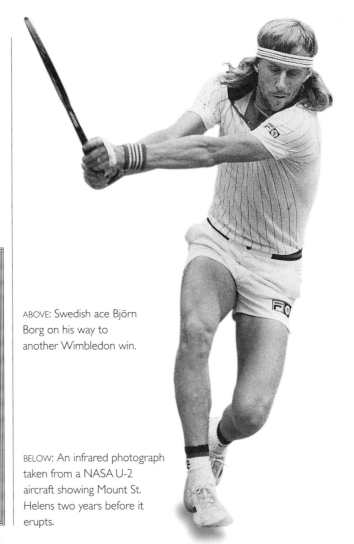

ABOVE: Swedish ace Björn Borg on his way to another Wimbledon win.

BELOW: An infrared photograph taken from a NASA U-2 aircraft showing Mount St. Helens two years before it erupts.

ABOVE: U.S. golfer Jack Nicklaus (b. 1940), the "Golden Bear," confirms his position as one of golf's greats.

ABOVE: Ayatollah Khomeini, charismatic fundamentalist leader of Iran, has many supporters for his return to conservative values.

ABOVE: Josip Tito, president of Yugoslavia, and his wife.

JOSIP TITO (BORN JOSIP BROZ) (1892–1980)

President Tito of Yugoslavia, who became head of the Yugoslav Communist party in 1937 and has been the country's leader since the postwar establishment of the new Federal Republic in 1945, has died. Viewed by Stalin as a revisionist, he pursued a policy of liberalism, and although he has been president for life since 1974 he has established a rotating leadership during recent years. The country's future without his leadership is uncertain.

NEW DIRECTION IN THE MOVIES

The late 1970s and early 1980s see the rise of a new generation of young director-producers whose work helps the cinema to recover from the blow inflicted on it by television. Large-scale action films, blockbusters, and science fiction sagas follow, and special effects almost take over as the stars of the films. Audiences flock back to the big screen.

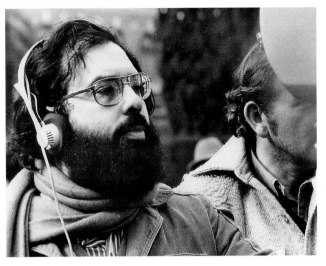

ABOVE: Francis Ford Coppola, enigmatic director most famous for his Mafia-based *Godfather* series.

ABOVE: Michael Cimino directs Robert de Niro on the set of *The Deer Hunter* (1978), the film that makes his name.

ABOVE: Golden boy Steven Spielberg, creator of *Jaws, Close Encounters of the Third Kind, ET,* and the *Indiana Jones* trilogy.

ABOVE: A scene from Star Wars, the film that launches George Lucas' career as a director.

ABOVE: Douglas Trumball, the special effects mastermind behind many science fiction films and the director of *Silent Running* (1972).

AIDS — A NEW KILLER

Iran releases the U.S. hostages after 444 days in captivity. Unrest increases in Poland and martial law is declared. François Mitterand is elected the first socialist president of France. President Sadat of Egypt is assassinated. France's new high-speed train reaches speeds of more than 186 miles per hour. A new disease — AIDS — is identified and the first successful heart-lung transplant takes place.

OPPOSITE: Prime Minister Margaret Thatcher meets French president François Mitterand.

1981

Jan	10	Greece joins the European Community (EC)	**Oct**	6	President Sadat of Egypt is assassinated
	20	U.S. hostages released from Tehran			
			Dec	13	Martial law declared in Poland
Feb	3	Gro Harlem Brundtland becomes first woman prime minister of Norway			
	23	Civil Guards storm Spanish Cortes (parliament) in abortive coup attempt			
Apr	12	American reusable space shuttle makes first flight			
	30	Polish Communist government approves limited reforms			
May	5	IRA activist Bobby Sands dies from hunger strike, Northern Ireland			
	10	François Mitterand becomes first socialist president of France			
July	29	Royal wedding of Prince Charles and Lady Diana Spencer, United Kingdom			

ABOVE: President Anwar Sadat of Egypt, who is assassinated this year.

ABOVE: American writer Susan Sontag, one of a group of Western intellectuals invited to tour Communist China.

ABOVE: Delegates from the States and U.S.S.R. meet in Geneva to discuss the limitation of intermediate nuclear forces in Europe.

ABOVE: Oil rigs begin to reap the rich harvest of North Sea oil.

ABOVE: American composer Samuel Barber, best known for his *Adagio*, dies.

UNREST IN POLAND

In Poland, the Communist government hands over to the army, which takes power under General Jaruzelski (b. 1923) as prime minister. He introduces some reforms in April to placate the independent trade union Solidarity, which is leading a general strike. Following demonstrations against food shortages and unrest throughout the country, he introduces martial law in December after pressure from the Soviet Union, curtailing all civil liberties and arresting Lech Walesa. Solidarity is banned in October 1982.

ATTEMPTED COUP

Right-wing members of the paramilitary Civil Guard storm the Cortes, the Spanish parliament, and attempt to overthrow the government. King Juan Carlos dons military uniform and instructs the army, which appears to support the coup, to rally behind the democratic government. The government quickly purges the army of former Franco supporters.

MITTERAND BECOMES PRESIDENT

François Mitterand (1916–96) becomes the first socialist president of France when he wins the presidential election, defeating the incumbent centrist Valéry Giscard d'Estaing. Mitterand's Socialist Party wins a landslide in the general election held in June; the new government includes three Communist ministers.

SADAT ASSASSINATED

Egyptian president Anwar Sadat is assassinated at a military parade by an Islamic extremist protesting against the peace deal with Israel. Sadat is succeeded by Vice-President Hosni Mubarak (b. 1928).

HOSTAGES RELEASED

The last 52 hostages are released from the U.S. embassy in Tehran, where they have been held by followers of the Ayatollah.

GREECE JOINS EC

The newly democratic Greece becomes the tenth nation to be admitted to the European Union.

JAILED HUNGER STRIKER WINS ELECTION

IRA activist Bobby Sands wins the Fermanagh and South Tyrone by-election in Northern Ireland, defeating the Unionists by a clear majority. Bobby Sands, who is on hunger strike in prison, dies a month later.

HIGH-SPEED TRAIN

In February France's new TGV (*train à grande vitesse*, or high-speed train) begins a regular service between Paris and Lyon. It sets a world speed record of 236 mph To reach such speeds, the TGV has specially-built tracks with steeply banked curves.

LEFT: April sees the launch of the first space shuttle, a reusable vehicle that can orbit the Earth and return under its own steam.

ABOVE: Modern art in a modern setting. Alexander Calder's stabile *Flamingo* outside the Federal Center in Chicago.

FIRST SPACE SHUTTLE FLIGHT

In April, America's first space shuttle *Columbia* makes its first flight, returning safely two days later. A second flight takes place in November.

AIDS IDENTIFIED

The U.S. Center for Disease Control identifies the first cases of what appears to be a new disease — AIDS (Acquired Immune Deficiency Syndrome). The condition affects a person's natural disease-combatting immune system and the first cases are identified in gay men.

RAIDERS OF THE LOST ARK

A new film, *Raiders of the Lost Ark*, is a great hit. It stars U.S. film actor Harrison Ford (b. 1942) who plays Indiana Jones, archaeologist and man of action, who overcomes a bunch of Nazis hunting for the lost Ark of the Covenant. The film is full of spectacular effects.

BOB MARLEY
(1945–1981)

Jamaican reggae artist Bob Marley (born Robert Nesta) has died of cancer. A Rastafarian, the singer and electric guitarist brought reggae to an international audience. Initially performing in a group of three known as the Wailers, Marley later went solo and gave performances worldwide. His latest album *Uprising* was produced last year. Among his best-known hits are "*No Woman No Cry*" and "*I Shot the Sheriff.*"

EXPLORING THE SOLAR SYSTEM

Since the beginning of space exploration in 1961, sophisticated probes have been sent to explore the solar system and bring back photographs of our nearest neighbors. More has been learnt about our home system in the last 30 years than over previous millennia.

ABOVE LEFT: Jupiter photographed from *Voyager I* in 1979.

ABOVE RIGHT: A thin coating of ice on Mars, recorded by *Viking Lander 2*.

RIGHT: Photomosaic of Mercury assembled from photographs taken by *Mariner 10*.

LEFT: The innermost of Jupiter's 16 moons, seen from *Voyager I*.

BELOW LEFT: Venus, seen as a crescent, from *Pioneer Venus I*.

BELOW RIGHT: Saturn photographed by the probe *Voyager 2* in 1980.

ABOVE: Salman Rushdie, Bombay-born author of *Midnight's Children*, a novel about the partition of India. Later in the decade he will incur the wrath of Muslim leader Ayatollah Khomeini.

MIDNIGHT'S CHILDREN

British novelist Salman Rushdie (b. 1947) publishes an epic novel, *Midnight's Children*. Telling the stories of characters born at the moment of India's independence, the novel shows Rushdie to be one of Britain's foremost novelists.

HEART-LUNG TRANSPLANT IS SUCCESSFUL

In California, Mary D. Golkhe receives the first successful transplant of a heart and a pair of lungs. Three earlier recipients of heart-lung transplants lived only a few days.

ENTER THE PC

U.S. firm IBM introduces its personal computer (the PC), using the Microsoft Disk Operating System (MS-DOS). It becomes a standard program throughout the computer industry.

REDS

U.S. film actor Warren Beatty (b. 1937) stars in, co-writes, and directs a new movie. *Reds* is the story of John Reed, journalist and founder-member of the American Communist party. The film is criticized for its disorganized structure, but is beautifully shot by Vittorio Storaro.

ABOVE: Dacca, Bangladesh, where President Zia ur-Rahman, leader of the Bangladesh Nationalist Party, is assassinated in May.

NEW MICROSCOPE

Physicists Gerd Binnig (b. 1947) of West Germany and Heinrich Roher of Switzerland invent the scanning tunnelling microscope, which can identify individual atoms.

AUSTRIAN STATE RADIO REGIONAL STUDIO

In Austria, Gustav Peichl has designed a new radio studio that combines the economical use of prefabricated concrete sections with striking high-tech elements such as polished chromium heating pipes.

ANTI-APARTHEID PROTESTS

Serious anti-apartheid demonstrations disrupt the South African rugby tour of New Zealand, which has been nicknamed the "Barbed Wire Tour." Similar angry protests had met the South Africans' visit to Great Britain in 1969.

CIVIL WAR IN LATIN AMERICA

Britain and Argentina go to war over ownership of the Falkland Islands. Israel drives the PLO out of Beirut and Christian Phalangists massacre Palestinian refugees. A state of emergency is declared in Nicaragua. Helmut Kohl becomes chancellor of Germany. The UN warns of destruction of the world's rainforests. Architecture adopts postmodernism, compact discs (CDs) appear on the market, and the U.S.S.R. puts a new space station into orbit.

1982

Mar	15	State of emergency declared in Nicaragua
Apr	2	Argentinian troops invade Falkland Islands (Malvinas)
	4	British Royal Navy task force sets sail for Falklands
	19	U.S.S.R. puts new space station into orbit
May	2	British submarine HMS *Conqueror* sinks Argentinian cruiser *General Belgrano*
	4	Argentinian missiles sink British destroyer HMS *Sheffield*
June	5	Israel invades Lebanon
	14	Argentinian forces surrender; Falklands War ends
July	23	International Whaling Commission votes for complete ban on whaling

Aug	30	Yasser Arafat and Palestinians leave Beirut
Sep	18	Palestinians massacred by Christian Phalangist militia
Oct	1	Helmut Kohl becomes chancellor, West Germany
	28	Socialists win election in Spain

LEFT: Helmut Kohl, the chancellor of West Germany.

FALKLANDS WAR

War breaks out between Argentina and Britain over ownership of the Falkland Islands. In April, the Argentinian junta under General Galtieri launches Operation Rosario and invades the Falkland Islands. The UN passes a resolution calling for Argentina to withdraw. A British task force is dispatched and, after a fierce conflict, Argentinian troops surrender and the islands are returned to Britain in June. Throughout the campaign, the British lose four warships and a container ship, and suffer 237 killed, as well as 18 civilians and 759 military personnel wounded. Argentina loses the battleship *Belgrano* and suffer more than 1,000 killed, including the crew of the *Belgrano*.

ISRAEL INVADES LEBANON

After an air bombardment Israeli forces invade Lebanon, headquarters of the Palestinian Liberation Organization (PLO) since its formation in 1964. Israeli and Syrian forces clash in southern Lebanon and Israeli forces surround 6,000 PLO guerrillas in West Beirut and demand their surrender. In July, Palestinian leader Yasser Arafat (b. 1929) offers to accept a UN Security Resolution recognizing Israel's right to exist in exchange for U.S. recognition of the PLO, but the United States refuses. By the end of August, the PLO has been driven out of Beirut.

EL SALVADOR

Civil war continues in El Salvador where, in 1980, human rights champion Oscar Romero was killed. Elections take place, accompanied by considerable violence, with left-wing parties refusing to participate. The Christian Democratic Party, headed by José Duarte, who has been president since 1980, is returned but is blocked by a coalition of right-wing parties.

ABOVE: A British Vulcan bomber plays its part in the Falklands conflict between Britain and Argentina.

PALESTINIANS MASSACRED

Following the assassination of Lebanese president-elect Bashir Gemayel, Christian Phalangists enter Palestinian refugee camps in West Beirut and kill more than 800 Palestinians.

SHINING PATH

In Peru, the Maoist guerrillas Sendero Luminoso (Shining Path), led by Dr. Renoso Guzman, become increasingly active, using terrorist tactics such as bombings and assassinations.

SOCIALISTS WIN IN SPAIN

In Spain, the Socialist Party of Felipe González (b. 1942) wins a landslide in the general election for the first time since the Civil War. He holds power until 1996.

INGRID BERGMAN
(1915–1982)

Swedish actress Ingrid Bergman has died. The English-speaking star (with Humphrey Bogart) of *Casablanca* (1942) had many other Hollywood successes during the 1940s. After a period in Europe she returned to Hollywood in 1956 to make *Anastasia* and *The Inn of Sixth Happiness* (1958). More recently she appeared on stage and television, and in Ingmar Bergman's film *Autumn Sonata* (1978).

ABOVE: Henry Fonda (with daughter Jane and Katharine Hepburn) wins his first and only Oscar for the film *On Golden Pond*.

KOHL BECOMES CHANCELLOR

The Social Democratic government of Helmut Schmidt falls and he is replaced as chancellor by the Christian Democrat Helmut Kohl (b. 1930), who holds power until 1998. Kohl does much to increase European unity in the EC, and to bring France and Germany closer.

NEW SOVIET SPACE STATION

The Soviet Union puts a new space station into orbit. It is *Salyut 7*, which replaces an earlier space station that has been in orbit for four years.

NICARAGUA

President Daniel Ortega (b. 1945) declares a state of emergency in Nicaragua, following guerrilla attacks on bridges and petroleum installations. Relations with the United States have deteriorated since Reagan became president, and U.S. aid to the country has been frozen since 1981. This year, the United States has begun actively attempting to destabilize the new Nicaraguan government by funding right-wing guerrillas known as Contras.

SOVIET LEADERS DIE

Soviet president Leonid Brezhnev dies, ushering in a period of weak leadership as two more leaders — Yuri Andropov and Konstantin Chernenko — both die within three years.

THE MARY ROSE IS RAISED

Archaeologists led by Margaret Rule raise the wreck of English king Henry VIII's warship *Mary Rose* to the surface off Portsmouth, England, after 437 years under water.

SHUTTLE LAUNCHES SATELLITE

The U.S. space shuttle *Columbia* carries two communications satellites in its cargo bay and puts them into orbit. The shuttle carries two specialists, who are not astronauts, as additional crew members.

CDS ARRIVE

Compact discs (CDs), which store sound digitally as microscopic pits and play it back with a laser beam, and CD players, go on sale. They are introduced by the Dutch company Philips and CBS/Sony of the United States.

FIRST LASER PRINTERS

The first laser printers for computers go on the market, produced by IBM.

POSTMODERN BUILDINGS

Designed by U.S. architect Michael Graves (b. 1934), the Portland Public Services Building in Oregon claims to be the first postmodern building. The colorful treatment of the façade, the play of patterns on the outer walls, and the use of ornamental statuary set this building apart from any other recent architectural project. A building in New York City, however, also claims to be post-modernism's "founding building." This is the AT&T Building designed by U.S. architects Philip Johnson and John Burgee. A highly controversial building, the skyscraper attracts immediate attention because of its enormous broken pediment, a historical allusion typical of the new style. It is nicknamed the "Chippendale skyscraper."

LEFT: The jubilant winning Italian soccer team hold the Jules Rimet trophy aloft after beating Germany to win the World Cup.

THE COLOR PURPLE

American writer Alice Walker (b. 1944) has published her first novel, *The Color Purple*. Walker's story of the life of an African-American woman will win her the Pulitzer Prize and international recognition.

THE HOUSE OF THE SPIRITS

Chilean writer Isabel Allende (b. 1942) gains international fame following the publication of her first novel, *The House of the Spirits*. A mixture of mythical elements and realism, the novel arose out of Allende's flight from Chile following the assassination of her uncle, Salvador Allende.

DESTRUCTION OF THE RAINFOREST

Environmentalists are concerned about the state of the world's rainforests after a UN environment program estimates that some 20 million acres of rainforest are being destroyed annually.

PAC-MAN FEVER

The Pac-Man computer game sweeps the America and Britain, becoming *Time* magazine's "Man of the Year."

ITALY WINS WORLD CUP

Italy wins the soccer World Cup for the third time at the final match staged in Spain. They beat Germany 3–1 in a disappointing final.

ABOVE: Russian premier Leonid Brezhnev dies and is buried in Moscow's Red Square. He is succeeded for a very short time by Yuri Andropov.

LEFT: Leader-in-waiting Mikhail Gorbachev; the death of Brezhnev begins the fall of the old guard and opens the way for liberalizers to come to power in the Soviet Union.

WHALING MORATORIUM

The International Whaling Commission agrees to a four-year moratorium on commercial whaling to begin 1985–86. However, catches made for scientific research continue, and much commercial whaling is disguised as "scientific."

CASA ROTONDA

Swiss-born architect Mario Botta's Casa Rotonda shows the flair of European architects for creating original forms. It is a cylindrically shaped house that plays inventively with volume.

GREENHAM WOMEN AND GERMAN GREENS

Civil war begins in Sri Lanka. A Soviet fighter shoots down a South Korean Boeing 747. Antinuclear protests take place throughout Europe against the siting of Cruise and Pershing missiles in Europe. German Greens win seats in the Bundestag. U.S. marines invade the island of Grenada. The AIDS virus is identified. A new device, the mouse, makes computer use easier. Steven Spielberg's film *ET*, starring a likeable extraterrestrial, becomes a smash hit.

OPPOSITE: Fiber optics, glass tubes which will revolutionize the telecommunications industry.

1983

Mar	23	U.S. president Reagan proposes new "Star Wars" defense system
July	27	Civil war in Sri Lanka between government and Tamil Tigers
Aug	21	Philippines opposition leader Benigno Aquino is assassinated
Sept	1	Soviet fighter shoots down South Korean Boeing 747
Oct	20	Speed of light redefined
	22	Antinuclear protests in Europe against siting of Cruise and Pershing missiles in Europe
	25	United States invades Grenada
Nov	28	European *Spacelab* goes into orbit
Dec	10	Raúl Alfonsín becomes president of Argentina

ABOVE: Boy George and his band Culture Club popularize gender-bending and crossdressing across the westernized world.

U.S.S.R. SHOOTS DOWN BOEING

A South Korean Boeing 747 civilian aircraft, flying over Sakhalin Island off the east coast of Siberia, is shot down by Soviet pilots. The 269 passengers all lose their lives; the U.S.S.R. claims the plane was on a spying mission. The attack increases tension between the U.S.S.R. and the West.

ANTINUCLEAR PROTESTS

Large antinuclear demonstrations take place in many European countries against the placing of U.S. Cruise and Pershing II missiles in Europe. The missiles increase the number of nuclear warheads in Europe and add to the arms race between the United States and Soviet Union. In Britain, women set up a permanent peace camp on Greenham Common, where 96 cruise missiles are to be located. The women established the camp in September 1981 and maintain a constant vigil for peace.

GERMAN GREENS

The Green Party (die Grünen) wins a 5.6% share of the vote in national elections to the Bundestag, so achieving its first representation in the German legislative chamber. Among those to win a seat is Petra Kelly (1947–92), environmentalist, antinuclear activist and cofounder of the Green Party. Since the European Green Party was formed in 1979, concerns about the environment and nuclear power have led to increasing support across Europe.

MILITARY RULE ENDS IN ARGENTINA

Raúl Alfonsín (b. 1927) becomes president of Argentina, ending eight years of military rule. The military's repressive measures affected all sections of society, but they have lost all authority since their defeat in the Falklands War in 1982.

UNITED STATES INVADES GRENADA

The presence of 1,000 U.S. students and a left-wing unelected government that had requested Cuban help with the construction of an international airport prompts the U.S. government to launch an invasion of the island of Grenada. Some 7,000 U.S. serviceman take two days to subdue a relatively untrained, ill-equipped and unsophisticated enemy. The Americans suffer 18 killed, 45 wounded; the Cubans 24 killed and 40 wounded; and the Grenadans 60 killed and 184 wounded.

MICE HELP KEYBOARDS

Apple Computer, Inc. introduces the computer mouse, a device that moves a pointer on screen and sends commands to the computer by the pressing of a button.

AQUINO ASSASSINATED

The opposition leader Benigno Aquino is assassinated at Manila airport as he returns from a three-year exile to fight the forthcoming general election. His death is widely blamed on the government of President Marcos, and fuels the opposition to his rule.

ABOVE: The Hummer or Humvee, a high-mobility multipurpose vehicle, replaces the faithful Jeep in the U.S. armed forces.

SRI LANKA

Civil war breaks out in Sri Lanka between government forces and northern Tamil separatists, the LiberationTigers of Tamil Eelam (LTTE), based in the Jaffna peninsula. It continues into the 1990s.

AIDS VIRUS IDENTIFIED

Researchers in France discover the virus that causes AIDS. It is labelled HIV-1, the Human Immune Deficiency Virus; U.S. researchers confirm the finding the following year. There is some doubt about who is first to identify the virus but certainty that AIDS itself is likely to become an epidemic.

"IMPROVED" PETUNIAS

Scientists in Germany and the United States transfer genes from a bacterium into cells from petunias, producing plants that are resistant to antibiotics.

FURTHER INTO SPACE

The European-built space laboratory *Spacelab* is put into orbit by the U.S. shuttle *Columbia*. In June, *Pioneer 10*, launched in 1972, becomes the first space probe to pass through the asteroid belt and travel beyond the solar system.

ET

US filmmaker Steven Spielberg (b. 1946) releases a new film, *ET*. A delightfully sentimental tale of an alien who visits Earth, it becomes a major box-office earner. Much of the film is cleverly shot from the eye-level of the ten-year-old boy who is the central character.

WORST EL NINO

Oceanographers report that the El Niño spell of extra-warm water along the coast of South America, which began in 1982, is the most intense ever recorded. It causes floods and droughts in many parts of the world.

ABOVE: U.S. troops on the ground during the two-day invasion of the tiny island of Grenada.

LEFT: The 82nd Airborne Division poised to land.

BELOW: A combined Marine and Army patrol during Operation Urgent Fury, the U.S. invasion of Grenada. The servicemen in the background are seated in a captured Soviet-built UAZ-469B light vehicle.

ADVANCES IN MEDICAL SCIENCE

Technological advances, partly developed for the space program, are successfully applied to the field of medicine. Computers, lasers, electronics, and nuclear science all take their place in diagnosis and surgical treatment.

RIGHT: Microsurgery uses powerful magnifying glasses, laser-guided instruments, and video screens for complex work.

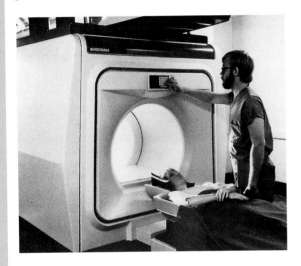

ABOVE: The Nuclear Magnetic Resonance Scanner is used to detect damage to, or cancers in, the bones and spine.

BELOW: Electrodes linked to a computer monitor the heart's rhythm and indicate any disruption to the patient's normal pattern.

TALKING CAMERA

The Minolta Company introduces a 35mm camera which "talks" to the user, warning of problems before the next shot.

SPEED OF LIGHT REDEFINED

An international committee redefines the speed of light as exactly 983,571,000 feet per second.

FASHIONABLE GENDER-BENDING

Gender-bending — sexually indeterminate dressing and lifestyle — becomes a fashionable youth subculture in America and Britain with the success of rock bands such as Culture Club, led by a gay singer, Boy George.

ARTIFICIAL HEART

Retired dentist Barney B. Clark, the first patient to be given an artificial Jarvik heart, dies after 112 days. The artificial heart does not fail but other organs do. The operation was carried out last year at the University of Utah. The artificial heart is made of plastic and metal and known as a Jarvik heart after its inventor, Robert Jarvik. It is to become useful as an interim measure while people wait for a suitable donor heart.

BALTHAZAR JOHANNES (JOHN) VORSTER
(1915–1983)

The Afrikaner Nationalist South African prime minister from 1966 to 1978, John Vorster, has died. He served as minister of justice during Hendrik Verwoerd's government (1961–66) and became prime minister after the former's assassination, continuing to enforce apartheid. He was forced to resign his position as state president in 1979 when found guilty of misappropriation of government funds.

ABOVE: The remains of the barracks at Beirut Airport, where 241 U.S. Marines die in a terrorist bomb attack. The Marines are in Lebanon to help keep the peace between Israel and Palestine.

THE MASK OF ORPHEUS

British composer Harrison Birtwistle (b. 1934) retells the Orpheus myth in his new opera. As well as the traditional language of opera (voices and instruments), Birtwistle uses taped musical inserts of harp chords dissected, analyzed and replayed by a computer to create rhythms faster and more complex than a human player could achieve.

AUSTRALIA WINS AMERICA'S CUP

Australia wins the America's Cup from the United States for the first time since 1851. John Betterand captained the Australian yachting challenge in *Australia II*, defeating Dennis Conner's *Liberty*.

RIGHT: Everybody's favorite alien, ET the extraterrestrial, star of Spielberg's box office success, *ET*.

THE CHALLENGER ACHIEVEMENT

More than a decade after the first moon-shot, the United States launches the space shuttle, a two-component vehicle comprising a rocket and an orbiter which can return to Earth. The first of the orbiters is the *Challenger*, launched in 1981 and in service until 1986. The idea is to carry out commercial, military, and scientific research. A major feature of the shuttle trips is the space walk, where astronauts leave the orbiter to carry out maintenance or construction work.

RIGHT: Astronauts F. Story Musgrave and Donald H. Peterson practice setting up a winch operation on the aft bulkhead.

BELOW: The astronauts spend almost four hours outside the *Challenger* as she orbits the Earth.

ABOVE: On a 1984 shuttle trip, astronaut Bruce McCandless II tests out the nitrogen-propelled, hand-controlled device called the Manned Maneuvering Unit (MMU), which allows great mobility. Previous spacewalkers were restricted by tethers, tying them to the mother ship.

LEFT: On a 1985 mission astronauts Sherwood C. Spring and Jerry L. Ross practice the assembling of components outside the shuttle.

AMRITSAR, BHOPAL, AND ACID RAIN

Sikh nationalists are massacred at the Golden Temple, Amritsar. Indian prime minister Indira Gandhi is assassinated in revenge. In Britain, the IRA bombs the Conservative Party Conference as part of a sustained campaign to get British troops out of Northern Ireland. Nations in Ottawa pledge to reduce carbon dioxide emissions, the source of acid rain, and toxic gas kills more than 2,000 in India. Women walk in space and Archbishop Tutu receives the Nobel Peace Prize.

1984

Feb	9	Soviet president Andropov dies. He is succeeded by Chernenko
	11	Iraq bombs nonmilitary targets in Iran
Apr	20	Demonstrations in West Germany against deployment of U.S. missiles in Europe
May	10	International Court of Justice at The Hague rules United States should end blockade of Nicaraguan ports
	10	Danish parliament votes to suspend payments to NATO as protest against siting of Pershing II and Cruise missiles in Europe
	24	Iranian warplanes attack oil tankers off coast of Saudi Arabia
June	6	Sikh nationalists killed when Indian troops storm Golden Temple, Amritsar

July	28	The 23rd Olympic Games open in Los Angeles
Aug	4	Tamils and Sinhalese clash in Sri Lanka
Sep	26	Britain agrees to hand over Hong Kong to China
Oct	12	IRA bombs Conservative Party Conference, Brighton, England
	31	Indian prime minister Indira Gandhi is assassinated
Nov	4	Sandanista Front win Nicaraguan elections
Dec	3	Toxic gas leak in Bhopal, India, kills and injures thousands

ABOVE: Mourners and the dead in Bhopal, the Indian city devastated by the leak of poisonous gas from the Union Carbide factory.

ABOVE: Ronald Reagan in Congress. The ex-actor has already served one term as president and this year is reelected for a second term.

LEFT: Indira Gandhi, the prime minister of India, with the Sikh bodyguard who later assassinates her.

GOLDEN TEMPLE MASSACRE

In June members of the Sikh nationalist group the Akali Dal seize the Golden Temple, Amritsar, India, in an attempt to establish an independent Sikh state called Khalistan. The Golden Temple is one of the Sikhs' holiest places. The Indian government launches an attack and troops storm and seize the temple. Fighting is fierce: Official figures give 493 nationalists and 83 soldiers killed. In October, the Indian prime minister Indira Gandhi is assassinated by her Sikh bodyguards, in revenge for the storming of the Golden Temple. Mrs. Gandhi's son Rajiv (1944–91) succeeds her to the premiership. The assassination provokes a Hindu backlash in which some 3,000 Sikhs are massacred.

BRIGHTON BOMBING

The IRA bomb the Conservative Party Conference in Brighton, England, narrowly avoiding killing prime minister Margaret Thatcher and her cabinet. Two people are killed and many injured in the blast, which wrecks the hotel they are staying in. The bomb is part of a sustained campaign by the IRA on the British mainland to force a British withdrawal from Northern Ireland.

FRANCOIS TRUFFAUT
(1932–1984)

The *nouvelle vague* French film director and critic François Truffaut has died. His first full-length film *Les Quatre Cents Coups* (1959) immediately made his reputation, and he consolidated this in 1962 with *Jules et Jim*. Many of his films form a loosely connected series featuring the actor Jean-Pierre Leaud, the boy hero of *Les Quatre Cents Coups*.

POISON GAS LEAK IN BHOPAL

Some 2,500 people are killed and thousands more injured when toxic gas escapes from the American-owned Union Carbide plant outside Bhopal, Madhya Pradesh, India. The leak is caused by the failure of two safety systems. Bhopal is declared a disaster zone.

BELOW: The blasted façade of the Grand Hotel, Brighton, where the IRA nearly succeeds in destroying the Conservative party.

ABOVE: The Anglo-French supersonic aircraft Concorde continues to fly the Atlantic in spite of protests by environmental activists.

HONG KONG TO BE RETURNED

Britain agrees to hand back Hong Kong to China in 1997. The 99-year lease on the New Territories runs out in 1997, making the rest of the colony unviable when they are returned to China. In the agreement, Hong Kong will be allowed to keep its capitalist system for at least 50 years and have considerable internal autonomy.

WALK IN SPACE

In June, Soviet cosmonaut Svetlana Savitskaya becomes the first woman to walk in space. She is followed in October by U.S. astronaut Kathryn D. Sullivan, who also walks in space.

FIRST CD-ROMS

Philips and Sony adapt the compact disc for computers, producing the first CD-ROMS (Compact Disc Read-Only Memory) for storing data.

OCEAN DRILLING

Eleven countries launch a ten-year program of drilling to explore the continental shelves, parts of the continents that lie under the sea.

STAATSGALERIE EXTENSION

British architects James Stirling and Michael Wilford create their own muted version of postmodernism (with classical details and primary colors) for this art gallery extension in Stuttgart, Germany.

ACID RAIN PLEDGE

Ten nations meet in Ottawa and pledge to reduce sulphur dioxide emissions by 30 percent to reduce acid rain, which has been found to be contaminating lakes and rivers and destroying forests in much of North America and Europe. Only in 1983 was it discovered to be caused by pollutants in the smoke from power stations and some factories.

JORDAN SELECTED

The Chicago Bulls select Brooklyn-born Michael Jordan (b. 1963), third in the basketball draft of college players.

LINDOW MAN FOUND

The remains of an Iron Age man are discovered preserved in a peat bog at Lindow Marsh, Cheshire, England; he appears to be the victim of a religious sacrifice.

OLYMPIC GAMES

The 23rd Olympics are held in Los Angeles. Many Communist countries boycott the games, which are the first to be privately financed, in retaliation for U.S. withdrawal in 1980. American sprinter Carl Lewis (b. 1961) achieves star status as he repeats Jesse Owens' haul of four golds. The women's marathon is an official Olympic event for the first time and is won by U.S. athlete Joan Benoit. Windsurfing, won by Holland's Stephen van den Berg, and synchronized swimming also become Olympic sports.

TUTU WINS NOBEL PRIZE

South African Anglican bishop and campaigner against apartheid Bishop Desmond Tutu (b. 1931) is awarded the Nobel Peace Prize. In 1985 he becomes the first black bishop of Johannesburg.

INDIRA PRIYAD ARSHINI GANDHI (1917–1984)

Indian prime minister Indira Gandhi has been assassinated by one of her guards. The daughter of Jawaharlal Nehru, she was educated partly at Oxford and was always politically active in the Congress party. She became prime minister in 1966 and lost her seat after a period of political upheaval in 1977. She was reelected in 1980.

PERESTROIKA AND LIVE AID

Mikhail Gorbachev becomes the new leader of the Soviet Union. He promises reforms. Ethiopia suffers the worst-ever recorded famine. Millions contribute to famine aid through massive Live Aid rock concerts. Greenpeace ship *Rainbow Warrior* is sunk in New Zealand by French agents. The death of Rock Hudson stimulates awareness of the AIDS epidemic. Scientists discover a hole in the ozone layer. The wreck of the *Titanic* is found. English soccer clubs are banned from Europe competitions.

1 9 8 5

Feb	8	ANC leader Nelson Mandela refuses offer of freedom, conditional on his renouncing violence
Mar	10	Soviet president Chernenko dies
	11	Mikhail Gorbachev becomes leader of the Soviet Union
	21	South African police fire on crowds on the 25th anniversary of the Sharpeville Massacre
Apr	11	Ramiz Alia becomes leader of Albania following death of Enver Hoxha
May	1	United States imposes trade sanctions on Nicaragua
	1	Solidarity supporters clash with police, Poland
	10	Sikh nationalists bomb Indian cities
July	11	Greenpeace ship *Rainbow Warrior* sunk in Auckland, New Zealand

July	18	Organization of African Unity holds conference in Addis Ababa; it announces that most African countries are on verge of economic collapse
Sep	2	Pol Pot resigns as leader of Khmer Rouge
	17	More than 2,000 die after earthquake, Mexico City
Oct	1	Israel attacks PLO headquarters, Tunis
	2	U.S. film star Rock Hudson dies of AIDS
Nov	15	Anglo-Irish Agreement signed giving Republic of Ireland consultative role in Northern Ireland
	29	Black union leaders form new trade union COSATU, South Africa

GORBACHEV PROMISES REFORM

Following the death of Konstantin Chernenko, Mikhail Gorbachev (b. 1931) becomes leader of the Soviet Union. He begins to reform the Communist system, promising *glasnost* (openness) and *perestroika* (restructuring).

ALBANIA OPENS UP

Enver Hoxha, leader of Albania since 1945, dies. His country had been isolated from the rest of Eastern Europe, taking its lead from China rather than the U.S.S.R., and is the poorest country in Europe. Slowly, the new government of Ramiz Alia (b. 1925) begins to end Albania's international isolation.

ABOVE: Tragedy in the Heysel Stadium, Brussels, as fans of soccer teams Liverpool and Juventus are crushed in a prematch brawl.

ANGLO-IRISH AGREEMENT

British prime minister Margaret Thatcher and Irish prime minister Garret Fitzgerald (b. 1926) sign the Anglo-Irish Agreement, which gives Ireland a consultative role in the running of Northern Ireland for the first time. The agreement is designed to counter the campaign of the IRA and to begin the process of finding a solution to the long-running troubles in Northern Ireland.

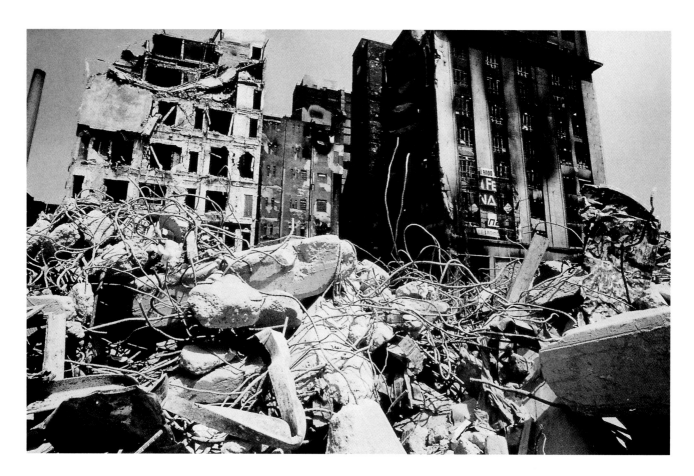

ABOVE: Ruins in Mexico City after the earthquake that hits the area in this year. Over 2,000 people are killed.

LIVE AID

Mass famine in Ethiopia leads Irish rock star Bob Geldof (b. 1954) to organize Live Aid, massive rock concerts, held in London and Philadelphia, to raise money for famine relief. Stars, who play for free, include Dire Straits, David Bowie, Queen, and Mick Jagger. The concerts raise $60 million and do much to raise the world's consciousness about famine and poverty in Africa. The famine in Ethiopia, which began in 1981 after drought and prolonged civil war, is the world's worst as recorded last year by film cameramen.

GEORGE ORSON WELLES
(1915–1985)

American film director and actor Orson Welles has died. His 1941 film *Citizen Kane*, in which he also starred, is greatly admired by film buffs, and his other work includes highly regarded films such as *The Magnificent Ambersons* (1942) and *Touch of Evil* (1958) (both cut and amended by the studio without his consent). As an actor Welles also leaves his famous performance as Harry Lime in *The Third Man* (1949). He will further be remembered for his panic-causing radio production of *War of the Worlds* in 1938.

KURDS ATTACK TURKEY

The Kurdistan Popular Liberation Army, formerly the Kurdish Worker's Party (KKK), begins military operations against the Turkish government.

RAINBOW WARRIOR SUNK

French secret agents sink the Greenpeace ship *Rainbow Warrior* in Auckland harbor, New Zealand. Environmental group Greenpeace sent the ship to the South Pacific to attempt to disrupt French nuclear tests on Mururoa Atoll, which are heavily criticized by all nations in the region.

OZONE HOLE DISCOVERED

Scientists of the British Antarctic Survey announce the discovery of a hole in the ozone layer over Antarctica. The discovery increases anxiety about global warming caused by carbon dioxide emissions.

AIDS EPIDEMIC

The World Health Organization (WHO) declares AIDS an epidemic. American film star Rock Hudson becomes the first celebrity to die of the disease, making people in the West more aware of its rapid spread.

BUCKYBALLS

U.S. chemist Richard E. Smalley makes new carbon molecules consisting of 60 atoms forming a hollow sphere. They are called buckminsterfullerenes, or buckyballs for short, after the inventor of the geodesic dome, R. Buckminster Fuller.

TITANIC LOCATED

Video cameras aboard an underwater search vessel locate the wreck of the liner *Titanic*, sunk in 1912, on the floor of the North Atlantic Ocean. The wreck is discovered off the Newfoundland coast in 13,200 feet of water.

GENETIC FINGERPRINTING

A team of British scientists led by Alec Jeffreys develops genetic fingerprinting, based on the fact that parts of the genetic code are unique to each person.

WOMEN'S RIGHTS

An international conference on women's rights takes place in Nairobi, Kenya; 10,000 women attend.

NATURAL DISASTERS

A massive earthquake hits Mexico City and kills 2,000. In Bangladesh, a cyclone and tidal wave kill 10,000.

YOUNG CHESS CHAMPION

The Russian Gary Kasparov (b. 1963) beats Anatoly Karpov (b. 1951), world champion and a fellow Russian, in one of the longest-running chess matches, to become the youngest-ever world chess champion.

RAN

Japanese film director Akira Kurosawa's *Ran* opens. A version of *King Lear*, set in 16th-century Japan, the film impresses audiences with its big set-piece battle scenes and strong characterization.

DEER FOR CHINA

Père David's deer, which became extinct in China in 1921, are sent to China from England, where they have been bred in captivity since 1894.

MARC CHAGALL
(1887–1985)

Little short of his centenary, the Russian-born Franco-Jewish painter Marc Chagall has died. He moved to France in 1922 and lived there for most of his life. He designed for the Ballets Russes and produced theatre posters, book illustrations and stained glass, as well as his many paintings. His style has been terms "fantastic art".

MAHABHARATA

English director Peter Brook (b. 1925) and French writer Jean-Claude Carrière (b. 1931) have produced a theatrical version of myths from the Hindu epic the *Mahabharata*. The production gains further recognition for Brook's Paris-based theatrical company, Les Bouffes du Nord.

ENGLISH SOCCER CLUBS BANNED

English soccer is devastated by two horrific events. In the northern town of Bradford, 56 die when an old wooden stand burns to the ground. Then at the European Cup Final between Liverpool and Juventus in the Heysel Stadium in Brussels, Belgium, 39 supporters of Turin club Juventus are crushed to death trying to get away from attacking Liverpool fans. English clubs are banned from European competitions and the tragedies force the English authorities to tackle hooliganism and the dilapidated state of English stadiums.

BELOW: The sinking hulk of *Rainbow Warrior*, the Greenpeace protest ship sunk in New Zealand by the French secret service.

STAR WARS

"Star Wars" is the nickname given to the Strategic Defense Initiative launched by President Ronald Reagan in 1983, which was to last as a research and development project for a decade. The plan is to devise a missile that can seek, catch, and destroy enemy missiles before they reach their target. Reagan sees it as the primary weapon in the battle against the "Evil Empire," his description of the Communist world.

LEFT: An artist's impression of a space-based nuclear power source to fuel the Star Wars missile, seen with its launcher, above.

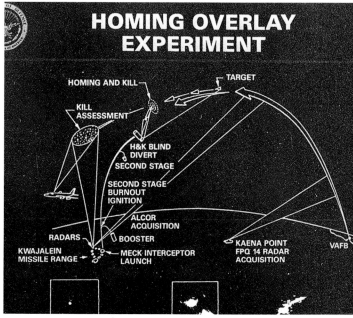

ABOVE: The tracker component of the project, which seeks and finds enemy intercontinental ballistic missiles.

ABOVE: Diagram to show how the Star Wars missiles would intercept the enemy and what ground support would be needed.

ABOVE: The Killl Mechanism of the Star Wars missile. A non-explosive "warhead," its metal ribs are wrapped around the neck of the defense missile during flight and unfurl seconds before impact. The force of the collision destroys the enemy missile.

RIGHT: The Airborne Optical Adjunct (AOA) is developed to optically identify and track warhead targets and to guide ground-based interceptors.

CHERNOBYL — NUCLEAR EXPLOSION

A major nuclear accident occurs at Chernobyl in the Soviet Union. Radioactive gas spreads across Europe. U.S. space shuttle *Challenger* explodes seconds after takeoff. Mrs. Corazon Aquino topples Marcos in the Philippines. "Baby Doc" is overthrown in Haiti. The United States launches air strikes against Libya. New architectural landmarks include the Hong Kong Bank and Lloyds Building. Canadian author Margaret Atwood publishes a chilling feminist dystopia. And Halley's Comet returns.

OPPOSITE: The space shuttle *Challenger* explodes on takeoff, killing all aboard.

1986

Jan	1	Spain and Portugal join the EC
	25	Gorbachev announces 25-year plan for elimination of nuclear weapons
	28	U.S. space shuttle *Challenger* explodes
Feb	7	Haitian president Jean-Claude Duvalier flees to France
	9	Halley's Comet makes closest approach to the Sun
	24	Marcos flees Philippines; Corazon Aquino sworn in as president
	28	Olaf Palme, Sweden's prime minister, is assassinated
Apr	11	Brian Keenan, lecturer in Beirut, is taken hostage
	15	U.S. bombers from British bases attack Libya
	17	John McCarthy, acting bureau chief for Worldwide Television, Beirut, is taken hostage
Apr	26	Major nuclear accident occurs at Chernobyl, Soviet Union
June	12	President Botha declares state of emergency in South Africa
	20	Conference in Paris of 120 nations calls for sanctions against South Africa because of its apartheid policies
July	29	Argentina wins World Cup in Mexico
Aug	21	Toxic gas kills 1,700 in northern Cameroon
Oct	19	President Machel of Mozambique and other government officials are killed in an air crash
	20	Israeli nuclear technician Mordechai Vanunu kidnapped in London after revealing nuclear secrets. He is held in Israel

ABOVE: The map used by Caspar Weinberger, Secretary of Defense, at a White House briefing to the U.S. Air Force during the Libyan action.

RIGHT: A Libyan patrol boat on guard in the Gulf of Sidra during the U.S. raids on Libya in retaliation for terrorist attacks on their troops in mainland Europe.

JORGE LUIS BORGES
(1899–1986)

The highly regarded Argentine writer Jorge Luis Borges has died. His work consists mostly of essays or short narratives which engage the reader in the labyrinths of his complex metaphysical and multidimensional inventions. Because of increasing blindness he has dictated his ever-briefer essays since 1953. He was director of the Argentine National Library from 1955. The best-known collection of his works in Europe is *Labyrinths* (1962).

SIMONE DE BEAUVOIR
(1908–1986)

French writer and feminist Simone de Beauvoir, author of *The Second Sex*, has died. She was the fiercely independent companion of Jean-Paul Sartre and collaborated with him in producing the socialist paper *Les Temps Modernes* after the war. Her many published works include novels and autobiographical writings, and *Adieu: A Farewell to Sartre* (1984), about the last ten years of Sartre's life.

HAITIAN DICTATOR OVERTHROWN
The self-styled ruler for life of Haiti, Jean-Claude Duvalier, known as "Baby Doc," son of the dictator "Papa Doc," is toppled from power. Between them they have ruled the impoverished island since 1957, with the help of the dreaded Tonton Macoutes secret police. Duvalier flees to France, taking his considerable looted wealth with him. A military government takes over.

CHERNOBYL DISASTER
A nuclear power station at Chernobyl in Ukraine, Soviet Union, explodes causing a radioactive cloud to drift over northern Europe. Although a full meltdown and nuclear catastrophe are avoided, radioactive contamination in the area kills and maims many people. It is estimated that many thousands may die in the future.

STATE OF EMERGENCY IN SOUTH AFRICA
President Botha declares a state of emergency in South Africa as the government prepares for major anti-apartheid demonstrations on the tenth anniversary of the Soweto uprising. The move is criticized internationally and increases opposition to the white-only government among the black population.

EC MEMBERS
Spain and Portugal join the European Community as its 11th and 12th members.

UNITED STATES STRIKES LIBYA
Following the death of U.S. servicemen in a bomb attack on Berlin, the United States names Libya as responsible for the act and launch an air strike against Libya, destroying military installations around Tripoli and Benghazi. Some of the U.S. aircraft leave from British bases.

MACHEL KILLED
President Samora Machel of Mozambique and 28 government officials are killed in an air crash. South Africa is suspected, as part of its policy of destabilizing its black neighbors in order to weaken their opposition to the apartheid government.

CHALLENGER EXPLODES
The U.S. space shuttle *Challenger* explodes at Cape Canaveral just 73 seconds after takeoff. The explosion, which is seen by millions on television, kills all seven members of the crew and is the worst space disaster to date. Failure of rubber seals on a fuel line is blamed.

SPACE STATION MIR
The Soviet Union puts space station *Mir* into orbit around the Earth; it continues to function until the end of the century.

BELOW: Chernobyl power station, U.S.S.R., three days after the worst nuclear accident the world has yet seen.

ABOVE: Mrs. Corazon Aquino (left) is sworn in as president of the Philippines. Her mother-in-law stands by her side.

HONG KONG BANK
British architect Norman Foster (b. 1935) designs a remarkable new building, the Hong Kong Bank. The structure is radical with the main elements supported on eight great masts and the floors hung from horizontal reinforcing struts. The structure is clearly visible from the outside, and gives the bank its distinctive lines.

AQUINO TAKES POWER IN PHILIPPINES
Mrs. Corazon Aquino (b. 1933), widow of the assassinated opposition leader, overthrows President Ferdinand Marcos. This follows mass demonstrations forcing him from office after he blatantly rigs the presidential election held in February.

LLOYD'S BUILDING
The new Lloyd's Building in London, designed by architect Richard Rogers, is dominated by its shining steel-clad stair towers and its vast 12-story glass hall. Brightly illuminated at night, the building becomes a new London landmark.

THE HANDMAID'S TALE
Canadian author Margaret Atwood (b. 1939) publishes a groundbreaking new novel. A feminist dystopia, it imagines a world in which fertile women become baby-producers for those who cannot have their own.

HALLEY'S COMET RETURNS
In February, Halley's Comet, returning after 76 years, makes its closest approach to the Sun. The space probe *Giotto* gets to within 373 miles of the nucleus and records valuable data.

ARGENTINA WINS WORLD CUP
The 52 games of the Mexico soccer World Cup draw 2.5 million spectators to the stadiums. Argentina triumphs in the final with a 3–2 win over Germany.

NEWS FROM URANUS
Space probe *Voyager 2* flies close to Uranus and sends back pictures of the planet; it discovers two more rings and ten more moons.

BELOVED
A new novel by American author Toni Morrison (b. 1931) has been published. Entitled *Beloved*, it tells the (true) story of a runaway slave who kills her daughter when she is about to be recaptured, to save her from a life of slavery. It wins the author the Pulitzer Prize.

A "NEW" DINOSAUR
The fossilized bones of a huge flesh-eating dinosaur, previously unknown, are discovered by an amateur palaeontologist, William Walker, in a clay pit in southern England.

ROUND THE WORLD NONSTOP
Pilots Richard D. Rutan and Jeana Yeager fly round the world nonstop without refuelling, in *Voyager*, an experimental aircraft. The journey takes nine days.

PORTABLE PHONES
The first portable telephones appear. Although the size of a briefcase, they are an improvement on the first battery-operated cordless telephone of the late 1960s.

REFUGEES

Conflicts and unrest all over the world result in huge numbers of refugees. Governments, charities, and aid agencies have their work cut out to feed, shelter, and reestablish people uprooted by political, military, and climatic circumstances beyond their control.

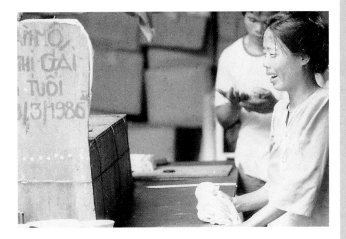

LEFT: Afghani refugees in Iran collect water from a traditional irrigation system, the *khanat*.

ABOVE: "Boat people," refugees from South Vietnam, rescued from the South China Sea.

BELOW: An Afghani refugee in the settlement at Nazdasht, Iran, is able to maintain her pastoral way of life.

BELOW: Sumo and Miskito refugees being repatriated from Honduras (where they had fled in 1981) to Nicaragua.

ABOVE: Afghani refugees at Peshawar, Pakistan, sitting it out until they can return to their homeland.

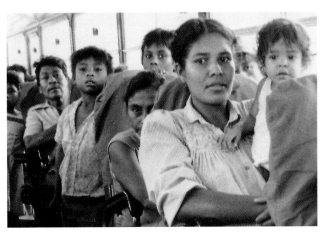

U.S. AND U.S.S.R. END ARMS RACE

The United States and the Soviet Union sign a treaty agreeing to eliminate intermediate-range nuclear weapons. British envoy Terry Waite is taken hostage in Beirut. Under the Montreal Protocol, 70 nations agree to limit the production of CFCs. Irangate causes a scandal in the United States. The UN begins a peace mission to end the Iran–Iraq war. Work begins on an Anglo-French Channel Tunnel. Van Gogh's painting *Irises* fetches an all-time record price.

OPPOSITE: The particle beam fusion accelerator, capable of generating 100 trillion watts of power.

1987

Jan 20 Archbishop's envoy Terry Waite is taken hostage in Beirut

Feb 5 Iran launches missile attack on Baghdad, Iraq

26 Tower Commission reports on Iran-Contra scandal

Mar 6 Cross-channel ferry capsizes off coast of Belgium

Apr 17 Tamils ambush buses, Sri Lanka

May 17 Iraqi Exocet missile hits USS *Stark* in Persian Gulf

Sep 11 UN Secretary-General Pérez de Cuéllar begins peace mission to end Iran-Iraq war

Oct 16 Hurricane sweeps across southeast England, the worst storm in Britain for 300 years

Nov 2 Soviet leader Gorbachev criticizes Stalin in a speech marking the 70th anniversary of the Russian Revolution.

8 IRA bombs explode at Armistice Day services, Enniskillen, Co. Fermanagh, Northern Ireland. Eleven killed

Dec 7 INF Treaty: U.S. president Reagan and Soviet leader Gorbachev agree to eliminate intermediate nuclear weapons

ABOVE: *Irises* by Vincent van Gogh (1853–90) sells for $48 million. Art has now become an investment commodity.

WAITE TAKEN HOSTAGE
Terry Waite (b. 1939), personal envoy of the Archbishop of Canterbury sent to Lebanon to negotiate the freedom of Western hostages in the country, is himself taken hostage by Hezbollah in Lebanon. Between 1983 and 1992, nearly 100 Westerners are grabbed off the streets of Beirut and held hostage for as long as seven years in guarded, underground cells throughout Lebanon.

IRANGATE
The profit from arms sent to Iran as part of a deal to free U.S. hostages in Lebanon is being used to support the right-wing Contra rebels fighting against the Nicaraguan government, contrary to the decision of U.S. Congress to stop supporting the Contras. The full extent of the Irangate conspiracy is revealed in the report of the Tower Commission set up to investigate the affair. The Tower Commission finds that President Reagan did not deliberately mislead the American people but seems to be unaware of important aspects of the operation.

INF TREATY
The Soviet Union and the United States sign an historic agreement to remove and dismantle all short- and intermediate-range nuclear weapons. The treaty requires the destruction of 1,752 Soviet and 859 U.S. missiles with ranges from 300 to 3,400 miles.

THE LAST EMPEROR
A new film by Italian Bernardo Bertolucci (b. 1940) has opened. *The Last Emperor* tells the story of the last Manchu ruler. A roaring success with both audiences and critics, it wins nine Oscars in 1988.

SCHINKELPLATZ
Architect Rob Krier uses a muted style, combining classical and traditional details, to produce housing in Berlin on a human scale to blend in with older buildings nearby.

TOP PRICE FOR IRISES
The painting *Irises* by Van Gogh fetches $48 million, a world record for art of all types. It confirms that he is the artist most in demand by international collectors. Three years later, in 1990, Van Gogh tops even this price when his *Portrait of Dr Gachet* fetches $80 million.

ZEEBRUGGE DISASTER
On March 6 a cross-channel ferry capsizes off Zeebrugge, Belgium; 187 people die. It later transpires that the bow doors were left open.

COMPUTER COMPATABILITY
Apple Computer, Inc. announces new Macintosh machines that can use software designed for the rival IBM machines.

ENTER SMART CARDS
A new type of credit card, the Smart Card, is introduced. It contains electronic chips, a tiny keyboard and display, and can process and store data.

CFC BAN AGREED
Seventy nations sign a protocol in Montreal to maintain use of CFCs (chlorofluorocarbons) at 1986 levels and to reduce levels by half by 1999. CFCs are believed to have caused a 90 percent thinning of the ozone layer over Antarctica. Ozone gas filters out harmful radiation from the Sun.

CHANNEL TUNNEL
Work on boring a tunnel under the English Channel between England and France begins on the English side. Work on the French side begins a year later.

A STAR EXPLODES
Astronomers in the southern hemisphere see a supernova (an exploding star) in a nearby galaxy.

USING GENETICS AGAINST CRIME
Genetic fingerprinting is first used in Britain to convict a criminal. The technique was developed in 1985 by Alec Jeffreys of the University of Leicester, who found that each person's core sequence of DNA is unique and can be used to determine family relationships.

DIGITAL TAPES
Digital audio tapes, which produce high-quality sound, go on sale. They are introduced by Aiwa in Japan.

RUGBY UNION
New Zealand wins the Webb Ellis Trophy in the inaugural Rugby Union World Cup, played in Australia and New Zealand. The All Blacks beat France 29–9 in the final of the 16-team event.

ANDY WARHOL
(1926–1987)

American artist and filmmaker Andy Warhol has died. One of the leading exponents of pop art, his early days as a commercial designer may have influenced his silkscreen-produced repeated images of cans of soup and a photographic image of Marilyn Monroe. His avant-garde film factory in Greenwich Village produced works such as *Chelsea Girls* (1967). In 1968 his real life became much more eventful than his films when he was shot and seriously injured by the radical feminist Valerie Solanas.

FRED ASTAIRE
(1899–1987)

The inimitable American dancer, actor, and singer Fred Astaire (real name Frederick Austerlitz) has died. After 1920s Broadway successes with his sister Adele, he moved on to Hollywood when she married Lord Charles Cavendish. He had several dancing partners but the best-known was Ginger Rogers. They danced together with apparently effortless grace in *The Gay Divorcee* (1934), *Top Hat* (1935), *Swing Time* (1936), and seven others. Despite his "retirement" in 1946 he continued to make musicals, and to act on screen until the late 1970s.

BUSH AND BHUTTO COME TO POWER

Ethnic and regional unrest begins in the Baltic states. Chilean dictator Pinochet steps down, clearing the way for democracy to return to Chile. A terrorist bomb explodes on a jumbo jet over Lockerbie, Scotland. The United States shoots down an Iranian airbus by accident. Drugs dominate the Seoul Olympics. Benazir Bhutto becomes the first Islamic woman prime minister. U.S. climatologist warns that the "greenhouse effect" has begun.

OPPOSITE: Benazir Bhutto, the first woman prime minister of Pakistan.

1988

Jan	26	Australia celebrates 200th anniversary of arrival of white settlers. Aborigines hold protests and declare it a time of mourning
Feb	13	Winter Olympics in Calgary, Canada
Mar	13	Seikan Tunnel opens, linking islands of Honshu and Hokkaido, Japan
May	13	Soviet troops begin withdrawal from Afghanistan
July	3	USS Vincennes shoots down an Iranian airbus
	6	Oil rig Piper Alpha explodes, killing 290 people
	18	Nelson Mandela's 70th birthday; the event is marked by worldwide calls for his release
Aug	8	Iran-Iraq ceasefire ends eight years of war
Sep	17	Olympic Games open in Seoul, South Korea
Oct	3	Chad and Libya formally end war that has been going on since 1965
	6	Chilean dictator General Pinochet steps down after losing referendum
Nov	8	Republican George Bush wins U.S. presidential elections
	16	Estonian parliament votes to give itself rights to veto laws from Moscow
Dec	2	Benazir Bhutto is sworn in as prime minister of Pakistan
	7	Soviet leader Mikhail Gorbachev announces plans to reduce Red Army
	21	Pan Am Flight 103 jumbo jet is blown up over Lockerbie, Scotland

UNREST IN BALTIC STATES

Ethnic and regional unrest grows in the Baltic states and Georgia as Gorbachev tries to reform the Soviet Union without breaking it up. Discontent with economic failure and lack of civil liberties leads to growing unrest and demands for autonomy and even independence from the 15 republics of the U.S.S.R.. In December, Gorbachev announces huge unilateral cuts in the Red Army, including massive reductions in the armies kept in Eastern Europe.

PINOCHET STEPS DOWN

The Chilean military dictator General Pinochet (b. 1915) loses a referendum on democracy and steps down after 15 years in power. During his presidency, 3,000 people have been assassinated, 1,000 "disappeared," 200,000 tortured, and a further 5,000–6,000 victims may have been buried in unmarked graves. In December 1989 Patricio Aylwin Azócar is elected president and democracy restored to Chile, with Pinochet gaining immunity for life.

BUSH BECOMES PRESIDENT

George Bush, vice-president for eight years, wins the U.S. presidential election and continues Reaganite policies.

ABOVE: An earthquake devastates Armenia.

LOCKERBIE DISASTER

In December Pan Am Flight 103 crashes after a terrorist bomb detonates over Lockerbie, Scotland. All 259 passengers die when the 747 crashes and 11 inhabitants of Lockerbie are killed by wreckage. Evidence points to Libya and two intelligence officers are held to be guilty. Libya refuses to give them up and UN sanctions are imposed. In 1999 the two will be flown to Holland to be tried under Scottish law.

IRANIAN AIRBUS SHOT DOWN BY MISTAKE

The USS *Vincennes* shoots down an Iranian airbus by mistake, killing all 290 passengers. Following the Iraqi Exocet air attack, directed at oil tankers en route to Iran which severely damaged the USS *Stark* in 1987, U.S. Navy warships in the Gulf have been on high alert. The Aegis automatic air defense system on the *Vincennes* picked up an aircraft, identified it as hostile, and shot it down. In fact, it was an airbus.

GREENHOUSE EFFECT

U.S. climatologist James E. Hansen predicts that the "greenhouse effect" in which a buildup of carbon dioxide in the atmosphere traps heat at the Earth's surface, has begun.

HUMAN GENOME PROJECT

A research scheme called the Human Genome Project begins; it plans to map the complete sequence of nucleic acids in human DNA.

LEFT: Vice-President George Bush and his wife Barbara hit the campaign trail in California on their way to the White House.

ENVIRONMENTALIST MURDERED

Brazilian environmentalist and labor leader Chico Mendez is assassinated by a cattle rancher. Mendez had been actively campaigning against the destruction of the Brazilian rainforests and had unionized itinerant rubber tappers (rubber tapping being sustainable use of rainforest). In 1987 he was awarded a UN ecology prize but had received many death threats.

SEIKAN TUNNEL COMPLETED

The Seikan Rail Tunnel connecting the Japanese islands of Honshu and Hokkaido is opened after 24 years' work. At nearly 34 miles long, it is the world's longest tunnel. It is also the final stage in the project to link Japan's four islands by train.

WOMAN MUSLIM LEADER

Benazir Bhutto (b. 1953), leader of the democratic Pakistan People's Party, is elected as Pakistan's prime minister. She is the first modern-day woman to be leader of a Muslim country.

MONTAG AUS LICHT

For years, German composer Karlheinz Stockhausen (b. 1928) has been engaged on a self-proclaimed masterpiece, a vast cycle of seven operas (one for each day of the week), known collectively as *Licht* ("light"). Now he has completed Monday.

WINTER OLYMPICS

Calgary in the Canadian Rockies is the venue for the 15th Winter Olympics, which have been extended from 12 to 16 days. Italian skier Alberto Tomba (b. 1966) wins two skiing golds and German ice skater Katarina Witt (b. 1965) becomes only the second woman to win back-to-back figure skating crowns.

ABOVE: Official investigators comb the wreckage of Pan Am Flight 103, which was blown up over the Scottish town of Lockerbie.

FIRST WOMAN BISHOP

Barbara Harris (b. 1930), a black woman priest, is elected the first woman bishop in the Anglican communion, to serve as suffragan bishop of Massachusetts.

FOSSIL BIRD

Spanish scientists report the discovery of a previously unknown fossil of a bird which lived about 125 million years ago; it appears to be a link between the earliest known bird, *Archaeopteryx*, and modern birds.

FAKE SHROUD

A fragment of cloth from the Turin Shroud — believed to be the winding sheet of Jesus — is given a radiocarbon test that shows it was probably made no earlier than 1350.

SOCCER WIN FOR HOLLAND

Holland finally wins a major soccer competition. Ruud Gullit and Marco Van Basten lead the team to victory at the European Championships in West Germany.

SEOUL OLYMPICS

Drugs dominate the 24th Olympic Games in Seoul, South Korea. Ben Johnson claims the 100m gold in a world record 9.79 seconds, but the Canadian is stripped of both medal and record when he fails a test for banned drugs. Known for her fashion sense and painted nails, American sprinter Florence Griffith-Joyner (Flo-Jo) shows she is a true champion, winning three golds and a silver. She dies tragically young in 1998.

THE END OF COMMUNIST RULE

The Cold War finally comes to an end as the Berlin Wall comes down, uniting West and East Germany. Eastern European countries — Hungary, Poland, Romania, and Czechoslovakia — move decisively away from Communist control. The last Soviet troops leave Afghanistan and the Angolan civil war comes to an end after 14 years of fighting. In China, troops suppress the prodemocracy movement. U.S. troops invade Panama. The Ayatollah issues a fatwa against author Salman Rushdie.

OPPOSITE: A Somalian refugee in Ethiopia waiting with her ration card for food.

1989

Jan	10	Cuban troops begin withdrawal from Angola	June	4	Solidarity wins elections with landslide, Poland
				23	Angolan president dos Santos and UNITA leader Savimbi sign declaration ending civil war
Feb	2	South African president Botha resigns; he is succeeded by F.W. de Klerk			
	3	Military coup overthrows 35-year dictatorship of President Alfredo Stroessner, Paraguay	Sep	10	Hungary opens borders for East Germans
	14	Ayatollah Khomeini issues fatwa against author Salman Rushdie		12	New Polish government is the first in Eastern Europe not under Communist rule since 1946
	15	Last Soviet troops leave Afghanistan after ten years		26	Last of 50,000 Vietnamese forces leave Cambodia
Mar	24	Oil tanker *Exxon Valdez* runs aground, causing massive oil spill	Oct	19	Earthquake hits California
			Nov	10	Berlin Wall demolished
Apr	17	In China, students call for democracy and march on Tiananmen Square	Dec	19	U.S. troops invade Panama to overthrow General Noriega
	20	Multiparty elections are held in Czechoslovakia, the first since 1946		30	Romanian dictator Nicolae Ceausescu executed

For the month of May 1989

SEX

FULL NAME   REG. No.

COUNTRY

MARITAL STATUS

ACCOMPANYING   DEPENDANTS

ZONE

DATE   SUB ZONE No.

PARAGUAYAN DICTATORSHIP ENDS

General Alfredo Stroessner, ruler of Paraguay, is overthrown in a coup after 35 years in power and replaced by General Andrés Rodríguez, who wins the presidential election held in May. The fall of Stroessner removes the longest-standing military dictatorship in South America.

AYATOLLAH ISSUES FATWA

In Iran, Ayatollah Khomeini issues a fatwa or death threat against Salman Rushdie, the British author of *The Satanic Verses*, because of the book's supposed blasphemous content. Rushdie goes into hiding, only emerging cautiously when the threat is partly lifted in September 1998.

POLAND ADOPTS NON-COMMUNIST GOVERNMENT

Polish trade union Solidarity is legalized after talks between its leader, Lech Walesa, and the government. The Catholic Church is given a status unprecedented in Europe, and Poland begins to move towards multiparty democracy. In August the Solidarity candidate Tadeusz Mazowiecki is elected prime minister as the Communist General Jaruzelski (b. 1923) remains president. The new government is the first non-Communist government in Eastern Europe since the late 1940s.

HUNGARY OPENS BORDERS

The Hungarian Army dismantles the border fence with Austria as a symbol of the strengthening democratic reforms in the country. When the border posts are opened in September, many East Germans take the opportunity to flee to the West across Hungary's open borders.

COMMUNISM COLLAPSES

Hungary becomes a multiparty democracy as the Communist party gives up power and changes its name and ideology. In the same month, the East German government collapses after mass demonstrations in the major cities led by the New Forum, a democratic pressure group calling for reform.

BERLIN WALL FALLS

In November, the government opens East Germany's borders and demolishes the wall separating East and West Berlin, uniting the city divided since 1945. In both Bulgaria and Czechoslovakia, the Communist party renounces its monopoly on power as both governments fall. In December, the playwright Vaclav Havel (b. 1936) wins the election as the first non-Communist president of Czechoslovakia since 1948.

SAN FRANCISCO EARTHQUAKE

An earthquake caused by the San Andreas Fault strikes San Francisco and Oakland, California, killing 62 people and causing widespread damage and fires.

CEAUSESCU EXECUTED

Street fighting breaks out in Bucharest as the Committee for National Salvation, backed by the Army, attacks buildings held by the state secret police, the Securitate. Romanian dictator Nicolae Ceausescu and his wife flee Bucharest. They are swiftly recaptured and killed by a firing squad on Christmas Day for "crimes against the people." The Romanian Communist Party is abolished and the ruling National Salvation Front promises free elections as the country moves towards democracy.

OPERATION JUST CAUSE

Some 12,000 U.S. troops invade Panama to oust General Manuel Noriega who has become implicated with Central American drug dealers as well as human rights abuses. In the fighting, 220 Panamanians and 314 soldiers are killed. The American forces suffer 23 dead and 324 wounded. Three civilians are killed.

STUDENTS KILLED IN TIANANMEN SQUARE

Students and other prodemocracy protesters occupying Tiananmen Square in Beijing, China, are fired on by the Red Army as it reoccupies the square. Many hundreds are killed and thousands later imprisoned as the prodemocracy movement is suppressed throughout China.

SOVIETS WITHDRAW FROM AFGHANISTAN

The last Soviet troops leave Afghanistan after a ten-year occupation. The long drawn-out guerrilla war has cost the U.S.S.R. more than 15,000 killed, 311 missing, and 35,478 wounded. The Afghans lose over 100,000 killed.

THE PROTECTING VEIL

This new cello piece by British composer John Tavener (b. 1944) is hailed as a powerful example of the "new simplicity" in music. Its spiritual content makes it popular and it goes to the top of the CD charts.

CLOSE-UP OF NEPTUNE

Space probe *Voyager 2* passes within 3,106 miles of Neptune after a journey of more than 12 years, sending back clear pictures and discovering a Great Dark Spot and fierce winds.

IVORY TRADE BANNED

The Convention on International Trade in Endangered Species agrees to a total ban on trading in ivory. In Kenya, 12 tons of elephant tusks are burnt as a sign of commitment to stamping out the trade.

ECSTASY FUELS RAVE SCENE

The development of the rave scene youth subculture is fuelled by the drug ecstasy and techno dance music. Tens of thousands of teenagers and people in their 20s are attracted to acid-house rave parties.

OPPOSITE: After almost 30 years, the Berlin Wall comes down as the Eastern bloc crumbles and the Cold War finally ends.

ABOVE: Batman, the caped crusader, in somber mood amid props and sets reminiscent of the dystopian *Metropolis*.

LEFT: Unrest in Middle America as the downside of Reagonomics strikes home, just after their champion leaves office.

BELOW LEFT: Somalian refugees at the Hartisheik camp in Ethiopia make do with whatever is at hand to make a home.

BATMAN

American star Michael Keaton's portrayal of the caped do-gooder is more brooding than the lighthearted version of earlier cartoons and films; this is helped by the sets and props. This new version of Batman breaks box office records within months of opening.

HILLSBOROUGH SOCCER DISASTER

Overcrowding kills 95 Liverpool fans at an F.A. Cup semifinal at Hillsborough in Sheffield, U.K. It is the highest death toll in British sports history and forces further reform of the game.

EXXON VALDEZ OIL DISASTER

The *Exxon Valdez* oil tanker runs aground in Prince William Sound, Alaska. Almost 11 million gallons of crude oil spills into the sea and spreads over 900 square miles of coast, devastating marine life.

RIGHT: A boom is used to try and scrape surface oil off the water.

BELOW: The cleanup team move in to assess the damage to the coastline and plan a strategy to make good the damage.

ABOVE: A golden-eye duck, one of the innocent victims of the spill.

ABOVE: Aerial view of the huge extent of the damage.

INTO THE NEW MILLENNIUM

In the 1990s the political map is redrawn. The Soviet Union crumbles, and more than 70 years of Soviet communism come to an end, leaving the United States as a solitary superpower. The collapse of Communism in Eastern Europe exposes ethnic tensions and war breaks out in the Balkans. However, in South Africa the oppressive apartheid system is finally dismantled. Peace also comes to war-torn Central America. In the world of science, distant planets such as Venus and Mercury are mapped.

OPPOSITE: Firefighters in the burning Kuwaiti oil fields during the Gulf War of 1991.

1990–1999

KEY EVENTS OF THE DECADE

- SOVIET UNION COLLAPSES
- GULF WAR
- APARTHEID ENDS
- YUGOSLAVIA BREAKS UP
- UN EARTH SUMMIT
- WAR IN BOSNIA
- RWANDAN CIVIL WAR
- DEATH OF PRINCESS DIANA
- COLLAPSE OF ASIAN ECONOMIES

- HALE-BOPP COMET
- HUBBLE SPACE TELESCOPE LAUNCHED
- PLANET VENUS IS MAPPED
- CLONING TAKES OFF
- ANIMATRONICS COME TO CINEMA
- CENTENARY OLYMPIC GAMES
- SINGLE EUROPEAN CURRENCY

WORLD POPULATION 5.295 MILLION

GERMANY UNITES, MANDELA IS FREED

ANC leader Nelson Mandela is released from prison after 27 years in captivity. Iraq invades Kuwait, prompting an immediate response from the United Nations and the United States. Tension rises as U.S. forces mass on the Saudi Arabian border. East and West Germany are finally united. The Soviet Union begins to crumble as Lithuania declares independence. The Hubble Space Telescope is launched but proves to be defective. A new handheld computer games console goes on sale.

1990

Feb	**2**	President F.W. de Klerk ends 20-year ban on ANC
	21	Namibia becomes an independent state
	25	U.S.-backed Violeta Chamorro wins Nicaraguan elections
Mar	**11**	Lithuania declares independence from Soviet Union
Apr	**24**	Hubble Space Telescope is launched into orbit
May	**29**	Boris Yeltsin elected president of Russian Federation
June	**8**	Russian Federation declares itself a sovereign state
July	**19**	Iraqi troops mass on Kuwaiti border

Aug	**2**	Iraqi forces invade Kuwait. Emir flees to Saudi Arabia
	6	UN Security Council imposes sanctions against Iraq
	24	Hostage Brian Keenan, held in Lebanon since 1986, is released
Sep	**28**	Serbian parliament strips Kosovo of autonomy, Yugoslavia
Oct	**2**	East and West Germany are reunited
Dec	**9**	Slobodan Milosevic is elected president of Serbia in the country's first free elections for 50 years

MANDELA FREED

The South African government under President de Klerk (b. 1936) lifts the ban on the African National Congress (ANC) and other anti-apartheid parties and frees ANC leader Nelson Mandela after 27 years in prison. Talks begin on moving South Africa towards multiracial democracy.

NAMIBIA INDEPENDENT

The last white-run colony in Africa gains its independence as South Africa relinquishes its hold on South West Africa, renamed Namibia. The former German colony had been administered by South Africa since 1919 under League of Nations and UN mandates. Sam Nujoma (b. 1929), the leader of the SWAPO opposition, is elected president.

IRAQ INVADES KUWAIT

Iraq invades the neighboring oil-rich sheikdom of Kuwait. The Emir flees to Saudi Arabia. Iraq's unprovoked invasion and potential threat to Saudi Arabia prompt an almost immediate reaction. The United Nations declares sanctions against Iraq and, in Operation Desert Shield, the United States airlifts 2,300 troops to Saudi Arabia within 18 hours. Iraqi leader Saddam Hussein (b. 1937) makes a formal peace treaty with long-term enemy Iran.

GERMANY UNITED

East and West Germany are reunited after pro-unity parties in East Germany win a majority in elections held in March and open talks with West Germany. In July the government cedes sovereignty over economic, monetary, and social policy to West Germany and the Deutschmark becomes the official currency. Elections held across Germany in December return Christian Democrat Helmut Kohl to power.

ABOVE: Free at last, ANC leader Nelson Mandela meets President George Bush in the White House.

THE EUROPEAN

A new concept in journalism, *The European* is founded as an English-language newspaper, dealing with news from a European perspective, but fails in the end.

POSSESSION

British writer A.S. Byatt (b. 1938) has published what is her best novel. Full of symbols and symmetries, it recreates the Victorian world (and writings) of the biographers' subject as well as their obsession with, and possession of, their quarry.

ABOVE: Hubble Space Telescope deployed from space shuttle *Discovery*.

ABOVE: Martina Navratilova takes the Pilkington Glass Ladies Singles Trophy at Eastbourne, England, as an appetizer for her Wimbledon triumph a month later.

BURMESE ELECTIONS

The National League for Democracy wins multiparty elections in Burma but the army refuses to hand over power. The League's cofounder is Aung San Suu Kyi (b. 1945), who has been under house arrest since 1989 because of her opposition to the ruling military junta. She is awarded the Nobel Peace Prize in 1991.

NICARAGUAN ELECTIONS

Elections held in Nicaragua are won by U.S.-backed Violeta Barrios de Chamorro. A month later the United States lifts sanctions and by the end of June the Contras are disbanded. In 1991, U.S. president Bush pledges economic support for Nicaragua. The cost to Nicaragua of economic sanctions and the Contra war is estimated at $15 billion, with some 30,000 people killed.

NEWS FROM NEPTUNE

U.S. space probe *Voyager 2* flies within 3,000 miles of Neptune, reporting four rings, six new moons, and a stormy surface like that of Jupiter.

GAME BOY

Japanese computer manufacturer Nintendo launch Game Boy, the first programmable handheld computer games console. It is an instant success.

BACK TO EARTH

Space shuttle *Columbia* returns to Earth after six years in orbit, bringing the Long Duration Exposure Facility, a railroad car-sized container of scientific experiments.

STRETCHABLE CERAMICS

Japanese researchers announce the development of ceramics that can be stretched at temperatures of about 2,912° F during manufacture.

HUBBLE DEFECTIVE

The Hubble Space Telescope is launched by space shuttle *Discovery* from Kennedy Space Center. Orbiting at an altitude of 375 miles above the Earth, it is designed to see further into space than any Earthbound telescope. However, its main mirror is found to be flawed, distorting the images and limiting the telescope's usefulness.

SUCCESS FOR NAVRATILOVA

Czech-born American tennis star Martina Navratilova becomes queen of Wimbledon when she achieves her ninth singles title. She beats American player Zina Garrison in the final.

GERMANY WINS WORLD CUP

Defending champions Argentina scratch and fight to reach the final in Rome at the 14th soccer World Cup but lose a disappointing match to Germany.

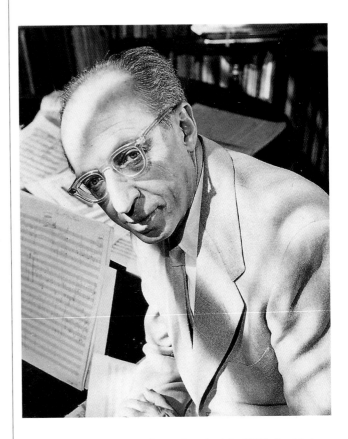

RIGHT: American composer Aaron Copeland (b. 1900) dies. He is best known for his ballet *Appalachian Spring* (1944).

ABOVE: In the White House, the States and Russia agree to terms laying down the foundations for a future arms limitation agreement.

BELOW: A helicopter gunship covers the USS *Dwight D. Eisenhower* as she sails through the Suez Canal to the Mediterranean.

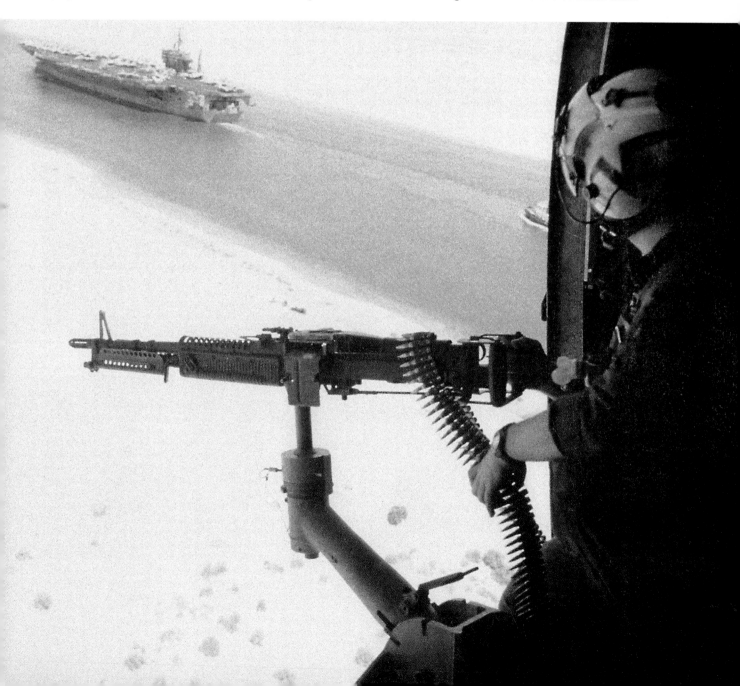

THE SOVIET UNION COLLAPSES

The Warsaw Pact is dissolved. A Communist coup takes place in the Soviet Union. Boris Yeltsin comes to power. Mikhail Gorbachev resigns as leader of the Soviet Union. The U.S.S.R. comes to an end, 74 years after the Russian Revolution. Operation Desert Storm launches the Gulf War and a U.S.-led multinational operation liberates Kuwait from Iraqi occupation. Croatia and Slovenia declare independence and Yugoslavia begins to break up.

OPPOSITE: Iraqi forces set light to oil wells outside Kuwait City as they retreat from the region.

1991

Jan	15	Iraq fails to meet UN deadline for withdrawal from Kuwait
	16	Operation Desert Storm begins. U.S.-led operation begins air offensive to liberate Kuwait
	18	Iraq sends Scud missiles against Israel
Feb	22	Retreating Iraqi forces torch Kuwaiti oil wells
	24	U.S.-led troops begin ground offensive against Iraqi forces
	28	Gulf War ends
	17	Serbia suspends provisional Kosovo constitution
Apr	30	Kurdish refugees move into "safe havens"
May	28	Ethiopian People's Revolutionary Democratic Front captures Addis Ababa
	31	Civil war ends in Angola
June	17	Population Registration Act ends apartheid in South Africa
	25	Republics of Croatia and Slovenia declare independence
July	31	U.S. president Bush and Soviet leader Gorbachev sign Strategic Arms Reduction Treaty (START) to reduce numbers of long-range nuclear weapons
Aug	19	Hard-line Communists stage coup against Soviet leader Mikhail Gorbachev
Sep	25	Peace accord ends civil war in El Salvador
Dec	25	Mikhail Gorbachev resigns; U.S.S.R. comes to an end

U.S.S.R. CRUMBLES

As Soviet control is removed from eastern Germany, the Warsaw Pact is formally dissolved. Inside the Soviet Union, Latvia and Estonia vote in referenda for independence, following the lead set by Lithuania. The U.S.S.R. continues to fall apart as domestic, economic, and political pressures mount. In August, hard-line Communists seize power while President Gorbachev is on holiday. The coup fails as Boris Yeltsin, president of Russia, leads popular resistance against it. As a result, Gorbachev's hold on power is seriously weakened and Ukraine and other states push for independence from the U.S.S.R. In December, Russia, Belarus, and Ukraine set up the Commonwealth of Independent States (CIS). The U.S.S.R. collapses and Gorbachev resigns on Christmas Day, bringing Communist Party rule and the Soviet Union to an end.

AIDS

The announcement that U.S. sports star Magic Johnson is HIV positive, and the death from AIDS of British rock singer Freddie Mercury increase public awareness of the rapid worldwide spread of AIDS.

GULF WAR

In January, the United States leads allied forces in an air attack, code-named Operation Desert Thunder, against Saddam Hussein's capital, Baghdad, Iraq. Following a month of intensive bombing, ground forces begin to liberate Kuwait in February, achieving their objective within four days and driving Iraqi forces out of Kuwait. During the retreat, oil wells are torched, causing serious pollution. At the end of the war, allied casualties are 95 killed and 370 wounded. The Iraqis suffered 30,000 killed in air attacks and the ground war and lost 20,000 prisoners with 270 tanks destroyed.

ASTEROID PHOTOGRAPHED

The *Galileo* space probe passes within 995 miles of the asteroid Gaspra and photographs it. This is the first-ever asteroid photograph taken in space.

PREHISTORIC REMAINS

The preserved body of a man who died around 3300 B.C. is found in a glacier in the Austrian Alps. Probably a hunter, he is tattooed on his back, knees, and ankles, and has a bow and a quiver of arrows.

ABOVE: A submarine bomb disposal expert attaches an explosive charge to an Iraqi mine in the Persian Gulf during the Gulf War.

ABOVE: An F-117A stealth fighter aircraft of the 37th Tactical Fighter Wing rolls towards the runway for the flight back home after Operation Desert Storm.

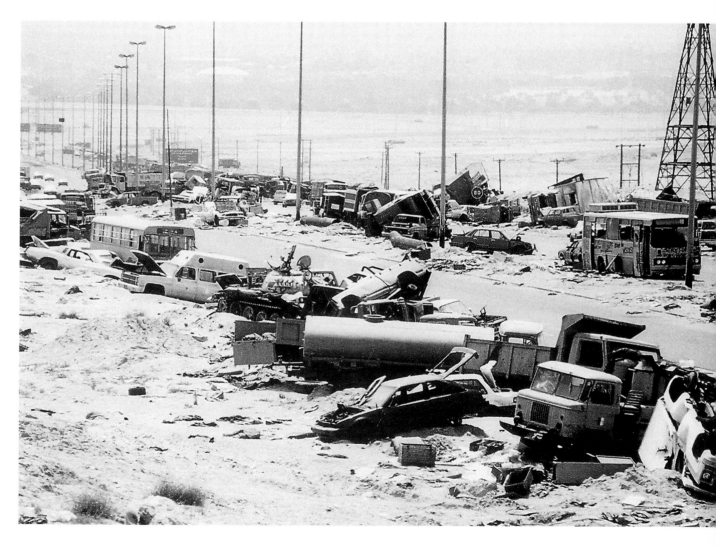

ABOVE: Demolished vehicles line Highway 8, the route that fleeing Iraqi forces took as they retreated from Kuwait.

ABOVE: Haitians, who had fled during the U.S. invasion, are repatriated and return home to their villages.

ABOVE: The UN Commissioner for Refugees, Sadako Ogata, visits refugees returning to Somalia after the civil war.

APARTHEID ENDS

In February, President de Klerk announces plans to repeal all apartheid laws in South Africa. Legislation is passed to end racial controls on land ownership and in June all remaining discriminatory laws are repealed. The United States ends sanctions against South Africa, and the country is readmitted into world sport.

ETHIOPIA AND SOMALIA

After a lengthy civil war, President Mengistu flees Ethiopia as 17 years of Marxist rule are brought to an end. Neighboring Somalia, meanwhile, collapses into anarchy as rival warlords fight for control following the overthrow of President Siyad Barrah in January.

JFK

A new film has been released about U.S. president Kennedy and the conspiracy theory surrounding his assassination. Directed by U.S. film director Oliver Stone (b. 1946), it stars American actor Kevin Costner (b. 1955) as the New Orleans district attorney.

MAPPING VENUS

While orbiting Venus, the U.S. unmanned spacecraft *Magellan* compiles a map of the surface, using radar signals.

POWELL OVERTAKES BEAMON

U.S. long jumper Mike Powell beats Bob Beamon's famous leap of 29 feet 2½ inches by 1½ inches at the World Athletics Championships in Tokyo. The world record had stood since the 1968 Olympics.

NATURAL DISASTERS

In April a typhoon, traveling at 145 miles per hour, strikes Bangladesh, killing more than 139,000 people and making ten million homeless. In June, Mt. Pinatubo, a Philippine volcano dormant for 600 years, erupts, killing more than 700 people.

CONFLICT IN YUGOSLAVIA

The delicate balance between Catholic, Muslim, and Orthodox ethnic groups that held together under the tough rule of President Tito is now unravelling. Ethnic tensions between the different communities are rising and Yugoslavia is falling apart as Slovenia and Croatia declare their independence, exacerbated by newly elected Serbian leader Slobodan Milosevic (b. 1941) who is emphasizing ethnic differences to consolidate his power base. The Serb-dominated Yugoslav National Army (JNA) tries to prevent the breakup of the country and attacks Croatia, starting a lengthy and bitter war between the two states.

THE SILENCE OF THE LAMBS

Welsh actor Anthony Hopkins (b. 1937) plays Hannibal Lecter, psychiatrist turned serial killer, in a new film, *The Silence of the Lambs,* which has opened this year. U.S. film star Jodie Foster (b. 1962) plays an FBI agent. A chilling movie, the horror is tightly controlled by director Jonathan Demme.

YUGOSLAVIA CRUMBLES AND LOS ANGELES BURNS

Interracial war breaks out in former Yugoslavia, and the abhorrent term "ethnic cleansing" enters the language as evidence is televised of death camps in Bosnia. Race riots erupt in Los Angeles, after the savage beating of a young black motorist. The UN Earth Summit meets in Rio de Janeiro to discuss the future of planet Earth, Disneyland comes to Europe, and Expo 92 is held in Spain.

1992

Feb	1	UN-negotiated peace comes into effect in El Salvador
	8	Winter Olympics open
Mar	1	Bosnia-Herzegovina declares independence following referendum
	2	Violence breaks out in Sarajevo between Serbs, Croats, and Muslims
	22	Communist rule ends in Albania after 45 years
Apr	8	Serb and federal army forces begin bombardment of Sarajevo as violence escalates in Bosnia Mujaheddin rebels take control in Afghanistan
	29	All-white jury acquits police of beating black American, precipitating riots, Los Angeles

July	25	Olympic Games open in Barcelona
Aug	13	United Nations condemns Serbian policy of so-called "ethnic cleansing," describing it as a war crime
Sep	25	New canal links Main and Danube rivers, Germany
Nov	3	Democrat Bill Clinton wins U.S. presidential elections

ABOVE: General "Stormin'" Norman Schwartzkopf, commander-in-chief, speaks to soldiers during Operation Desert Shield.

ABOVE: General Colin Powell consults the Pentagon while visiting troops during Operation Desert Shield.

WAR IN BOSNIA

After the former Yugoslav province of Bosnia votes for independence, a vicious war erupts as Croatia and Serbia attempt to carve up Bosnia along ethnic lines, threatening its multiracial nature in a campaign known as "ethnic cleansing." Bosnian Serbs backed by the Yugoslav National Army attack the fledgling country, which they wish to remain part of Greater Serbia. They overrun 70 percent of the country and set up a Serb government in Pale. In August, evidence emerges of Serbian death camps where Bosnian prisoners are kept in appalling conditions.

MUJAHEDDIN VICTORIOUS

Mujaheddin rebels in Afghanistan take control after a lengthy civil war, overthrowing the Communist government of President Najibullah. The Mujaheddin led the resistance to the Soviet occupation of the country from 1979–89, and fought on to remove the Communist government.

L.A. RACE RIOTS

Race riots erupt in Los Angeles after police officers, who savagely beat a young black man, Rodney King, and are witnessed on video, are acquitted by an all-white jury. The verdict outrages the black community and reveals the extent of racial discrimination still experienced by many Americans.

CLINTON WINS ELECTION

Bill Clinton (b. 1946) from Arkansas wins the presidential election for the Democrats, only the second time in 24 years that a Democrat has gained the White House. However, Clinton's record of draft-dodging and marital infidelity infuriates right-wing Republicans, who campaign incessantly against him and his government.

LAST EUROPEAN COMMUNIST GOVERNMENT

In Albania, the last Communist government in Europe ends after the opposition Democrat party wins a majority in the general election.

ABOVE: A microwave map of the whole sky compiled from a year's worth of data from NASA's Cosmic Background Explorer.

OPERATION RESTORE HOPE

In Somalia, United Nations military observers arrive in the capital Mogadishu to help distribute food aid. In what is code-named Operation Restore Hope, some 17,000 soldiers drawn from the United States and ten other UN countries attempt to impose order to allow relief to be distributed. In a raid by U.S. Rangers to capture the Somali warlord Mohammad Farrah Aidid, in October 1993, 18 soldiers are killed and 73 wounded.

EL SALVADOR

The United Nations finally brokers peace in El Salvador. The FMLN is granted the status of a political party. Peace talks began in 1990. It is estimated that about 100,000 people died in El Salvador between 1979 and 1990.

ABOVE: Riots and fires in Los Angeles follow after black motorist Rodney King was beaten up by the LAPD.

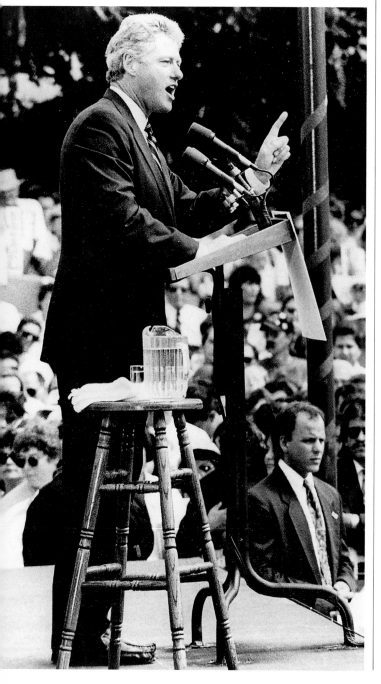

LEFT: Presidential candidate and Democrat Bill Clinton campaigns in Albuquerque, New Mexico, a key state in the election battle.

PERUVIAN GUERRILLA WAR

In Peru, Maoist leader Dr. Renoso Guzman is captured by the Army and police special forces, bringing an end to the activities of the Shining Path. The campaign of bombings, assassination, and terror has caused the deaths of more than 23,000 men and women since it began in 1982.

EXPO 92, SEVILLE

In April, Expo 92, the first Exposition Universelle for 22 years, opens in Seville, Spain. Nations from around the world display their innovations and achievements in industry, science, and the arts. One of the lasting monuments will be Alamillo Bridge. Designed by Spanish architect and civil engineer Santiago Calatrava, it is one of the most beautiful of all modern bridges. Its harplike, cable-styled construction makes it an instant success.

GENETICALLY ENGINEERED WHEAT

U.S. biologists report in June that they have developed the first genetically engineered wheat, which is proof against a powerful herbicide.

WATER LINK

In Germany, a new canal opens linking the Main and Danube rivers. This completes a river and canal trade route from the Baltic Sea to the Black Sea.

DISNEYLAND COMES TO PARIS
Disneyland comes to Europe and the whole Disney culture — from the themed worlds to the cavalcades and wandering Disney characters brought to life — is transported to Paris.

SATELLITE CAPTURED
Three astronauts aboard the space shuttle *Endeavor* do a space walk to capture *Intelsat 6*, a communications satellite which has drifted into the wrong orbit. They put it back into the right orbit.

BIG BANG NEWS
NASA scientists announce that their Cosmic Background Explorer (COBE) satellite, launched in 1989, has detected 15 billion-year-old clouds of matter that relate to the Big Bang. American astrophysicist George Fitzgerald Smoot (b. 1945), who heads COBE's team of analysts, announces that the satellite had found fluctuations in the background radiation, preserved from about 300,000 years after the Big Bang. The variations gave rise to stars, galaxies, and other cosmic structures.

ANTI-COLUMBUS DEMONSTRATIONS
Demonstrations against the celebrations of the 500th anniversary of the arrival of Christopher Columbus in the New World take place in many Latin American countries.

METHANE UNDER THE OCEAN
U.S. scientists find deposits of methane hydrate off the coast of northern North America, which may prove to be a huge source of natural gas.

EARTH SUMMIT
In June, representatives from 178 counties meet in an "Earth Summit" — the UN Conference on Environment and Development — in Rio de Janeiro, Brazil. Most agree to phase out CFC gases, which cause depletion of the ozone layer, to preserve forests and protect biodiversity.

WOMEN PRIESTS
The Church of England Synod votes to allow women to be ordained as priests. Ten women were ordained to the Anglican priesthood in Australia in 1992.

WINTER OLYMPICS
Twelve sites around Albertville in France are the venue for the 16th Winter Olympics. Short-track speed skating and freestyle moguls skiing become Olympic events. Sixteen-year-old Toni Nieminen takes ski-jumping gold on the big hill and in the team event and bronze on the small hill.

OLYMPIC GAMES
The emphasis returns to athletics at the 25th Olympic Games in Barcelona, Spain. In the long jump, U.S. athlete Carl Lewis (b. 1961) wins a gold for the third successive Games, while Vitali Sherbo, of a post-Soviet Union team, dominates men's gymnastics and the American basketball "Dream Team" sweeps all before it.

ABOVE: Astronauts Hieb, Akers, and Thuot reel in the *Intelsat 6* satellite as part of the nine-day STS-49 Mission.

ISRAEL AND PLO SIGN FOR PEACE

Israel and the PLO sign an historic peace accord. In Russia, the army crushes an attempted coup against Yeltsin's government. The European single market comes into force. Aborigines finally achieve recognition of their land rights in Australia. Explorers cross Antarctica on foot. New Zealander Jane Campion becomes the first woman film director to win the Palme d'Or, and Spielberg's film *Schindler's List* opens to critical acclaim.

1993

Jan	1	EC's single market comes into force
	1	Czechoslovakia divides
Feb	26	World Trade Center bombed
Mar	17	Ballet star Rudolf Nureyev dies aged 55
May	24	Eritrea gains independence
Sep	13	PLO and Israel sign peace agreement
Oct	4	Army crushes potential coup, Moscow
	15	Nelson Mandela and President de Klerk jointly win Nobel Peace Prize
Nov	1	Maastricht Treaty comes into force, European Community
Dec	22	Aborigines win land rights, Australia

MIDDLE EAST PEACE ACCORD

In Washington, D.C., Prime Minister Rabin of Israel and the Palestine Liberation Organization (PLO) leader Yasser Arafat sign a treaty handing over control of the Gaza Strip and the West Bank city of Jericho to the Palestinians. Secret talks between the two sides in the Norwegian capital of Oslo have led to this historic agreement, which is designed to be the first stage in the gradual handing over of Israeli-occupied territory to the Palestinians in return for their recognition of the state of Israel.

SINGLE EUROPEAN MARKET

The European single market comes into force, removing all obstacles to the free movement of trade, services, and people throughout the European Community. The Maastricht Treaty, establishing a single currency by 1999, comes into force and the European Community (EC) becomes the European Union (EU).

LANDMARK SPIELBERGS

U.S. film director Steven Spielberg has released two remarkable but highly contrasting movies. His *Jurassic Park* involves genetically recreated dinosaurs that run amok in the theme park to end all theme parks and is a commercial coup. More somber is *Schindler's List*. Based on Thomas Keneally's book *Schindler's Ark* and shot almost entirely in black and white, this moving film is concerned with the Holocaust and is Spielberg's account of Oskar Schindler, the German businessman who rescued Jews from the death camps by employing them in his factory. Liam Neeson (b. 1952) stars as Schindler. An epilogue shows actual survivors, and Schindler's widow, at Schindler's grave in Israel.

CZECHOSLOVAKIA DIVIDES
Following the success of pro-independence parties in Slovakia, Czechoslovakia splits amicably in two, with both the Czech Republic and Slovakia becoming independent states.

COMMUNIST COUP FAILS
A hardline Communist coup against the Russian government of Boris Yeltsin is crushed when the army storms the White House, the parliament building in Moscow. The coup reveals levels of discontent in Russia caused by the failure of economic reforms.

ANOTHER SUPERNOVA
Spanish astronomer Francisco García announces that he has discovered another supernova (exploding star), some 11 million light years distant.

ABOVE: Rudolph Nureyev, probably the best-known ballet dancer of his generation, dies in Paris. He is seen here dancing in the States.

RUDOLF HAMETOVICH NUREYEV
(1938–1993)

The great Russian ballet dancer Rudolf Nureyev has died in Paris of an AIDS-related disease. In 1961, Nureyev defected from the Kirov Ballet while visiting Paris, and in 1962 made his debut at Covent Garden with the great ballerina Margot Fonteyn. They formed a partnership that transformed ballet. From 1983 to 1989 Nureyev was artistic director to the Paris Opera. As a solo dancer he performed with the world's greatest companies.

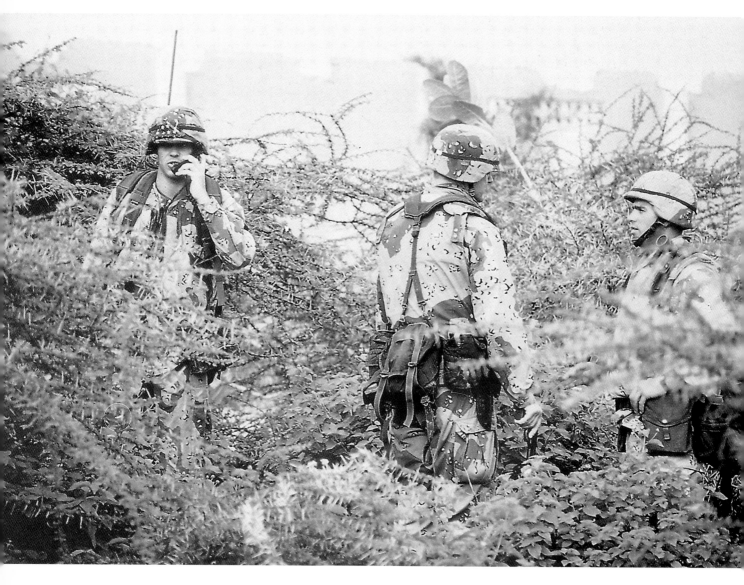

ABOVE: U.S. Marines take part in the multinational relief effort Operation Restore Hope in Mogadishu, Somalia.

WAR IN BOSNIA

UN forces are deployed as peacekeepers in war-torn Bosnia. However, Bosnian Serbs continue to shell the regional capital of Sarajevo. Croatian forces shell the town of Mostar.

FRANCIS VINCENT (FRANK) ZAPPA (1940–1993)

American rock musician Frank Zappa has died after a two-year battle with prostate cancer. Always at the forefront of experimental rock as guitarist, singer, and music writer, Zappa founded the group Mothers of Invention in the 1960s. Their first album *Freak Out!* was released in 1966. Zappa's first solo album was *Lumpy Gravy* (1968) and his final album *Yellow Shark*, appeared this year.

FIRST WOMAN ATTORNEY-GENERAL

Janet Reno (b. 1938) becomes the first woman attorney-general of the United States. The start of her new career is marred by a disaster during which more than 70 members of a cult religion die at Waco, Texas, while being besieged by the FBI.

"DONT ASK, DON'T TELL"

In the States, President Clinton reaches an agreement with the Department of Defense whereby gays can serve in the military provided that they neither openly declare their homosexuality nor engage in homosexual activity.

FERMAT'S LAST THEOREM

British mathematician Andrew Wiles claims to have proved Fermat's Last Theorem, a mathematical proposition put forward in 1627 by Pierre de Fermat — who omitted the proof.

5,000 MILE TELESCOPE

In August, the Very Long Baseline Array, huge radio telescope dishes at ten different sites scattered over 5,000 miles, begins operation.

HUBBLE CORRECTED

During five spacewalks, astronauts aboard the space shuttle *Endeavor* "capture" the Hubble Space Telescope, correct its faults, and update it.

ROMANOVS FINGERPRINTED

Genetic material from the British relatives of the Romanovs, the last Russian Tsars, are compared with material taken from the supposed remains of Nicholas II and his family. Genetic fingerprinting methods prove that the remains are genuine.

SUPERMODEL STARS

Supermodels of the fashion industry, such as Cindy Crawford, Christy Turlington, and Linda Evangelista, become stars, known internationally in their own right.

REICHSTAG

In probably the most important artistic aspect of German reunification, Alex Schultes wins the architectural competition to design the administrative district around the Reichstag.

PIANO WINS PALME D'OR

New Zealand film director Jane Campion (b. 1954) becomes the first woman to win the prestigious Palme d'Or at Cannes for her latest film *The Piano*. The film stars Holly Hunter (b. 1958), who also gets an award for her portrayal of the mute heroine who finds expression through her piano playing.

ABOVE: President George Bush and Russian premier Boris Yeltsin, who has just survived an attempted coup by Communist hardliners.

ERITREA INDEPENDENT

The former Italian colony of Eritrea, which has been joined to Ethiopia since 1952, wins its independence. This is in reward for its role in overthrowing the Mengistu government.

ABORIGINAL LAND RIGHTS

In Australia, the federal parliament passes the Native Title Act, recognizing Aboriginal rights to make claims on land taken away from them by early European settlers. The Act follows years of campaigning by Aboriginal rights groups.

FIRST WALK ACROSS ANTARCTICA

English explorer Ranulph Fiennes (b. 1945) and Mike Stroud become the first people to cross Antarctica on foot. After 95 days they are picked up 350 miles from the sea, having walked 1,347 miles pulling sleds loaded with supplies.

HOUSE

British sculptor Rachel Whiteread (b. 1963) inspires controversy with her sculpture *House*. It is a cast of a house in London's East End, made by pouring in concrete and then removing the walls and roof. Whiteread's work is shown in Paris, Chicago, and Berlin.

MANDELA FOR PRESIDENT

South Africa holds multiracial elections and Mandela becomes the country's first black president. Violence breaks out in Rwanda. The IRA announces a ceasefire in Northern Ireland. Russian forces invade breakaway Chechnya. Dead animals pickled in formaldehyde are a talking point in the art world and the long-awaited Channel Tunnel is opened. Fossil remains in Ethiopia help to date human prehistory.

OPPOSITE: Displaced persons — internal refugees in Rwanda — seek safety in Kibeho Camp.

1994

Feb	5	Serb mortar bomb hits crowded market place, Sarajevo
	23	Ceasefire between Serbia and Croatia, Bosnia
Apr	6	The presidents of Burundi and Rwanda are killed in a plane crash; mass violence erupts in Rwanda
	26	First multiracial elections begin in South Africa, resulting in victory for the African National Congress (ANC)
May	1	Brazilian racing champion Ayrton Senna killed
	6	Channel Tunnel opens
	10	Nelson Mandela sworn in as first black president of South Africa
Aug	14	"Carlos the Jackal," most wanted terrorist, is arrested
	31	Irish Republican Army (IRA) declares ceasefire, Northern Ireland
Sep	19	U.S. troops invade Haiti
Dec	11	Russian forces invade Chechnya, following its declaration of independence

ABOVE: *Away from the Flock*, Damien Hirst's contribution to "Sensation," the exhibition of work by young British artists.

PRESIDENT MANDELA

Nelson Mandela becomes the first black president of South African following the victory of the African National Congress (ANC) in the country's first multiracial democratic elections.

MASS SLAUGHTER IN RWANDA

Genocide breaks out in Rwanda as the Hutu-dominated army and Hutu extremists massacre 500,000 people from the Tutsi majority. The Tutsis establish control and two million Hutus flee for their lives into neighboring Zaire. The genocide and mass exodus follow the death in a plane crash of the presidents of both Rwanda and neighboring Burundi, which experiences similar massacres.

NORTHERN IRELAND CEASEFIRE

Following the Anglo–Irish Downing Street Declaration between the prime ministers of Britain and Ireland, John Major (b. 1943) and Albert Reynolds (b. 1932), to bring peace to Northern Ireland, the Irish Republican Army (IRA) declare a ceasefire. This allows Sinn Fein, their political representatives, to take part in the peace talks.

CHANNEL TUNNEL OPENS

The Channel Tunnel is open. Running under the sea between England and France, it provides a high-speed rail link.

RIGHT: The huge ozone hole over the Antarctic, mapped by the Russian *Meteor 3* satellite.

RUSSIANS INVADE CHECHNYA

Russian troops occupy the rebel Caucasian province of Chechnya after it unilaterally declared independence from Russia. The capital, Grozny, is levelled to the ground in the fighting, which continues until an agreement is reached which in effect grants the province de facto independence. The final Russian troops withdraw in January 1997. In May 1997, Russia and Chechnya sign a peace agreement formally ending the separatist war.

YEMEN CIVIL WAR

Tension, which has existed between the Northern and Southern Yemen elites since last year, explodes into war. This follows sporadic clashes when the southern leadership declares secession, formal unification having taken place in 1990. The fighting involves armor and artillery and in July the Northern forces capture Aden, which had been bombarded with SCUD missiles. In a frenzy of religious zeal the northerners destroyed the only brewery in the Arabian peninsula.

FINNISH DIAMONDS

Diamond deposits are discovered in northern Finland, leading to hopes that there are very large deposits in the region.

PEACE IN COLOMBIA
In Colombia, the government reaches peace with four left-wing guerrilla groups.

SARAJEVO BOMBED
In February a Serb 120-mm mortar bomb hits a crowded market place in Sarajevo, killing 68 people and seriously wounding 200 more. Subsequently, Serb forces bombard safe areas in Goradze and Srebrenica. NATO authorizes air strikes on Serbian posts, galvanizing the Contact Group of United States, Britain, Russia, and Germany.

AWAY FROM THE FLOCK SHOCKS
British artist Damien Hirst (b. 1965) provokes controversy and debate in the media with his work. This year sees *Away from the Flock*, featuring a dead lamb preserved in a glass tank of formaldehyde. Last year he used a similar technique to display *Mother and Child Divided*, a cow and calf sliced in half.

U.S. INTO HAITI
The U.S. Army lands on the island of Haiti to restore civilian rule after a military coup deposed Jean-Bertrand Aristide, the democratically elected president, in September 1991. Presidential elections held in August 1995 result in victory for René Préval, a close associate of Aristide.

PULP FICTION
American director Quentin Tarantino (b. 1963), of *Reservoir Dogs* fame, produces a new film — *Pulp Fiction*. It stars John Travolta and Harvey Keitel, and is inspired by thrillers of the 1950s and 1960s.

KANSAI AIRPORT
One of the largest civil engineering projects of recent years, Japan's new airport has opened. The buildings are designed by Renzo Piano and are sited on a specially created artificial island.

COMET HITS JUPITER
Chunks of Comet Shoemaker-Levy 9 collide with the planet Jupiter in July, producing fiery plumes of gas; the comet had broken up in Jupiter's magnetic field.

MISSING LINK
The uncertainty surrounding human origins becomes a little clearer when anthropologists announce the discovery in Ethiopia of fossils of *Australopithecus ramidus*, the earliest direct ancestors of humans. The fossils are 4.4 million years old.

MASS SUICIDE
Members of an international religious cult, Order of the Solar Temple, commit mass suicide in Switzerland and Canada. It is one of a number of mass suicides and other events by members of religious cults heralding the end of the millennium.

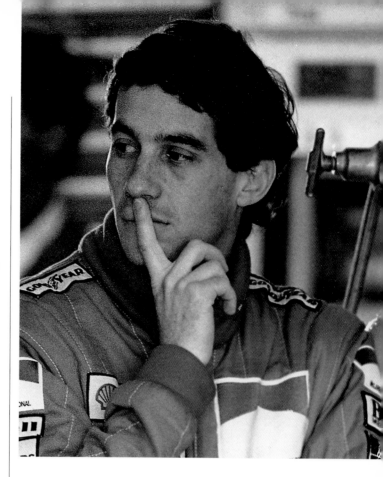

ABOVE: Brazilian racing champion Ayrton Senna is killed when his car crashes in the Grand Prix race at Monza, Italy.

EUTHANASIA PERMITTED
Oregon voters support Measure 16 permitting euthanasia in regulated circumstances.

WINTER OLYMPICS
The 17th Winter Olympics take place in the Norwegian town of Lillehammer just two years after the previous Winter Games. Television revenues are the reason for splitting the winter and summer games.

LARA BREAKS RECORD
West Indian cricketer Brian Lara (b. 1969) smashes the England cricket team for a world record 375 runs in the test match in Antigua.

BRAZIL WINS WORLD CUP
Brazil wins a record fourth soccer World Cup. The controversial decision to stage the World Cup in the United States, not a soccer power, is a success and leads to the formation of Major League Soccer in that country.

AYRTON SENNA
(1960–1994)

Brazilian motor racing legend Ayrton Senna has died after a 190mph crash in the San Marino Grand Prix at Monza in Italy. In his tragically short career he won 41 Grand Prix races and was three times Formula One world racing champion, in 1988, 1990, and 1992.

PEACE IN BOSNIA

The Dayton Peace Accord ends three years' fighting in Bosnia. A terrorist bomb explodes in Oklahoma. Israeli prime minister Yitzhak Rabin is assassinated. Worldwide outrage follows renewed nuclear testing and the execution of writer and human rights campaigner Ken Saro-Wiwa. An earthquake devastates the port of Kobe, Japan. Astronomers discover a brown dwarf and a talking pig becomes an unlikely film star.

OPPOSITE: The U.S. space shuttle *Atlantis* photographed from the Russian *Mir* space station.

1995

Jan	1	Austria, Finland, and Sweden join EU
	6	Tamils sign ceasefire in Sri Lanka but fighting resumes
	17	Earthquake devastates Kobe, Japan
Mar	20	Turkish forces launch attack against Kurds
Apr	19	Bomb in Oklahoma City
July	11	Serbs capture UN-designated safe area of Srebrenica, Bosnia
	20	Serbs attack UN safe haven, Bihac, Bosnia
Aug	4	Croatian forces invade Serb-inhabited region of Krajina, Croatia
	30	NATO begins attacks on Serb positions, Bosnia
Nov	1	Peace accord signed in Dayton, Ohio, between Bosnia, Serbia, and Croatia

Nov	4	Israeli prime minister Yitzhak Rabin is assassinated
	11	Nigerian writer and human rights campaigner Ken Saro-Wiwa executed
Dec	28	International protests following French nuclear tests

ABOVE: Yitzhak Rabin, who is shot dead in Tel Aviv.

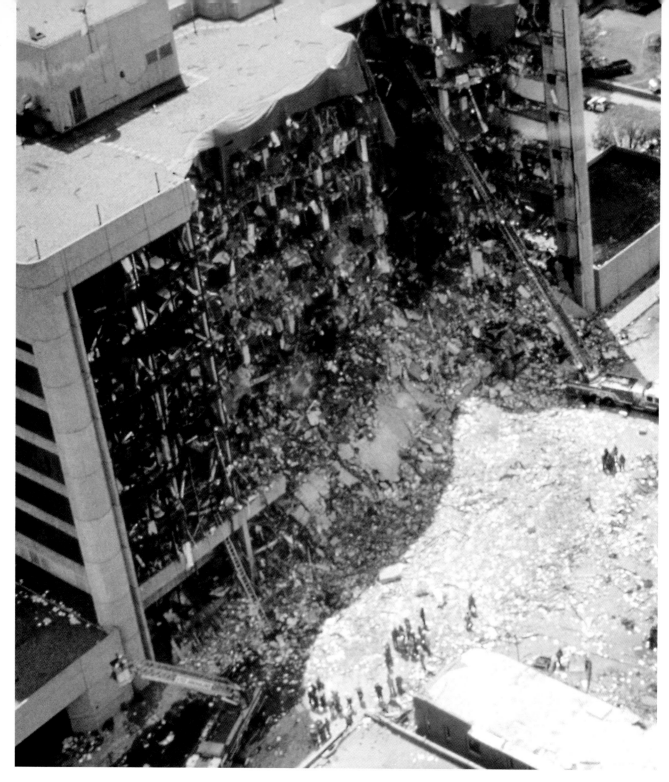

BOSNIAN CRISIS

In July, the Serbs overrun the UN-protected zones of Srebrenica and massacre the male population. They also besiege Bihac. The following month Serbs bombard Sarajevo, killing 37 people and leading NATO to attack infrastructure targets in Serb-held Bosnia. Following pressure on the Bosnian Serb leader Radovan Karadzic by President Milosevic of Serbia, heavy weapons are withdrawn from around Sarajevo. In November, at Dayton, Ohio, a peace agreement is signed, bringing an end to the Bosnian conflict: It splits the state 51-49 between the Bosnian and Croat Federation and the Republika Srpska (Bosnian Serbs). The settlement creates a unified Bosnia but in fact divides the country into two self-governing parts, a Muslim-Croat federation and a Bosnian-Serb republic.

ABOVE: Ruins of the Alfred Murrah Federal Building in Oklahoma City after a bomb has blown it up. A fanatical right-winger, Timothy McVeigh, will later be charged with planting the bomb.

LEFT: Filmmaker and comic Woody Allen directs *Mighty Aphrodite*, a comedy about love, marriage, and adopted children, perhaps as an antidote to the bad press he is receiving about his relationship with his adopted daughter.

ABOVE: A Bosnian Serb refugee from Krajina waits patiently in a government center. The plan is to reintegrate refugees into society.

OKLAHOMA BOMBING
Federal government offices in Oklahoma City are blown up in a rare terrorist bombing in the United States. The blast kills 167 people. Two men are later indicted for the crime; both are associated with far-right militias, which are fanatically opposed to the federal government.

SRI LANKA
Despite a temporary ceasefire, fighting resumes between the government and the Tamils. A state of emergency is reintroduced.

FRENCH NUCLEAR TESTING
In defiance of world opinion, France renews underground nuclear testing on Mururoa Atoll in the South Pacific. France carries out a series of tests before ending them in January 1996 and signing the Nuclear Test-Ban Treaty, which it had previously refused to do.

RABIN ASSASSINATED
Prime Minister Yitzhak Rabin is assassinated by a Hebrew fanatic in Tel Aviv, Israel, soon after leaving a peace rally. He is succeeded by Simon Peres. However, Rabin's assassination jeopardizes the peace process with the Palestinians when Peres loses the general election in May 1996 to the right-winger Benyamin Netanyahu (b. 1949), who is opposed to the land for peace deal.

BROWN DWARF DISCOVERED
Astronomers discover a brown dwarf, a strange object smaller than a star but larger than a planet. The existence of brown dwarfs has long been suspected but never proved.

SARO-WIWA EXECUTED
In Nigeria, the dissident writer and human rights campaigner Ken Saro-Wiwa (1941–95) and eight others are executed by the military government, prompting international outrage. Saro-Wiwa has led the protests by the Ogoni people of southern Nigeria against exploitation of their land by international oil companies; his death causes Nigeria to be suspended from the Commonwealth and sanctions imposed.

NEW EU MEMBERS
Austria, Sweden, and Finland join the EU, bringing its members up to 13. Many other states, including the Czech Republic, Hungary, Poland, Estonia, Slovenia, and Cyprus, queue up to join.

POWDER HER FACE
British composer Thomas Adès attracts critical praise for his opera *Powder her Face*. It is based on the sometimes scandalous life of Margaret, Duchess of Argyll.

MILKY WAY BLACK HOLE
U.S. astronomers report detecting signs of a black hole in our own galaxy, the Milky Way.

ANTIATOMS
A team of German, Italian, and Swiss physicists make the first antiatoms. They last for only a fraction of a second before colliding with ordinary atoms and vanishing.

ORBITING JUPITER
In December the U.S. spacecraft *Galileo*, launched in 1989, goes into orbit around Jupiter, and starts sending pictures and data back to Earth.

KOBE EARTHQUAKE
The Great Hanshin earthquake devastates Kobe in Japan. More than 2,700 lose their lives and more than 1,000 buildings are destroyed, as well as the region's roads and power supplies. The earthquake measured 7.2 on the Richter scale and is the worst earthquake to hit Japan since 1923.

ROAD PROTESTERS
In Britain, environmentalists protest against the building of a new road through ancient British woodland. They tunnel into the forest floor and build tree houses to prevent the felling of 10,000 trees. The protesters are evicted but their cause attracts considerable publicity and sympathy.

BANNING LIVE ANIMAL EXPORTS
Animal rights activists achieve a temporary ban on exporting live animals from a British port. They claim that animals are carried in overcrowded conditions and deprived of food and water for long periods, and aim for an EU ban on such practices.

TALIBAN, HUTUS, AND BRITISH BEEF

Taliban seizes Kabul in Afghanistan and imposes strict Islamic law. The Guatemalan civil war ends after 36 years of fighting. Tutsis attack Hutu refugees in Zaire. Prime minister Benazir Bhutto is dismissed from office. U.S. president Bill Clinton is elected for a second term. The EU bans British beef after fears of BSE. A bomb blast mars the centenary Olympic Games.

1 9 9 6

Feb	17	Space probe NEAR is launched	**Oct**	21	UN reports that 250,000 Hutu refugees have fled Zaire
Mar	13	Sixteen schoolchildren and their teacher killed by gunman in Dunblane, Scotland	**Nov**	5	Bill Clinton is elected U.S. president for second term
	25	EU ban export of British beef after BSE fears		15	Tutsi rebels defeat extremist Hutu militiamen
Apr	29	UN war crimes tribunal opens in The Hague, Netherlands, to investigate alleged crimes against humanity in Yugoslav civil war	**Dec**	17	Tupac guerrillas seize hostages, Lima, Peru
				29	Civil war ends in Guatemala
July	27	Bomb explodes at Olympic Games, Atlanta			
Aug	31	Iraqi aircraft violate UN no-fly zone			
Sep	3	United States launches cruise missiles against Iraq			
	27	Taliban takes control of Kabul, Afghanistan			

ABOVE: A U.S. military engineeer directs traffic across the pontoon bridge built to link Croatia and Bosnia-Herzegovina.

BELOW: A U.S. Howitzer at work during Operation Joint Endeavor, part of the response to the crisis in former Yugoslavia.

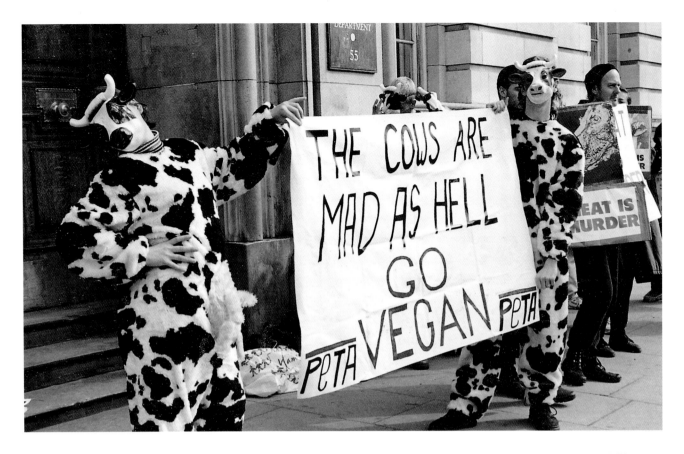

ABOVE: Animal rights activists demonstrate in London as BSE is discovered in cattle and is feared to affect human beings.

TALIBAN TAKE KABUL

The Islamic fundamentalist Taliban militia take control of Afghanistan's capital, Kabul, imposing strict Islamic law and forcing women to wear a full veil in public and all men to grow beards. Their control of the country is far from complete, but Taliban brings a measure of peace to Afghanistan not enjoyed since the Russian invasion in 1979.

RWANDAN REFUGEES

More than one million Hutu refugees from Rwanda living in refugee camps are attacked by Tutsis supported by the Rwandan government, driving them from their camps. Many die from cholera and other diseases, causing a major humanitarian crisis in Zaire and destabilizing the government of President Mobutu (b. 1930). During November, 400,000 of the Hutus return home to Rwanda after the extremists responsible for the 1994 genocide in Rwanda are driven out of the refugee camps.

BENAZIR BHUTTO DISMISSED

In Pakistan, Prime Minister Benazir Bhutto (b. 1953) is again dismissed by the president for corruption for the second time in her career. Bhutto, daughter of the former prime minister Zulfikar Ali Bhutto, who was overthrown and then executed by the military in 1978, first became prime minister in 1988 after the fall of the military government but was dismissed in 1990. She won reelection in 1993 but persistent charges of corruption against her, and in particular her husband, remove her from power once again.

CLINTON WINS SECOND TERM

U.S. president Bill Clinton wins a second term in office against Republican Bob Dole, taking 49 percent of the popular vote against 41 percent for Dole. Democrats fail to win Congress, and face problems getting legislation through against Republican opposition.

KURDS CAPTURE SULAIMANIYA

The Kurdish Democratic Party (KDP), fighting with Iraqi assistance, capture the city of Sulaimaniya, stronghold of the umbrella anti-Iraqi organization the Patriotic Union of Kurdistan (PUK). The KDP shell a Kurdish refugee camp in Iran. Sulaimaniya is recaptured in October.

TUPAC GUERRILLAS SEIZE HOSTAGES

Movimiento Revolucionario Tupac Amaru (MRTA) guerrillas seize 460 hostages at the Japanese ambassador's residence in Lima, Peru. All but 72 hostages are released through negotiations. In April 1997, Peruvian special forces storm the residence, kill the 14 members of MRTA and release the hostages.

HUGE DINOSAUR

Fossil bones of a huge carnivorous dinosaur are found in the Sahara. The dinosaur is larger than the famous *Tyrannosaurus rex*, but similar to another dinosaur found in South America eight months earlier.

PEACE IN GUATEMALA

Left-wing guerrillas in Guatemala sign peace with the government and end 36 years of civil war. Two years later, the Roman Catholic Church reports that the civil war has caused the deaths of 150,000 members of the rural Native American majority with a further 50,000 listed as missing.

TOP: An Italian soldier clearing landmines at Praca in Bosnia. When the fighting is over, the mines present a danger to civilians.

ABOVE: A U.S. soldier mans an IFOR (International Force) checkpoint on the road that leads to Tuzla, Bosnia-Herzegovina.

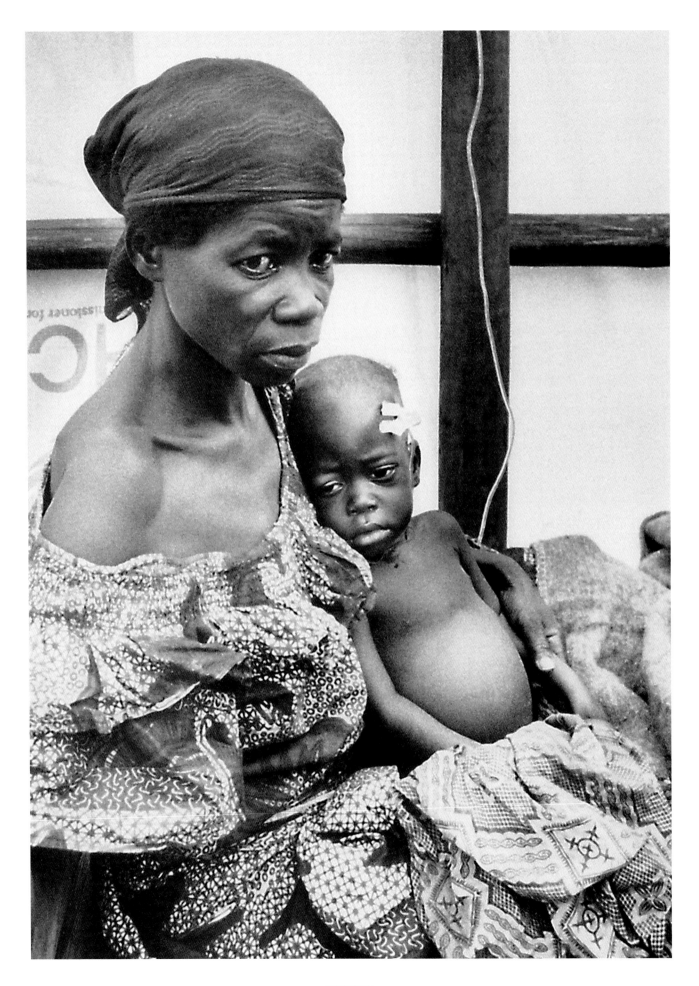

TRAINSPOTTING

The film *Trainspotting* is premiered. Starring Robert Carlyle, the film is based on a novel by Irving Welsh and takes a sometimes funny, sometimes brutal look at the Scottish drug scene.

TOY STORY

A new film, *Toy Story*, opens. It features the adventures of a group of toys and is the first full-length feature film to be made completely by computer animation.

ASTEROID PROBE

Space probe NEAR (Near Earth Asteroid Rendezvous) is launched on February 17 to investigate the asteroid Eros, a rugged 25-mile-long lump of rock between Mars and Jupiter.

MAD COW DISEASE

British scientists report a new variant of a rare fatal illness of the human nervous system, Creutzfeldt-Jakob Disease (CJD), linked to eating beef from cattle infected with bovine spongiform encephalopathy (BSE), or mad cow disease. BSE was identified in 1986 in cows fed with animal protein from sheep infected with a nervous disease, scrapie. In March, the EU bans the export of British beef.

LEFT: Refugees from Zaire shelter in Nyaragusu Camp, Kigoma, Tanzania. Diseases such as cholera are a problem in the camps.

SUBMARINE SUICIDES

North Korean infiltrators commit suicide when their Sang-O-class submarine with 26 men on board runs aground off South Korea in September. Thirteen were killed by South Korean forces, while ten appear to have been executed by an officer who, rather than be captured, committed suicide.

CENTENARY OLYMPICS

The 100th Olympic Games are held in Atlanta. Eleven thousand athletes from 197 nations attend. Kerri Strug's brave vault with an injured ankle helps the American women's team to gold in gymnastics, while Canadian Donovan Bailey claims gold and a world record time of 9.84 seconds in the 100m. The undoubted star of the track is Michael Johnson, of the United States, who achieves a double in the 200m and 400m, winning the 200m in the fastest time ever. Michelle Smith takes three swimming golds and a bronze back home to Ireland. Sport, however, is again obscured by violence when a bomb explodes in Olympic Park, killing two and injuring 11.

TINY MOTORS

U.S. engineers announce the construction of micromotors about 1mm (.039in) square, which can drive gears thinner than a human hair.

BELOW: Zairean refugees flee the fighting in their country, cramming into small boats to cross Lake Tanganyika to Tanzania.

DEATH OF A PRINCESS

Diana, Princess of Wales dies suddenly in a car crash in Paris. Financial crisis hits Southeast Asia when the value of the Thai baht collapses. Socialists and Social Democrats dominate European elections. Hong Kong reverts to Chinese control. Scientists successfully clone a sheep — the first ever. The world watches three-tailed comet Hale-Bopp as it passes the Earth, and girl power hits the charts.

OPPOSITE: Thousands leave flowers at the gates of Kensington Palace, London, in honor of a dead princess.

1997

Jan	1	Kofi Annan of Ghana becomes UN Secretary-General
	26	Violence in Albania after collapse of pyramid saving schemes
Feb	27	Announcement that British geneticists have cloned a sheep
Apr	22	Peruvian special forces storm the occupied Japanese embassy in Lima, killing 14 Tupac guerrillas and releasing their hostages
May	1	Labour Party wins British general election
	12	Russia and Chechnya sign peace agreement
	26	Tutsi rebels take Kinshasa, Zaire. They rename the country the Democratic Republic of Congo
June	1	Socialist Party wins general election in France
	2	Timothy McVeigh found guilty of Oklahama City bombing
July	1	Hong Kong reverts to Chinese control
	2	Economic crisis begins in Southeast Asia
Aug	31	Diana, Princess of Wales, is killed in a car crash. Dodi Fayed, her escort, also dies in the accident

ABOVE: The Spice Girls, living embodiment of "girl power" at the première of their film *Spice — the Movie.*

EUROPEAN ELECTIONS

In Britain Tony Blair (b. 1953) leads the Labour Party to a landslide victory after 18 years of Conservative government. Victories for the French Socialists in June and the German Social Democrats in September 1998, removing Helmut Kohl after 16 years in power, lead to Socialist or Social Democratic governments in almost every Western European nation.

HONG KONG

A British crown colony since 1841, Hong Kong reverts to Chinese rule. The Chinese agree to respect existing laws and economic structures, although democratic institutions are swiftly replaced by an assembly appointed by Beijing.

MOTHER TERESA OF CALCUTTA
(born AGNES GONXHA BOJAXHIU)
(1910–1997)

The Yugoslav-born Roman Catholic missionary Mother Teresa, whose work in Calcutta is known throughout the world, has died. In 1928 Mother Teresa joined the Sisters of Loretto in Calcutta and taught in their convent until 1948 when she left to work alone with the poor. In 1950 she founded her sisterhood, the Order of the Missionaries of Charity, which now has some 2,000 sisters, caring for the poor and sick.

DEATH OF DIANA

Diana, Princess of Wales, is killed in a car crash in Paris. Her death causes an international outpouring of grief and leads to a sharp fall in the popularity of the British monarchy, whom many consider treated her poorly during her life. An estimated two billion people worldwide watch the funeral service on television. Her campaign to rid the world of landmines is successful in 1998, when an international treaty forbidding their use is signed in Ottawa.

FINANCIAL COLLAPSE

The collapse in value of the Thai baht leads to a financial crisis throughout Southeast Asia as banks collapse and currencies lose their value. The crisis, caused by excessive national debt and poor financial controls, spreads to Japan, Indonesia, and Russia, and then in 1999 to Brazil. Although the International Monetary Fund launches a rescue package for affected countries, the economic downturn creates chaos throughout the world's markets and leads to fears of a recession to match that of the 1930s.

MOBUTU DEFEATED

President Mobutu, leader and dictator of Zaire since 1965, loses power after rebels led by Laurent Kabilia overthrow his government. As leader, Mobutu treated Zaire as his personal bank account, bleeding the country dry and causing economic ruin.

FINANCIAL COLLAPSE IN ALBANIA

The small eastern European country of Albania descends into anarchy after the collapse of corrupt pyramid investment schemes. Albanians who have lost all their savings take to the streets, looting weapons from the army and attacking the government. Foreign nationals are evacuated and the government calls elections, which result in a landslide victory for the opposition Socialist Party in June.

BRITISH/RUSSIAN AGREEMENT

In March the British and Russian governments sign an agreement on joint military training and information exchange on new weapons.

SPICE POWER

Girl power in the form of the Spice Girls — Posh, Baby, Sporty, Scary, and Ginger — is the latest success in the world of pop. The all-girl British band is achieving worldwide success with a string of bestselling numbers.

E. COLI MAPPED

An American team of geneticists led by Fred Blattner compile the complete genetic code of the bacterium *Escherichia coli,* which contains more than 4,200 genes. Some forms of *E. coli* cause food poisoning; this year an outbreak of *E. coli* bacteria derived from eating contaminated meat occurs in the UK.

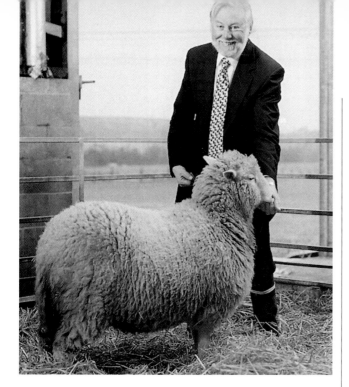

ABOVE: Dolly the sheep, the world's first adult animal clone, with Dr. Ron James, head of PPL Therapeutics at Edinburgh's Roslin Institute.

ABOVE: Sarajevo, the Serbian capital, begins to rebuild as peace settles in the troubled countries of the former Yugoslavia.

THE FULL MONTY

A new British film is gaining unexpected success internationally. Directed by Peter Cattaneo, *The Full Monty* features a group of unemployed men in the north of England who turn to stripping to earn a living, extracting hilarious comedy from social deprivation.

DOLLY THE SHEEP

Scottish scientists announce that they have cloned a sheep from a cell taken from an adult animal; the sheep is nicknamed Dolly. This is the first successful cloning using nonreproductive cells. DNA from an adult cell was combined with an unfertilized egg that had had its DNA removed.

HALE-BOPP

Comet Hale-Bopp, a comet with three tails, nears the Sun in April. A mass of rock, dust, and ice, the comet is named after the two American astronomers who first saw it: Alan Hale and Thomas Bopp. The comet will not return for 2,400 years.

CULT SUICIDE

As Comet Hale-Bopp appears, the brightest comet visible for 400 years, 39 members of the Heaven's Gate cult in San Diego, commit mass suicide. The cult's members believed that they were to escape Earth's destruction by rendez-vousing with a space vehicle obscured by the comet.

GUGGENHEIM MUSEUM

One of the most striking of recent buildings is the Guggenheim Museum in Bilbao. Designed by Frank O. Gehry, the building has a striking metal-clad façade in which curved forms seem to invite the visitor into a mysterious space.

FLOODS CAUSE HOMELESSNESS

Flash floods make 70,000 homeless in the Czech Republic, Germany, and Poland.

TIGER WOODS

U.S. golfer Eldrick "Tiger" Woods wins the Masters golf tournament, aged 21, by a 12-stroke victory at Augusta.

McDONALD'S CLEARED

The longest trial in English history ends when fast food chain McDonald's is cleared of damaging the environment. McDonald's sued two protesters, David Morris and Helen Steel, for distributing leaflets criticizing the American chain's environmental record.

OFF TO SATURN

The spacecraft *Cassini/Huygens* is launched on a voyage to Saturn to arrive in 2004.

DIANA, PRINCESS OF WALES (1961–1997)

The world is shocked by the sudden and violent death of Diana, Princess of Wales, who has been killed in Paris during a car chase involving the press. The former wife of HRH the Prince of Wales (they divorced in 1996), she had been a constant focus of media attention since taking on her public role. She was actively involved in the work of many charities, but since 1994 had been working principally for the International Red Cross. Recently she had spearheaded the campaign against land mines. She was in the company of Dodi Fayed when she was killed.

SEX, TRUTH, AND RECONCILIATION

In the United States, President Clinton avoids impeachment, following investigation into an alleged affair. In South Africa, the Truth and Reconciliation Committee publishes its report. Tension rises again in Serbia. Former Chilean dictator Pinochet is arrested. Terrorists bomb U.S. embassies in Kenya and Tanzania. The Good Friday Peace Agreement brings peace to Northern Ireland. A hurricane devastates Central America. Viagra is the new wonder drug for impotence.

OPPOSITE: Bill Clinton, seen here with his wife and daughter, has a troubled year in office.

1998

Jan	21	Investigation launched into President Clinton's alleged affair with White House intern
Mar	5	NASA scientists announce evidence of water on Moon
Apr	10	Good Friday Peace Agreement brings peace settlement for Northern Ireland
May	6	Mudslides devastate towns in Italy
	20	Indonesian president Suharto resigns following riots
	28	Pakistan explodes five nuclear devices
Aug	7	Terrorists bomb U.S. embassies in Nairobi, Kenya, and Dar-es-Salaam, Tanzania
Sept	24	Iran lifts fatwa on author Salman Rushdie
Oct	12	Nato threatens air strike against Serbia
	18	International observers arrive in Serbian province of Kosovo
	18	Former Chilean dictator General Augusto Pinochet arrested in London
	24	Troops from South Africa and Botswana enter Lesotho
	29	Truth and Reconciliation Committee publishes report, South Africa
Dec	16	American and British air strikes against Iraq

ABOVE: Frank Sinatra, "Ol' Blue Eyes," dies this year.

CLINTON SEX SCANDAL

President Clinton is accused of having an affair with a White House intern and asking her to lie about it. The allegations are investigated by a independent prosecutor, Kenneth Starr, and eventually lead to an attempt by the U.S. Congress to impeach the president for perjury and other offenses in November. The president gives evidence to the House of Representatives, which is televised, but despite pressure from Republicans, Clinton is not impeached.

GOOD FRIDAY AGREEMENT

In Northern Ireland, political parties from Unionist and Nationalist communities sign the Good Friday Peace Agreement setting up an elected assembly and new institutions linking the North with the Republic. The agreement, which is overseen by Northern Ireland Secretary Mo Mowlam (b. 1949), also sets up a process to encourage paramilitary groups to decommission their weapons. The Unionist leader, David Trimble, and the Nationalist John Hume jointly receive the 1998 Nobel Peace Prize for their work in securing the agreement.

TITANIC

Starring Leonardo di Caprio and Kate Winslett, the disaster movie *Titanic* is the most expensive film ever made and a smash hit, taking 11 Academy Awards.

SUHARTO RESIGNS

In Indonesia, following economic collapse, demonstrators force the resignation of President Suharto, leader since 1967. He is succeeded by his deputy, Jusuf Habibie, who promises to end corruption and nepotism in government.

U.S. EMBASSIES BOMBED

Islamic fundamentalists bomb the U.S. embassies in Nairobi, Kenya, and Dar-es-Salaam, Tanzania, killing 257 people and injuring hundreds more. In retaliation, U.S. warships launch Tomahawk cruise missiles at targets in Afghanistan and Sudan in an attempt to kill Osama bin Laden, the Saudi millionaire who has been identified with terrorist bombings against U.S. targets in Africa and the Middle East. The cruise missile attack does not kill him. U.S. intelligence incorrectly identified a pharmaceuticals factory in Khartoum, Sudan, as a chemical warfare factory.

KOSOVO

International observers are sent to the Serbian province of Kosovo to police a ceasefire agreed between Kosovan freedom fighters and the Serbian army after NATO threatens air strikes against Serbia. The province, which is almost entirely Albanian in population, is fighting for independence from Serbia, which suspended the provincial constitution in March 1991 and introduced repressive measures against the Albanian population. The war is the latest chapter in the disintegration of the former Yugoslavia which began in 1991.

TRUTH AND RECONCILIATION

The report of the Truth and Reconciliation Commission, chaired by Nobel Peace Prize-winner Archbishop Desmond Tutu, is published. The Commission took evidence from many people in an attempt to reconcile the differences left by apartheid. The report condemns apartheid as a crime against humanity but finds the ruling African National Congress (ANC) as well as white-only parties to have been guilty of human rights violations.

PINOCHET ARRESTED

Former Chilean dictator Augusto Pinochet is arrested in London after Spanish judges apply for his extradition to Spain to face charges of murder and torture. Following legal debates over whether Pinochet has legal immunity, in 1999 the High Court decides that he does not have immunity and the British Home Secretary Jack Straw (b. 1946) orders his extradition.

LESOTHO

The Pretoria government, South Africa, sends troops into Lesotho to restore calm following civil unrest.

OPERATION DESERT FOX

The United States and Britain carry out air strikes against Iraqi targets following Saddam Hussein's noncompliance with UN weapons inspectors. The U.S. Navy, U.S. Air Force and RAF launch 650 attacks, the U.S. Navy launches 325 Tomahawk cruise missiles, and U.S. Air Force B-52s 90 cruise missiles against 100 targets including Republican Guard barracks and chemical and biological warfare installations in Iraq.

BIRTHDAY LETTERS

Britain's Poet Laureate Ted Hughes (1930–98) publishes poems he has written about the suicide of his first wife, American poet Sylvia Plath. The book, which appears just before Hughes's death, wins critical acclaim and sells in large numbers.

NUCLEAR TESTING

India joins the nuclear club by testing nuclear devices in Rajasthan. Pakistan retaliates by testing five devices, although both pledge to sign the Nuclear Test-Ban Treaty at some stage.

FAST-SELLING VIAGRA

Viagra, a new treatment for impotence, has become the fastest-selling prescription drug.

ITALIAN EARTHQUAKE

Frescoes by Italian artist Giotto are destroyed after an earthquake in Assisi. There is controversy over whether the works of art could have been better protected.

CODE COMPLETED

For the first time, scientists compile the complete code of an invertebrate animal, a tiny worm.

FLYING GALAXIES

Astronomers discover that the galaxies in space are flying apart at ever-increasing speeds against the force of gravity.

CIRCADIAN CLOCK

Research shows that nearly all living organisms, not just people, have a built-in mechanism, the "circadian clock," which uses light and temperature to keep track of night and day.

WINTER OLYMPICS

The Winter Olympics in Nagano, Japan, are a resounding success in front of huge crowds. The speed skating record book is rewritten with the use of the clap skate, invented in Holland. The new skates, named for the noise they make, have a spring-loaded hinge at the front which allows the racer's heel to rise without lifting the blade of the skate from the ice. Dutch skaters win five golds and six other medals and five world records are broken. The Czech Republic score a shock ice hockey win by beating the NHL professionals of Canada and America, and American Tara Lipinski captures figure skating gold.

FRANCE WINS WORLD CUP

France wins the football World Cup in Paris. The defeat of Brazil in the final was surrounded by intrigue over the poor performance of Brazilian star Ronaldo.

DRUGS DOMINATE TOUR DE FRANCE

The Tour de France is disrupted by revelations of drug use by cyclists and team support for the abuse. The discovery of a team masseur carrying banned drugs leads to a police investigation, arrests, and then protests by racers, who complain of victimization. Cycling's top event is completed but the sport's image is tarnished.

BASEBALL

Mark McGwire, the first-baseman for the St. Louis Cardinals, hits his 62nd home run of the season to pass Roger Maris's tally. His race with Sammy Sosa of the Chicago Cubs to reach the record entrances baseball fans. McGwire finishes with 70 homers, Sosa with 66.

POL POT DEAD

The body of the former leader of the Khmer Rouge, Pol Pot, has been put on display in northern Cambodia. Due for trial, he may have committed suicide or have been murdered. During his rule over Cambodia (1975–79) he was responsible for some 1.7 million deaths.

DEVASTATING HURRICANE

Hurricane Mitch causes devastation in Honduras, Nicaragua, El Salvador, and Guatemala before heading across Mexico into the Caribbean. More than 10,000 people are killed, and whole towns are swept away.

BELOW: The "Agreement," the document produced as a result of the Northern Ireland peace talks, is torn up by a Unionist supporter.

BLOODY AND VIOLENT END TO THE CENTURY

War breaks out in the Balkans when Nato begins air strikes against the Serbian military targets in Yugoslavia. The action intensifies Serbian "cleansing" of ethnic Albanians and thousands flee Kosovo. The single European currency is introduced and the EU Commission resigns after evidence of fraud. King Hussein of Jordan dies. New research suggests flirting is good for you. A series of earthquakes in Turkey leaves thousands dead. Russian military battle in Grozny, Chechnya, as Christmas approaches.

OPPOSITE: Nelson Mandela bows out of South African politics.

1999

Jan	1	European single currency begins	**Apr**	5	Two Libyans suspected of Lockerbie bombing in The Netherlands for trial
	24	Cash-for-votes scandal hits International Olympic Committee (IOC); subsequently six members resign	**May**	17	Ehud Barak elected prime minister of Israel in landslide victory
				26	Indian aircraft attack guerrillas in Indian part of Kashmir and lose two planes
Feb	4	Russians attempt to create artificial moon			
	7	King Hussein of Jordan dies aged 64	**Aug**	17	Turkey rocked by first of a series of devastating earthquakes, thousands die
	15	Abdullah Ocalan, leader of the Kurdish Workers Party, is captured in Nairobi by Turkish special forces			
	23	Britain completes destruction of its stocks of anti-personnel mines	**Sep**	1	Anti-independence militia gangs rampage in East Timor
Mar	7	US threatens trade war against Europe for importing bananas from former US colonies in the Caribbean and Africa	**Nov**	10	After many denials, Russia moves military forces against Chechnya
	15	All members of the European Commission resign over fraud	**Dec**	14	USA relinquishes control over Panama Canal
	24	Nato begins air strikes against Serbia		31	Boris Yeltsin, Russian president, resigns
	31	Serb forces capture three US soldiers			

NEW NATO MEMBERS

Hungary, Poland and the Czech Republic join NATO, the first former Communist countries in Eastern Europe to do so. All three countries are also applying to join the EU.

SINGLE EUROPEAN CURRENCY

The European single currency begins in eleven EU nations, including France and Germany but not Britain. The Euro, which can only be used in paper transactions, will initially run alongside the different national currencies but will replace them in 2002, when the national currencies will be abolished and Euro notes and coins will circulate freely.

FRAUD IN EU

All twenty members of the EU Commission resign following a report into alleged fraud, which finds the executive guilty of mismanagement, corruption and nepotism. Former Italian prime minister Romano Prodi is appointed new president of the Commission.

NATO BOMBS YUGOSLAVIA

In March aircraft and cruise missiles from twelve Nato nations launch air attacks against more than 40 targets in Yugoslavia after Serbia refuses to accede to peace negotiations over Kosovo. Serb troops in Kosovo force ethnic Kosovan Albanians across neighbouring borders. By the end of March some 300,000 have been displaced. Three US soldiers from the 1st Infantry Division are captured at Kumanovo, Macedonia, by Serb forces who have crossed the border. US politician Jesse Jackson later negotiates their release.

INSTITUTIONAL RACISM

In the UK, the inquiry into the murder of a black teenager, Stephen Lawrence, finds that the police had mishandled the case and are guilty of institutional racism. In the US, a white supremacist is convicted of murdering a black man, James Byrd, in Texas.

BERLIN IS GERMANY'S CAPITAL

For the first time since the war, Berlin becomes the capital of Germany again as the government moves back from Bonn. Since the fall of the Berlin Wall in 1990 and the reunification of Germany, Berlin has been extensively rebuilt to accommodate the new government buildings.

CIVIL WAR IN SIERRA LEONE

Fighting intensifies in Sierra Leone when forces of the Revolutionary United Front (RUF) loot and burn Freetown. President Kabbah has criticized Liberia for supporting the rebels. Civil war began in 1991. In 1996, Ahmed Kabbah was democratically elected president but was overthrown nine months later by the RUF. In 1997, supported by 5,000 men from the Nigerian backed ECOMOG force, he returned to power, but the RUF continues its fight.

KURDISH LEADER CAPTURED

Turkish special forces in Nairobi capture the Kurdish leader Abdullah Öçalan. The capture precipitates protests throughout Europe as Kurds blame Greek diplomats for allowing their leader to be captured.

NEW ISRAELI PRIME MINISTER

Labour leader and Israel's most decorated soldier, Ehud Barak, is elected Israel's new prime minister, defeating right-winger Binyamin Netanyahu in a landslide victory. Barak's election will pave the way for a fresh start to Middle East peace talks.

SISTINE CHAPEL CEILING

The cleaning of Michelangelo's famous painted ceiling in the Vatican's Sistine Chapel is completed. It shows the familiar paintings in an unfamiliar light, much brighter in colour. Experts are divided over the result, some saying that the cleaning has brought the ceiling as close as possible to its original condition, others saying that the work has been too radical.

MIRROR FAILURE

A Russian attempt to create an artificial "moon" to light up dark areas of the country fails when a space mirror does not unfurl from space station *Mir*.

STARDUST TRIP

Space probe *Stardust* sets off on a 5 billion-km (3 billion-mi) journey to rendezvous with Comet Wild-2, carrying instruments to collect dust from the comet in order to learn more about it.

EXTRA-TERRESTRIAL CHAIR

The first academic chair for an astronomer to search for extra-terrestrial intelligence is founded at the University of California at Berkeley; first professor is William Welch.

GM FOODS DEBATE

In the UK, the safety of genetically modified foods comes under intense debate following a demand from pressure groups and some scientists for the UK government to impose a moratorium on new GM crops.

FLIRTING IS GOOD FOR YOU

Research published in the American magazine *Psychology Today* suggests that flirting may be designed to ensure that we attract the right mate. According to some research, flirting, far from being superficial party behaviour, may be a deeply ingrained means of exchanging vital information about the health and reproductive fitness of a potential partner.

THE WHOLE WOMAN

Australian feminist Germaine Greer publishes *The Whole Woman*, a sequel to *The Female Eunuch*, one of the landmark books of the Women's Liberation Movement. In her new book, Greer states that feminism has lost its way and women need to get angry again.

MICHAEL JORDAN RETIRES — AGAIN

Michael Jordan, on whose back professional basketball rose to international prominence, announces his second retirement. Jordan led the Chicago Bulls to six NBA titles; three before his first retirement and three after.

LOCKERBIE SUSPECTS

In April, the two Libyan intelligence officers believed to be responsible for the Lockerbie explosion in 1988, are flown to an air force base in Holland to be tried under Scottish law.

BANANA WAR

The US threatens a trade war with Europe, claiming that Europe favours bananas imported from former US colonies in the Caribbean and Africa. Caribbean-producing countries St Lucia and Dominica threaten to stall World Trade Organization talks.

KING HUSSEIN (IBN TALAL) OF JORDAN (1935–1999)

King Hussein of Jordan has died after a battle with cancer. Educated at Harrow and Sandhurst in England, he had ruled Jordan for 46 years and is widely accredited as an influential peace-maker in the troubled Middle East. More than 50 foreign leaders and 800,000 Jordanians gathered for his funeral.

ABOVE A family of Kosovan Albanians flee Serbian torture and executions.

BELOW: A distressed young Albanian demonstrates the misery of conflict.

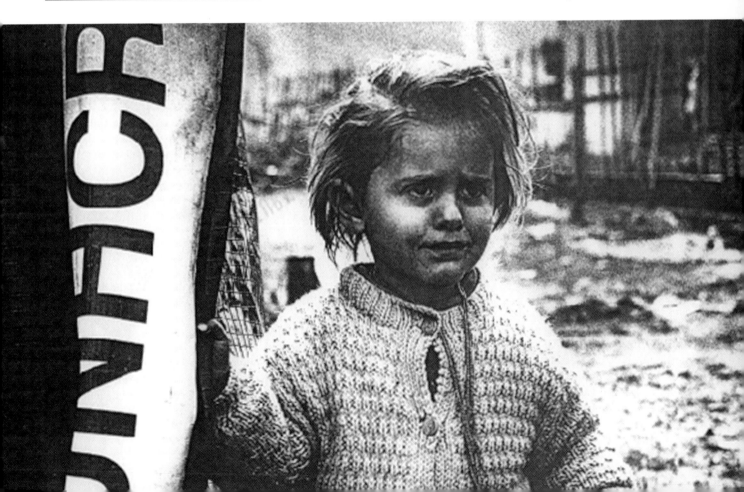

WAR CRIME INDICTMENT

As diplomats work to reduce differences between the West and Russia over plans to end the Kosovo crisis, the International War-Crimes Tribunal announces that it plans to indict Serb leader Slobodan Milosevic, therefore reducing his incentive to compromise. Meanwhile, NATO announces that it is to increase to 50,000 the number of troops on standby in neighbouring Macedonia — though for what purpose is unclear. By June, Serbia announces agreement to a peace deal proposed by Russian, European and American envoys.

COLD WAR REVISITED

An American congressional committee reveals that China has stolen classified information on every deployed warhead in their missile system. The spying had gone on for more that 20 years at Los Alamos National Laboratory and appears to be continuing. The US government seems powerless to stop the information flow but promises to tighten security at government laboratories.

KASHMIR CONFLICT FLARES UP

Indian aircraft attacks guerrillas operating out of Kashmir on the Indian side, however, there is a price — two aircraft are lost. India accuses the Pakistani army of supplying military equipment to the guerrillas. Twice before the two countries have fought a war over this territory. By June tension reaches its highest level for 30 years. India's prime minister, Atal Behari Vajpayee, says the campaign will continue until the infiltrators are driven out.

BACK TO TIANANMEN SQUARE

Ten years after the killings in Tiananman Square, China prepares for the anniversary by closing foreign satellite TV channels and blocking the internet. In an unprecedented legal action, the relatives of some of the victims in the original demonstration submit evidence

BELOW: Izmit, Turkey is hit at 03.01 hours by an earthquake measuring 7.4 on the Richter scale. Rescue operations become a race against time as air runs out for survivors trapped under collapsed buildings.

to a Chinese court demanding a criminal investigation into the role played by officials and troops at the time.

ANC LANDSLIDE
The African National Congress wins almost two thirds of the vote in South Africa's second non-racial election, in June. It falls one seat short of a two-thirds majority in parliament. The ANC forms a coalition with the Inkatha Freedom Party giving a combined majority of more than three to one.

GREENPEACE FROZEN OUT
British Nuclear Fuels secure a Dutch court order to freeze Greenpeace's international bank account after arguing that the organisation's protests caused extensive delays in preparing two controversial shipments of reprocessed plutonium to be shipped from France back to Japan. Both Britain and France had banned Greenpeace vessels from their waters. Greenpeace argues that the 20 tons of plutonium is a dangerous shipment and a waste of money.

RELENTLESS RAINS AND FLOODING
Rivers in the Ganges, Brahmaputra and Meghna basins overflow displacing nearly one million people as seasonal rains fall relentlessly in Bangladesh. Meanwhile, in China emergency workers battle to contain the flow of water from the Yangtze river and its tributaries. The water has been rising since June and by August, fed by tropical storm Olga, an estimated 1.8 million people move from the flood plains in central and east China.

BLACK SKY
In south east Asia the sky was again painted black by smog from burning forests in Indonesia. Last year, the smog clouds reached Singapore and Malaysia causing sickness in the populations.

POPE OUT, THEN IN BY ANOTHER ROUTE
Pope John Paul is banned by China from visiting Hong Kong during his Asian tour because of the Vatican's ties with Taiwan. The pope still intends to visit the mainland via Macau.

A SOLAR ECLIPSE
Millions of onlookers are attracted to watch the path of a solar eclipse as it passes over Europe, the Middle East and Asia. Watching this natural phenomenon, many are anxious to dispel the idea that it is a precursor to an apocalypse as the century draws to an end. Others are concerned to avoid blindness while enjoying the view.

TURKEY EARTHQUAKE
The industrial north west of Turkey is struck by a massive earthquake. The town of Izmit is the focus of destruction. Over 13,000 people are missing, many buried in shoddily constructed apartment blocks. A hospital and a military base is destroyed. An oil refinery

ABOVE: Communications and freedom: by the end of the century laptop computers such as the iBook and mobile telephones afford a change of living style that is one life-style revolution for the coming decade.

is set alight. The government is criticized for contributing to a feeble rescue effort as international organisations dig for survivors and more than 200,000 people are made homeless. Three months later, in November, a second big earthquake hits a town 200 km west of Ankara, the capital. Over 500 people are killed.

DEATH WISH GRANTED
Plans to legalize euthanasia and doctor-assisted suicide are published by the Dutch government. This action formalizes practices already carried out and accepted in the country. Working to very strict guidelines children as young as 12 would be entitled to request death. If approved, The Netherlands will become the first country in the world to legalize mercy killings.

BLOOD MONEY
IG Farben was the world's largest chemical company during WWII, and one of its subsidiaries produced lethal gases used to kill camp inmates in Nazi Germany. In August, more than 50 years after the end of the war, the shareholders agree to establish a $1.6 million fund to compensate former slave labourers. The move fails to satisfy survivor groups who are demanding an estimated $15 million, liquidating the company's assets, to be distributed to its victims.

INDEPENDENCE FIGHT
In Dili, East Timor, as the August 30 referendum draws near, anti-independence thugs launch attacks on the UN and pro-independence groups. By September 1, these militias go on the rampage. Most East Timorese vote for independence, but the violence becomes overwhelming throughout September until it is eventually brought under control by a United Nations force led by Australia. More than 300,000 Timorese have been left homeless in an effort to escape attack by rampaging mobs. Indonesia cancels a four-year-old security agreement with Australia in protest at its attitude.

ABOVE: The newly constructed interior of the Reichstag building sees the first full session of the Bundestag in April as government power returns to Germany's historic capital.

RUSSIA DEFENDS ITS SOVEREIGNTY

In September, after more than three weeks of Russian artillery and air strikes, the guerrillas who invaded Dagastan are forced back into Chechnya in southern Russia. 30,000 soldiers are sent to Russia's border with Chechnya whose Islamic militants are accused of recent civilian bombings. Air attacks start against what the Kremlin describes as terrorist targets. In November, it is estimated that over 180,000 Chechen civilians have fled their homes. By December, Russian ground forces in Chechnya enter Grozny, the capital, fighting a dirty war of retribution.

JAPAN'S WOMEN COME LAST

Women in Japan finally get access to the birth control pill four decades after their counterparts in other industrialized countries. In contrast, it took just six months for the male dominated Japanese society to approve the sale of Viagra, the popular anti-impotence drug.

BATTERED BY FLOYD

More than 3.5 million people move out of the path of Hurricane Floyd as it works its way up the east coast of America. States of emergency are declared in several states as the country's largest evacuation in history begins. Florida and Georgia are declared disaster areas.

HAPPY BIRTHDAY?

China celebrates 50 years of communism. An edition of the American based *Time* magazine containing articles on human rights in China is banned. The Chinese authorities crack down on the banned Falun Gong movement — said to have more adherents than China's Communist Party — accusing it of being 'superstitious, evil thinking' and an organisation that 'sabotages social stability'. Government agencies arrest unknown numbers of followers in security sweeps across Beijing after a silent protest in Tiananmen Square by supporters of the movement.

BELOW: Hurricane Floyd over the Americas. This weather satellite image helps predict the path of damage lying in wait. Flooding affects more than 200,000 in the USA and even more in Central America.

Hurricane Floyd
GOES-8 Colorized IR Image

ABOVE: By the end of 1999, use of the electronic World Wide Web and Internet leads to e-commerce becoming a household activity for communications and day-to-day activities such as shopping.

PAKISTAN COUP

In mid-October, Pakistan's army overthrows Nawaz Sharif's government after it tries to sack General Pervez Musharraf from the top military job. Troops seize Mr Sharif, airports and TV studio as the General promises to maintain stability. Governments all over the world condemn the coup. The Commonwealth suspends Pakistan as the country's constitution is suspended.

WALL REMEMBERED

Germans and other Europeans celebrate the 10th anniversary of the fall of the Berlin wall. At much the same time, prison sentences given to East Germany's 1989 head of state — Egon Krenz — and other top communists who oversaw the shooting of would-be escapers to the West are upheld on appeal.

WORLD CHAMPIONS AGAIN

Australia are the first national side to win the Rugby World Cup for a second time when they defeat France in the final at Cardiff's Millennium stadium in Wales. France were the rank outsider who against the odds defeated the New Zealand All Blacks in the semi-final to cause a major upset in the competition.

ASSASSINATION

Five men gun down Armenia's Prime Minister Vazgen Sarkisian and seven other officials in the parliamentary chamber. The attack is caught on television and stuns the nation. The gunmen take dozens of hostages but surrender after a 12 hour siege. Their leader accuses the government of letting the country disintegrate and of rampant corruption. The five are charged with terrorism.

FAT GET FATTER

The US-based Centres for Disease Control and Prevention publish a study which concludes that nearly 20 per cent of Americans are obese and that one in two adults are overweight.

CHINA ROCKET IN ORBIT

China successfully launches its first spacecraft becoming the third country after the former Soviet Union and America, to develop and launch a space vehicle capable of carrying a person into space.

BATTLE IN SEATTLE

World Trade Organization talks in Seattle, USA, face violent demonstrations not seen in America since the seventies. Protesters are dissatisfied with the industrialized countries manipulation of the markets in their favour at the expense of poorer countries. Many leaders appear on television looking shocked by the persistence and aggression of the mainly middle class demonstrators.

PANAMA CANAL HANDED OVER

Panama is soon to have full sovereignty over all its territory as the 51-mile-long canal cut through the mountains and policed by the Americans is handed back to its rightful owners. With 14,000 ships passing through the canal each year, the canal has huge earning potential said to be worth at least $5 billion. The project to build the canal was the most complex and expensive undertaken by the United States outside its borders. It was a project that became a source of American pride and international power for most of the century.

BERLIN AGREES COMPENSATION

Germany at last agrees to a $5 billion pay out to survivors forced by the Nazis to work in German factories. The German taxpayer bears the lions' share of the burden, only a minority of the companies that exploited the labour of enslaved citizens agree to contribute. About 12 million people were press-ganged to serve the Nazi war effort.

BRITISH-IRISH COUNCIL MEET

The momentum of the peace process in Northern Ireland is maintained in December at the first meeting of the British-Irish Council held in London set up as a result of the Good Friday Agreement.

YELTSIN RESIGNS

In a typically dramatic gesture, Boris Yeltsin resigns as Russia's president on New Year's eve amid speculation that he has secured a deal to suppress corruption allegations concerning his years in power.

PARTY TIMES

From the International Date Line, in the Pacific Ocean, the midnight deadline spreads inexorably west. Millennium Island and Kiribati start the fireworks, and are followed by spectacular displays in Auckland and Sydney. In China, fires light the Great Wall from end to end. In the desert of Africa, Timbuktu celebrates in the same spirit as ice-bound Anchorage in Alaska. The world parties in expectation: at the start of the 20th century, the life expectancy for a woman was 40 years, 100 years later it has doubled and the population stands at six billion. In non-industrialized nations there remains over 2 billion people still without electricity and even more with no sanitation. Thus the 21st century begins.

BELOW: Midnight, the final moment of the second Millennium, over Southampton Water, England.

1999 ⟶ 2000

LEFT: Jan 1 2000, daybreak in Tongan waters in the Pacific Ocean. To the west, the rest of the world awaits the midnight hour to start celebrations, as these islanders begin their day.

BELOW: The London Eye: a giant ferris wheel that fails to make its deadline. Built to herald the new millennium it was bedevilled by safety problems. The Millennium Dome, however, also on the banks of the Thames, is completed just in time and is the focus of the capital's effort to welcome in the New Year. It stages exhibitions and performances designed to attract visitors.

Sydney's Harbour Bridge and Opera House:
one million people watch 22 tonnes of fireworks light the midnight sky.

ABOVE: West Beijing: revellers at the newly built
China Century Monument, designed in the
style of the Temple of Heaven used by Chinese
emperors to perform major ceremonial rites,
express their joy as the century turns.

ABOVE: Jerusalem, fireworks explode over the Church of Nativity, the traditional birthplace of Jesus, in Manger Square, Bethlehem.

RIGHT: Cairo, a new millennium concert in the shadow of the 4,500-year-old pyramids. A mix of ancient civilization and 20th century techno-wizardry combines to start another 1,000 year period.

ABOVE RIGHT: Moscow, as their president resigns, a boy gazes into the future as he watches the new century sky above Red Square.

LEFT: Berlin, the Brandenberg Gate during Germany's festivities. Over a million are estimated to join the all-night party in this historic district.

FAR LEFT: Sarajevo, Bosnians see in the New Year close to the National Theatre lit against a background of exploding fireworks after years of war in the 1990s.

BELOW LEFT: Dubrovnik, the ancient Croatian city draws thousands into the main square to celebrate. CNN, the American TV company, announces the city is in its top ten places in the world to celebrate the New Year 2000.

BELOW: The Vatican City, Pope John Paul II watches the fireworks from his balcony at the Vatican at the start of the Christian third millennium. His message to followers is one of joy and peace.

LEFT: Paris, by popular vote the most visually stunning event in Europe. Fireworks burst from the Eiffel Tower as millions party on the boulevards by night.

BELOW: London welcomes in the new millennium. The River Thames and the Houses of Parliament are reflected in the light of fireworks as the river is lit by a 'wall of fire'. Thousands pack the riverbanks to watch the display.